The Complete
Mediterranean Diet Cookbook

1800	Vibrant, Healthy and Tasty Mediterranean recipes with 60-Day Meal Plans To Start your Mediterranean Journey with Ease

Jodie G. Blanding

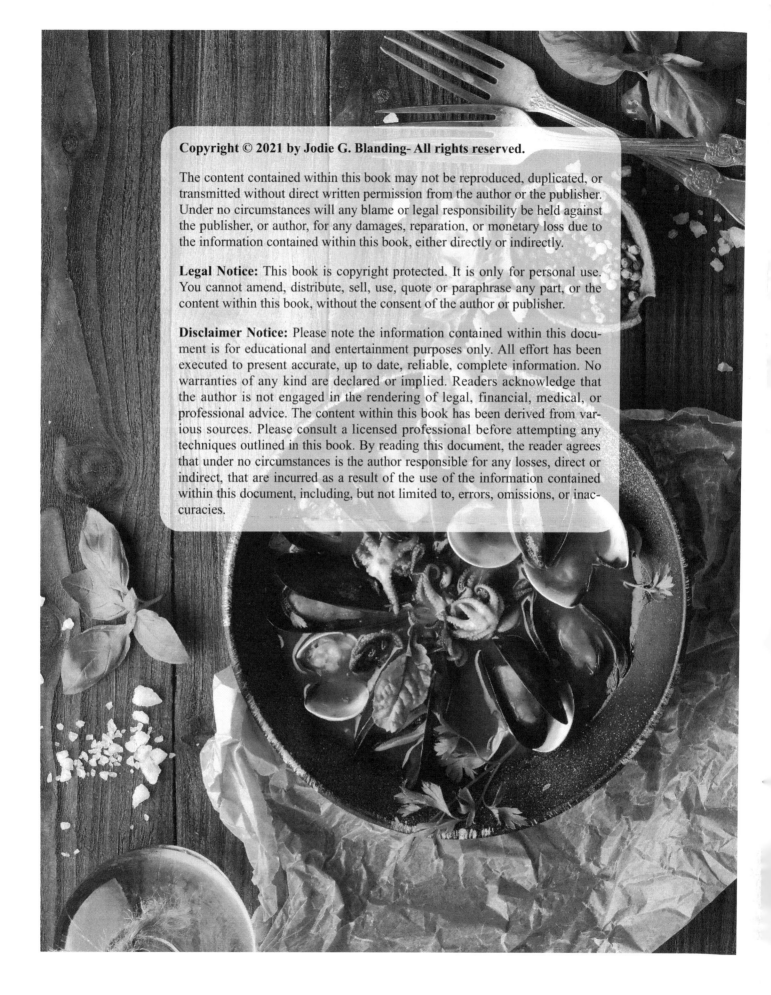

CONTENTS

CHAPTER 3 VEGETABLE MAINS AND MEATLESS RECIPES.................................33

CHAPTER 5 POULTRY AND MEATS RECIPES...............75

Introduction

The term "diet" for most of us spells out deprivation, extreme hunger, and bland and boring foods that we are forced to eat in order to lose weight. However, with the Mediterranean diet, none of those apply.

The Mediterranean diet is endowed with an unlimited assortment of fresh, healthy, natural, and wholesome foods from all food groups. Although there is a greater focus on certain components, no natural components are excluded. Mediterranean diet devotees can enjoy their favorite dishes as they learn to appreciate how nourishing the freshest healthy and natural foods can be. This diet is primarily based on the eating habits of the original inhabitants of the coasts of Greece, Italy, Spain, Morocco, and France. Because of their temperate climate and location, seasonal fruit, vegetables, and seafood from these regions' nutritional foundation.

The easiest way to understand the Mediterranean diet is to picture eating as though it's summer every day. It might also give you a déjà vu moment by reminding you of the foods you enjoyed most on a summer vacation or at the beach. In truth, there is never a dull moment with the Mediterranean diet!

All fun aside, Mediterranean Cookbook for Beginners 2022 will help you find great pleasure in food, knowing that every bite you take will provide your body with the healthiest nutrition. When your food tastes like you are on a perpetual vacation, its easy ad exciting to stay on the bandwagon!

Chapter 1 Understanding the Mediterranean Diet

What the Mediterranean Diet Is

Essentially, following a Mediterranean diet means eating in the way that the people in the Mediterranean region traditionally ate.

A traditional diet from the Mediterranean region includes a generous portion of fresh produce, whole grains, and legumes, as well as some healthful fats and fish.

The general guidelines of the diet recommend that people eat:

• a wide variety of vegetables, fruits, and whole grains

• healthful fats, such as nuts, seeds, and olive oil

• moderate amounts of dairy and fish

• very little white meat and red meat

• few eggs

• red wine in moderation

The American Heart AssociationTrusted Source note that the average Mediterranean diet contains a high percentage of calories from fat.

Although more than half of the calories from fat come from monounsaturated fats, such as olive oil, the diet may not be right for people who need to limit their fat intake.

Worst Foods to Eat and the Reasons

Which items are prohibited from the Mediterranean diet? There aren't any hard and fast rules here. However, there are several things that you should avoid when consuming Mediterranean-style meals.

1. Foods that have been heavily processed.

Let's be honest: Many foods have been processed in some way. A processed can of beans is one in which the beans have been boiled before being canned. Because olives are turned into oil, olive oil has been treated. However, when experts talk about restricting processed foods, they really mean limiting high-sodium frozen meals. Limit soda, sweets, and candy as well. It's processed, according to the saying, if the ingredient list includes things your great-grandparents wouldn't recognize as food. You're fine to go if you buy packaged foods that are as close to their whole-food form as possible, such as frozen fruit or vegetables with no extra ingredients.

2. Meat that has been processed.

Red meat, such as steak, should be consumed in moderation on the Mediterranean diet. What about red meat that has been processed, such as bacon and hot dogs? These foods should be avoided or limited as much as feasible. According to a study conducted in the British Medical Journal, routinely consuming red meat, particularly processed types, is linked to an increased risk of mortality.

3. Butter.

It is another dish that should be avoided if you're following a Mediterranean diet. Rather, use olive oil, which has a lot of heart-health benefits and is lower in saturated fat than butter. Butter includes 7gms of saturated fat per tablespoon, whereas olive oil has roughly two gms, as per the USDA National Nutrient Database.

4. Grain that has been refined.

Whole grains including farro, couscous, millet, and brown rice are staples in the Mediterranean diet. You'll want to minimize your intake of refined grains like white pasta and white bread if you're following this eating plan.

5. Alcohol.

Red wine should be your alcoholic beverage of choice if you're following the Mediterranean diet. This is due to the fact that red wine has health benefits, especially for the heart. However, it is necessary to limit alcohol consumption to one drink per day for women and men over the age of 65 and two drinks per day for men 65 and younger. A drink is defined as five ounces of wine, twelve ounces of beer, or 1.5 ounces of 80-proof liquor.

The Top 5 Tips for Success

1. Treat Yourself Like Company

The Mediterranean diet is as much about how you eat as it is about what you eat. The Mediterranean people have a respect for and appreciation of food that inspires them to set beautiful (though often very simple) tables. Bring out the good china, put some fresh flowers in a canning jar, light some candles, or eat outside on the patio. However you choose to do it, treat every meal as though you were having guests.

2. Learn to Savor

Turn off the TV, even if you're eating alone. Put away the work, the cell phone, and any other distractions. Even if you're having dinner for one, focus on the delicious food you're eating. Really taste what's on your plate and start appreciating the pleasure of flavor.

3. Become a Social Eater

Inviting friends and family over for a simple summer lunch or a casual dinner party is a great way to incorporate the Mediterranean approach to dining into your own life. For the Mediterranean people, eating is as much about the company as it is about the food, and meals really do taste better when you share them.

4. Learn to Make Substitutions

Very few things are off-limits in the Mediterranean diet, but moderation is key. If you're craving something you don't think you should be eating, like greasy French fries or salty potato chips, learn to make substitutions. You may find that the thing that stands in for your favorite junk food becomes your new favorite!

5. Try Something New Each Week

Eating the Mediterranean way should be fun, exciting, and even a little exotic. Try to choose one unfamiliar fruit, vegetable, fish, or other ingredient each week. It'll keep things interesting and enhance that sense of voyaging to another land.

Eating Out on the Mediterranean Diet

Eating out on the Mediterranean diet is very easy, and the trend toward healthier menus and vegetarian and vegan offerings makes it easier than ever before.

Some of the best restaurants for the Mediterranean diet are seafood houses, farm-to-table establishments, and Italian, Spanish, Greek, and Provençal (Southern French) restaurants. Vegetarian restaurants also offer a wide variety of delicious pasta dishes and entrées that are made healthfully and with fresh ingredients.

Here are a few guidelines to follow when dining out on the Mediterranean diet:

• Go easy on the bread basket. Although bread is welcomed on the Mediterranean diet, you don't want to add too many calories to your meal before your entrée hits the table. When you do eat bread, ask that olive oil and pepper be brought to the table instead of butter.

• Order food that is broiled, baked, sautéed (in olive oil, not butter), grilled, braised, roasted, poached, or steamed. Avoid any entrée that is breaded or deep-fried.

• Try to include a fresh salad with your meal, but skip the creamy dressings. Instead, ask for vinaigrette or olive oil and vinegar.

• If you order a meat entrée, chances are that the portion will be much larger than those favored on the Mediterranean diet. This is also usually true when having pasta. If this is the case, ask the server to either box half of it up before serving you or to bring you a carryout box along with the entrée. Then just put about half of the portion into the box before you start eating and enjoy it another day.

• For the most part, opt for fruit or a cheese plate for dessert. Other good choices for a sweet treat are sorbet and baked fruit dishes. By all means, have a piece of chocolate cake or a crème brûlée now and then, but make it a rare treat and share it with someone or take half of it home.

The Mediterranean diet is all about enjoying great food in pleasant surroundings and with wonderful people. This makes restaurant dining a natural part of the diet, so try not to stress too much about where and what to eat. Most restaurants have plenty of Mediterranean-friendly choices.

BASIC KITCHEN CONVERSIONS & EQUIVALENTS

DRY MEASUREMENTS CONVERSION CHART

3 TEASPOONS = 1 TABLESPOON = 1/16 CUP

6 TEASPOONS = 2 TABLESPOONS = 1/8 CUP

12 TEASPOONS = 4 TABLESPOONS = 1/4 CUP

24 TEASPOONS = 8 TABLESPOONS = 1/2 CUP

36 TEASPOONS = 12 TABLESPOONS = 3/4 CUP

48 TEASPOONS = 16 TABLESPOONS = 1 CUP

METRIC TO US COOKING CONVERSIONS

OVEN TEMPERATURES

120 °C = 250 °F

160 °C = 320 °F

180° C = 350 °F

205 °C = 400 °F

220 °C = 425 °F

LIQUID MEASUREMENTS CONVERSION CHART

8 FLUID OUNCES = 1 CUP = 1/2 PINT = 1/4 QUART

16 FLUID OUNCES = 2 CUPS = 1 PINT = 1/2 QUART

32 FLUID OUNCES = 4 CUPS = 2 PINTS = 1 QUART = 1/4 GALLON

128 FLUID OUNCES = 16 CUPS = 8 PINTS = 4 QUARTS = 1 GALLON

BAKING IN GRAMS

1 CUP FLOUR = 140 GRAMS

1 CUP SUGAR = 150 GRAMS

1 CUP POWDERED SUGAR = 160 GRAMS

1 CUP HEAVY CREAM = 235 GRAMS

VOLUME

1 MILLILITER = 1/5 TEASPOON

5 ML = 1 TEASPOON

15 ML = 1 TABLESPOON

240 ML = 1 CUP OR 8 FLUID OUNCES

1 LITER = 34 FL. OUNCES

WEIGHT

1 GRAM = .035 OUNCES

100 GRAMS = 3.5 OUNCES

500 GRAMS = 1.1 POUNDS

1 KILOGRAM = 35 OUNCES

US TO METRIC COOKING CONVERSIONS

1/5 TSP = 1 ML

1 TSP = 5 ML

1 TBSP = 15 ML

1 FL OUNCE = 30 ML

1 CUP = 237 ML

1 PINT (2 CUPS) = 473 ML

1 QUART (4 CUPS) = .95 LITER

1 GALLON (16 CUPS) = 3.8 LITERS

1 OZ = 28 GRAMS

1 POUND = 454 GRAMS

BUTTER

1 CUP BUTTER = 2 STICKS = 8 OUNCES = 230 GRAMS = 8 TABLESPOONS

WHAT DOES 1 CUP EQUAL

1 CUP = 8 FLUID OUNCES

1 CUP = 16 TABLESPOONS

1 CUP = 48 TEASPOONS

1 CUP = 1/2 PINT

1 CUP = 1/4 QUART

1 CUP = 1/16 GALLON

1 CUP = 240 ML

BAKING PAN CONVERSIONS

1 CUP ALL-PURPOSE FLOUR = 4.5 OZ

1 CUP ROLLED OATS = 3 OZ 1 LARGE EGG = 1.7 OZ

1 CUP BUTTER = 8 OZ 1 CUP MILK = 8 OZ

1 CUP HEAVY CREAM = 8.4 OZ

1 CUP GRANULATED SUGAR = 7.1 OZ

1 CUP PACKED BROWN SUGAR = 7.75 OZ

1 CUP VEGETABLE OIL = 7.7 OZ

1 CUP UNSIFTED POWDERED SUGAR = 4.4 OZ

BAKING PAN CONVERSIONS

9-INCH ROUND CAKE PAN = 12 CUPS

10-INCH TUBE PAN =16 CUPS

11-INCH BUNDT PAN = 12 CUPS

9-INCH SPRINGFORM PAN = 10 CUPS

9 X 5 INCH LOAF PAN = 8 CUPS

9-INCH SQUARE PAN = 8 CUPS

Chapter 2 Breakfast Recipes

Chapter 2 Breakfast Recipes

Yummy Lentil Stuffed Pitas

Servings:4 | Cooking Time:20 Minutes

Ingredients:
- 4 pitta breads, halved horizontally
- 2 tbsp olive oil
- 1 tomato, cubed
- 1 red onion, chopped
- 1 garlic clove, minced
- ¼ cup parsley, chopped
- 1 cup lentils, rinsed
- ¼ cup lemon juice
- Salt and black pepper to taste

Directions:
1. Bring a pot of salted water to a boil over high heat. Pour in the lentils and lower the heat. Cover and let it simmer for 15 minutes or until lentils are tender, adding more water if needed. Drain and set aside.
2. Warm the olive oil in a skillet over medium heat and cook the onion and garlic and for 3 minutes until soft and translucent. Stir in tomato, lemon juice, salt, and pepper and cook for another 10 minutes. Add the lentils and parsley to the skillet and stir to combine. Fill the pita bread with the lentil mixture. Roll up and serve immediately. Enjoy!

Nutrition Info:
- Per Serving: Calories: 390;Fat: 2g;Protein: 29g;Carbs: 68g.

Red Pepper Coques With Pine Nuts

Servings:4 | Cooking Time: 45 Minutes

Ingredients:
- Dough:
- 3 cups almond flour
- ½ teaspoon instant or rapid-rise yeast
- 2 teaspoons raw honey
- 1⅓ cups ice water
- 3 tablespoons extra-virgin olive oil
- 1½ teaspoons sea salt
- Red Pepper Topping:
- 4 tablespoons extra-virgin olive oil, divided
- 2 cups jarred roasted red peppers, patted dry and sliced
- thinly
- 2 large onions, halved and sliced thin
- 3 garlic cloves, minced
- ¼ teaspoon red pepper flakes
- 2 bay leaves
- 3 tablespoons maple syrup
- 1½ teaspoons sea salt
- 3 tablespoons red whine vinegar
- For Garnish:
- ¼ cup pine nuts (optional)
- 1 tablespoon minced fresh parsley

Directions:
1. Make the Dough:
2. Combine the flour, yeast, and honey in a food processor, pulse to combine well. Gently add water while pulsing. Let the dough sit for 10 minutes.
3. Mix the olive oil and salt in the dough and knead the dough until smooth. Wrap in plastic and refrigerate for at least 1 day.
4. Make the Topping:
5. Heat 1 tablespoon of olive oil in a nonstick skillet over medium heat until shimmering.
6. Add the red peppers, onions, garlic, red pepper flakes, bay leaves, maple syrup, and salt. Sauté for 20 minutes or until the onion is caramelized.
7. Turn off the heat and discard the bay leaves. Remove the onion from the skillet and baste with wine vinegar. Let them sit until ready to use.
8. Make the Coques:
9. Preheat the oven to 500ºF. Grease two baking sheets with 1 tablespoon of olive oil.
10. Divide the dough ball into four balls, then press and shape them into equal-sized oval. Arrange the ovals on the baking sheets and pierce each dough about 12 times.
11. Rub the ovals with 2 tablespoons of olive oil and bake for 7 minutes or until puffed. Flip the ovals halfway through the cooking time.
12. Spread the ovals with the topping and pine nuts, then bake for an additional 15 minutes or until well browned.
13. Remove the coques from the oven and spread with parsley. Allow to cool for 10 minutes before serving.

Nutrition Info:
- Per Serving: Calories: 658;Fat: 23.1g;Protein: 3.4g;Carbs: 112.0g.

Baked Eggs In Avocado

Servings:2 | Cooking Time: 10 To 15 Minutes

Ingredients:
- 1 ripe large avocado
- 2 large eggs
- Salt and freshly ground black pepper, to taste
- 4 tablespoons jarred pesto,
- for serving
- 2 tablespoons chopped tomato, for serving
- 2 tablespoons crumbled feta cheese, for serving (optional)

Directions:
1. Preheat the oven to 425ºF.
2. Slice the avocado in half, remove the pit and scoop out a generous tablespoon of flesh from each half to create a hole big enough to fit an egg.
3. Transfer the avocado halves (cut-side up) to a baking sheet.
4. Crack 1 egg into each avocado half and sprinkle with salt and pepper.
5. Bake in the preheated oven for 10 to 15 minutes, or until the eggs are cooked to your preferred doneness.
6. Remove the avocado halves from the oven. Scatter each avocado half evenly with the jarred pesto, chopped tomato, and crumbled feta cheese (if desired). Serve immediately.

Nutrition Info:
- Per Serving: Calories: 301;Fat: 25.9g;Protein: 8.1g;Carbs: 9.8g.

Basil Scrambled Eggs

Servings:2 | Cooking Time: 8 Minutes

Ingredients:
- 4 large eggs
- 2 tablespoons grated Gruyère cheese
- 2 tablespoons finely chopped fresh basil
- 1 tablespoon plain Greek
- yogurt
- 1 tablespoon olive oil
- 2 cloves garlic, minced
- Sea salt and freshly ground pepper, to taste

Directions:
1. In a large bowl, beat together the eggs, cheese, basil, and yogurt with a whisk until just combined.
2. Heat the oil in a large, heavy nonstick skillet over medium-low heat. Add the garlic and cook until golden, about 1 minute.

3. Pour the egg mixture into the skillet over the garlic. Work the eggs continuously and cook until fluffy and soft.

4. Season with sea salt and freshly ground pepper to taste. Divide between 2 plates and serve immediately.

Nutrition Info:
- Per Serving: Calories: 243;Fat: 19.7g;Protein: 15.6g;Carbs: 3.4g.

Luxurious Fruit Cocktail

Servings:6 | Cooking Time:10 Min + Cooling Time

Ingredients:
- ½ cup olive oil
- 2 cups cubed honeydew melon
- 2 cups cubed cantaloupe
- 2 cups red seedless grapes
- 1 lemon, juiced and zested
- ½ cup slivered almonds
- 1 cup sliced strawberries
- 1 cup blueberries
- ¼ cup honey

Directions:
1. In a bowl, place melon, cantaloupe, grapes, strawberries, blueberries, and lemon zest. Toss to coat and set aside.

2. Mix the honey and lemon juice in a bowl and whisk until the honey is well incorporated. Carefully pour in the olive oil and mix well. Drizzle over the fruit and toss to combine. Transfer to the fridge covered and let chill for at least 4 hours. Stir well and top with slivered almonds before serving.

Nutrition Info:
- Per Serving: Calories: 326;Fat: 19g;Protein: 2g;Carbs: 43g.

Mushroom And Caramelized Onion Musakhan

Servings:4 | Cooking Time: 1 Hour 5 Minutes

Ingredients:
- 2 tablespoons sumac, plus more for sprinkling
- 1 teaspoon ground allspice
- ½ teaspoon ground cardamom
- ½ teaspoon ground cumin
- 3 tablespoons extra-virgin olive oil, divided
- 2 pounds portobello mushroom caps, gills removed, caps
- halved and sliced ½ inch thick
- 3 medium white onions, coarsely chopped
- ¼ cup water
- Kosher salt, to taste
- 1 whole-wheat Turkish flatbread
- ¼ cup pine nuts
- 1 lemon, wedged

Directions:
1. Preheat the oven to 350ºF.

2. Combine 2 tablespoons of sumac, allspice, cardamom, and cumin in a small bowl. Stir to mix well.

3. Heat 2 tablespoons of olive oil in an oven-proof skillet over medium-high heat until shimmering.

4. Add the mushroom to the skillet and sprinkle with half of sumac mixture. Sauté for 8 minutes or until the mushrooms are tender. You may need to work in batches to avoid overcrowding. Transfer the mushrooms to a plate and set side.

5. Heat 1 tablespoon of olive oil in the skillet over medium-high heat until shimmering.

6. Add the onion and sauté for 20 minutes or until caramelized. Sprinkle with remaining sumac mixture, then cook for 1 more minute.

7. Pour in the water and sprinkle with salt. Bring to a simmer.

8. Turn off the heat and put the mushroom back to the skillet.

9. Place the skillet in the preheated oven and bake for 30 minutes.

10. Remove the skillet from the oven and let the mushroom sit for 10 minutes until cooled down.

11. Heat the Turkish flatbread in a baking dish in the oven for 5 minutes or until warmed through.

12. Arrange the bread on a large plate and top with mushrooms, onions, and roasted pine nuts. Squeeze the lemon wedges over and sprinkle with more sumac. Serve immediately.

Nutrition Info:
- Per Serving: Calories: 336;Fat: 18.7g;Protein: 11.5g;Carbs: 34.3g.

Carrot & Pecan Cupcakes

Servings:6 | Cooking Time:30 Minutes

Ingredients:
- 2 tbsp olive oil
- 1 ½ cups grated carrots
- ¼ cup pecans, chopped
- 1 cup oat bran
- 1 cup wholewheat flour
- ½ cup all-purpose flour
- ½ cup old-fashioned oats
- 3 tbsp light brown sugar
- 1 tsp vanilla extract
- ½ lemon, zested
- 1 tsp baking powder
- 2 tsp ground cinnamon
- 2 tsp ground ginger
- ½ tsp ground nutmeg
- ¼ tsp salt
- 1¼ cups soy milk
- 2 tbsp honey
- 1 egg

Directions:
1. Preheat oven to 350 °F. Mix whole-wheat flour, all-purpose flour, oat bran, oats, sugar, baking powder, cinnamon, nutmeg, ginger, and salt in a bowl; set aside.

2. Beat egg with soy milk, honey, vanilla, lemon zest, and olive oil in another bowl. Pour this mixture into the flour mixture and combine to blend, leaving some lumps. Stir in carrots and pecans. Spoon batter into greased muffin cups. Bake for about 20 minutes. Prick with a toothpick and if it comes out easily, the cakes are cooked done. Let cool and serve.

Nutrition Info:
- Per Serving: Calories: 346;Fat: 10g;Protein: 13g;Carbs: 59g.

Lemon Cardamom Buckwheat Pancakes

Servings:2 | Cooking Time:20 Minutes

Ingredients:
- ½ cup buckwheat flour
- ½ tsp cardamom
- ½ tsp baking powder
- ½ cup milk
- ¼ cup plain Greek yogurt
- 1 egg
- 1 tsp lemon zest
- 1 tbsp honey

Directions:
1. Mix the buckwheat flour, cardamom, and baking powder in a medium bowl. Whisk the milk, yogurt, egg, lemon zest, and honey in another bowl. Add the wet ingredients to the dry ingredients and stir until the batter is smooth.

2. Spray a frying pan with non-stick cooking oil and cook the pancakes over medium heat until the edges begin to brown. Flip and cook on the other side for 3 more minutes. Serve.

Nutrition Info:
- Per Serving: Calories: 196;Fat: 6g;Protein: 10g;Carbs: 27g.

White Pizzas With Arugula And Spinach

Servings:4 | Cooking Time: 20 Minutes

Ingredients:
- 1 pound refrigerated fresh pizza dough
- 2 tablespoons extra-virgin olive oil, divided
- ½ cup thinly sliced onion
- 2 garlic cloves, minced
- 3 cups baby spinach
- 3 cups arugula
- 1 tablespoon water
- ¼ teaspoon freshly ground black pepper
- 1 tablespoon freshly squeezed lemon juice
- ½ cup shredded Parmesan cheese
- ½ cup crumbled goat cheese
- Cooking spray

Directions:
1. Preheat the oven to 500°F. Spritz a large, rimmed baking sheet with cooking spray.
2. Take the pizza dough out of the refrigerator.
3. Heat 1 tablespoon of the oil in a large skillet over medium heat. Add the onion to the skillet and cook for 4 minutes, stirring constantly. Add the garlic and cook for 1 minute, stirring constantly.
4. Stir in the spinach, arugula, water and pepper. Cook for about 2 minutes, stirring constantly, or until all the greens are coated with oil and they start to cook down. Remove the skillet from the heat and drizzle with the lemon juice.
5. On a lightly floured work surface, form the pizza dough into a 12-inch circle or a 10-by-12-inch rectangle, using a rolling pin or by stretching with your hands.
6. Place the dough on the prepared baking sheet. Brush the dough with the remaining 1 tablespoon of the oil. Spread the cooked greens on top of the dough to within ½ inch of the edge. Top with the Parmesan cheese and goat cheese.
7. Bake in the preheated oven for 10 to 12 minutes, or until the crust starts to brown around the edges.
8. Remove from the oven and transfer the pizza to a cutting board. Cut into eight pieces before serving.

Nutrition Info:
- Per Serving: Calories: 521;Fat: 31.0g;Protein: 23.0g;Carbs: 38.0g.

Tomato Eggs With Fried Potatoes

Servings:2 | Cooking Time:20 Minutes

Ingredients:
- 2 tbsp + ½ cup olive oil
- 3 medium tomatoes, puréed
- 1 tbsp fresh tarragon, chopped
- 1 garlic clove, minced
- Salt and black pepper to taste
- 3 potatoes, cubed
- 4 fresh eggs
- 1 tsp fresh oregano, chopped

Directions:
1. Warm 2 tbsp of olive oil in a saucepan over medium heat. Add the garlic and sauté for 1 minute. Pour in the tomatoes, tarragon, salt, and pepper. Reduce the heat and cook for 5-8 minutes or until the sauce is thickened and bubbly.
2. Warm the remaining olive oil in a skillet over medium heat. Fry the potatoes for 5 minutes until crisp and browned on the outside, then cover and reduce heat to low. Steam potatoes until done. Carefully crack the eggs into the tomato sauce.
3. Cook over low heat until the eggs are set in the sauce, about 6 minutes. Remove the potatoes from the pan, drain them on paper towels, and place them in a bowl. Sprinkle with salt and pepper and top with oregano. Carefully remove the eggs with a slotted spoon and place them on a plate with the potatoes. Spoon sauce over and serve.

Nutrition Info:
- Per Serving: Calories: 1146;Fat: 69g;Protein: 26g;Carbs: 45g.

Pesto Salami & Cheese Egg Cupcakes

Servings:6 | Cooking Time:25 Minutes

Ingredients:
- ½ cup roasted red peppers, chopped
- 1 tbsp olive oil
- 5 eggs, whisked
- 4 oz Italian dry salami, sliced
- 1/3 cup spinach, chopped
- ¼ cup ricotta cheese, crumbled
- Salt and black pepper to taste
- 1 ½ tbsp basil pesto

Directions:
1. Preheat the oven to 380 °F. Brush 6 ramekin cups with olive oil and line them with dry salami slices. Top with spinach, ricotta cheese, and roasted peppers. Whisk the eggs with pesto, salt, and pepper in a bowl and pour over the peppers. Bake for 15 minutes and serve warm.

Nutrition Info:
- Per Serving: Calories: 120;Fat: 8g;Protein: 10g;Carbs: 2g.

Tomato Scrambled Eggs With Feta Cheese

Servings:4 | Cooking Time:25 Minutes

Ingredients:
- ¼ cup olive oil
- 2 Roma tomatoes, chopped
- ¼ cup minced red onion
- 2 garlic cloves, minced
- ½ tsp dried oregano
- ½ tsp dried thyme
- 8 large eggs
- Salt and black pepper to taste
- ¾ cup feta cheese, crumbled
- ¼ cup fresh cilantro, chopped

Directions:
1. Warm the olive oil in a large skillet over medium heat. Add the chopped tomatoes and red onion and sauté for 10 minutes or until the tomatoes are soft. Add the garlic, oregano, and thyme and sauté for another 1-2 minutes until the liquid reduces.
2. In a medium bowl, whisk together the eggs, salt, and pepper until well combined. Add the eggs to the skillet, reduce the heat to low, and scramble until set and creamy, using a spatula to move them constantly, 3-4 minutes. Remove the skillet from the heat, stir in the feta and cilantro, and serve.

Nutrition Info:
- Per Serving: Calories: 338;Fat: 28g;Protein: 16g;Carbs: 6g.

Crustless Tiropita (greek Cheese Pie)

Servings:6 | Cooking Time: 35 To 40 Minutes

Ingredients:
- 4 tablespoons extra-virgin olive oil, divided
- ½ cup whole-milk ricotta cheese
- 1¼ cups crumbled feta cheese
- 1 tablespoon chopped fresh dill
- 2 tablespoons chopped fresh mint
- ½ teaspoon lemon zest
- ¼ teaspoon freshly ground black pepper
- 2 large eggs
- ½ teaspoon baking powder

Directions:
1. Preheat the oven to 350ºF. Coat the bottom and sides of a baking dish with 2 tablespoons of olive oil. Set aside.
2. Mix together the ricotta and feta cheese in a medium bowl and stir with a fork until well combined. Add the dill, mint, lemon zest, and black pepper and mix well.

3. In a separate bowl, whisk together the eggs and baking powder. Pour the whisked eggs into the bowl of cheese mixture. Blend well.

4. Slowly pour the mixture into the coated baking dish and drizzle with the remaining 2 tablespoons of olive oil.

5. Bake in the preheated oven for about 35 to 40 minutes, or until the pie is browned around the edges and cooked through.

6. Cool for 5 minutes before slicing into wedges.

Nutrition Info:
• Per Serving: Calories: 181;Fat: 16.6g;Protein: 7.0g;Carbs: 1.8g.

Spinach Cheese Pie

Servings:8 | Cooking Time: 25 Minutes

Ingredients:
• 2 tablespoons extra-virgin olive oil
• 1 onion, chopped
• 1 pound frozen spinach, thawed
• ¼ teaspoon ground nutmeg
• ¼ teaspoon garlic salt
• ¼ teaspoon freshly ground

black pepper
• 4 large eggs, divided
• 1 cup grated Parmesan cheese, divided
• 2 puff pastry doughs, at room temperature
• 4 hard-boiled eggs, halved
• Nonstick cooking spray

Directions:
1. Preheat the oven to 350°F. Spritz a baking sheet with nonstick cooking spray and set aside.

2. Heat a large skillet over medium-high heat. Add the olive oil and onion and sauté for about 5 minutes, stirring occasionally, or until translucent.

3. Squeeze the excess water from the spinach, then add to the skillet and cook, uncovered, so that any excess water from the spinach can evaporate.

4. Season with the nutmeg, garlic salt, and black pepper. Remove from heat and set aside to cool.

5. Beat 3 eggs in a small bowl. Add the beaten eggs and ½ cup of Parmesan cheese to the spinach mixture, stirring well.

6. Roll out the pastry dough on the prepared baking sheet. Layer the spinach mixture on top of the dough, leaving 2 inches around each edge.

7. Once the spinach is spread onto the pastry dough, evenly place the hard-boiled egg halves throughout the pie, then cover with the second pastry dough. Pinch the edges closed.

8. Beat the remaining 1 egg in the bowl. Brush the egg wash over the pastry dough.

9. Bake in the preheated oven for 15 to 20 minutes until golden brown.

10. Sprinkle with the remaining ½ cup of Parmesan cheese. Cool for 5 minutes before cutting and serving.

Nutrition Info:
• Per Serving: Calories: 417;Fat: 28.0g;Protein: 17.0g;Carbs: 25.0g.

Dulse, Avocado, And Tomato Pitas

Servings:4 | Cooking Time: 30 Minutes

Ingredients:
• 2 teaspoons coconut oil
• ½ cup dulse, picked through and separated
• Ground black pepper, to taste
• 2 avocados, sliced
• 2 tablespoons lime juice
• ¼ cup chopped cilantro
• 2 scallions, white and light green parts, sliced
• Sea salt, to taste
• 4 whole wheat pitas, sliced in half

• 4 cups chopped romaine
• 4 plum tomatoes, sliced

Directions:
1. Heat the coconut oil in a nonstick skillet over medium heat until melted.

2. Add the dulse and sauté for 5 minutes or until crispy. Sprinkle with ground black pepper and turn off the heat. Set aside.

3. Put the avocado, lime juice, cilantro, and scallions in a food processor and sprinkle with salt and ground black pepper. Pulse to combine well until smooth.

4. Toast the pitas in a baking pan in the oven for 1 minute until soft.

5. Transfer the pitas to a clean work surface and open. Spread the avocado mixture over the pitas, then top with dulse, romaine, and tomato slices.

6. Serve immediately.

Nutrition Info:
• Per Serving: Calories: 412;Fat: 18.7g;Protein: 9.1g;Carbs: 56.1g.

5-ingredient Quinoa Breakfast Bowls

Servings:1 | Cooking Time: 17 Minutes

Ingredients:
• ¼ cup quinoa, rinsed
• ¾ cup water, plus additional as needed
• 1 carrot, grated
• ½ small broccoli head, finely

chopped
• ¼ teaspoon salt
• 1 tablespoon chopped fresh dill

Directions:
1. Add the quinoa and water to a small pot over high heat and bring to a boil.

2. Once boiling, reduce the heat to low. Cover and cook for 5 minutes, stirring occasionally.

3. Stir in the carrot, broccoli, and salt and continue cooking for 1o to 12 minutes, or until the quinoa is cooked though and the vegetables are fork-tender. If the mixture gets too thick, you can add additional water as needed.

4. Add the dill and serve warm.

Nutrition Info:
• Per Serving: Calories: 219;Fat: 2.9g;Protein: 10.0g;Carbs: 40.8g.

Avocado Toast With Goat Cheese

Servings:2 | Cooking Time: 2 To 3 Minutes

Ingredients:
• 2 slices whole-wheat thin-sliced bread
• ½ avocado
• 2 tablespoons crumbled goat cheese
• Salt, to taste

Directions:
1. Toast the bread slices in a toaster for 2 to 3 minutes on each side until browned.

2. Scoop out the flesh from the avocado into a medium bowl and mash it with a fork to desired consistency. Spread the mash onto each piece of toast.

3. Scatter the crumbled goat cheese on top and season as needed with salt.

4. Serve immediately.

Nutrition Info:
• Per Serving: Calories: 136;Fat: 5.9g;Protein: 5.0g;Carbs: 17.5g.

Feta & Olive Breakfast

Servings:4 | Cooking Time:15 Minutes

Ingredients:
- ¼ cup extra-virgin olive oil
- 4 feta cheese squares
- 3 cups mixed olives, drained
- 3 tbsp lemon juice
- 1 tsp lemon zest
- 1 tsp dried dill
- Pita bread for serving

Directions:
1. In a small bowl, whisk together the olive oil, lemon juice, lemon zest, and dill. Place the feta cheese on a serving plate and add the mixed olives. Pour the dressing all over the feta cheese. Serve with toasted pita bread.

Nutrition Info:
- Per Serving: Calories: 406;Fat: 38.2g;Protein: 7.9g;Carbs: 8g.

Fresh Mozzarella & Salmon Frittata

Servings:4 | Cooking Time:15 Minutes

Ingredients:
- 1 ball fresh mozzarella cheese, chopped
- 2 tsp olive oil
- 8 fresh eggs
- ½ cup whole milk
- 1 spring onion, chopped
- ¼ cup chopped fresh basil
- Salt and black pepper to taste
- 3 oz smoked salmon, chopped

Directions:
1. Preheat your broiler to medium. Whisk the eggs with milk, spring onion, basil, pepper, and salt in a bowl. Heat the olive oil in a skillet over medium heat and pour in the egg mixture.
2. Top with mozzarella cheese and cook for 3–5 minutes until the frittata is set on the bottom and the egg is almost set but still moist on top. Scatter over the salmon and place the skillet under the preheated broiler for 1-2 minutes or until set and slightly puffed. Cut the frittata into wedges. Enjoy!

Nutrition Info:
- Per Serving: Calories: 351;Fat: 13g;Protein: 52g;Carbs: 6g.

Herby Artichoke Frittata With Ricotta

Servings:2 | Cooking Time:20 Minutes

Ingredients:
- 4 oz canned artichoke hearts, quartered
- 2 tbsp olive oil
- 4 large eggs
- 1 tsp dried herbs
- Salt and black pepper to taste
- 1 cup kale, chopped
- 8 cherry tomatoes, halved
- ½ cup crumbled ricotta cheese

Directions:
1. Preheat oven to 360 °F. In a bowl, whisk the eggs, herbs, salt, and pepper and whisk well with a fork. Set aside. Warm the olive oil in a skillet over medium heat. Sauté the kale, artichoke, and cherry tomatoes until just wilted, 1-2 minutes.
2. Pour the egg mixture over and let it cook for 3-4 minutes until the eggs begin to set on the bottom. Sprinkle with ricotta cheese on top. Place the skillet under the preheated broiler for 5 minutes until the frittata is firm in the center and golden brown on top. Invert the frittata onto a plate and slice in half. Serve warm.

Nutrition Info:
- Per Serving: Calories: 527;Fat: 47g;Protein: 21g;Carbs: 10g.

Vegetable & Egg Sandwiches

Servings:2 | Cooking Time:15 Minutes

Ingredients:
- 1 Iceberg lettuce, separated into leaves
- 1 tbsp olive oil
- 1 tbsp butter
- 2 fontina cheese slices, grated
- 3 eggs
- 4 slices multigrain bread
- 3 radishes, sliced
- ½ cucumber, sliced
- 2 pimiento peppers, chopped
- Salt and red pepper to taste

Directions:
1. Warm the oil in a skillet over medium heat. Crack in the eggs and cook until the whites are set. Season with salt and red pepper; remove to a plate. Brush the bread slices with butter and toast them in the same skillet for 2 minutes per side.
2. Arrange 2 bread slices on a flat surface and put them over the eggs. Add in the remaining ingredients and top with the remaining slices. Serve immediately.

Nutrition Info:
- Per Serving: Calories: 487;Fat: 13g;Protein: 24g;Carbs: 32g.

Apple & Pumpkin Muffins

Servings:12 | Cooking Time:30 Minutes

Ingredients:
- ½ cup butter, melted
- 1 ½ cups granulated sugar
- ½ cup sugar
- ¾ cup flour
- 2 tsp pumpkin pie spice
- 1 tsp baking soda
- ¼ tsp salt
- ¼ tsp nutmeg
- 1 apple, grated
- 1 can pumpkin puree
- ½ cup full-fat yogurt
- 2 large egg whites

Directions:
1. Preheat the oven to 350 F. In a bowl, mix sugars, flour, pumpkin pie spice, baking soda, salt, and nutmeg. In a separate bowl, mix apple, pumpkin puree, yogurt, and butter.
2. Slowly mix the wet ingredients into the dry ingredients. Using a mixer on high, whip the egg whites until stiff and fold them into the batter. Pour the batter into a greased muffin tin, filling each cup halfway. Bake for 25 minutes or until a fork inserted in the center comes out clean. Let cool.

Nutrition Info:
- Per Serving: Calories: 259;Fat: 8.2g;Protein: 3g;Carbs: 49.1g.

Sunday Pancakes In Berry Sauce

Servings:4 | Cooking Time:20 Minutes

Ingredients:
- Pancakes
- 6 tbsp olive oil
- 1 cup flour
- 1 tsp baking powder
- ¼ tsp salt
- 2 large eggs
- 1 lemon, zested and juiced
- ½ tsp vanilla extract
- ½ tsp dark rum
- Berry Sauce
- 1 cup mixed berries
- 3 tbsp sugar
- 1 tbsp lemon juice
- ½ tsp vanilla extract

Directions:
1. In a large bowl, combine the flour, baking powder, and salt and whisk to break up any clumps. Add 4 tablespoons of olive oil, eggs, lemon zest and juice, rum, and vanilla extract and whisk to combine well. Brush a frying pan with butter over medium heat and cook the pancakes for 5-7 minutes, flipping once until bubbles begin to form.
2. To make the sauce, pour the mixed berries, lemon juice, va-

nilla, and sugar in a small saucepan over medium heat. Cook for 3-4 minutes until bubbly, adding a little water if the mixture is too thick. Mash the berries with a fork and stir until smooth. Pour over the pancakes and serve.

Nutrition Info:
- Per Serving: Calories: 275;Fat: 26g;Protein: 4g;Carbs: 8g.

Avocado & Peach Power Smoothie

Servings:2 | Cooking Time:10 Minutes

Ingredients:
- 1 tbsp sesame seeds
- 1 tsp sugar
- 2 peaches, cored and chopped
- ½ cup Greek yogurt
- ½ ripe avocado, chopped
- 2 tbsp flax meal
- 1 tsp vanilla extract
- 1 tsp orange extract

Directions:
1. Blend the sesame seeds, sugar, peaches, yogurt, avocado, flax meal, vanilla, orange extract, and honey in your food processor until smooth. Pour the mixture into 2 bowls. Serve.

Nutrition Info:
- Per Serving: Calories: 213;Fat: 13g;Protein: 6g;Carbs: 23g.

Honey Breakfast Smoothie

Servings:1 | Cooking Time:10 Minutes

Ingredients:
- 1 tbsp olive oil
- 2 tbsp almond butter
- 1 cup almond milk
- ¼ cup blueberries
- 1 tbsp ground flaxseed
- 1 tsp honey
- ½ tsp vanilla extract
- ¼ tsp ground cinnamon

Directions:
1. In a blender, mix the almond milk, blueberries, almond butter, flaxseed, olive oil, stevia vanilla, and cinnamon and pulse until smooth and creamy. Add more milk or water to achieve your desired consistency. Serve at room temperature.

Nutrition Info:
- Per Serving: Calories: 460;Fat: 40.2g;Protein: 9g;Carbs: 20g.

Brown Rice Salad With Cheese

Servings:4 | Cooking Time:10 Minutes

Ingredients:
- 2 tbsp olive oil
- ½ cup brown rice
- 1 lb watercress
- 1 Roma tomato, sliced
- 4 oz feta cheese, crumbled
- 2 tbsp fresh basil, chopped
- Salt and black pepper to taste
- 2 tbsp lemon juice
- ¼ tsp lemon zest

Directions:
1. Bring to a boil salted water in a pot over medium heat. Add in the rice and cook for 15-18 minutes. Drain and let cool completely. Whisk the olive oil, lemon zest, lemon juice, salt, and pepper in a salad bowl. Add in the watercress, cooled rice, and basil and toss to coat. Top with feta cheese and tomato. Serve immediately.

Nutrition Info:
- Per Serving: Calories: 480;Fat: 24g;Protein: 14g;Carbs: 55g.

Power Green Smoothie

Servings:1 | Cooking Time:10 Minutes

Ingredients:
- 1 tbsp extra-virgin olive oil
- 1 avocado, peeled and pitted
- 1 cup milk
- ½ cup watercress
- ½ cup baby spinach leaves
- ½ cucumber, peeled and seeded
- 10 mint leaves, stems removed
- ½ lemon, juiced

Directions:
1. In a blender, mix avocado, milk, baby spinach, watercress, cucumber, olive oil, mint, and lemon juice and blend until smooth and creamy. Add more milk or water to achieve your desired consistency. Serve chilled or at room temperature.

Nutrition Info:
- Per Serving: Calories: 330;Fat: 30.2g;Protein: 4g;Carbs: 19g.

Zucchini & Tomato Cheese Tart

Servings:6 | Cooking Time:60 Minutes

Ingredients:
- 3 tbsp olive oil
- 5 sun-dried tomatoes, chopped
- 1 prepared pie crust
- 1 onion, chopped
- 2 garlic cloves, minced
- 2 zucchinis, chopped
- 1 red bell pepper, chopped
- 6 Kalamata olives, sliced
- 1 tsp fresh dill, chopped
- ½ cup Greek yogurt
- 1 cup feta cheese, crumbled
- 4 eggs
- 1 ½ cups milk
- Salt and black pepper to taste

Directions:
1. Preheat the oven to 380°F. Warm the olive oil in a skillet over medium heat and sauté garlic and onion for 3 minutes. Add in bell pepper and zucchini and sauté for another 3 minutes. Stir in olives, dill, salt, and pepper for 1-2 minutes and add tomatoes and feta cheese. Mix well and turn the heat off.
2. Press the crust gently into a lightly greased pie dish and prick it with a fork. Bake in the oven for 10-15 minutes until pale gold. Spread the zucchini mixture over the pie crust. Whisk the eggs with salt, pepper, milk, and yogurt in a bowl, then pour over the zucchini layer. Bake for 25-30 minutes until golden brown. Let cool before serving.

Nutrition Info:
- Per Serving: Calories: 220;Fat: 16g;Protein: 10g;Carbs: 14g.

Vegetable & Cheese Frittata

Servings:4 | Cooking Time:30 Minutes

Ingredients:
- 2 tbsp olive oil
- ½ lb cauliflower florets
- ½ cup skimmed milk
- 6 eggs
- 1 red bell pepper, chopped
- ½ cup fontina cheese, grated
- ½ tsp red pepper
- ½ tsp turmeric
- Salt and black pepper to taste

Directions:
1. Preheat oven to 360°F. In a bowl, beat the eggs with milk. Add in fontina cheese, red pepper, turmeric, salt, and pepper. Mix in red bell pepper. Warm olive oil in a skillet over medium heat, pour in the egg mixture and cook for 4-5 minutes. Set aside.
2. Blanch the cauliflower florets in a pot for 5 minutes until tender. Spread over the egg mixture. Place the skillet in the oven and bake for 15 minutes or until golden brown. Allow cooling for a few minutes before slicing. Serve warm.

Nutrition Info:
- Per Serving: Calories: 312;Fat: 18g;Protein: 21g;Carbs: 17g.

Ritzy Garden Burgers

Servings:6 | Cooking Time: 30 Minutes

Ingredients:
- 1 tablespoon avocado oil
- 1 yellow onion, diced
- ½ cup shredded carrots
- 4 garlic cloves, halved
- 1 can black beans, rinsed and drained
- 1 cup gluten-free rolled oats
- ¼ cup oil-packed sun-dried tomatoes, drained and chopped
- ½ cup sunflower seeds, toasted
- 1 teaspoon chili powder
- 1 teaspoon paprika
- 1 teaspoon ground cumin
- ½ cup fresh parsley, stems removed
- ¼ teaspoon ground red pepper flakes
- ¾ teaspoon sea salt
- ¼ teaspoon ground black pepper
- ¼ cup olive oil
- For Serving:
- 6 whole-wheat buns, split in half and toasted
- 2 ripe avocados, sliced
- 1 cup kaiware sprouts or mung bean sprouts
- 1 ripe tomato, sliced

Directions:
1. Line a baking sheet with parchment paper.
2. Heat 1 tablespoon of avocado oil in a nonstick skillet over medium heat.
3. Add the onion and carrots and sauté for 10 minutes or until the onion is caramelized.
4. Add the garlic and sauté for 30 seconds or until fragrant.
5. Transfer them into a food processor, then add the remaining ingredients, except for the olive oil. Pulse until chopped fine and the mixture holds together. Make sure not to purée the mixture.
6. Divide and form the mixture into six 4-inch diameter and ½-inch thick patties.
7. Arrange the patties on the baking sheet and wrap the sheet in plastic. Put the baking sheet in the refrigerator and freeze for at least an hour until firm.
8. Remove the baking sheet from the refrigerator, let them sit under room temperature for 10 minutes.
9. Heat the olive oil in a nonstick skillet over medium-high heat until shimmering.
10. Fry the patties in the skillet for 15 minutes or until lightly browned and crispy. Flip the patties halfway through the cooking time. You may need to work in batches to avoid overcrowding.
11. Assemble the buns with patties, avocados, sprouts, and tomato slices to make the burgers.

Nutrition Info:
- Per Serving: Calories: 613;Fat: 23.1g;Protein: 26.2g;Carbs: 88.3g.

Bell Pepper & Cheese Egg Scramble

Servings:4 | Cooking Time:20 Minutes

Ingredients:
- ½ cup fresh mozzarella cheese, crumbled
- 2 tsp olive oil
- 1 cup bell peppers, chopped
- 2 garlic cloves, minced
- 6 large eggs, beaten
- Salt to taste
- 2 tbsp fresh cilantro, chopped

Directions:
1. Warm the olive oil in a large skillet over medium heat. Add the peppers and sauté for 5 minutes, stirring occasionally. Add the garlic and cook for 1 minute. Stir in the eggs and salt and cook for 2-3 minutes until the eggs begin to set on the bottom. Top with mozzarella cheese and cook the eggs for about 2 more minutes, stirring slowly, until the eggs are soft-set and custardy. Sprinkle with cilantro and serve.

Nutrition Info:
- Per Serving: Calories: 259;Fat: 16g;Protein: 29g;Carbs: 2g.

Brown Rice And Black Bean Burgers

Servings:8 | Cooking Time: 40 Minutes

Ingredients:
- 1 cup cooked brown rice
- 1 can black beans, drained and rinsed
- 1 tablespoon olive oil
- 2 tablespoons taco or seasoning
- ½ yellow onion, finely diced
- 1 beet, peeled and grated
- 1 carrot, peeled and grated
- 2 tablespoons no-salt-added tomato paste
- 2 tablespoons apple cider vinegar
- 3 garlic cloves, minced
- ¼ teaspoon sea salt
- Ground black pepper, to taste
- 8 whole-wheat hamburger buns
- Toppings:
- 16 lettuce leaves, rinsed well
- 8 tomato slices, rinsed well
- Whole-grain mustard, to taste

Directions:
1. Line a baking sheet with parchment paper.
2. Put the brown rice and black beans in a food processor and pulse until mix well. Pour the mixture in a large bowl and set aside.
3. Heat the olive oil in a nonstick skillet over medium heat until shimmering.
4. Add the taco seasoning and stir for 1 minute or until fragrant.
5. Add the onion, beet, and carrot and sauté for 5 minutes or until the onion is translucent and beet and carrot are tender.
6. Pour in the tomato paste and vinegar, then add the garlic and cook for 3 minutes or until the sauce is thickened. Sprinkle with salt and ground black pepper.
7. Transfer the vegetable mixture to the bowl of rice mixture, then stir to mix well until smooth.
8. Divide and shape the mixture into 8 patties, then arrange the patties on the baking sheet and refrigerate for at least 1 hour.
9. Preheat the oven to 400ºF.
10. Remove the baking sheet from the refrigerator and allow to sit under room temperature for 10 minutes.
11. Bake in the preheated oven for 40 minutes or until golden brown on both sides. Flip the patties halfway through the cooking time.
12. Remove the patties from the oven and allow to cool for 10 minutes.
13. Assemble the buns with patties, lettuce, and tomato slices. Top the filling with mustard and serve immediately.

Nutrition Info:
- Per Serving: Calories: 544;Fat: 20.0g;Protein: 15.8g;Carbs: 76.0g.

Lime Watermelon Yogurt Smoothie

Servings:6 | Cooking Time:5 Minutes

Ingredients:
- ½ cup almond milk
- 2 cups watermelon, cubed
- ½ cup Greek yogurt
- ½ tsp lime zest

Directions:
1. In a food processor, blend watermelon, almond milk, lime zest, and yogurt until smooth. Serve into glasses.

Nutrition Info:
- Per Serving: Calories: 260;Fat: 10g;Protein: 2g;Carbs: 6g.

Apple-oat Porridge With Cranberries

Servings:4 | Cooking Time:15 Minutes

Ingredients:
- 3 green apples, cored, peeled and cubed
- 2 cups milk
- ½ cup walnuts, chopped
- 3 tbsp maple syrup
- ½ cup steel cut oats
- ½ tsp cinnamon powder
- ½ cup cranberries, dried
- 1 tsp vanilla extract

Directions:
1. Warm the milk in a pot over medium heat and stir in apples, maple syrup, oats, cinnamon powder, cranberries, vanilla extract, and 1 cup water. Simmer for 10 minutes. Ladle the porridge into serving bowls, top with walnuts, and serve.

Nutrition Info:
- Per Serving: Calories: 160;Fat: 3g;Protein: 6g;Carbs: 4g.

Grilled Caesar Salad Sandwiches

Servings:2 | Cooking Time: 5 Minutes

Ingredients:
- ¾ cup olive oil, divided
- 2 romaine lettuce hearts, left intact
- 3 to 4 anchovy fillets
- Juice of 1 lemon
- 2 to 3 cloves garlic, peeled
- 1 teaspoon Dijon mustard
- ¼ teaspoon Worcestershire
- sauce
- Sea salt and freshly ground pepper, to taste
- 2 slices whole-wheat bread, toasted
- Freshly grated Parmesan cheese, for serving

Directions:
1. Preheat the grill to medium-high heat and oil the grates.
2. On a cutting board, drizzle the lettuce with 1 to 2 tablespoons of olive oil and place on the grates.
3. Grill for 5 minutes, turning until lettuce is slightly charred on all sides. Let lettuce cool enough to handle.
4. In a food processor, combine the remaining olive oil with the anchovies, lemon juice, garlic, mustard, and Worcestershire sauce.
5. Pulse the ingredients until you have a smooth emulsion. Season with sea salt and freshly ground pepper to taste. Chop the lettuce in half and place on the bread.
6. Drizzle with the dressing and serve with a sprinkle of Parmesan cheese.

Nutrition Info:
- Per Serving: Calories: 949;Fat: 85.6g;Protein: 12.9g;Carbs: 34.1g.

Basic Tortilla De Patatas

Servings:4 | Cooking Time:35 Minutes

Ingredients:
- 1 ½ lb gold potatoes, peeled and sliced
- ½ cup olive oil
- 1 sweet onion, thinly sliced
- 8 eggs
- ½ dried oregano
- Salt to taste

Directions:
1. Heat the olive oil in a skillet over medium heat. Fry the potatoes for 8-10 minutes, stirring often. Add in onion, oregano, and salt and cook for 5-6 minutes until the potatoes are tender and slightly golden; set aside.
2. In a bowl, beat the eggs with a pinch of salt. Add in the potato mixture and mix well. Pour into the skillet and cook for about 10-12 minutes. Flip the tortilla using a plate, and cook for 2 more minutes until nice and crispy. Slice and serve.

Nutrition Info:
- Per Serving: Calories: 440;Fat: 34g;Protein: 14g;Carbs: 22g.

Quick & Easy Bread In A Mug

Servings:1 | Cooking Time:10 Minutes

Ingredients:
- 1 tbsp olive oil
- 3 tbsp flour
- 1 large egg
- ½ tsp dried thyme
- ¼ tsp baking powder
- ½ tsp salt

Directions:
1. In a heat-resistant ramekin, mix the flour, olive oil, egg, thyme, baking powder, and salt with a fork. Place in the microwave and heat for 80 seconds on high. Run a knife around the edges and flip around to remove the bread. Slice in half to use it to make sandwiches.

Nutrition Info:
- Per Serving: Calories: 232;Fat: 22.2g;Protein: 8g;Carbs: 1.1g.

Berry & Cheese Omelet

Servings:4 | Cooking Time:10 Minutes

Ingredients:
- 2 tbsp olive oil
- 6 eggs, whisked
- 1 tsp cinnamon powder
- 1 cup ricotta cheese
- 4 oz berries

Directions:
1. Whisk eggs, cinnamon powder, ricotta cheese, and berries in a bowl. Warm the olive oil in a skillet over medium heat and pour in the egg mixture. Cook for 2 minutes, turn the egg and cook for 2 minutes more. Serve immediately.

Nutrition Info:
- Per Serving: Calories: 256;Fat: 18g;Protein: 15.6g;Carbs: 7g.

Za'atar Pizza

Servings:4 | Cooking Time: 1o To 12 Minutes

Ingredients:
- 1 sheet puff pastry
- ¼ cup extra-virgin olive oil
- ⅓ cup za'atar seasoning

Directions:
1. Preheat the oven to 350ºF. Line a baking sheet with parchment paper.
2. Place the puff pastry on the prepared baking sheet. Cut the pastry into desired slices.
3. Brush the pastry with the olive oil. Sprinkle with the za'atar seasoning.
4. Put the pastry in the oven and bake for 10 to 12 minutes, or until edges are lightly browned and puffed up.
5. Serve warm.

Nutrition Info:
- Per Serving: Calories: 374;Fat: 30.0g;Protein: 3.0g;Carbs: 20.0g.

Pumpkin-yogurt Parfaits

Servings:4 | Cooking Time:5 Min + Chilling Time

Ingredients:
- 1 can pumpkin puree
- 4 tsp honey
- 1 tsp pumpkin pie spice
- ¼ tsp ground cinnamon
- 2 cups Greek yogurt
- 1 cup honey granola
- 2 tbsp pomegranate seeds

Directions:
1. Mix the pumpkin puree, honey, pumpkin pie spice, and cinnamon in a large bowl. Layer the pumpkin mix, yogurt, and granola in small glasses. Repeat the layers. Top with pomegranate seeds. Chill for at least 3 hours before serving.

Nutrition Info:
- Per Serving: Calories: 264;Fat: 9.2g;Protein: 15g;Carbs: 35g.

Cheese & Mushroom Muffins

Servings:6 | Cooking Time:40 Minutes

Ingredients:
- 6 eggs
- Salt and black pepper to taste
- 1 cup Gruyere cheese, grated
- 1 yellow onion, chopped
- 1 cup mushrooms, sliced
- ½ cup green olives, chopped

Directions:
1. Beat the eggs, salt, pepper, Gruyere cheese, onion, mushrooms, and green olives in a bowl. Pour into a silicone muffin tray and bake for 30 minutes at 360 F. Serve warm.

Nutrition Info:
- Per Serving: Calories: 120;Fat: 6g;Protein: 8g;Carbs: 10g.

Samosas In Potatoes

Servings:8 | Cooking Time: 30 Minutes

Ingredients:
- 4 small potatoes
- 1 teaspoon coconut oil
- 1 small onion, finely chopped
- 1 small piece ginger, minced
- 2 garlic cloves, minced
- 2 to 3 teaspoons curry powder
- Sea salt and freshly ground black pepper, to taste
- ¼ cup frozen peas, thawed
- 2 carrots, grated
- ¼ cup chopped fresh cilantro

Directions:
1. Preheat the oven to 350ºF.
2. Poke small holes into potatoes with a fork, then wrap with aluminum foil.
3. Bake in the preheated oven for 30 minutes until tender.
4. Meanwhile, heat the coconut oil in a nonstick skillet over medium-high heat until melted.
5. Add the onion and sauté for 5 minutes or until translucent.
6. Add the ginger and garlic to the skillet and sauté for 3 minutes or until fragrant.
7. Add the curry power, salt, and ground black pepper, then stir to coat the onion. Remove them from the heat.
8. When the cooking of potatoes is complete, remove the potatoes from the foil and slice in half.
9. Hollow to potato halves with a spoon, then combine the potato fresh with sautéed onion, peas, carrots, and cilantro in a large bowl. Stir to mix well.
10. Spoon the mixture back to the tomato skins and serve immediately.

Nutrition Info:
- Per Serving: Calories: 131;Fat: 13.9g;Protein: 3.2g;Carbs: 8.8g.

Energy Nut Smoothie

Servings:1 | Cooking Time:10 Minutes

Ingredients:
- 1 tbsp extra-virgin olive oil
- ½ cup Greek yogurt
- ½ cup almond milk
- ½ orange, zested and juiced
- 1 tbsp pistachios, chopped
- 1 tsp honey
- ½ tsp ground allspice
- ¼ tsp ground cinnamon
- ¼ tsp vanilla extract

Directions:
1. Place the yogurt, almond milk, orange zest and juice, olive oil, pistachios, honey, allspice, cinnamon, and vanilla in a blender and pulse until smooth and creamy. Add a little water to achieve your desired consistency. Serve in a chilled glass.

Nutrition Info:
- Per Serving: Calories: 264;Fat: 22.2g;Protein: 6g;Carbs: 12g.

Eggs Florentine With Pancetta

Servings:2 | Cooking Time:20 Minutes

Ingredients:
- 1 English muffin, toasted and halved
- ¼ cup chopped pancetta
- 2 tsp hollandaise sauce
- 1 cup spinach
- Salt and black pepper to taste
- 2 large eggs

Directions:
1. Place pancetta in a pan over medium heat and cook for 5 minutes until crispy; reserve. Add the baby spinach and cook for 2-3 minutes in the same pan until the spinach wilts. Fill a pot with 3 inches of water over medium heat and bring to a boil. Add 1 tbsp of vinegar and reduce the heat.
2. Crack the eggs one at a time into a small dish and gently pour into the simmering water. Poach the eggs for 2-3 minutes until the whites are set, but the yolks are still soft; remove with a slotted spoon. Divide the spinach between muffin halves and top with pancetta and poached eggs. Spoon the hollandaise sauce on top and serve.

Nutrition Info:
- Per Serving: Calories: 173;Fat: 7g;Protein: 11g;Carbs: 17g.

Avocado & Tuna Sandwiches

Servings:4 | Cooking Time:15 Minutes

Ingredients:
- 2 cans tuna, packed in olive oil
- 4 bun breads, sliced in half
- 2 tbsp garlic aioli
- 1 avocado, mashed
- 1 tbsp chopped capers
- 1 tsp chopped fresh cilantro

Directions:
1. Cut each round of bun in half and set aside. Add the tuna and oil into a bowl, and mix in the aioli, avocado, capers, and cilantro. Mix well with a fork. Toast the bread, remove and spread the tuna salad onto each quarter. Serve warm.

Nutrition Info:
- Per Serving: Calories: 436;Fat: 36g;Protein: 22.9g;Carbs: 5g.

Honey & Feta Frozen Yogurt

Servings:4 | Cooking Time:5 Minutes + Freezing Time

Ingredients:
- 1 tbsp honey
- 1 cup Greek yogurt
- ½ cup feta cheese, crumbled
- 2 tbsp mint leaves, chopped

Directions:
1. In a food processor, blend yogurt, honey, and feta cheese until smooth. Transfer to a wide dish, cover with plastic wrap, and put in the freezer for 2 hours or until solid. When frozen, spoon into cups, sprinkle with mint, and serve.

Nutrition Info:
- Per Serving: Calories: 170;Fat: 12g;Protein: 7g;Carbs: 13g.

Cauliflower Breakfast Porridge

Servings:2 | Cooking Time: 5 Minutes

Ingredients:
- 2 cups riced cauliflower
- ¾ cup unsweetened almond milk
- 4 tablespoons extra-virgin olive oil, divided
- 2 teaspoons grated fresh orange peel (from ½ orange)
- ½ teaspoon almond extract or
- vanilla extract
- ½ teaspoon ground cinnamon
- ⅛ teaspoon salt
- 4 tablespoons chopped walnuts, divided
- 1 to 2 teaspoons maple syrup (optional)

Directions:
1. Place the riced cauliflower, almond milk, 2 tablespoons of olive oil, orange peel, almond extract, cinnamon, and salt in a medium saucepan.
2. Stir to incorporate and bring the mixture to a boil over medium-high heat, stirring often.
3. Remove from the heat and add 2 tablespoons of chopped walnuts and maple syrup (if desired).
4. Stir again and divide the porridge into bowls. To serve, sprinkle each bowl evenly with remaining 2 tablespoons of walnuts and olive oil.

Nutrition Info:
- Per Serving: Calories: 381;Fat: 37.8g;Protein: 5.2g;Carbs: 10.9g.

Cheese Egg Quiche

Servings:6 | Cooking Time:45 Minutes

Ingredients:
- 1 tbsp melted butter
- 1 ¼ cups crumbled feta
- ½ cup ricotta, crumbled
- 2 tbsp chopped fresh mint
- 1 tbsp chopped fresh dill
- ½ tsp lemon zest
- Black pepper to taste
- 2 large eggs, beaten

Directions:
1. Preheat the oven to 350 F. In a medium bowl, combine the feta and ricotta cheeses and blend them well with a fork. Stir in the mint, dill, lemon zest, and black pepper. Slowly add the eggs to the cheese mixture and blend well. Pour the batter into a greased baking dish and drizzle with melted butter. Bake until lightly browned, 35-40 minutes. Serve.

Nutrition Info:
- Per Serving: Calories: 182;Fat: 17g;Protein: 7g;Carbs: 2g.

Quick Pumpkin Oatmeal

Servings:4 | Cooking Time:15 Minutes

Ingredients:
- ¼ cup pumpkin seeds
- ½ cup milk
- 1 cup old-fashioned oats
- 1 cup pumpkin puree
- 2 tbsp superfine sugar
- ½ tsp ground cinnamon
- 1 ¾ cups water
- ¼ tsp sea salt

Directions:
1. Place milk, salt, and 1 ¾ cups of water in a pot over medium heat and bring to a boil. Mix in oats, then lower the heat and simmer for 5 minutes, stirring periodically.
2. Let sit covered for 5 minutes more. Combine with pumpkin puree, cinnamon, and sugar. Top with pumpkin seeds and serve.

Nutrition Info:
- Per Serving: Calories: 143;Fat: 5.4g;Protein: 5g;Carbs: 20.8g.

Warm Bulgur Breakfast Bowls With Fruits

Servings:6 | Cooking Time: 15 Minutes

Ingredients:
- 2 cups unsweetened almond milk
- 1½ cups uncooked bulgur
- 1 cup water
- ½ teaspoon ground cinnamon
- 2 cups frozen (or fresh, pit-ted) dark sweet cherries
- 8 dried (or fresh) figs, chopped
- ½ cup chopped almonds
- ¼ cup loosely packed fresh mint, chopped

Directions:
1. Combine the milk, bulgur, water, and cinnamon in a medium saucepan, stirring, and bring just to a boil.
2. Cover, reduce the heat to medium-low, and allow to simmer for 10 minutes, or until the liquid is absorbed.
3. Turn off the heat, but keep the pan on the stove, and stir in the frozen cherries (no need to thaw), figs, and almonds. Cover and let the hot bulgur thaw the cherries and partially hydrate the figs, about 1 minute.
4. Fold in the mint and stir to combine, then serve.

Nutrition Info:
- Per Serving: Calories: 207;Fat: 6.0g;Protein: 8.0g;Carbs: 32.0g.

Eggplant, Spinach, And Feta Sandwiches

Servings:2 | Cooking Time: 6 To 8 Minutes

Ingredients:
- 1 medium eggplant, sliced into ½-inch-thick slices
- 2 tablespoons olive oil
- Sea salt and freshly ground pepper, to taste
- 5 to 6 tablespoons hummus
- 4 slices whole-wheat bread, toasted
- 1 cup baby spinach leaves
- 2 ounces feta cheese, soft-ened

Directions:
1. Preheat the grill to medium-high heat.
2. Salt both sides of the sliced eggplant, and let sit for 20 minutes to draw out the bitter juices.
3. Rinse the eggplant and pat dry with a paper towel.
4. Brush the eggplant slices with olive oil and season with sea salt and freshly ground pepper to taste.
5. Grill the eggplant until lightly charred on both sides but still slightly firm in the middle, about 3 to 4 minutes per side.
6. Spread the hummus on the bread slices and top with the spinach leaves, feta cheese, and grilled eggplant. Top with the other slice of bread and serve immediately.

Nutrition Info:
- Per Serving: Calories: 493;Fat: 25.3g;Protein: 17.1g;Carbs: 50.9g.

Easy Pizza Pockets

Servings:2 | Cooking Time: 0 Minutes

Ingredients:
- ½ cup tomato sauce
- ½ teaspoon oregano
- ½ teaspoon garlic powder
- ½ cup chopped black olives
- 2 canned artichoke hearts,
- drained and chopped
- 2 ounces pepperoni, chopped
- ½ cup shredded Mozzarella cheese
- 1 whole-wheat pita, halved

Directions:
1. In a medium bowl, stir together the tomato sauce, oregano, and garlic powder.
2. Add the olives, artichoke hearts, pepperoni, and cheese. Stir to mix.
3. Spoon the mixture into the pita halves and serve.

Nutrition Info:
- Per Serving: Calories: 375;Fat: 23.5g;Protein: 17.1g;Carbs: 27.1g.

Tomato And Egg Scramble

Servings:4 | Cooking Time: 20 Minutes

Ingredients:
- 2 tablespoons extra-virgin olive oil
- ¼ cup finely minced red onion
- 1½ cups chopped fresh tomatoes
- 2 garlic cloves, minced
- ½ teaspoon dried thyme
- ½ teaspoon dried oregano
- 8 large eggs
- ½ teaspoon salt
- ¼ teaspoon freshly ground black pepper
- ¾ cup crumbled feta cheese
- ¼ cup chopped fresh mint leaves

Directions:
1. Heat the olive oil in a large skillet over medium heat.
2. Sauté the red onion and tomatoes in the hot skillet for 10 to 12 minutes, or until the tomatoes are softened.
3. Stir in the garlic, thyme, and oregano and sauté for 2 to 4 minutes, or until the garlic is fragrant.
4. Meanwhile, beat the eggs with the salt and pepper in a medium bowl until frothy.
5. Pour the beaten eggs into the skillet and reduce the heat to low. Scramble
6. for 3 to 4 minutes, stirring constantly, or until the eggs are set.
7. Remove from the heat and scatter with the feta cheese and mint. Serve warm.

Nutrition Info:
- Per Serving: Calories: 260;Fat: 21.9g;Protein: 10.2g;Carbs: 5.8g.

Olive & Poppy Seed Bread

Servings:6 | Cooking Time:40 Min + Rising Time

Ingredients:
- ¼ cup olive oil
- 4 cups whole-wheat flour
- 3 tbsp oregano, chopped
- 2 tsp dry yeast
- 1 cup black olives, sliced
- 1 cup lukewarm water
- ½ cup feta cheese, crumbled
- 1 tbsp poppy seeds
- 1 egg, beaten

Directions:
1. In a bowl, combine flour, water, yeast, and olive oil and knead the dough well. Transfer to a bowl and let sit covered with plastic wrap to rise until doubled in size for 60 minutes.
2. Remove the wrap and fold in oregano, black olives, and feta cheese. Place on a floured surface and knead again. Shape the dough into 6 balls and place them in a lined baking sheet. Cover and let rise for another 40 minutes. Preheat the oven to 390 °F. Brush the balls with the egg and sprinkle with the poppy seeds. Bake for 25-30 minutes. Serve.

Nutrition Info:
- Per Serving: Calories: 260;Fat: 8g;Protein: 7g;Carbs: 40g.

Veg Mix And Blackeye Pea Burritos

Servings:6 | Cooking Time: 40 Minutes

Ingredients:
- 1 teaspoon olive oil
- 1 red onion, diced
- 2 garlic cloves, minced
- 1 zucchini, chopped
- 1 tomato, diced
- 1 bell pepper, any color, de-
- seeded and diced
- 1 can blackeye peas
- 2 teaspoons chili powder
- Sea salt, to taste
- 6 whole-grain tortillas

Directions:
1. Preheat the oven to 325ºF.
2. Heat the olive oil in a nonstick skillet over medium heat or until shimmering.
3. Add the onion and sauté for 5 minutes or until translucent.
4. Add the garlic and sauté for 30 seconds or until fragrant.
5. Add the zucchini and sauté for 5 minutes or until tender.
6. Add the tomato and bell pepper and sauté for 2 minutes or until soft.
7. Fold in the black peas and sprinkle them with chili powder and salt. Stir to mix well.
8. Place the tortillas on a clean work surface, then top them with sautéed vegetables mix.
9. Fold one ends of tortillas over the vegetable mix, then tuck and roll them into burritos.
10. Arrange the burritos in a baking dish, seam side down, then pour the juice remains in the skillet over the burritos.
11. Bake in the preheated oven for 25 minutes or until golden brown.
12. Serve immediately.

Nutrition Info:
- Per Serving: Calories: 335;Fat: 16.2g;Protein: 12.1g;Carbs: 8.3g.

Hummus Toast With Pine Nuts & Ricotta

Servings:2 | Cooking Time:5 Minutes

Ingredients:
- 2 whole-wheat bread slices, toasted
- 1 tsp water
- 1 tbsp hummus
- 2 tsp ricotta cheese, crumbled
- ½ lemon, juiced
- 2 tsp pine nuts

Directions:
1. Whisk hummus, water, and lemon juice in a bowl and spread over toasted slices. Sprinkle ricotta cheese and pine nuts.

Nutrition Info:
- Per Serving: Calories: 150;Fat: 8g;Protein: 6g;Carbs: 15g.

One-pan Tomato-basil Eggs

Servings:2 | Cooking Time:25 Minutes

Ingredients:
- 2 tsp olive oil
- 2 eggs, whisked
- 2 tomatoes, cubed
- 1 tbsp basil, chopped
- 1 green onion, chopped
- Salt and black pepper to taste

Directions:
1. Warm the oil in a skillet over medium heat and sauté tomatoes, green onion, salt, and pepper for 5 minutes. Stir in eggs and cook for another 10 minutes. Serve topped with basil.

Nutrition Info:
- Per Serving: Calories: 310;Fat: 15g;Protein: 12g;Carbs: 18g.

Maple-vanilla Yogurt With Walnuts

Servings:4 | Cooking Time:10 Minutes

Ingredients:
- 2 cups Greek yogurt
- ¾ cup maple syrup
- 1 cup walnuts, chopped
- 1 tsp vanilla extract
- 2 tsp cinnamon powder

Directions:
1. Combine yogurt, walnuts, vanilla, maple syrup, and cinnamon powder in a bowl. Let sit in the fridge for 10 minutes.

Nutrition Info:
- Per Serving: Calories: 400;Fat: 25g;Protein: 11g;Carbs: 40g.

Berry-yogurt Smoothie

Servings:1 | Cooking Time:5 Minutes

Ingredients:
- ½ cup Greek yogurt
- ¼ cup milk
- ½ cup fresh blueberries
- 1 tsp vanilla sugar
- 2 ice cubes

Directions:
1. Pulse the Greek yogurt, milk, vanilla sugar, and berries in your blender until the berries are liquefied. Add the ice cubes and blend on high until thick and smooth. Serve.

Nutrition Info:
- Per Serving: Calories: 230;Fat: 8.8g;Protein: 16g;Carbs: 23g.

Almond Iced-coffee

Servings:1 | Cooking Time:5 Minutes

Ingredients:
- 1 cup brewed black coffee, warm
- 1 tbsp olive oil
- 1 tsp MCT oil
- 1 tbsp heavy cream
- ½ tsp almond extract
- ½ tsp ground cinnamon

Directions:
1. Pour the warm coffee (not hot) into a blender. Add the olive oil, heavy cream, MCT oil, almond extract, and cinnamon. Blend well until smooth and creamy. Drink warm and enjoy.

Nutrition Info:
- Per Serving: Calories: 128;Fat: 14.2g;Protein: 0g;Carbs: 0g.

Super Cheeses And Mushroom Tart

Servings:4 | Cooking Time: 1 Hour 30 Minutes

Ingredients:
- Crust:
- 1¾ cups almond flour
- 1 tablespoon raw honey
- ¾ teaspoon sea salt
- ¼ cup extra-virgin olive oil
- ⅓ cup water
- Filling:
- 2 tablespoons extra-virgin olive oil, divided
- 1 pound white mushrooms, trimmed and sliced thinly
- Sea salt, to taste
- 1 garlic clove, minced
- 2 teaspoons minced fresh thyme
- ¼ cup shredded Mozzarella cheese
- ½ cup grated Parmesan cheese
- 4 ounces part-skim ricotta cheese
- Ground black pepper, to taste
- 2 tablespoons ground basil

Directions:
1. Make the Crust:
2. Preheat the oven to 350°F.
3. Combine the flour, honey, salt and olive oil in a large bowl. Stir to mix well. Gently mix in the water until a smooth dough forms.
4. Drop walnut-size clumps from the dough in the single layer on a tart pan. Press the clumps to coat the bottom of the pan.
5. Bake the crust in the preheated oven for 50 minutes or until firm and browned. Rotate the pan halfway through.
6. Make the Filling:
7. While baking the crust, heat 1 tablespoon of olive oil in a non-stick skillet over medium-high heat until shimmering.
8. Add the mushrooms and sprinkle with ½ teaspoon of salt. Sauté for 15 minutes or until tender.
9. Add the garlic and thyme and sauté for 30 seconds or until fragrant.
10. Make the Tart:
11. Meanwhile, combine the cheeses, salt, ground black pepper, and 1 tablespoon of olive oil in a bowl. Stir to mix well.
12. Spread the cheese mixture over the crust, then top with the mushroom mixture.
13. Bake in the oven for 20 minutes or until the cheeses are frothy and the tart is heated through. Rotate the pan halfway through the baking time.
14. Remove the tart from the oven. Allow to cool for at least 10 minutes, then sprinkle with basil. Slice to serve.

Nutrition Info:
- Per Serving: Calories: 530;Fat: 26.6g;Protein: 11.7g;Carbs: 63.5g.

Artichoke Omelet With Goat Cheese

Servings:2 | Cooking Time:20 Minutes

Ingredients:
- 1 cup canned artichoke hearts, chopped
- 1 tsp butter
- 4 eggs
- Salt and black pepper to taste
- 2 small tomato, chopped
- 4 oz goat cheese, crumbled

Directions:
1. Whisk the eggs with salt and pepper in a bowl. Melt butter in a skillet over medium heat and pour in the eggs, swirling the skillet until the base is golden, 4 minutes. Add the tomato, artichoke, and goat cheese and fold over the omelet. Serve.

Nutrition Info:
- Per Serving: Calories: 310;Fat: 20g;Protein: 23g;Carbs: 16g.

Open-faced Margherita Sandwiches

Servings:4 | Cooking Time: 5 Minutes

Ingredients:
- 2 whole-wheat submarine or hoagie rolls, sliced open horizontally
- 1 tablespoon extra-virgin olive oil
- 1 garlic clove, halved
- 1 large ripe tomato, cut into 8 slices
- ¼ teaspoon dried oregano
- 1 cup fresh Mozzarella, sliced
- ¼ cup lightly packed fresh basil leaves, torn into small pieces
- ¼ teaspoon freshly ground black pepper

Directions:
1. Preheat the broiler to High with the rack 4 inches under the heating element.
2. Put the sliced bread on a large, rimmed baking sheet and broil for 1 minute, or until the bread is just lightly toasted. Remove from the oven.
3. Brush each piece of the toasted bread with the oil, and rub a garlic half over each piece.
4. Put the toasted bread back on the baking sheet. Evenly divide the tomato slices on each piece. Sprinkle with the oregano and top with the cheese.
5. Place the baking sheet under the broiler. Set the timer for 1½ minutes, but check after 1 minute. When the cheese is melted and the edges are just starting to get dark brown, remove the sandwiches from the oven.
6. Top each sandwich with the fresh basil and pepper before serving.

Nutrition Info:
- Per Serving: Calories: 93;Fat: 2.0g;Protein: 10.0g;Carbs: 8.0g.

Classic Spanish Tortilla With Tuna

Servings:4 | Cooking Time:30 Minutes

Ingredients:
- 7 oz canned tuna packed in water, flaked
- 2 plum tomatoes, seeded and diced
- 2 tbsp olive oil
- 6 large eggs, beaten
- 2 small potatoes, diced
- 2 green onions, chopped
- 1 roasted red bell pepper, sliced
- 1 tsp dried tarragon

Directions:
1. Preheat your broiler to high. Heat the olive oil in a skillet over medium heat. Fry the potatoes for 7 minutes until slightly soft. Add the green onions and cook for 3 minutes. Stir in the tuna, tomatoes, peppers, tarragon, and eggs. Cook for 8-10 minutes until the eggs are bubbling from the bottom and the bottom is slightly brown. Place the skillet under the preheated broiler for 5-6 minutes or until the middle is set and the top is slightly brown. Serve sliced into wedges.

Nutrition Info:
- Per Serving: Calories: 422;Fat: 21g;Protein: 14g;Carbs: 46g.

Avocado And Egg Toast

Servings:2 | Cooking Time: 8 Minutes

Ingredients:
- 2 tablespoons ground flaxseed
- ½ teaspoon baking powder
- 2 large eggs, beaten
- 1 teaspoon salt, plus additional for serving
- ½ teaspoon freshly ground black pepper, plus additional for serving
- ½ teaspoon garlic powder, sesame seed, caraway seed, or other dried herbs (optional)
- 3 tablespoons extra-virgin olive oil, divided
- 1 medium ripe avocado, peeled, pitted, and sliced
- 2 tablespoons chopped ripe tomato

Directions:
1. In a small bowl, combine the flaxseed and baking powder, breaking up any lumps in the baking powder.
2. Add the beaten eggs, salt, pepper, and garlic powder (if desired) and whisk well. Let sit for 2 minutes.
3. In a small nonstick skillet, heat 1 tablespoon of olive oil over medium heat. Pour the egg mixture into the skillet and let cook undisturbed until the egg begins to set on bottom, 2 to 3 minutes.
4. Using a rubber spatula, scrape down the sides to allow uncooked egg to reach the bottom. Cook for an additional 2 to 3 minutes.
5. Once almost set, flip like a pancake and allow the top to fully cook, another 1 to 2 minutes.
6. Remove from the skillet and allow to cool slightly, then slice into 2 pieces.
7. Top each piece with avocado slices, additional salt and pepper, chopped tomato, and drizzle with the remaining 2 tablespoons of olive oil. Serve immediately.

Nutrition Info:
- Per Serving: Calories: 297;Fat: 26.1g;Protein: 8.9g;Carbs: 12.0g.

Kale Egg Cupcakes

Servings:2 | Cooking Time:40 Minutes

Ingredients:
- 1 whole-grain bread slice
- 4 large eggs, beaten
- 3 tbsp milk
- Salt and black pepper to taste
- ½ tsp onion powder
- ¼ tsp garlic powder
- ¾ cup chopped kale

Directions:
1. Heat the oven to 350 °F. Break the bread into pieces and divide between 2 greased ramekins. Mix the eggs, milk, salt, onion powder, garlic powder, pepper, and kale in a medium bowl. Pour half of the egg mixture into each ramekin and bake for 25 minutes or until the eggs are set. Serve and enjoy!

Nutrition Info:
- Per Serving: Calories: 213;Fat: 12g;Protein: 17g;Carbs: 13g.

Savory Breakfast Oatmeal

Servings:2 | Cooking Time: 15 Minutes

Ingredients:
- ½ cup steel-cut oats
- 1 cup water
- 1 medium cucumber, chopped
- 1 large tomato, chopped
- 1 tablespoon olive oil
- Pinch freshly grated Parme-
- san cheese
- Sea salt and freshly ground pepper, to taste
- Flat-leaf parsley or mint, chopped, for garnish

Directions:
1. Combine the oats and water in a medium saucepan and bring to a boil over high heat, stirring continuously, or until the water is absorbed, about 15 minutes.
2. Divide the oatmeal between 2 bowls and scatter the tomato and cucumber on top. Drizzle with the olive oil and sprinkle with the Parmesan cheese.
3. Season with salt and pepper to taste. Serve garnished with the

parsley.

Nutrition Info:
- Per Serving: Calories: 197;Fat: 8.9g;Protein: 6.3g;Carbs: 23.1g.

Oat & Raspberry Pudding
Servings:2 | Cooking Time:5 Minutes

Ingredients:
- 1 cup almond milk
- ½ cup rolled oats
- 1 tbsp chia seeds
- 2 tsp honey
- 1 cup raspberries, pureed
- 1 tbsp yogurt

Directions:
1. Toss the oats, almond milk, chia seeds, honey, and raspberries in a bowl. Serve in bowls topped with yogurt.

Nutrition Info:
- Per Serving: Calories: 410;Fat: 32g;Protein: 7g;Carbs: 34g.

Spicy Tofu Tacos With Cherry Tomato Salsa
Servings:4 | Cooking Time: 11 Minutes

Ingredients:
- Cherry Tomato Salsa:
- ¼ cup sliced cherry tomatoes
- ½ jalapeño, deseeded and sliced
- Juice of 1 lime
- 1 garlic clove, minced
- Sea salt and freshly ground black pepper, to taste
- 2 teaspoons extra-virgin olive oil
- Spicy Tofu Taco Filling:
- 4 tablespoons water, divided
- ½ cup canned black beans, rinsed and drained
- 2 teaspoons fresh chopped chives, divided
- ¾ teaspoon ground cumin, divided
- ¾ teaspoon smoked paprika, divided
- Dash cayenne pepper (optional)
- ¼ teaspoon sea salt
- ¼ teaspoon freshly ground black pepper
- 1 teaspoon extra-virgin olive oil
- 6 ounces firm tofu, drained, rinsed, and pressed
- 4 corn tortillas
- ¼ avocado, sliced
- ¼ cup fresh cilantro

Directions:
1. Make the Cherry Tomato Salsa:
2. Combine the ingredients for the salsa in a small bowl. Stir to mix well. Set aside until ready to use.
3. Make the Spicy Tofu Taco Filling:
4. Add 2 tablespoons of water into a saucepan, then add the black beans and sprinkle with 1 teaspoon of chives, ½ teaspoon of cumin, ¼ teaspoon of smoked paprika, and cayenne. Stir to mix well.
5. Cook for 5 minutes over medium heat until heated through, then mash the black beans with the back of a spoon. Turn off the heat and set aside.
6. Add remaining water into a bowl, then add the remaining chives, cumin, and paprika. Sprinkle with cayenne, salt, and black pepper. Stir to mix well. Set aside.
7. Heat the olive oil in a nonstick skillet over medium heat until shimmering.
8. Add the tofu and drizzle with taco sauce, then sauté for 5 minutes or until the seasoning is absorbed. Remove the tofu from the skillet and set aside.
9. Warm the tortillas in the skillet for 1 minutes or until heated through.
10. Transfer the tortillas onto a large plate and top with tofu, mashed black beans, avocado, cilantro, then drizzle the tomato salsa over. Serve immediately.

Nutrition Info:

- Per Serving: Calories: 240;Fat: 9.0g;Protein: 11.6g;Carbs: 31.6g.

Detox Juice
Servings:1 | Cooking Time:5 Minutes

Ingredients:
- ½ grapefruit
- ½ lemon
- 3 cups cavolo nero
- 1 cucumber
- ¼ cup fresh parsley leaves
- ¼ pineapple, cut into wedges
- ½ green apple
- 1 tsp grated fresh ginger

Directions:
1. In a mixer, place the cavolo nero, parsley, cucumber, pineapple, grapefruit, apple, lemon, and ginger and pulse until smooth. Serve in a tall glass.

Nutrition Info:
- Per Serving: Calories: 255;Fat: 0.9g;Protein: 9.5g;Carbs: 60g.

Spinach & Prosciutto Crostini
Servings:1 | Cooking Time:5 Minutes

Ingredients:
- 1 tsp olive oil
- 2 prosciutto slices
- 2 ciabatta slices, toasted
- 1 tbsp Dijon mustard
- Salt and black pepper to taste
- 1 tomato, sliced
- ¼ cup baby spinach

Directions:
1. Smear Dijon mustard on one side of each ciabatta slice and top with prosciutto, tomato, spinach, salt, and pepper on each slice. Drizzle with olive oil and serve.

Nutrition Info:
- Per Serving: Calories: 250;Fat: 12g;Protein: 9g;Carbs: 18g.

Creamy Vanilla Oatmeal
Servings:4 | Cooking Time: 40 Minutes

Ingredients:
- 4 cups water
- Pinch sea salt
- 1 cup steel-cut oats
- ¾ cup unsweetened almond
- milk
- 2 teaspoons pure vanilla extract

Directions:
1. Add the water and salt to a large saucepan over high heat and bring to a boil.
2. Once boiling, reduce the heat to low and add the oats. Mix well and cook for 30 minutes, stirring occasionally.
3. Fold in the almond milk and vanilla and whisk to combine. Continue cooking for about 10 minutes, or until the oats are thick and creamy.
4. Ladle the oatmeal into bowls and serve warm.

Nutrition Info:
- Per Serving: Calories: 117;Fat: 2.2g;Protein: 4.3g;Carbs: 20.0g.

Spicy Black Bean And Poblano Dippers
Servings:8 | Cooking Time: 21 Minutes

Ingredients:
- 2 tablespoons avocado oil, plus more for brushing the dippers
- 1 can black beans, drained and rinsed
- 1 poblano, deseeded and quartered
- 1 jalapeño, halved and deseeded
- ½ cup fresh cilantro, leaves

and tender stems
- 1 yellow onion, quartered
- 2 garlic cloves
- 1 teaspoon chili powder
- 1 teaspoon ground cumin
- 1 teaspoon sea salt
- 24 organic corn tortillas

Directions:
1. Preheat the oven to 400ºF. Line a baking sheet with parchment paper and grease with avocado oil.
2. Combine the remaining ingredients, except for the tortillas, in a food processor, then pulse until chopped finely and the mixture holds together. Make sure not to purée the mixture.
3. Warm the tortillas on the baking sheet in the preheated oven for 1 minute or until softened.
4. Add a tablespoon of the mixture in the middle of each tortilla. Fold one side of the tortillas over the mixture and tuck to roll them up tightly to make the dippers.
5. Arrange the dippers on the baking sheet and brush them with avocado oil. Bake in the oven for 20 minutes or until well browned. Flip the dippers halfway through the cooking time.
6. Serve immediately.

Nutrition Info:
- Per Serving: Calories: 388;Fat: 6.5g;Protein: 16.2g;Carbs: 69.6g.

Artichoke & Spinach Frittata
Servings:4 | Cooking Time:55 Minutes

Ingredients:
- 4 oz canned artichokes, chopped
- 2 tsp olive oil
- ½ cup whole milk
- 8 eggs
- 1 cup spinach, chopped
- 1 garlic clove, minced
- ½ cup Parmesan, crumbled
- 1 tsp oregano, dried
- 1 Jalapeño pepper, minced
- Salt to taste

Directions:
1. Preheat oven to 360 F. Warm the olive oil in a skillet over medium heat and sauté garlic and spinach for 3 minutes.
2. Beat the eggs in a bowl. Stir in artichokes, milk, Parmesan cheese, oregano, jalapeño pepper, and salt. Add in spinach mixture and toss to combine. Transfer to a greased baking dish and bake for 20 minutes until golden and bubbling. Slice into wedges and serve.

Nutrition Info:
- Per Serving: Calories: 190;Fat: 14g;Protein: 10g;Carbs: 5g.

Dilly Salmon Frittata
Servings:4 | Cooking Time:35 Minutes

Ingredients:
- 2 tbsp olive oil
- 1 cup cream cheese
- 1 cup smoked salmon, chopped
- 8 eggs, whisked
- 1 tsp dill, chopped
- 2 tbsp milk
- Salt and black pepper to taste

Directions:
1. Preheat oven to 360 °F. In a bowl, place all the ingredients and stir to combine. Warm olive oil in a pan over medium heat and pour in the mixture. Cook until the base is set, about 3-4 minutes. Place the pan in the oven and bake until the top is golden, about 5 minutes. Serve sliced into wedges.

Nutrition Info:
- Per Serving: Calories: 418;Fat: 37g;Protein: 19.6g;Carbs: 3g.

Banana Corn Fritters
Servings:2 | Cooking Time: 10 Minutes

Ingredients:
- ½ cup yellow cornmeal
- ¼ cup flour
- 2 small ripe bananas, peeled and mashed
- 2 tablespoons unsweetened almond milk
- 1 large egg, beaten
- ½ teaspoon baking powder
- ¼ to ½ teaspoon ground chipotle chili
- ¼ teaspoon ground cinnamon
- ¼ teaspoon sea salt
- 1 tablespoon olive oil

Directions:
1. Stir together all ingredients except for the olive oil in a large bowl until smooth.
2. Heat a nonstick skillet over medium-high heat. Add the olive oil and drop about 2 tablespoons of batter for each fritter. Cook for 2 to 3 minutes until the bottoms are golden brown, then flip. Continue cooking for 1 to 2 minutes more, until cooked through. Repeat with the remaining batter.
3. Serve warm.

Nutrition Info:
- Per Serving: Calories: 396;Fat: 10.6g;Protein: 7.3g;Carbs: 68.0g.

Couscous & Cucumber Bowl
Servings:4 | Cooking Time:15 Minutes

Ingredients:
- 2 tbsp olive oil
- ¾ cup couscous
- 1 cup water
- 1 yellow onion, chopped
- 2 garlic cloves, minced
- 2 cups canned chickpeas
- Salt to taste
- 15 oz canned tomatoes, diced
- 1 cucumber, cut into ribbons
- ½ cup black olives, chopped
- 1 tbsp lemon juice
- 1 tbsp mint leaves, chopped

Directions:
1. Cover the couscous with salted boiling water, cover, and let it sit for about 5 minutes. Then fluff with a fork and set aside.
2. Warm the olive oil in a skillet over medium heat and sauté onion and garlic for 3 minutes until soft. Stir in chickpeas, salt, and tomatoes for 1-2 minutes. Turn off the heat and mix in olives, couscous, and lemon juice. Transfer to a bowl and top with cucumber ribbons and mint to serve.

Nutrition Info:
- Per Serving: Calories: 350;Fat: 11g;Protein: 12g;Carbs: 50g.

Chili & Cheese Frittata
Servings:6 | Cooking Time:35 Minutes

Ingredients:
- 2 tbsp olive oil
- 12 fresh eggs
- ¼ cup half-and-half
- Salt and black pepper to taste
- ½ chili pepper, minced
- 2 ½ cups shredded mozzarella

Directions:
1. Preheat oven to 350 °F. Whisk the eggs in a bowl. Add the half-and-half, salt, and black and stir to combine. Warm the olive oil in a skillet over medium heat. Sauté the chili pepper for 2-3 minutes. Sprinkle evenly with mozzarella cheese. Pour eggs over cheese in the skillet. Place the skillet in the oven and bake for 20–25 minutes until just firm. Let cool the frittata for a few minutes and cut into wedges. Serve hot.

Nutrition Info:

- Per Serving: Calories: 381;Fat: 31g;Protein: 25g;Carbs: 2g.

Hot Zucchini & Egg Nests

Servings:4 | Cooking Time:25 Minutes

Ingredients:
- 2 tbsp olive oil
- 4 eggs
- 1 lb zucchinis, shredded
- Salt and black pepper to taste
- ½ red chili pepper, minced
- 2 tbsp parsley, chopped

Directions:
1. Preheat the oven to 360 °F. Combine zucchini, salt, pepper, and olive oil in a bowl. Form nest shapes with a spoon onto a greased baking sheet. Crack an egg into each nest and season with salt, pepper, and chili pepper. Bake for 11 minutes. Serve topped with parsley.

Nutrition Info:
- Per Serving: Calories: 141;Fat: 11.6g;Protein: 7g;Carbs: 4.2g.

Cream Peach Smoothie

Servings:1 | Cooking Time:5 Minutes

Ingredients:
- 1 large peach, sliced
- 6 oz peach Greek yogurt
- 2 tbsp almond milk
- 2 ice cubes

Directions:
1. Blend the peach, yogurt, almond milk, and ice cubes in your food processor until thick and creamy. Serve and enjoy!

Nutrition Info:
- Per Serving: Calories: 228;Fat: 3g;Protein: 11g;Carbs: 41.6g.

Tomato & Spinach Egg Wraps

Servings:2 | Cooking Time:15 Minutes

Ingredients:
- 1 tbsp parsley, chopped
- 1 tbsp olive oil
- ¼ onion, chopped
- 3 sun-dried tomatoes, chopped
- 3 large eggs, beaten
- 2 cups baby spinach, torn
- 1 oz feta cheese, crumbled
- Salt to taste
- 2 whole-wheat tortillas, warm

Directions:
1. Warm the olive oil in a pan over medium heat. Sauté the onion and tomatoes for about 3 minutes. Add the beaten eggs and stir to scramble them, about 4 minutes. Add the spinach and parsley stir to combine. Sprinkle the feta cheese over the eggs. Season with salt to taste. Divide the mixture between the tortillas. Roll them up and serve.

Nutrition Info:
- Per Serving: Calories: 435;Fat: 28g;Protein: 17g;Carbs: 31g.

Cinnamon Oatmeal With Dried Cranberries

Servings:2 | Cooking Time: 8 Minutes

Ingredients:
- 1 cup almond milk
- 1 cup water
- Pinch sea salt
- 1 cup old-fashioned oats
- ½ cup dried cranberries
- 1 teaspoon ground cinnamon

Directions:
1. In a medium saucepan over high heat, bring the almond milk, water, and salt to a boil.
2. Stir in the oats, cranberries, and cinnamon. Reduce the heat to medium and cook for 5 minutes, stirring occasionally.
3. Remove the oatmeal from the heat. Cover and let it stand for 3 minutes. Stir before serving.

Nutrition Info:
- Per Serving: Calories: 107;Fat: 2.1g;Protein: 3.2g;Carbs: 18.2g.

Mushroom & Zucchini Egg Muffins

Servings:4 | Cooking Time:20 Minutes

Ingredients:
- 2 tbsp olive oil
- 1 cup Parmesan, grated
- 1 onion, chopped
- 1 cup mushrooms, sliced
- 1 red bell pepper, chopped
- 1 zucchini, chopped
- Salt and black pepper to taste
- 8 eggs, whisked
- 2 tbsp chives, chopped

Directions:
1. Preheat the oven to 360 °F. Warm the olive oil in a skillet over medium heat and sauté onion, bell pepper, zucchini, mushrooms, salt, and pepper for 5 minutes until tender. Mix with eggs and season with salt and pepper. Distribute the mixture across muffin cups and top with the Parmesan cheese. Sprinkle with chives and bake for 10 minutes. Serve.

Nutrition Info:
- Per Serving: Calories: 60;Fat: 4g;Protein: 5g;Carbs: 4g.

Maple Peach Smoothie

Servings:2 | Cooking Time:5 Minutes

Ingredients:
- 2 cups almond milk
- 2 cups peaches, chopped
- 1 cup crushed ice
- ½ tsp ground ginger
- 1 tbsp maple syrup

Directions:
1. In a food processor, mix milk, peaches, ice, maple syrup, and ginger until smooth. Serve.

Nutrition Info:
- Per Serving: Calories: 639;Fat: 58g;Protein: 7g;Carbs: 34.2g.

Mushroom-pesto Baked Pizza

Servings:2 | Cooking Time: 15 Minutes

Ingredients:
- 1 teaspoon extra-virgin olive oil
- ½ cup sliced mushrooms
- ½ red onion, sliced
- Salt and freshly ground black pepper
- ¼ cup store-bought pesto sauce
- 2 whole-wheat flatbreads
- ¼ cup shredded Mozzarella cheese

Directions:
1. Preheat the oven to 350ºF.
2. In a small skillet, heat the oil over medium heat. Add the mushrooms and onion, and season with salt and pepper. Sauté for 3 to 5 minutes until the onion and mushrooms begin to soften.
3. Spread 2 tablespoons of pesto on each flatbread.
4. Divide the mushroom-onion mixture between the two flatbreads. Top each with 2 tablespoons of cheese.
5. Place the flatbreads on a baking sheet and bake for 10 to 12 minutes until the cheese is melted and bubbly. Serve warm.

Nutrition Info:
- Per Serving: Calories: 348;Fat: 23.5g;Protein: 14.2g;Carbs: 28.1g.

Nut & Plum Parfait

Servings:4 | Cooking Time:10 Minutes

Ingredients:
- 1 tbsp honey
- 1 cup plums, chopped
- 2 cups Greek yogurt
- 1 tsp cinnamon powder
- 1 tbsp almonds, chopped
- 1 tbsp walnuts, chopped
- ¼ cup pistachios, chopped

Directions:
1. Place a skillet over medium heat and add in plums, honey, cinnamon powder, almonds, walnuts, pistachios, and ¼ cup water. Cook for 5 minutes. Share Greek yogurt into serving bowls and top with plum mixture and toss before serving.

Nutrition Info:
- Per Serving: Calories: 200;Fat: 5g;Protein: 4g;Carbs: 42g.

Hot Egg Scramble

Servings:4 | Cooking Time:35 Minutes

Ingredients:
- 2 tbsp olive oil
- 1 small red onion, chopped
- 1 bell green pepper, chopped
- ½ tsp red pepper flakes
- 1 jalapeño, cut into strips
- 3 medium tomatoes, chopped
- Salt and black pepper to taste
- 1 tbsp ground cumin
- 1 tsp ground coriander
- 4 large eggs, lightly beaten

Directions:
1. Warm the olive oil in a skillet over medium heat. Add the onion and cook until soft and translucent, 5-7 minutes. Add the peppers and continue to cook for another 4-5 minutes until soft. Add in the tomatoes and season to taste. Stir in the cumin and coriander. Simmer for 10 minutes. Add the eggs, stirring them into the mixture to distribute. Cover the skillet and cook until the eggs are set but still fluffy and tender, 5-6 more minutes. Serve topped with red pepper flakes.

Nutrition Info:
- Per Serving: Calories: 171;Fat: 12.1g;Protein: 8.1g;Carbs: 8g.

Lazy Blueberry Oatmeal

Servings:2 | Cooking Time:10 Min + Chilling Time

Ingredients:
- ⅔ cup milk
- ⅓ cup quick rolled oats
- ¼ cup blueberries
- 1 tsp honey
- ½ tsp ground cinnamon
- ¼ tsp ground cloves

Directions:
1. Layer the oats, milk, blueberries, honey, cinnamon, and cloves into 2 mason jars. Cover and store in the refrigerator overnight. Serve cold and enjoy!

Nutrition Info:
- Per Serving: Calories: 82;Fat: 2.2g;Protein: 2g;Carbs: 14.1g.

Parmesan Oatmeal With Greens

Servings:2 | Cooking Time: 18 Minutes

Ingredients:
- 1 tablespoon olive oil
- ¼ cup minced onion
- 2 cups greens (arugula, baby spinach, chopped kale, or Swiss chard)
- ¾ cup gluten-free old-fashioned oats
- 1½ cups water, or low-sodium chicken stock
- 2 tablespoons Parmesan cheese
- Salt, to taste
- Pinch freshly ground black pepper

Directions:
1. Heat the olive oil in a saucepan over medium-high heat. Add the minced onion and sauté for 2 minutes, or until softened.
2. Add the greens and stir until they begin to wilt. Transfer this mixture to a bowl and set aside.
3. Add the oats to the pan and let them toast for about 2 minutes. Add the water and bring the oats to a boil.
4. Reduce the heat to low, cover, and let the oats cook for 10 minutes, or until the liquid is absorbed and the oats are tender.
5. Stir the Parmesan cheese into the oats, and add the onion and greens back to the pan. Add additional water if needed, so the oats are creamy and not dry.
6. Stir well and season with salt and black pepper to taste. Serve warm.

Nutrition Info:
- Per Serving: Calories: 257;Fat: 14.0g;Protein: 12.2g;Carbs: 30.2g.

Chia & Almond Oatmeal

Servings:2 | Cooking Time:10 Min + Chilling Time

Ingredients:
- ¼ tsp almond extract
- ½ cup milk
- ½ cup rolled oats
- 2 tbsp almonds, sliced
- 2 tbsp sugar
- 1 tsp chia seeds
- ¼ tsp ground cardamom
- ¼ tsp ground cinnamon

Directions:
1. Combine the milk, oats, almonds, sugar, chia seeds, cardamom, almond extract, and cinnamon in a mason jar and shake well. Keep in the refrigerator for 4 hours. Serve.

Nutrition Info:
- Per Serving: Calories: 131;Fat: 6.2g;Protein: 4.9g;Carbs: 17g.

Egg Bake

Servings:2 | Cooking Time: 30 Minutes

Ingredients:
- 1 tablespoon olive oil
- 1 slice whole-grain bread
- 4 large eggs
- 3 tablespoons unsweetened almond milk
- ½ teaspoon onion powder
- ¼ teaspoon garlic powder
- ¾ cup chopped cherry tomatoes
- ¼ teaspoon salt
- Pinch freshly ground black pepper

Directions:
1. Preheat the oven to 375ºF.
2. Coat two ramekins with the olive oil and transfer to a baking sheet. Line the bottom of each ramekin with ½ of bread slice.
3. In a medium bowl, whisk together the eggs, almond milk, onion powder, garlic powder, tomatoes, salt, and pepper until well combined.
4. Pour the mixture evenly into two ramekins. Bake in the preheated oven for 30 minutes, or until the eggs are completely set.
5. Cool for 5 minutes before serving.

Nutrition Info:
- Per Serving: Calories: 240;Fat: 17.4g;Protein: 9.0g;Carbs: 12.2g.

Tomato And Egg Breakfast Pizza

Servings:2 | Cooking Time: 15 Minutes

Ingredients:
- 2 slices of whole-wheat naan bread
- 2 tablespoons prepared pesto
- 1 medium tomato, sliced
- 2 large eggs

Directions:
1. Heat a large nonstick skillet over medium-high heat. Place the naan bread in the skillet and let warm for about 2 minutes on each side, or until softened.
2. Spread 1 tablespoon of the pesto on one side of each slice and top with tomato slices.
3. Remove from the skillet and place each one on its own plate.
4. Crack the eggs into the skillet, keeping them separated, and cook until the whites are no longer translucent and the yolk is cooked to desired doneness.
5. Using a spatula, spoon one egg onto each bread slice. Serve warm.

Nutrition Info:
- Per Serving: Calories: 429;Fat: 16.8g;Protein: 18.1g;Carbs: 12.0g.

Spinach Frittata With Roasted Peppers

Servings:4 | Cooking Time:30 Minutes

Ingredients:
- 2 tbsp olive oil
- 1 cup roasted peppers, chopped
- ½ cup milk
- 8 eggs
- Salt and black pepper to taste
- 1 tsp oregano, dried
- ½ cup red onions, chopped
- 4 cups baby spinach
- 1 cup goat cheese, crumbled

Directions:
1. Beat the eggs with salt, pepper, and oregano in a bowl. Warm the olive oil in a skillet over medium heat and sauté onions for 3 minutes until soft. Mix in spinach, milk, and goat cheese and pour over the eggs. Cook for 2-3 minutes until the base of the frittata is set. Place in preheated to 360°F oven and bake for 10-15 minutes until the top is golden. Top with roasted peppers.

Nutrition Info:
- Per Serving: Calories: 260;Fat: 5g;Protein: 15g;Carbs: 5g.

Roasted Tomato Panini

Servings:2 | Cooking Time: 3 Hours 6 Minutes

Ingredients:
- 2 teaspoons olive oil
- 4 Roma tomatoes, halved
- 4 cloves garlic
- 1 tablespoon Italian seasoning
- Sea salt and freshly ground
- pepper, to taste
- 4 slices whole-grain bread
- 4 basil leaves
- 2 slices fresh Mozzarella cheese

Directions:
1. Preheat the oven to 250°F. Grease a baking pan with olive oil.
2. Place the tomatoes and garlic in the baking pan, then sprinkle with Italian seasoning, salt, and ground pepper. Toss to coat well.
3. Roast in the preheated oven for 3 hours or until the tomatoes are lightly wilted.
4. Preheat the panini press.
5. Make the panini: Place two slices of bread on a clean work surface, then top them with wilted tomatoes. Sprinkle with basil and spread with Mozzarella cheese. Top them with remaining two slices of bread.
6. Cook the panini for 6 minutes or until lightly browned and the cheese melts. Flip the panini halfway through the cooking.
7. Serve immediately.

Nutrition Info:
- Per Serving: Calories: 323;Fat: 12.0g;Protein: 17.4g;Carbs: 37.5g.

Mediterranean Eggs (shakshuka)

Servings:4 | Cooking Time: 20 Minutes

Ingredients:
- 2 tablespoons extra-virgin olive oil
- 1 cup chopped shallots
- 1 teaspoon garlic powder
- 1 cup finely diced potato
- 1 cup chopped red bell peppers
- 1 can diced tomatoes, drained
- ¼ teaspoon ground cardamom
- ¼ teaspoon paprika
- ¼ teaspoon turmeric
- 4 large eggs
- ¼ cup chopped fresh cilantro

Directions:
1. Preheat the oven to 350°F.
2. Heat the olive oil in an ovenproof skillet over medium-high heat until it shimmers.
3. Add the shallots and sauté for about 3 minutes, stirring occasionally, until fragrant.
4. Fold in the garlic powder, potato, and bell peppers and stir to combine.
5. Cover and cook for 10 minutes, stirring frequently.
6. Add the tomatoes, cardamon, paprika, and turmeric and mix well.
7. When the mixture begins to bubble, remove from the heat and crack the eggs into the skillet.
8. Transfer the skillet to the preheated oven and bake for 5 to 10 minutes, or until the egg whites are set and the yolks are cooked to your liking.
9. Remove from the oven and garnish with the cilantro before serving.

Nutrition Info:
- Per Serving: Calories: 223;Fat: 11.8g;Protein: 9.1g;Carbs: 19.5g.

Easy Zucchini & Egg Stuffed Tomatoes

Servings:4 | Cooking Time:40 Minutes

Ingredients:
- 1 tbsp olive oil
- 1 small zucchini, grated
- 8 tomatoes, insides scooped
- 8 eggs
- Salt and black pepper to taste

Directions:
1. Preheat the oven to 360 °F. Place tomatoes on a greased baking dish. Mix the zucchini with olive oil, salt, and pepper. Divide the mixture between the tomatoes and crack an egg on each one. Bake for 20-25 minutes. Serve warm.

Nutrition Info:
- Per Serving: Calories: 280;Fat: 22g;Protein: 14g;Carbs: 12g.

Poached Egg & Avocado Toasts

Servings:4 | Cooking Time:15 Minutes

Ingredients:
- 4 bread slices, toasted
- 4 eggs
- 2 avocados, chopped
- ¼ cup chopped fresh cilantro
- 3 tbsp red wine vinegar
- 1 lemon, juiced and zested
- 1 garlic clove, minced
- Salt and black pepper to taste
- 1 tsp hot sauce

Directions:
1. Puree avocados, cilantro, lemon juice, lemon zest, garlic, 2 tbsp of vinegar, salt, black pepper, and hot sauce with an immersion blender in a bowl until smooth. Bring to a boil salted water in a pot over high heat.
2. Add in the remaining vinegar and a pinch of salt. Drop the eggs, one at a time, and poach for 2-3 minutes until the whites are set and yolks are cooked. Remove with a perforated spoon to a paper towel to drain. Spread the avocado mash on the bread toasts and top with poached eggs to serve.

Nutrition Info:
- Per Serving: Calories: 296;Fat: 24.3g;Protein: 8g;Carbs: 14g.

Chocolate-strawberry Smoothie

Servings:2 | Cooking Time:5 Minutes

Ingredients:
- 1 cup buttermilk
- 2 cups strawberries, hulled
- 1 cup crushed ice
- 3 tbsp cocoa powder
- 3 tbsp honey
- 2 mint leaves

Directions:
1. In a food processor, pulse buttermilk, strawberries, ice, cocoa powder, mint, and honey until smooth. Serve.

Nutrition Info:
- Per Serving: Calories: 209;Fat: 2.6g;Protein: 7g;Carbs: 47.2g.

Citrus French Toasts

Servings:4 | Cooking Time:30 Minutes

Ingredients:
- 1 tbsp butter
- 1 orange, juiced and zested
- 4 bread slices
- 1 ½ cups milk
- 2 eggs, beaten
- 1 tsp vanilla extract
- 1 tsp ground cinnamon
- 1 tbsp powdered sugar

Directions:
1. Beat milk, eggs, vanilla, orange zest, and orange juice in a bowl. Lay the bread in a rectangular baking dish in an even layer. Cover with the egg mixture and let it stand for 10 minutes, flipping once, to absorb well.
2. Melt the butter in a skillet over medium heat and fry the bread in batches until golden brown on both sides, about 6-8 minutes. Dust with powdered sugar and cinnamon. Serve.

Nutrition Info:
- Per Serving: Calories: 160;Fat: 7.3g;Protein: 6.9g;Carbs: 17g.

Banana & Chocolate Porridge

Servings:4 | Cooking Time:20 Minutes

Ingredients:
- 2 bananas
- 4 dried apricots, chopped
- 1 cup barley, soaked
- 2 tbsp flax seeds
- 1 tbsp cocoa powder
- 1 cup coconut milk
- ¼ tsp mint leaves
- 2 oz dark chocolate bars, grated
- 2 tbsp coconut flakes

Directions:
1. Place the barley in a saucepan along with the flaxseeds and two cups of water. Bring to a boil, then lower the heat and simmer for 12 minutes, stirring often.
2. Meanwhile, in a food processor, blend bananas, cocoa powder, coconut milk, apricots, and mint leaves until smooth. Once the barley is ready, stir in chocolate. Add in banana mixture. Garnish with coconut flakes. Serve.

Nutrition Info:
- Per Serving: Calories: 476;Fat: 22g;Protein: 10g;Carbs: 65g.

Chapter 3 Vegetable Mains And Meatless Recipes

Chapter 3 Vegetable Mains And Meatless Recipes

Zoodles With Beet Pesto

Servings:2 | Cooking Time: 50 Minutes

Ingredients:
- 1 medium red beet, peeled, chopped
- ½ cup walnut pieces
- ½ cup crumbled goat cheese
- 3 garlic cloves
- 2 tablespoons freshly squeezed lemon juice
- 2 tablespoons plus 2 teaspoons extra-virgin olive oil, divided
- ¼ teaspoon salt
- 4 small zucchinis, spiralized

Directions:
1. Preheat the oven to 375ºF.
2. Wrap the chopped beet in a piece of aluminum foil and seal well.
3. Roast in the preheated oven for 30 to 40 minutes until tender.
4. Meanwhile, heat a skillet over medium-high heat until hot. Add the walnuts and toast for 5 to 7 minutes, or until fragrant and lightly browned.
5. Remove the cooked beets from the oven and place in a food processor. Add the toasted walnuts, goat cheese, garlic, lemon juice, 2 tablespoons of olive oil, and salt. Pulse until smoothly blended. Set aside.
6. Heat the remaining 2 teaspoons of olive oil in a large skillet over medium heat. Add the zucchini and toss to coat in the oil. Cook for 2 to 3 minutes, stirring gently, or until the zucchini is softened.
7. Transfer the zucchini to a serving plate and toss with the beet pesto, then serve.

Nutrition Info:
- Per Serving: Calories: 423;Fat: 38.8g;Protein: 8.0g;Carbs: 17.1g.

Simple Braised Carrots

Servings:4 | Cooking Time:20 Minutes

Ingredients:
- 2 tbsp butter
- 1 lb carrots, cut into sticks
- ¾ cup water
- ¼ cup orange juice
- 1 tbsp honey
- Salt and white pepper to taste
- 1 tsp rosemary leaves

Directions:
1. Combine all the ingredients, except for the carrots and rosemary, in a heavy saucepan over medium heat and bring to a boil. Add carrots and cover. Turn the heat to a simmer and continue to cook for 5–8 minutes until carrots are soft when pierced with a knife. Remove the carrots to a serving plate. Then, increase heat to high and bring the liquid to a boil. Boil until the liquid has reduced and syrupy, about 4 minutes. Drizzle the sauce over the carrots and sprinkle with rosemary. Serve warm.

Nutrition Info:
- Per Serving: Calories: 122;Fat: 6g;Protein: 1g;Carbs: 17g.

Stir-fried Eggplant

Servings:2 | Cooking Time: 15 Minutes

Ingredients:
- 1 cup water, plus more as needed
- ½ cup chopped red onion
- 1 tablespoon finely chopped garlic
- 1 tablespoon dried Italian herb seasoning
- 1 teaspoon ground cumin
- 1 small eggplant, peeled and cut into ½-inch cubes
- 1 medium carrot, sliced
- 2 cups green beans, cut into 1-inch pieces
- 2 ribs celery, sliced
- 1 cup corn kernels
- 2 tablespoons almond butter
- 2 medium tomatoes, chopped

Directions:
1. Heat 1 tablespoon of water in a large soup pot over medium-high heat until it sputters.
2. Cook the onion for 2 minutes, adding a little more water as needed.
3. Add the garlic, Italian seasoning, cumin, and eggplant and stir-fry for 2 to 3 minutes, adding a little more water as needed.
4. Add the carrot, green beans, celery, corn kernels, and ½ cup of water and stir well. Reduce the heat to medium, cover, and cook for 8 to 10 minutes, stirring occasionally, or until the vegetables are tender.
5. Meanwhile, in a bowl, stir together the almond butter and ½ cup of water.
6. Remove the vegetables from the heat and stir in the almond butter mixture and chopped tomatoes. Cool for a few minutes before serving.

Nutrition Info:
- Per Serving: Calories: 176;Fat: 5.5g;Protein: 5.8g;Carbs: 25.4g.

Chargrilled Vegetable Kebabs

Servings:4 | Cooking Time:26 Minutes

Ingredients:
- 2 red bell peppers, cut into squares
- 2 zucchinis, sliced into half-moons
- 6 portobello mushroom caps, quartered
- ¼ cup olive oil
- 1 tsp Dijon mustard
- 1 tsp fresh rosemary, chopped
- 1 garlic clove, minced
- Salt and black pepper to taste
- 2 red onions, cut into wedges

Directions:
1. Preheat your grill to High. Mix the olive oil, mustard, rosemary, garlic, salt, and pepper in a bowl. Reserve half of the oil mixture for serving. Thread the vegetables in alternating order onto metal skewers and brush them with the remaining oil mixture. Grill them for about 15 minutes until browned, turning occasionally. Transfer the kebabs to a serving platter and remove the skewers. Drizzle with reserved oil mixture and serve.

Nutrition Info:
- Per Serving: Calories: 96;Fat: 9.2g;Protein: 1.1g;Carbs: 3.6g.

Cauliflower Steaks With Arugula

Servings:4 | Cooking Time: 20 Minutes

Ingredients:
- Cauliflower:
- 1 head cauliflower
- Cooking spray
- ½ teaspoon garlic powder
- 4 cups arugula
- Dressing:
- 1½ tablespoons extra-virgin olive oil
- 1½ tablespoons honey mustard
- 1 teaspoon freshly squeezed lemon juice

Directions:
1. Preheat the oven to 425ºF.
2. Remove the leaves from the cauliflower head, and cut it in half lengthwise. Cut 1½-inch-thick steaks from each half.
3. Spritz both sides of each steak with cooking spray and season both sides with the garlic powder.
4. Place the cauliflower steaks on a baking sheet, cover with foil, and roast in the oven for 10 minutes.
5. Remove the baking sheet from the oven and gently pull back the foil to avoid the steam. Flip the steaks, then roast uncovered for 10 minutes more.
6. Meanwhile, make the dressing: Whisk together the olive oil, honey mustard and lemon juice in a small bowl.
7. When the cauliflower steaks are done, divide into four equal portions. Top each portion with one-quarter of the arugula and dressing.
8. Serve immediately.

Nutrition Info:
- Per Serving: Calories: 115;Fat: 6.0g;Protein: 5.0g;Carbs: 14.0g.

Vegan Lentil Bolognese

Servings:2 | Cooking Time: 50 Minutes

Ingredients:
- 1 medium celery stalk
- 1 large carrot
- ½ large onion
- 1 garlic clove
- 2 tablespoons olive oil
- 1 can crushed tomatoes
- 1 cup red wine
- ½ teaspoon salt, plus more as needed
- ½ teaspoon pure maple syrup
- 1 cup cooked lentils (prepared from ½ cup dry)

Directions:
1. Add the celery, carrot, onion, and garlic to a food processor and process until everything is finely chopped.
2. In a Dutch oven, heat the olive oil over medium-high heat. Add the chopped mixture and sauté for about 10 minutes, stirring occasionally, or until the vegetables are lightly browned.
3. Stir in the tomatoes, wine, salt, and maple syrup and bring to a boil.
4. Once the sauce starts to boil, cover, and reduce the heat to medium-low. Simmer for 30 minutes, stirring occasionally, or until the vegetables are softened.
5. Stir in the cooked lentils and cook for an additional 5 minutes until warmed through.
6. Taste and add additional salt, if needed. Serve warm.

Nutrition Info:
- Per Serving: Calories: 367;Fat: 15.0g;Protein: 13.7g;Carbs: 44.5g.

Buttery Garlic Green Beans

Servings:6 | Cooking Time:25 Minutes

Ingredients:
- 2 tbsp butter
- 1 lb green beans, trimmed
- 4 cups water
- 6 garlic cloves, minced
- 1 shallot, chopped
- Celery salt to taste
- ½ tsp red pepper flakes

Directions:
1. Pour 4 cups of water in a pot over high heat and bring to a boil. Cut the green beans in half crosswise. Reduce the heat and add in the green beans. Simmer for 6-8 minutes until crisp-tender but still vibrant green. Drain beans and set aside.
2. Melt the butter in a pan over medium heat and sauté garlic and shallot for 3 minutes until the garlic is slightly browned and fragrant. Stir in the beans and season with celery salt. Cook for 2–3 minutes. Serve topped with red pepper flakes.

Nutrition Info:
- Per Serving: Calories: 65;Fat: 4g;Protein: 2g;Carbs: 7g.

Mini Crustless Spinach Quiches

Servings:6 | Cooking Time: 20 Minutes

Ingredients:
- 2 tablespoons extra-virgin olive oil
- 1 onion, finely chopped
- 2 cups baby spinach
- 2 garlic cloves, minced
- 8 large eggs, beaten
- ¼ cup unsweetened almond
- milk
- ½ teaspoon sea salt
- ¼ teaspoon freshly ground black pepper
- 1 cup shredded Swiss cheese
- Cooking spray

Directions:
1. Preheat the oven to 375ºF. Spritz a 6-cup muffin tin with cooking spray. Set aside.
2. In a large skillet over medium-high heat, heat the olive oil until shimmering. Add the onion and cook for about 4 minutes, or until soft. Add the spinach and cook for about 1 minute, stirring constantly, or until the spinach softens. Add the garlic and sauté for 30 seconds. Remove from the heat and let cool.
3. In a medium bowl, whisk together the eggs, milk, salt and pepper.
4. Stir the cooled vegetables and the cheese into the egg mixture. Spoon the mixture into the prepared muffin tins. Bake for about 15 minutes, or until the eggs are set.
5. Let rest for 5 minutes before serving.

Nutrition Info:
- Per Serving: Calories: 218;Fat: 17.0g;Protein: 14.0g;Carbs: 4.0g.

Baked Veggie Medley

Servings:4 | Cooking Time:70 Minutes

Ingredients:
- 2 tbsp olive oil
- ½ lb green beans, trimmed
- 1 tomato, chopped
- 1 potato, sliced
- ½ tbsp tomato paste
- 2 tbsp chopped fresh parsley
- 1 tsp sweet paprika
- 1 onion, sliced
- 1 cup mushrooms, sliced
- 1 celery stalk, chopped
- 1 red bell pepper, sliced
- 1 eggplant, sliced
- ½ cup vegetable broth
- Salt and black pepper to taste

Directions:
1. Preheat oven to 375°F. Warm oil in a skillet over medium heat

and sauté onion, bell pepper, celery, and mushrooms for 5 minutes until tender. Stir in paprika and tomato paste for 1 minute. Pour in the vegetable broth and stir. Combine the remaining ingredients in a baking pan and mix in the sautéed vegetable. Bake covered with foil for 40-50 minutes.

Nutrition Info:
• Per Serving: Calories: 175;Fat: 8g;Protein: 5.2g;Carbs: 25.2g.

Spicy Kale With Almonds

Servings:4 | Cooking Time:25 Minutes

Ingredients:
• 2 tbsp olive oil
• ¼ cup slivered almonds
• 1 lb chopped kale
• ¼ cup vegetable broth
• 1 lemon, juiced and zested
• 1 garlic clove, minced
• 1 tbsp red pepper flakes
• Salt and black pepper to taste

Directions:
1. Warm olive oil in a pan over medium heat and sauté garlic, kale, salt, and pepper for 8-9 minutes until soft. Add in lemon juice, lemon zest, red pepper flakes, and vegetable broth and continue cooking until the liquid evaporates, about 3-5 minutes. Garnish with almonds and serve.

Nutrition Info:
• Per Serving: Calories: 123;Fat: 8.1g;Protein: 4g;Carbs: 10.8g.

Veggie Rice Bowls With Pesto Sauce

Servings:2 | Cooking Time: 1 Minute

Ingredients:
• 2 cups water
• 1 cup arborio rice, rinsed
• Salt and ground black pepper, to taste
• 2 eggs
• 1 cup broccoli florets
• ½ pound Brussels sprouts
• 1 carrot, peeled and chopped
• 1 small beet, peeled and cubed
• ¼ cup pesto sauce
• Lemon wedges, for serving

Directions:
1. Combine the water, rice, salt, and pepper in the Instant Pot. Insert a trivet over rice and place a steamer basket on top. Add the eggs, broccoli, Brussels sprouts, carrots, beet cubes, salt, and pepper to the steamer basket.
2. Lock the lid. Select the Manual mode and set the cooking time for 1 minute at High Pressure.
3. When the timer beeps, perform a natural pressure release for 10 minutes, then release any remaining pressure. Carefully open the lid.
4. Remove the steamer basket and trivet from the pot and transfer the eggs to a bowl of ice water. Peel and halve the eggs. Use a fork to fluff the rice.
5. Divide the rice, broccoli, Brussels sprouts, carrot, beet cubes, and eggs into two bowls. Top with a dollop of pesto sauce and serve with the lemon wedges.

Nutrition Info:
• Per Serving: Calories: 590;Fat: 34.1g;Protein: 21.9g;Carbs: 50.0g.

Zucchini Ribbons With Ricotta

Servings:4 | Cooking Time:10 Minutes

Ingredients:
• 3 tbsp olive oil
• 1 garlic clove, minced
• 1 tsp lemon zest
• 1 tbsp lemon juice
• 4 zucchinis, cut into ribbons
• Salt and black pepper to taste

• 2 tbsp chopped fresh parsley
• ½ ricotta cheese, crumbled

Directions:
1. Whisk 2 tablespoons oil, garlic, salt, pepper, and lemon zest, and lemon juice in a bowl. Warm the remaining olive oil in a skillet over medium heat. Season the zucchini ribbons with salt and pepper and add them to the skillet; cook for 3-4 minutes per side. Transfer to a serving bowl and drizzle with the dressing, sprinkle with parsley and cheese and serve.

Nutrition Info:
• Per Serving: Calories: 134;Fat: 2g;Protein: 2g;Carbs: 4g.

Simple Honey-glazed Baby Carrots

Servings:2 | Cooking Time: 6 Minutes

Ingredients:
• ⅔ cup water
• 1½ pounds baby carrots
• 4 tablespoons almond butter
• ½ cup honey
• 1 teaspoon dried thyme
• 1½ teaspoons dried dill
• Salt, to taste

Directions:
1. Pour the water into the Instant Pot and add a steamer basket. Place the baby carrots in the basket.
2. Secure the lid. Select the Manual mode and set the cooking time for 4 minutes at High Pressure.
3. Once cooking is complete, do a quick pressure release. Carefully open the lid.
4. Transfer the carrots to a plate and set aside.
5. Pour the water out of the Instant Pot and dry it.
6. Press the Sauté button on the Instant Pot and heat the almond butter.
7. Stir in the honey, thyme, and dill.
8. Return the carrots to the Instant Pot and stir until well coated. Sauté for another 1 minute.
9. Taste and season with salt as needed. Serve warm.

Nutrition Info:
• Per Serving: Calories: 575;Fat: 23.5g;Protein: 2.8g;Carbs: 90.6g.

Homemade Vegetarian Moussaka

Servings:4 | Cooking Time:80 Minutes

Ingredients:
• 2 tbsp olive oil
• 1 yellow onion, chopped
• 2 garlic cloves, chopped
• 2 eggplants, halved
• ½ cup vegetable broth
• Salt and black pepper to taste
• ½ tsp paprika
• ¼ cup parsley, chopped
• 1 tsp basil, chopped
• 1 tsp hot sauce
• 1 tomato, chopped
• 2 tbsp tomato puree
• 6 Kalamata olives, chopped
• ½ cup feta cheese, crumbled

Directions:
1. Preheat oven to 360ºF. Remove the tender center part of the eggplants and chop it. Arrange the eggplant halves on a baking tray and drizzle with some olive oil. Roast for 35-40 minutes.
2. Warm the remaining olive oil in a skillet over medium heat and add eggplant flesh, onion, and garlic and sauté for 5 minutes until tender. Stir in the vegetable broth, salt, pepper, basil, hot sauce, paprika, tomato, and tomato puree. Lower the heat and simmer for 10-15 minutes. Once the eggplants are ready, remove them from the oven and fill them with the mixture. Top with Kalamata olives and feta cheese. Return to the oven and bake for 10-15 minutes. Sprinkle with parsley.

Nutrition Info:

• Per Serving: Calories: 223;Fat: 14g;Protein: 6.9g;Carbs: 23g.

Paprika Cauliflower Steaks With Walnut Sauce

Servings:2 | Cooking Time: 30 Minutes

Ingredients:
• Walnut Sauce:
• ½ cup raw walnut halves
• 2 tablespoons virgin olive oil, divided
• 1 clove garlic, chopped
• 1 small yellow onion, chopped
• ½ cup unsweetened almond milk
• 2 tablespoons fresh lemon juice
• Salt and pepper, to taste
• Paprika Cauliflower:
• 1 medium head cauliflower
• 1 teaspoon sweet paprika
• 1 teaspoon minced fresh thyme leaves

Directions:
1. Preheat the oven to 350ºF.
2. Make the walnut sauce: Toast the walnuts in a large, ovenproof skillet over medium heat until fragrant and slightly darkened, about 5 minutes. Transfer the walnuts to a blender.
3. Heat 1 tablespoon of olive oil in the skillet. Add the garlic and onion and sauté for about 2 minutes, or until slightly softened. Transfer the garlic and onion into the blender, along with the almond milk, lemon juice, salt, and pepper. Blend the ingredients until smooth and creamy. Keep the sauce warm while you prepare the cauliflower.
4. Make the paprika cauliflower: Cut two 1-inch-thick "steaks" from the center of the cauliflower. Lightly moisten the steaks with water and season both sides with paprika, thyme, salt, and pepper.
5. Heat the remaining 1 tablespoon of olive oil in the skillet over medium-high heat. Add the cauliflower steaks and sear for about 3 minutes until evenly browned. Flip the cauliflower steaks and transfer the skillet to the oven.
6. Roast in the preheated oven for about 20 minutes until crisp-tender.
7. Serve the cauliflower steaks warm with the walnut sauce on the side.

Nutrition Info:
• Per Serving: Calories: 367;Fat: 27.9g;Protein: 7.0g;Carbs: 22.7g.

Garlicky Zucchini Cubes With Mint

Servings:4 | Cooking Time: 10 Minutes

Ingredients:
• 3 large green zucchinis, cut into ½-inch cubes
• 3 tablespoons extra-virgin olive oil
• 1 large onion, chopped
• 3 cloves garlic, minced
• 1 teaspoon salt
• 1 teaspoon dried mint

Directions:
1. Heat the olive oil in a large skillet over medium heat.
2. Add the onion and garlic and sauté for 3 minutes, stirring constantly, or until softened.
3. Stir in the zucchini cubes and salt and cook for 5 minutes, or until the zucchini is browned and tender.
4. Add the mint to the skillet and toss to combine, then continue cooking for 2 minutes.
5. Serve warm.

Nutrition Info:
• Per Serving: Calories: 146;Fat: 10.6g;Protein: 4.2g;Carbs: 11.8g.

Quick Steamed Broccoli

Servings:2 | Cooking Time: 0 Minutes

Ingredients:
• ¼ cup water
• 3 cups broccoli florets
• Salt and ground black pepper, to taste

Directions:
1. Pour the water into the Instant Pot and insert a steamer basket. Place the broccoli florets in the basket.
2. Secure the lid. Select the Manual mode and set the cooking time for 0 minutes at High Pressure.
3. Once cooking is complete, do a quick pressure release. Carefully open the lid.
4. Transfer the broccoli florets to a bowl with cold water to keep bright green color.
5. Season the broccoli with salt and pepper to taste, then serve.

Nutrition Info:
• Per Serving: Calories: 16;Fat: 0.2g;Protein: 1.9g;Carbs: 1.7g.

Creamy Polenta With Mushrooms

Servings:2 | Cooking Time: 30 Minutes

Ingredients:
• ½ ounce dried porcini mushrooms (optional but recommended)
• 2 tablespoons olive oil
• 1 pound baby bella (cremini) mushrooms, quartered
• 1 large shallot, minced
• 1 garlic clove, minced
• 1 tablespoon flour
• 2 teaspoons tomato paste
• ½ cup red wine
• 1 cup mushroom stock (or reserved liquid from soaking the porcini mushrooms, if using)
• ½ teaspoon dried thyme
• 1 fresh rosemary sprig
• 1½ cups water
• ½ teaspoon salt
• ⅓ cup instant polenta
• 2 tablespoons grated Parmesan cheese

Directions:
1. If using the dried porcini mushrooms, soak them in 1 cup of hot water for about 15 minutes to soften them. When they're softened, scoop them out of the water, reserving the soaking liquid. Mince the porcini mushrooms.
2. Heat the olive oil in a large sauté pan over medium-high heat. Add the mushrooms, shallot, and garlic, and sauté for 10 minutes, or until the vegetables are wilted and starting to caramelize.
3. Add the flour and tomato paste, and cook for another 30 seconds. Add the red wine, mushroom stock or porcini soaking liquid, thyme, and rosemary. Bring the mixture to a boil, stirring constantly until it thickens. Reduce the heat and let it simmer for 10 minutes.
4. Meanwhile, bring the water to a boil in a saucepan and add salt.
5. Add the instant polenta and stir quickly while it thickens. Stir in the Parmesan cheese. Taste and add additional salt, if needed. Serve warm.

Nutrition Info:
• Per Serving: Calories: 450;Fat: 16.0g;Protein: 14.1g;Carbs: 57.8g.

Baked Vegetable Stew

Servings:6 | Cooking Time:70 Minutes

Ingredients:
- 1 can diced tomatoes, drained with juice reserved
- 3 tbsp olive oil
- 1 onion, chopped
- 2 tbsp fresh oregano, minced
- 1 tsp paprika
- 4 garlic cloves, minced
- 1 ½ lb green beans, sliced
- 1 lb Yukon Gold potatoes, peeled and chopped
- 1 tbsp tomato paste
- Salt and black pepper to taste
- 3 tbsp fresh basil, chopped

Directions:
1. Preheat oven to 360°F. Warm the olive oil in a skillet over medium heat. Sauté onion and garlic for 3 minutes until softened. Stir in oregano and paprika for 30 seconds. Transfer to a baking dish and add in green beans, potatoes, tomatoes, tomato paste, salt, pepper, and 1 ½ cups of water; stir well. Bake for 40-50 minutes. Sprinkle with basil. Serve.

Nutrition Info:
- Per Serving: Calories: 121;Fat: 0.8g;Protein: 4.2g;Carbs: 26g.

Butternut Noodles With Mushrooms

Servings:4 | Cooking Time: 12 Minutes

Ingredients:
- ¼ cup extra-virgin olive oil
- 1 pound cremini mushrooms, sliced
- ½ red onion, finely chopped
- 1 teaspoon dried thyme
- ½ teaspoon sea salt
- 3 garlic cloves, minced
- ½ cup dry white wine
- Pinch of red pepper flakes
- 4 cups butternut noodles
- 4 ounces grated Parmesan cheese

Directions:
1. In a large skillet over medium-high heat, heat the olive oil until shimmering. Add the mushrooms, onion, thyme, and salt to the skillet. Cook for about 6 minutes, stirring occasionally, or until the mushrooms start to brown. Add the garlic and sauté for 30 seconds. Stir in the white wine and red pepper flakes.
2. Fold in the noodles. Cook for about 5 minutes, stirring occasionally, or until the noodles are tender.
3. Serve topped with the grated Parmesan.

Nutrition Info:
- Per Serving: Calories: 244;Fat: 14.0g;Protein: 4.0g;Carbs: 22.0g.

Tradicional Matchuba Green Beans

Servings:4 | Cooking Time:15 Minutes

Ingredients:
- 1 ¼ lb narrow green beans, trimmed
- 3 tbsp butter, melted
- 1 cup Moroccan matbucha
- 2 green onions, chopped
- Salt and black pepper to taste

Directions:
1. Steam the green beans in a pot for 5-6 minutes until tender. Remove to a bowl, reserving the cooking liquid. In a skillet over medium heat, melt the butter. Add green onions, salt, and black pepper and cook until fragrant. Lower the heat and put in the green beans along with some of the reserved water. Simmer for 3-4 minutes. Serve the green beans with the Sabra Moroccan matbucha as a dip.

Nutrition Info:
- Per Serving: Calories: 125;Fat: 8.6g;Protein: 2.2g;Carbs: 9g.

Parsley & Olive Zucchini Bake

Servings:6 | Cooking Time:1 Hour 40 Minutes

Ingredients:
- 3 tbsp olive oil
- 1 can tomatoes, diced
- 2 lb zucchinis, sliced
- 1 onion, chopped
- Salt and black pepper to taste
- 3 garlic cloves, minced
- ¼ tsp dried oregano
- ¼ tsp red pepper flakes
- 10 Kalamata olives, chopped
- 2 tbsp fresh parsley, chopped

Directions:
1. Preheat oven to 325ºF. Warm the olive oil in a saucepan over medium heat. Sauté zucchini for about 3 minutes per side; transfer to a bowl. Stir-fry the onion and salt in the same saucepan for 3-5 minutes, stirring occasionally until onion soft and lightly golden. Stir in garlic, oregano, and pepper flakes and cook until fragrant, about 30 seconds.
2. Add in olives, tomatoes, salt, and pepper, bring to a simmer, and cook for about 10 minutes, stirring occasionally. Return the zucchini, cover, and transfer the pot to the oven. Bake for 10-15 minutes. Sprinkle with parsley and serve.

Nutrition Info:
- Per Serving: Calories: 164;Fat: 6g;Protein: 1.5g;Carbs: 7.7g.

Marinara Zoodles

Servings:4 | Cooking Time:65 Minutes

Ingredients:
- 2 cans crushed tomatoes
- 2 tbsp olive oil
- 16 oz zucchini noodles
- 1 can diced tomatoes,
- 1 onion, chopped
- 4 garlic cloves, minced
- 1 tbsp dried Italian seasoning
- 1 tsp dried oregano
- Sea salt to taste
- ¼ tsp red pepper flakes
- ¼ cup Romano cheese, grated

Directions:
1. Warm olive oil in a pot over medium heat and sauté onion and garlic for 5 minutes, stirring frequently until fragrant. Pour in tomatoes, oregano, Italian seasoning, salt, and red pepper flakes. Bring just to a boil, then lower the heat, and simmer for 10-15 minutes. Stir in the zucchini noodles and cook for 3-4 minutes until the noodles are slightly softened. Scatter with Romano cheese and serve.

Nutrition Info:
- Per Serving: Calories: 209;Fat: 9g;Protein: 8.1g;Carbs: 27.8g.

Grilled Za´atar Zucchini Rounds

Servings:4 | Cooking Time:20 Minutes

Ingredients:
- 2 tbsp olive oil
- 4 zucchinis, sliced
- 1 tbsp za'atar seasoning
- Salt to taste
- 2 tbsp parsley, chopped

Directions:
1. Preheat the grill on high. Cut the zucchini lengthways into ½-inch thin pieces. Brush the zucchini 'steaks' with olive oil and season with salt and za'atar seasoning. Grill for 6 minutes on both sides. Sprinkle with parsley and serve.

Nutrition Info:
- Per Serving: Calories: 91;Fat: 7.4g;Protein: 2.4g;Carbs: 6.6g.

Veggie-stuffed Portabello Mushrooms

Servings:6 | Cooking Time: 24 To 25 Minutes

Ingredients:

- 3 tablespoons extra-virgin olive oil, divided
- 1 cup diced onion
- 2 garlic cloves, minced
- 1 large zucchini, diced
- 3 cups chopped mushrooms
- 1 cup chopped tomato
- 1 teaspoon dried oregano
- ¼ teaspoon kosher salt
- ¼ teaspoon crushed red pepper
- 6 large portabello mushrooms, stems and gills removed
- Cooking spray
- 4 ounces fresh Mozzarella cheese, shredded

Directions:

1. In a large skillet over medium heat, heat 2 tablespoons of the oil. Add the onion and sauté for 4 minutes. Stir in the garlic and sauté for 1 minute.
2. Stir in the zucchini, mushrooms, tomato, oregano, salt and red pepper. Cook for 10 minutes, stirring constantly. Remove from the heat.
3. Meanwhile, heat a grill pan over medium-high heat.
4. Brush the remaining 1 tablespoon of the oil over the portabello mushroom caps. Place the mushrooms, bottom-side down, on the grill pan. Cover with a sheet of aluminum foil sprayed with non-stick cooking spray. Cook for 5 minutes.
5. Flip the mushroom caps over, and spoon about ½ cup of the cooked vegetable mixture into each cap. Top each with about 2½ tablespoons of the Mozzarella.
6. Cover and grill for 4 to 5 minutes, or until the cheese is melted.
7. Using a spatula, transfer the portabello mushrooms to a plate. Let cool for about 5 minutes before serving.

Nutrition Info:

- Per Serving: Calories: 111;Fat: 4.0g;Protein: 11.0g;Carbs: 11.0g.

Baked Potato With Veggie Mix

Servings:4 | Cooking Time:45 Minutes

Ingredients:

- 4 tbsp olive oil
- 1 lb potatoes, peeled and diced
- 2 red bell peppers, halved
- 1 lb mushrooms, sliced
- 2 tomatoes, diced
- 8 garlic cloves, peeled
- 1 eggplant, sliced
- 1 yellow onion, quartered
- ½ tsp dried oregano
- ¼ tsp caraway seeds
- Salt to taste

Directions:

1. Preheat the oven to 390°F. In a bowl, combine the bell peppers, mushrooms, tomatoes, eggplant, onion, garlic, salt, olive oil, oregano, and caraway seeds. Set aside. Arrange the potatoes on a baking dish and bake for 15 minutes. Top with the veggies mixture and bake for 15-20 minutes until tender.

Nutrition Info:

- Per Serving: Calories: 302;Fat: 15g;Protein: 8.5g;Carbs: 39g.

Creamy Sweet Potatoes And Collards

Servings:2 | Cooking Time: 35 Minutes

Ingredients:

- 1 tablespoon avocado oil
- 3 garlic cloves, chopped
- 1 yellow onion, diced
- ½ teaspoon crushed red pepper flakes
- 1 large sweet potato, peeled and diced
- 2 bunches collard greens, stemmed, leaves chopped into 1-inch squares
- 1 can diced tomatoes with juice
- 1 can red kidney beans or chickpeas, drained and rinsed
- 1½ cups water
- ½ cup unsweetened coconut milk
- Salt and black pepper, to taste

Directions:

1. In a large, deep skillet over medium heat, melt the avocado oil.
2. Add the garlic, onion, and red pepper flakes and cook for 3 minutes. Stir in the sweet potato and collards.
3. Add the tomatoes with their juice, beans, water, and coconut milk and mix well. Bring the mixture just to a boil.
4. Reduce the heat to medium-low, cover, and simmer for about 30 minutes, or until softened.
5. Season to taste with salt and pepper and serve.

Nutrition Info:

- Per Serving: Calories: 445;Fat: 9.6g;Protein: 18.1g;Carbs: 73.1g.

Roasted Asparagus With Hazelnuts

Servings:4 | Cooking Time:25 Minutes

Ingredients:

- 2 tbsp olive oil
- 1 lb asparagus, trimmed
- ¼ cup hazelnuts, chopped
- 1 lemon, juiced and zested
- Salt and black pepper to taste
- ½ tsp red pepper flakes

Directions:

1. Preheat oven to 425ºF. Arrange the asparagus on a baking sheet. Combine olive oil, lemon zest, lemon juice, salt, hazelnuts, and black pepper in a bowl and mix well. Pour the mixture over the asparagus. Place in the oven and roast for 15-20 minutes until tender and lightly charred. Serve topped with red pepper flakes.

Nutrition Info:

- Per Serving: Calories: 112;Fat: 10g;Protein: 3.2g;Carbs: 5.2g.

Grilled Vegetable Skewers

Servings:4 | Cooking Time: 10 Minutes

Ingredients:

- 4 medium red onions, peeled and sliced into 6 wedges
- 4 medium zucchini, cut into 1-inch-thick slices
- 2 beefsteak tomatoes, cut into quarters
- 4 red bell peppers, cut into 2-inch squares
- 2 orange bell peppers, cut into 2-inch squares
- 2 yellow bell peppers, cut into 2-inch squares
- 2 tablespoons plus 1 teaspoon olive oil, divided
- SPECIAL EQUIPMENT:
- 4 wooden skewers, soaked in water for at least 30 minutes

Directions:

1. Preheat the grill to medium-high heat.
2. Skewer the vegetables by alternating between red onion, zucchini, tomatoes, and the different colored bell peppers. Brush them with 2 tablespoons of olive oil.
3. Oil the grill grates with 1 teaspoon of olive oil and grill the vegetable skewers for 5 minutes. Flip the skewers and grill for 5 minutes more, or until they are cooked to your liking.
4. Let the skewers cool for 5 minutes before serving.

Nutrition Info:

- Per Serving: Calories: 115;Fat: 3.0g;Protein: 3.5g;Carbs: 18.7g.

Stir-fry Baby Bok Choy

Servings:6 | Cooking Time: 10 To 13 Minutes

Ingredients:
- 2 tablespoons coconut oil
- 1 large onion, finely diced
- 2 teaspoons ground cumin
- 1-inch piece fresh ginger, grated
- 1 teaspoon ground turmeric
- ½ teaspoon salt
- 12 baby bok choy heads, ends trimmed and sliced lengthwise
- Water, as needed
- 3 cups cooked brown rice

Directions:
1. Heat the coconut oil in a large pan over medium heat.
2. Sauté the onion for 5 minutes, stirring occasionally, or until the onion is translucent.
3. Fold in the cumin, ginger, turmeric, and salt and stir to coat well.
4. Add the bok choy and cook for 5 to 8 minutes, stirring occasionally, or until the bok choy is tender but crisp. You can add 1 tablespoon of water at a time, if the skillet gets dry until you finish sautéing.
5. Transfer the bok choy to a plate and serve over the cooked brown rice.

Nutrition Info:
- Per Serving: Calories: 443;Fat: 8.8g;Protein: 30.3g;Carbs: 75.7g.

Roasted Vegetable Medley

Servings:2 | Cooking Time:65 Minutes

Ingredients:
- 1 head garlic, cloves split apart, unpeeled
- 3 tbsp olive oil
- 2 carrots, cut into strips
- ¼ lb asparagus, chopped
- ½ lb Brussels sprouts, halved
- 2 cups broccoli florets
- 1 cup cherry tomatoes
- ½ fresh lemon, sliced
- Salt and black pepper to taste

Directions:
1. Preheat oven to 375ºF. Drizzle the garlic cloves with some olive oil and lightly wrap them in a small piece of foil. Place the packet in the oven and roast for 30 minutes. Place all the vegetables and the lemon slices into a large mixing bowl. Drizzle with the remaining olive oil and season with salt and pepper. Increase the oven to 400 F. Pour the vegetables on a sheet pan in a single layer, leaving the packet of garlic cloves on the pan. Roast for 20 minutes, shaking occasionally until tender. Remove the pan from the oven. Let the garlic cloves sit until cool enough to handle, then remove the skins. Top the vegetables with roasted garlic and serve.

Nutrition Info:
- Per Serving: Calories: 256;Fat: 15g;Protein: 7g;Carbs: 31g.

Simple Zoodles

Servings:2 | Cooking Time: 5 Minutes

Ingredients:
- 2 tablespoons avocado oil
- 2 medium zucchinis, spiralized
- ¼ teaspoon salt
- Freshly ground black pepper, to taste

Directions:
1. Heat the avocado oil in a large skillet over medium heat until it shimmers.
2. Add the zucchini noodles, salt, and black pepper to the skillet and toss to coat. Cook for 1 to 2 minutes, stirring constantly, until

tender.
3. Serve warm.

Nutrition Info:
- Per Serving: Calories: 128;Fat: 14.0g;Protein: 0.3g;Carbs: 0.3g.

Beet And Watercress Salad

Servings:4 | Cooking Time: 8 Minutes

Ingredients:
- 2 pounds beets, scrubbed, trimmed and cut into ¾-inch pieces
- ½ cup water
- 1 teaspoon caraway seeds
- ½ teaspoon table salt, plus more for seasoning
- 1 cup plain Greek yogurt
- 1 small garlic clove, minced
- 5 ounces watercress, torn into bite-size pieces
- 1 tablespoon extra-virgin
- olive oil, divided, plus more for drizzling
- 1 tablespoon white wine vinegar, divided
- Black pepper, to taste
- 1 teaspoon grated orange zest
- 2 tablespoons orange juice
- ¼ cup coarsely chopped fresh dill
- ¼ cup hazelnuts, toasted, skinned and chopped
- Coarse sea salt, to taste

Directions:
1. Combine the beets, water, caraway seeds and table salt in the Instant Pot. Set the lid in place. Select the Manual mode and set the cooking time for 8 minutes on High Pressure. When the timer goes off, do a quick pressure release.
2. Carefully open the lid. Using a slotted spoon, transfer the beets to a plate. Set aside to cool slightly.
3. In a small bowl, combine the yogurt, garlic and 3 tablespoons of the beet cooking liquid. In a large bowl, toss the watercress with 2 teaspoons of the oil and 1 teaspoon of the vinegar. Season with table salt and pepper.
4. Spread the yogurt mixture over a serving dish. Arrange the watercress on top of the yogurt mixture, leaving 1-inch border of the yogurt mixture.
5. Add the beets to now-empty large bowl and toss with the orange zest and juice, the remaining 2 teaspoons of the vinegar and the remaining 1 teaspoon of the oil. Season with table salt and pepper.
6. Arrange the beets on top of the watercress mixture. Drizzle with the olive oil and sprinkle with the dill, hazelnuts and sea salt.
7. Serve immediately.

Nutrition Info:
- Per Serving: Calories: 240;Fat: 15.0g;Protein: 9.0g;Carbs: 19.0g.

Roasted Vegetables And Chickpeas

Servings:2 | Cooking Time: 30 Minutes

Ingredients:
- 4 cups cauliflower florets (about ½ small head)
- 2 medium carrots, peeled, halved, and then sliced into quarters lengthwise
- 2 tablespoons olive oil, divided
- ½ teaspoon garlic powder,
- divided
- ½ teaspoon salt, divided
- 2 teaspoons za'atar spice mix, divided
- 1 can chickpeas, drained, rinsed, and patted dry
- ¾ cup plain Greek yogurt
- 1 teaspoon harissa spice paste

Directions:
1. Preheat the oven to 400ºF. Line a sheet pan with foil or parchment paper.
2. Place the cauliflower and carrots in a large bowl. Drizzle with

1 tablespoon olive oil and sprinkle with ¼ teaspoon of garlic powder, ¼ teaspoon of salt, and 1 teaspoon of za'atar. Toss well to combine.

3. Spread the vegetables onto one half of the sheet pan in a single layer.

4. Place the chickpeas in the same bowl and season with the remaining 1 tablespoon of oil, ¼ teaspoon of garlic powder, and ¼ teaspoon of salt, and the remaining za'atar. Toss well to combine.

5. Spread the chickpeas onto the other half of the sheet pan.

6. Roast for 30 minutes, or until the vegetables are tender and the chickpeas start to turn golden. Flip the vegetables halfway through the cooking time, and give the chickpeas a stir so they cook evenly.

7. The chickpeas may need an extra few minutes if you like them crispy. If so, remove the vegetables and leave the chickpeas until they're cooked to desired crispiness.

8. Meanwhile, combine the yogurt and harissa in a small bowl. Taste and add additional harissa as desired, then serve.

Nutrition Info:
• Per Serving: Calories: 468;Fat: 23.0g;Protein: 18.1g;Carbs: 54.1g.

Sweet Mustard Cabbage Hash
Servings:4 | Cooking Time:30 Minutes

Ingredients:
• 1 head Savoy cabbage, shredded
• 3 tbsp olive oil
• 1 onion, finely chopped
• 2 garlic cloves, minced
• ½ tsp fennel seeds
• ¼ cup red wine vinegar
• 1 tbsp mustard powder
• 1 tbsp honey
• Salt and black pepper to taste

Directions:
1. Warm olive oil in a pan over medium heat and sauté onion, fennel seeds, cabbage, salt, and pepper for 8-9 minutes.

2. In a bowl, mix vinegar, mustard, and honey; set aside. Sauté garlic in the pan for 30 seconds. Pour in vinegar mixture and cook for 10-15 minutes until the liquid reduces by half.

Nutrition Info:
• Per Serving: Calories: 181;Fat: 12g;Protein: 3.4g;Carbs: 19g.

Spicy Potato Wedges
Servings:4 | Cooking Time:30 Minutes

Ingredients:
• 1 ½ lb potatoes, peeled and cut into wedges
• 3 tbsp olive oil
• 1 tbsp minced fresh rosemary
• 2 tsp chili powder
• 3 garlic cloves, minced
• Salt and black pepper to taste

Directions:
1. Preheat the oven to 370ºF. Toss the wedges with olive oil, garlic, salt, and pepper. Spread out in a roasting sheet. Roast for 15-20 minutes until browned and crisp at the edges. Remove and sprinkle with chili powder and rosemary.

Nutrition Info:
• Per Serving: Calories: 152;Fat: 7g;Protein: 2.5g;Carbs: 21g.

Eggplant And Zucchini Gratin
Servings:6 | Cooking Time: 19 Minutes

Ingredients:
• 2 large zucchinis, finely chopped
• 1 large eggplant, finely chopped
• ¼ teaspoon kosher salt
• ¼ teaspoon freshly ground black pepper
• 3 tablespoons extra-virgin olive oil, divided
• ¾ cup unsweetened almond milk
• 1 tablespoon all-purpose flour
• ⅓ cup plus 2 tablespoons grated Parmesan cheese, divided
• 1 cup chopped tomato
• 1 cup diced fresh Mozzarella
• ¼ cup fresh basil leaves

Directions:
1. Preheat the oven to 425ºF.

2. In a large bowl, toss together the zucchini, eggplant, salt and pepper.

3. In a large skillet over medium-high heat, heat 1 tablespoon of the oil. Add half of the veggie mixture to the skillet. Stir a few times, then cover and cook for about 4 minutes, stirring occasionally. Pour the cooked veggies into a baking dish. Place the skillet back on the heat, add 1 tablespoon of the oil and repeat with the remaining veggies. Add the veggies to the baking dish.

4. Meanwhile, heat the milk in the microwave for 1 minute. Set aside.

5. Place a medium saucepan over medium heat. Add the remaining 1 tablespoon of the oil and flour to the saucepan. Whisk together until well blended.

6. Slowly pour the warm milk into the saucepan, whisking the entire time. Continue to whisk frequently until the mixture thickens a bit. Add ⅓ cup of the Parmesan cheese and whisk until melted. Pour the cheese sauce over the vegetables in the baking dish and mix well.

7. Fold in the tomatoes and Mozzarella cheese. Roast in the oven for 10 minutes, or until the gratin is almost set and not runny.

8. Top with the fresh basil leaves and the remaining 2 tablespoons of the Parmesan cheese before serving.

Nutrition Info:
• Per Serving: Calories: 122;Fat: 5.0g;Protein: 10.0g;Carbs: 11.0g.

Vegetable And Red Lentil Stew
Servings:6 | Cooking Time: 35 Minutes

Ingredients:
• 1 tablespoon extra-virgin olive oil
• 2 onions, peeled and finely diced
• 6½ cups water
• 2 zucchinis, finely diced
• 4 celery stalks, finely diced
• 3 cups red lentils
• 1 teaspoon dried oregano
• 1 teaspoon salt, plus more as needed

Directions:
1. Heat the olive oil in a large pot over medium heat.

2. Add the onions and sauté for about 5 minutes, stirring constantly, or until the onions are softened.

3. Stir in the water, zucchini, celery, lentils, oregano, and salt and bring the mixture to a boil.

4. Reduce the heat to low and let simmer covered for 30 minutes, stirring occasionally, or until the lentils are tender.

5. Taste and adjust the seasoning as needed.

Nutrition Info:
• Per Serving: Calories: 387;Fat: 4.4g;Protein: 24.0g;Carbs: 63.7g.

Stuffed Portobello Mushroom With Tomatoes

Servings:4 | Cooking Time: 15 Minutes

Ingredients:
- 4 large portobello mushroom caps
- 3 tablespoons extra-virgin olive oil
- Salt and freshly ground black pepper, to taste
- 4 sun-dried tomatoes
- 1 cup shredded mozzarella cheese, divided
- ½ to ¾ cup low-sodium tomato sauce

Directions:
1. Preheat the broiler on high.
2. Arrange the mushroom caps on a baking sheet and drizzle with olive oil. Sprinkle with salt and pepper.
3. Broil for 1o minutes, flipping the mushroom caps halfway through, until browned on the top.
4. Remove from the broil. Spoon 1 tomato, 2 tablespoons of cheese, and 2 to 3 tablespoons of sauce onto each mushroom cap.
5. Return the mushroom caps to the broiler and continue broiling for 2 to 3 minutes.
6. Cool for 5 minutes before serving.

Nutrition Info:
- Per Serving: Calories: 217;Fat: 15.8g;Protein: 11.2g;Carbs: 11.7g.

Roasted Caramelized Root Vegetables

Servings:6 | Cooking Time:40 Minutes

Ingredients:
- 1 sweet potato, peeled and cut into chunks
- 3 tbsp olive oil
- 2 carrots, peeled
- 2 beets, peeled
- 1 turnip, peeled
- 1 tsp cumin
- 1 tsp sweet paprika
- Salt and black pepper to taste
- 1 lemon, juiced
- 2 tbsp parsley, chopped

Directions:
1. Preheat oven to 400ºF. Cut the vegetables into chunks and toss them with olive oil and seasonings in a sheet pan. Drizzle with lemon juice and roast them for 35-40 minutes until vegetables are tender and golden. Serve topped with parsley.

Nutrition Info:
- Per Serving: Calories: 80;Fat: 4.8g;Protein: 1.5g;Carbs: 8.9g.

Roasted Vegetables

Servings:2 | Cooking Time: 35 Minutes

Ingredients:
- 6 teaspoons extra-virgin olive oil, divided
- 12 to 15 Brussels sprouts, halved
- 1 medium sweet potato, peeled and cut into 2-inch cubes
- 2 cups fresh cauliflower flo-
- rets
- 1 medium zucchini, cut into 1-inch rounds
- 1 red bell pepper, cut into 1-inch slices
- Salt, to taste

Directions:
1. Preheat the oven to 425ºF.
2. Add 2 teaspoons of olive oil, Brussels sprouts, sweet potato, and salt to a large bowl and toss until they are completely coated.
3. Transfer them to a large roasting pan and roast for 10 minutes, or until the Brussels sprouts are lightly browned.
4. Meantime, combine the cauliflower florets with 2 teaspoons of olive oil and salt in a separate bowl.
5. Remove from the oven. Add the cauliflower florets to the roasting pan and roast for 10 minutes more.
6. Meanwhile, toss the zucchini and bell pepper with the remaining olive oil in a medium bowl until well coated. Season with salt.
7. Remove the roasting pan from the oven and stir in the zucchini and bell pepper. Continue roasting for 15 minutes, or until the vegetables are fork-tender.
8. Divide the roasted vegetables between two plates and serve warm.

Nutrition Info:
- Per Serving: Calories: 333;Fat: 16.8g;Protein: 12.2g;Carbs: 37.6g.

Roasted Veggies And Brown Rice Bowl

Servings:4 | Cooking Time: 20 Minutes

Ingredients:
- 2 cups cauliflower florets
- 2 cups broccoli florets
- 1 can chickpeas, drained and rinsed
- 1 cup carrot slices
- 2 to 3 tablespoons extra-virgin olive oil, divided
- Salt and freshly ground black pepper, to taste
- Nonstick cooking spray
- 2 cups cooked brown rice
- 2 to 3 tablespoons sesame seeds, for garnish
- Dressing:
- 3 to 4 tablespoons tahini
- 2 tablespoons honey
- 1 lemon, juiced
- 1 garlic clove, minced
- Salt and freshly ground black pepper, to taste

Directions:
1. Preheat the oven to 400ºF. Spritz two baking sheets with nonstick cooking spray.
2. Spread the cauliflower and broccoli on the first baking sheet and the second with the chickpeas and carrot slices.
3. Drizzle each sheet with half of the olive oil and sprinkle with salt and pepper. Toss to coat well.
4. Roast the chickpeas and carrot slices in the preheated oven for 10 minutes, leaving the carrots tender but crisp, and the cauliflower and broccoli for 20 minutes until fork-tender. Stir them once halfway through the cooking time.
5. Meanwhile, make the dressing: Whisk together the tahini, honey, lemon juice, garlic, salt, and pepper in a small bowl.
6. Divide the cooked brown rice among four bowls. Top each bowl evenly with roasted vegetables and dressing. Sprinkle the sesame seeds on top for garnish before serving.

Nutrition Info:
- Per Serving: Calories: 453;Fat: 17.8g;Protein: 12.1g;Carbs: 61.8g.

Wilted Dandelion Greens With Sweet Onion

Servings:4 | Cooking Time: 15 Minutes

Ingredients:
- 1 tablespoon extra-virgin olive oil
- 2 garlic cloves, minced
- 1 Vidalia onion, thinly sliced
- ½ cup low-sodium vegetable
- broth
- 2 bunches dandelion greens, roughly chopped
- Freshly ground black pepper, to taste

Directions:
1. Heat the olive oil in a large skillet over low heat.
2. Add the garlic and onion and cook for 2 to 3 minutes, stirring occasionally, or until the onion is translucent.
3. Fold in the vegetable broth and dandelion greens and cook for

5 to 7 minutes until wilted, stirring frequently.
4. Sprinkle with the black pepper and serve on a plate while warm.

Nutrition Info:
- Per Serving: Calories: 81;Fat: 3.9g;Protein: 3.2g;Carbs: 10.8g.

Italian Hot Green Beans

Servings:4 | Cooking Time:25 Minutes

Ingredients:
- 2 tbsp olive oil
- 1 red bell pepper, diced
- 1 ½ lb green beans
- 4 garlic cloves, minced
- ½ tsp mustard seeds
- ½ tsp fennel seeds
- 1 tsp dried dill weed
- 2 tomatoes, chopped
- 1 cup cream of celery soup
- 1 tsp Italian herb mix
- 1 tsp chili powder
- Salt and black pepper to taste

Directions:
1. Warm the olive oil in a saucepan over medium heat. Add and fry the bell pepper and green beans for about 5 minutes, stirring periodically to promote even cooking. Add in the garlic, mustard seeds, fennel seeds, and dill and continue sautéing for an additional 1 minute or until fragrant. Add in the pureed tomatoes, cream of celery soup, Italian herb mix, chili powder, salt, and black pepper. Continue to simmer, covered, for 10-12 minutes until the green beans are tender.

Nutrition Info:
- Per Serving: Calories: 160;Fat: 9g;Protein: 5g;Carbs: 19g.

Spinach & Lentil Stew

Servings:4 | Cooking Time:40 Minutes

Ingredients:
- 2 tbsp olive oil
- 1 cup dry red lentils, rinsed
- 1 carrot, chopped
- 1 celery stalk, chopped
- 1 red onion, chopped
- 4 garlic cloves, minced
- 3 tomatoes, puréed
- 3 cups vegetable broth
- 1 tsp cayenne pepper
- ½ tsp ground cumin
- ½ tsp thyme
- 1 tsp turmeric
- 1 tbsp sweet paprika
- 1 cup spinach, chopped
- 1 cup fresh cilantro, chopped
- Salt and black pepper to taste

Directions:
1. Heat the olive oil in a pot over medium heat and sauté the garlic, carrot, celery, and onion until tender, about 4-5 minutes. Stir in cayenne pepper, cumin, thyme, paprika, and turmeric for 1 minute and add tomatoes; cook for 3 more minutes. Pour in vegetable broth and lentils and bring to a boil. Reduce the heat and simmer covered for 15 minutes. Stir in spinach and cook for 5 minutes until wilted. Adjust the seasoning and divide between bowls. Top with cilantro.

Nutrition Info:
- Per Serving: Calories: 310;Fat: 9g;Protein: 18.3g;Carbs: 41g.

Cauliflower Cakes With Goat Cheese

Servings:4 | Cooking Time:50 Minutes

Ingredients:
- ¼ cup olive oil
- 10 oz cauliflower florets
- 1 tsp ground turmeric
- 1 tsp ground coriander
- Salt and black pepper to taste
- ½ tsp ground mustard seeds
- 4 oz Goat cheese, softened
- 2 scallions, sliced thin
- 1 large egg, lightly beaten
- 2 garlic cloves, minced
- 1 tsp grated lemon zest
- 4 lemon wedges
- ¼ cup flour

Directions:
1. Preheat oven to 420°F. In a bowl, whisk 1 tablespoon oil, turmeric, coriander, salt, ground mustard, and pepper. Add in the cauliflower and toss to coat. Transfer to a greased baking sheet and spread it in a single layer. Roast for 20-25 minutes until cauliflower is well browned and tender. Transfer the cauliflower to a large bowl and mash it coarsely with a potato masher. Stir in Goat cheese, scallions, egg, garlic, and lemon zest until well combined. Sprinkle flour over cauliflower mixture and stir to incorporate. Shape the mixture into 10-12 cakes and place them on a sheet pan. Chill to firm, about 30 minutes. Warm the remaining olive oil in a skillet over medium heat. Fry the cakes for 5-6 minutes on each side until deep golden brown and crisp. Serve with lemon wedges.

Nutrition Info:
- Per Serving: Calories: 320;Fat: 25g;Protein: 13g;Carbs: 12g.

Stir-fried Kale With Mushrooms

Servings:4 | Cooking Time:10 Minutes

Ingredients:
- 1 cup cremini mushrooms, sliced
- 4 tbsp olive oil
- 1 small red onion, chopped
- 2 cloves garlic, thinly sliced
- 1 ½ lb curly kale
- 2 tomatoes, chopped
- 1 tsp dried oregano
- 1 tsp dried basil
- ½ tsp dried rosemary
- ½ tsp dried thyme
- Salt and black pepper to taste

Directions:
1. Warm the olive oil in a saucepan over medium heat. Sauté the onion and garlic for about 3 minutes or until they are softened. Add in the mushrooms, kale, and tomatoes, stirring to promote even cooking. Turn the heat to a simmer, add in the spices and cook for 5-6 minutes until the kale wilt.

Nutrition Info:
- Per Serving: Calories: 221;Fat: 16g;Protein: 9g;Carbs: 19g.

Tomatoes Filled With Tabbouleh

Servings:4 | Cooking Time:25 Minutes

Ingredients:
- 3 tbsp olive oil, divided
- 8 medium tomatoes
- ½ cup water
- ½ cup bulgur wheat
- 1 ½ cups minced parsley
- ⅓ cup minced fresh mint
- 2 scallions, chopped
- 1 tsp sumac
- Salt and black pepper to taste
- 1 lemon, zested

Directions:
1. Place the bulgur wheat and 2 cups of salted water in a pot and bring to a boil. Lower the heat and simmer for 10 minutes or until tender. Remove the pot from the heat and cover with a lid. Let it sit for 15 minutes.
2. Preheat the oven to 400°F. Slice off the top of each tomato and scoop out the pulp and seeds using a spoon into a sieve set over a bowl. Drain and discard any excess liquid; chop the remaining pulp and place it in a large mixing bowl. Add in parsley, mint, scallions, sumac, lemon zest, lemon juice, bulgur, pepper, and salt, and mix well.
3. Spoon the filling into the tomatoes and place the lids on top. Drizzle with olive oil and bake for 15-20 minutes until the tomatoes are tender. Serve and enjoy!

Nutrition Info:
- Per Serving: Calories: 160;Fat: 7g;Protein: 5g;Carbs: 22g.

Tasty Lentil Burgers

Servings:4 | Cooking Time:25 Minutes

Ingredients:
- 1 cup cremini mushrooms, finely chopped
- 1 cup cooked green lentils
- ½ cup Greek yogurt
- ½ lemon, zested and juiced
- ½ tsp garlic powder
- ½ tsp dried oregano
- 1 tbsp fresh cilantro, chopped
- Salt to taste
- 3 tbsp extra-virgin olive oil
- ¼ tsp tbsp white miso
- ¼ tsp smoked paprika
- ¼ cup flour

Directions:
1. Pour ½ cup of lentils in your blender and puree partially until somewhat smooth, but with many whole lentils still remaining. In a small bowl, mix the yogurt, lemon zest and juice, garlic powder, oregano, cilantro, and salt. Season and set aside. In a medium bowl, mix the mushrooms, 2 tablespoons of olive oil, miso, and paprika. Stir in all the lentils. Add in flour and stir until the mixture everything is well incorporated. Shape the mixture into patties about ¾-inch thick. Warm the remaining olive oil in a skillet over medium heat. Fry the patties until browned and crisp, about 3 minutes. Turn and fry on the second side. Serve with the reserved yogurt mixture.

Nutrition Info:
- Per Serving: Calories: 215;Fat: 13g;Protein: 10g;Carbs: 19g.

Rainbow Vegetable Kebabs

Servings:4 | Cooking Time:30 Minutes

Ingredients:
- 1 cup mushrooms, cut into quarters
- 6 mixed bell peppers, cut into squares
- 4 red onions, cut into 6 wedges
- 4 zucchini, cut into half-moons
- 2 tomatoes, cut into quarters
- 3 tbsp herbed oil

Directions:
1. Preheat your grill to medium-high. Alternate the vegetables onto bamboo skewers. Grill them for 5 minutes on each side until the vegetables begin to char. Remove them from heat and drizzle with herbed oil.

Nutrition Info:
- Per Serving: Calories: 238;Fat: 12g;Protein: 6g;Carbs: 34.2g.

Minty Broccoli & Walnuts

Servings:2 | Cooking Time:10 Minutes

Ingredients:
- 1 garlic clove, minced
- ½ cups walnuts, chopped
- 3 cups broccoli florets, steamed
- 1 tbsp mint, chopped
- ½ lemon, juiced
- Salt and black pepper to taste

Directions:
1. Mix walnuts, broccoli, garlic, mint, lemon juice, salt, and pepper in a bowl. Serve chilled.

Nutrition Info:
- Per Serving: Calories: 210;Fat: 7g;Protein: 4g;Carbs: 9g.

Lentil And Tomato Collard Wraps

Servings:4 | Cooking Time: 0 Minutes

Ingredients:
- 2 cups cooked lentils
- 5 Roma tomatoes, diced
- ½ cup crumbled feta cheese
- 10 large fresh basil leaves, thinly sliced
- ¼ cup extra-virgin olive oil
- 1 tablespoon balsamic vinegar
- 2 garlic cloves, minced
- ½ teaspoon raw honey
- ½ teaspoon salt
- ¼ teaspoon freshly ground black pepper
- 4 large collard leaves, stems removed

Directions:
1. Combine the lentils, tomatoes, cheese, basil leaves, olive oil, vinegar, garlic, honey, salt, and black pepper in a large bowl and stir until well blended.
2. Lay the collard leaves on a flat work surface. Spoon the equal-sized amounts of the lentil mixture onto the edges of the leaves. Roll them up and slice in half to serve.

Nutrition Info:
- Per Serving: Calories: 318;Fat: 17.6g;Protein: 13.2g;Carbs: 27.5g.

Roasted Artichokes

Servings:4 | Cooking Time:50 Minutes

Ingredients:
- 4 artichokes, stalk trimmed and large leaves removed
- 2 lemons, freshly squeezed
- 4 tbsp extra-virgin olive oil
- 4 cloves garlic, chopped
- 1 tsp fresh rosemary
- 1 tsp fresh basil
- 1 tsp fresh parsley
- 1 tsp fresh oregano
- Salt and black pepper to taste
- 1 tsp red pepper flakes
- 1 tsp paprika

Directions:
1. Preheat oven to 395ºF. In a small bowl, thoroughly combine the garlic with herbs and spices; set aside. Cut the artichokes in half vertically and scoop out the fibrous choke to expose the heart with a teaspoon.
2. Rub the lemon juice all over the entire surface of the artichoke halves. Arrange them on a parchment-lined baking dish, cut side up, and brush them evenly with olive oil. Stuff the cavities with the garlic/herb mixture. Cover them with aluminum foil and bake for 30 minutes. Discard the foil and bake for another 10 minutes until lightly charred. Serve.

Nutrition Info:
- Per Serving: Calories: 220;Fat: 14g;Protein: 6g;Carbs: 21g.

Zoodles With Walnut Pesto

Servings:4 | Cooking Time: 10 Minutes

Ingredients:
- 4 medium zucchinis, spiralized
- ¼ cup extra-virgin olive oil, divided
- 1 teaspoon minced garlic, divided
- ½ teaspoon crushed red pepper
- ¼ teaspoon freshly ground black pepper, divided
- ¼ teaspoon kosher salt, divided
- 2 tablespoons grated Parmesan cheese, divided
- 1 cup packed fresh basil leaves
- ¾ cup walnut pieces, divided

Directions:
1. In a large bowl, stir together the zoodles, 1 tablespoon of the

olive oil, ½ teaspoon of the minced garlic, red pepper, ⅛ teaspoon of the black pepper and ⅛ teaspoon of the salt. Set aside.

2. Heat ½ tablespoon of the oil in a large skillet over medium-high heat. Add half of the zoodles to the skillet and cook for 5 minutes, stirring constantly. Transfer the cooked zoodles into a bowl. Repeat with another ½ tablespoon of the oil and the remaining zoodles. When done, add the cooked zoodles to the bowl.

3. Make the pesto: In a food processor, combine the remaining ½ teaspoon of the minced garlic, ⅛ teaspoon of the black pepper and ⅛ teaspoon of the salt, 1 tablespoon of the Parmesan, basil leaves and ¼ cup of the walnuts. Pulse until smooth and then slowly drizzle the remaining 2 tablespoons of the oil into the pesto. Pulse again until well combined.

4. Add the pesto to the zoodles along with the remaining 1 tablespoon of the Parmesan and the remaining ½ cup of the walnuts. Toss to coat well.

5. Serve immediately.

Nutrition Info:
• Per Serving: Calories: 166;Fat: 16.0g;Protein: 4.0g;Carbs: 3.0g.

Stuffed Portobello Mushrooms With Spinach

Servings:4 | Cooking Time: 20 Minutes

Ingredients:
• 8 large portobello mushrooms, stems removed
• 3 teaspoons extra-virgin olive oil, divided
• 1 medium red bell pepper, diced
• 4 cups fresh spinach
• ¼ cup crumbled feta cheese

Directions:
1. Preheat the oven to 450°F.
2. Using a spoon to scoop out the gills of the mushrooms and discard them. Brush the mushrooms with 2 teaspoons of olive oil.
3. Arrange the mushrooms (cap-side down) on a baking sheet. Roast in the preheated oven for 20 minutes.
4. Meantime, in a medium skillet, heat the remaining olive oil over medium heat until it shimmers.
5. Add the bell pepper and spinach and sauté for 8 to 10 minutes, stirring occasionally, or until the spinach is wilted.
6. Remove the mushrooms from the oven to a paper towel-lined plate. Using a spoon to stuff each mushroom with the bell pepper and spinach mixture. Scatter the feta cheese all over.
7. Serve immediately.

Nutrition Info:
• Per Serving: Calories: 115;Fat: 5.9g;Protein: 7.2g;Carbs: 11.5g.

Brussels Sprouts Linguine

Servings:4 | Cooking Time: 25 Minutes

Ingredients:
• 8 ounces whole-wheat linguine
• ⅓ cup plus 2 tablespoons extra-virgin olive oil, divided
• 1 medium sweet onion, diced
• 2 to 3 garlic cloves, smashed
• 8 ounces Brussels sprouts,
chopped
• ½ cup chicken stock
• ⅓ cup dry white wine
• ½ cup shredded Parmesan cheese
• 1 lemon, quartered

Directions:
1. Bring a large pot of water to a boil and cook the pasta for about 5 minutes, or until al dente. Drain the pasta and reserve 1 cup of the pasta water. Mix the cooked pasta with 2 tablespoons of the olive oil. Set aside.

2. In a large skillet, heat the remaining ⅓ cup of the olive oil over medium heat. Add the onion to the skillet and sauté for about 4 minutes, or until tender. Add the smashed garlic cloves and sauté for 1 minute, or until fragrant.
3. Stir in the Brussels sprouts and cook covered for 10 minutes. Pour in the chicken stock to prevent burning. Once the Brussels sprouts have wilted and are fork-tender, add white wine and cook for about 5 minutes, or until reduced.
4. Add the pasta to the skillet and add the pasta water as needed.
5. Top with the Parmesan cheese and squeeze the lemon over the dish right before eating.

Nutrition Info:
• Per Serving: Calories: 502;Fat: 31.0g;Protein: 15.0g;Carbs: 50.0g.

Baked Beet & Leek With Dilly Yogurt

Servings:4 | Cooking Time:40 Minutes

Ingredients:
• 5 tbsp olive oil
• ½ lb leeks, thickly sliced
• 1 lb red beets, sliced
• 1 cup yogurt
• 2 garlic cloves, finely minced
• ¼ tsp cumin, ground
• ¼ tsp dried parsley
• ¼ cup parsley, chopped
• 1 tsp dill
• Salt and black pepper to taste

Directions:
1. Preheat the oven to 390°F. Arrange the beets and leeks on a greased roasting dish. Sprinkle with some olive oil, cumin, dried parsley, black pepper, and salt. Bake in the oven for 25-30 minutes. Transfer to a serving platter. In a bowl, stir in yogurt, dill, garlic, and the remaining olive oil. Whisk to combine. Drizzle the veggies with the yogurt sauce and top with fresh parsley to serve.

Nutrition Info:
• Per Serving: Calories: 281;Fat: 18.7g;Protein: 6g;Carbs: 24g.

Grilled Eggplant "steaks" With Sauce

Servings:6 | Cooking Time:20 Minutes

Ingredients:
• 2 lb eggplants, sliced lengthways
• 6 tbsp olive oil
• 5 garlic cloves, minced
• 1 tsp dried oregano
• ½ tsp red pepper flakes
• ½ cup Greek yogurt
• 3 tbsp chopped fresh parsley
• 1 tsp grated lemon zest
• 2 tsp lemon juice
• 1 tsp ground cumin
• Salt and black pepper to taste

Directions:
1. In a bowl, whisk half of the olive oil, yogurt, parsley, lemon zest and juice, cumin, and salt; set aside until ready to serve. Preheat your grill to High. Rub the eggplant steaks with the remaining olive oil, oregano, salt, and pepper. Grill them for 4-6 minutes per side until browned and tender; transfer to a serving platter. Drizzle yogurt sauce over eggplant.

Nutrition Info:
• Per Serving: Calories: 112;Fat: 7g;Protein: 2.6g;Carbs: 11.3g.

Authentic Mushroom Gratin

Servings:4 | Cooking Time:25 Minutes

Ingredients:
• 2 lb Button mushrooms, cleaned
• 2 tbsp olive oil
• 2 tomatoes, sliced
• 2 tomato paste
• ½ cup Parmesan cheese, grated
• ½ cup dry white wine

- ¼ tsp sweet paprika
- ½ tsp dried basil
- ½ tsp dried thyme
- Salt and black pepper to taste

Directions:
1. Preheat oven to 360°F. Combine tomatoes, tomato paste, wine, oil, mushrooms, paprika, black pepper, salt, basil, and thyme in a baking dish. Bake for 15 minutes. Top with Parmesan and continue baking for 5 minutes until the cheese melts.

Nutrition Info:
- Per Serving: Calories: 162;Fat: 8.6g;Protein: 9g;Carbs: 12.3g.

Braised Cauliflower With White Wine

Servings:4 | Cooking Time: 12 To 16 Minutes

Ingredients:
- 3 tablespoons plus 1 teaspoon extra-virgin olive oil, divided
- 3 garlic cloves, minced
- ⅛ teaspoon red pepper flakes
- 1 head cauliflower, cored and cut into 1½-inch florets
- ¼ teaspoon salt, plus more
- for seasoning
- Black pepper, to taste
- ⅓ cup vegetable broth
- ⅓ cup dry white wine
- 2 tablespoons minced fresh parsley

Directions:
1. Combine 1 teaspoon of the oil, garlic and pepper flakes in small bowl.
2. Heat the remaining 3 tablespoons of the oil in a skillet over medium-high heat until shimmering. Add the cauliflower and ¼ teaspoon of the salt and cook for 7 to 9 minutes, stirring occasionally, or until florets are golden brown.
3. Push the cauliflower to sides of the skillet. Add the garlic mixture to the center of the skillet. Cook for about 30 seconds, or until fragrant. Stir the garlic mixture into the cauliflower.
4. Pour in the broth and wine and bring to simmer. Reduce the heat to medium-low. Cover and cook for 4 to 6 minutes, or until the cauliflower is crisp-tender. Off heat, stir in the parsley and season with salt and pepper.
5. Serve immediately.

Nutrition Info:
- Per Serving: Calories: 143;Fat: 11.7g;Protein: 3.1g;Carbs: 8.7g.

Potato Tortilla With Leeks And Mushrooms

Servings:2 | Cooking Time: 50 Minutes

Ingredients:
- 1 tablespoon olive oil
- 1 cup thinly sliced leeks
- 4 ounces baby bella (cremini) mushrooms, stemmed and sliced
- 1 small potato, peeled and sliced ¼-inch thick
- 5 large eggs, beaten
- ½ cup unsweetened almond
- milk
- 1 teaspoon Dijon mustard
- ½ teaspoon dried thyme
- ½ teaspoon salt
- Pinch freshly ground black pepper
- 3 ounces Gruyère cheese, shredded

Directions:
1. Preheat the oven to 350ºF.
2. Heat the olive oil in a large sauté pan (nonstick is best) over medium-high heat. Add the leeks, mushrooms, and potato slices and sauté until the leeks are golden and the potatoes start to brown, about 10 minutes.
3. Reduce the heat to medium-low, cover, and let the vegetables cook for another 10 minutes, or until the potatoes begin to soften. If the potato slices stick to the bottom of the pan, add 1 to 2 tablespoons of water to the pan, but be careful because it may splatter.

4. Meanwhile, combine the beaten eggs, milk, mustard, thyme, salt, pepper, and cheese in a medium bowl and whisk everything together.
5. When the potatoes are soft enough to pierce with a fork or knife, turn off the heat.
6. Transfer the cooked vegetables to an oiled ovenproof pan (nonstick is best) and arrange them in a nice layer along the bottom and slightly up the sides of the pan.
7. Pour the egg mixture over the vegetables and give it a light shake or tap to distribute the eggs evenly through the vegetables.
8. Bake for 25 to 30 minutes, or until the eggs are set and the top is golden and puffed.
9. Remove from the oven and cool for 5 minutes before cutting and serving.

Nutrition Info:
- Per Serving: Calories: 541;Fat: 33.1g;Protein: 32.8g;Carbs: 31.0g.

Zucchini Crisp

Servings:2 | Cooking Time: 20 Minutes

Ingredients:
- 4 zucchinis, sliced into ½-inch rounds
- ½ cup unsweetened almond milk
- 1 teaspoon fresh lemon juice
- 1 teaspoon arrowroot powder
- ½ teaspoon salt, divided
- ½ cup whole wheat bread
- crumbs
- ¼ cup nutritional yeast
- ¼ cup hemp seeds
- ½ teaspoon garlic powder
- ¼ teaspoon crushed red pepper
- ¼ teaspoon black pepper

Directions:
1. Preheat the oven to 375ºF. Line two baking sheets with parchment paper and set aside.
2. Put the zucchini in a medium bowl with the almond milk, lemon juice, arrowroot powder, and ¼ teaspoon of salt. Stir to mix well.
3. In a large bowl with a lid, thoroughly combine the bread crumbs, nutritional yeast, hemp seeds, garlic powder, crushed red pepper and black pepper. Add the zucchini in batches and shake until the slices are evenly coated.
4. Arrange the zucchini on the prepared baking sheets in a single layer.
5. Bake in the preheated oven for about 20 minutes, or until the zucchini slices are golden brown.
6. Season with the remaining ¼ teaspoon of salt before serving.

Nutrition Info:
- Per Serving: Calories: 255;Fat: 11.3g;Protein: 8.6g;Carbs: 31.9g.

Simple Broccoli With Yogurt Sauce

Servings:4 | Cooking Time:25 Minutes

Ingredients:
- 2 tbsp olive oil
- 1 head broccoli, cut into florets
- 2 garlic cloves, minced
- ½ cup Greek yogurt
- Salt and black pepper to taste
- 2 tsp fresh dill, chopped

Directions:
1. Warm olive oil in a pan over medium heat and sauté broccoli, salt, and pepper for 12 minutes. Mix Greek yogurt, dill, and garlic in a small bowl. Drizzle the broccoli with the sauce.

Nutrition Info:

- Per Serving: Calories: 104;Fat: 7.7g;Protein: 4.5g;Carbs: 6g.

Sautéed Green Beans With Tomatoes

Servings:4 | Cooking Time: 20 Minutes

Ingredients:
- ¼ cup extra-virgin olive oil
- 1 large onion, chopped
- 4 cloves garlic, finely chopped
- 1 pound green beans, fresh or frozen, cut into 2-inch pieces
- 1½ teaspoons salt, divided
- 1 can diced tomatoes
- ½ teaspoon freshly ground black pepper

Directions:
1. Heat the olive oil in a large skillet over medium heat.
2. Add the onion and garlic and sauté for 1 minute until fragrant.
3. Stir in the green beans and sauté for 3 minutes. Sprinkle with ½ teaspoon of salt.
4. Add the tomatoes, remaining salt, and pepper and stir to mix well. Cook for an additional 12 minutes, stirring occasionally, or until the green beans are crisp and tender.
5. Remove from the heat and serve warm.

Nutrition Info:
- Per Serving: Calories: 219;Fat: 13.9g;Protein: 4.0g;Carbs: 17.7g.

Ratatouille

Servings:4 | Cooking Time: 30 Minutes

Ingredients:
- 4 tablespoons extra-virgin olive oil, divided
- 1 cup diced zucchini
- 2 cups diced eggplant
- 1 cup diced onion
- 1 cup chopped green bell pepper
- 1 can no-salt-added diced tomatoes
- ½ teaspoon garlic powder
- 1 teaspoon ground thyme
- Salt and freshly ground black pepper, to taste

Directions:
1. Heat 2 tablespoons of olive oil in a large saucepan over medium heat until it shimmers.
2. Add the zucchini and eggplant and sauté for 10 minutes, stirring occasionally. If necessary, add the remaining olive oil.
3. Stir in the onion and bell pepper and sauté for 5 minutes until softened.
4. Add the diced tomatoes with their juice, garlic powder, and thyme and stir to combine. Continue cooking for 15 minutes until the vegetables are cooked through, stirring occasionally. Sprinkle with salt and black pepper.
5. Remove from the heat and serve on a plate.

Nutrition Info:
- Per Serving: Calories: 189;Fat: 13.7g;Protein: 3.1g;Carbs: 14.8g.

Chili Vegetable Skillet

Servings:4 | Cooking Time:30 Minutes

Ingredients:
- 1 cup condensed cream of mushroom soup
- 1 ½ lb eggplants, cut into chunks
- 1 cup cremini mushrooms, sliced
- 4 tbsp olive oil
- 1 carrot, thinly sliced
- 1 can tomatoes
- ½ cup red onion, thinly sliced
- 2 garlic cloves, minced
- 1 tsp fresh rosemary
- 1 tsp chili pepper
- Salt and black pepper to taste

- 2 tbsp parsley, chopped
- ¼ cup Parmesan cheese, grated

Directions:
1. Warm the olive oil in a skillet over medium heat. Add in the eggplant and cook until golden brown on all sides, about 5 minutes; set aside. Add in the carrot, onion, and mushrooms and sauté for 4 more minutes to the same skillet. Add in garlic, rosemary, and chili pepper. Cook for another 30-40 seconds. Add in 1 cup of water, cream of mushroom soup, and tomatoes. Bring to a boil and lower the heat; simmer covered for 5 minutes. Mix in sautéed eggplants and parsley and cook for 10 more minutes. Sprinkle with salt and black pepper. Serve topped with Parmesan cheese.

Nutrition Info:
- Per Serving: Calories: 261;Fat: 18.7g;Protein: 5g;Carbs: 23g.

Creamy Cauliflower Chickpea Curry

Servings:4 | Cooking Time: 15 Minutes

Ingredients:
- 3 cups fresh or frozen cauliflower florets
- 2 cups unsweetened almond milk
- 1 can low-sodium chickpeas, drained and rinsed
- 1 can coconut milk
- 1 tablespoon curry powder
- ¼ teaspoon garlic powder
- ¼ teaspoon ground ginger
- ⅛ teaspoon onion powder
- ¼ teaspoon salt

Directions:
1. Add the cauliflower florets, almond milk, chickpeas, coconut milk, curry powder, garlic powder, ginger, and onion powder to a large stockpot and stir to combine.
2. Cover and cook over medium-high heat for 10 minutes, stirring occasionally.
3. Reduce the heat to low and continue cooking uncovered for 5 minutes, or until the cauliflower is tender.
4. Sprinkle with the salt and stir well. Serve warm.

Nutrition Info:
- Per Serving: Calories: 409;Fat: 29.6g;Protein: 10.0g;Carbs: 29.8g.

Fried Eggplant Rolls

Servings:4 | Cooking Time: 10 Minutes

Ingredients:
- 2 large eggplants, trimmed and cut lengthwise into ¼-inch-thick slices
- 1 teaspoon salt
- 1 cup shredded ricotta cheese
- 4 ounces goat cheese, shredded
- ¼ cup finely chopped fresh basil
- ½ teaspoon freshly ground black pepper
- Olive oil spray

Directions:
1. Add the eggplant slices to a colander and season with salt. Set aside for 15 to 20 minutes.
2. Mix together the ricotta and goat cheese, basil, and black pepper in a large bowl and stir to combine. Set aside.
3. Dry the eggplant slices with paper towels and lightly mist them with olive oil spray.
4. Heat a large skillet over medium heat and lightly spray it with olive oil spray.
5. Arrange the eggplant slices in the skillet and fry each side for 3 minutes until golden brown.
6. Remove from the heat to a paper towel-lined plate and rest for 5 minutes.
7. Make the eggplant rolls: Lay the eggplant slices on a flat

work surface and top each slice with a tablespoon of the prepared cheese mixture. Roll them up and serve immediately.

Nutrition Info:
• Per Serving: Calories: 254;Fat: 14.9g;Protein: 15.3g;Carbs: 18.6g.

Mushroom & Cauliflower Roast
Servings:4 | Cooking Time:35 Minutes

Ingredients:
• 2 tbsp olive oil
• 4 cups cauliflower florets
• 1 celery stalk, chopped
• 1 cup mushrooms, sliced
• 10 cherry tomatoes, halved
• 1 yellow onion, chopped
• 2 garlic cloves, minced
• 2 tbsp dill, chopped
• Salt and black pepper to taste

Directions:
1. Preheat the oven to 340ºF. Line a baking sheet with parchment paper. Place in cauliflower florets, olive oil, mushrooms, celery, tomatoes, onion, garlic, salt, and pepper and mix to combine. Bake for 25 minutes. Serve topped with dill.

Nutrition Info:
• Per Serving: Calories: 380;Fat: 15g;Protein: 12g;Carbs: 17g.

Asparagus & Mushroom Farro
Servings:2 | Cooking Time:40 Minutes

Ingredients:
• ½ oz dried porcini mushrooms, soaked
• 2 tbsp olive oil
• 1 cup hot water
• 3 cups vegetable stock
• ½ large onion, minced
• 1 garlic clove
• 1 cup fresh mushrooms, sliced
• ½ cup farro
• ½ cup dry white wine
• ½ tsp dried thyme
• ½ tsp dried marjoram
• 4 oz asparagus, chopped
• 2 tbsp grated Parmesan cheese

Directions:
1. Drain the soaked mushrooms, reserving the liquid, and cut them into slices. Warm the olive oil in a saucepan oven over medium heat. Sauté the onion, garlic, and soaked and fresh mushrooms for 8 minutes. Stir in the farro for 1-2 minutes. Add the wine, thyme, marjoram, reserved mushroom liquid, and a ladleful of stock. Bring it to a boil.
2. Lower the heat and cook for about 20 minutes, stirring occasionally and adding another ladleful of stock, until the farro is cooked through but not overcooked. Stir in the asparagus and the remaining stock. Cook for 3-5 more minutes or until the asparagus is softened. Sprinkle with Parmesan cheese and serve warm.

Nutrition Info:
• Per Serving: Calories: 341;Fat: 16g;Protein: 13g;Carbs: 26g.

Grilled Romaine Lettuce
Servings:4 | Cooking Time: 3 To 5 Minutes

Ingredients:
• Romaine:
• 2 heads romaine lettuce, halved lengthwise
• 2 tablespoons extra-virgin olive oil
• Dressing:
• ½ cup unsweetened almond
milk
• 1 tablespoon extra-virgin olive oil
• ¼ bunch fresh chives, thinly chopped
• 1 garlic clove, pressed
• 1 pinch red pepper flakes

Directions:
1. Heat a grill pan over medium heat.
2. Brush each lettuce half with the olive oil. Place the lettuce halves, flat-side down, on the grill. Grill for 3 to 5 minutes, or until the lettuce slightly wilts and develops light grill marks.
3. Meanwhile, whisk together all the ingredients for the dressing in a small bowl.
4. Drizzle 2 tablespoons of the dressing over each romaine half and serve.

Nutrition Info:
• Per Serving: Calories: 126;Fat: 11.0g;Protein: 2.0g;Carbs: 7.0g.

5-ingredient Zucchini Fritters
Servings:14 | Cooking Time: 5 Minutes

Ingredients:
• 4 cups grated zucchini
• Salt, to taste
• 2 large eggs, lightly beaten
• ⅓ cup sliced scallions (green
and white parts)
• ⅔ all-purpose flour
• ⅛ teaspoon black pepper
• 2 tablespoons olive oil

Directions:
1. Put the grated zucchini in a colander and lightly season with salt. Set aside to rest for 10 minutes. Squeeze out as much liquid from the grated zucchini as possible.
2. Pour the grated zucchini into a bowl. Fold in the beaten eggs, scallions, flour, salt, and pepper and stir until everything is well combined.
3. Heat the olive oil in a large skillet over medium heat until hot.
4. Drop 3 tablespoons mounds of the zucchini mixture onto the hot skillet to make each fritter, pressing them lightly into rounds and spacing them about 2 inches apart.
5. Cook for 2 to 3 minutes. Flip the zucchini fritters and cook for 2 minutes more, or until they are golden brown and cooked through.
6. Remove from the heat to a plate lined with paper towels. Repeat with the remaining zucchini mixture.
7. Serve hot.

Nutrition Info:
• Per Serving: Calories: 113;Fat: 6.1g;Protein: 4.0g;Carbs: 12.2g.

Chickpea Lettuce Wraps With Celery
Servings:4 | Cooking Time: 0 Minutes

Ingredients:
• 1 can low-sodium chickpeas, drained and rinsed
• 1 celery stalk, thinly sliced
• 2 tablespoons finely chopped red onion
• 2 tablespoons unsalted tahini
• 3 tablespoons honey mustard
• 1 tablespoon capers, undrained
• 12 butter lettuce leaves

Directions:
1. In a bowl, mash the chickpeas with a potato masher or the back of a fork until mostly smooth.
2. Add the celery, red onion, tahini, honey mustard, and capers to the bowl and stir until well incorporated.
3. For each serving, place three overlapping lettuce leaves on a plate and top with ¼ of the mashed chickpea filling, then roll up. Repeat with the remaining lettuce leaves and chickpea mixture.

Nutrition Info:
• Per Serving: Calories: 182;Fat: 7.1g;Protein: 10.3g;Carbs: 19.6g.

Easy Zucchini Patties

Servings:2 | Cooking Time: 5 Minutes

Ingredients:
- 2 medium zucchinis, shredded
- 1 teaspoon salt, divided
- 2 eggs
- 2 tablespoons chickpea flour
- 1 tablespoon chopped fresh mint
- 1 scallion, chopped
- 2 tablespoons extra-virgin olive oil

Directions:
1. Put the shredded zucchini in a fine-mesh strainer and season with ½ teaspoon of salt. Set aside.
2. Beat together the eggs, chickpea flour, mint, scallion, and remaining ½ teaspoon of salt in a medium bowl.
3. Squeeze the zucchini to drain as much liquid as possible. Add the zucchini to the egg mixture and stir until well incorporated.
4. Heat the olive oil in a large skillet over medium-high heat.
5. Drop the zucchini mixture by spoonful into the skillet. Gently flatten the zucchini with the back of a spatula.
6. Cook for 2 to 3 minutes or until golden brown. Flip and cook for an additional 2 minutes.
7. Remove from the heat and serve on a plate.

Nutrition Info:
- Per Serving: Calories: 264;Fat: 20.0g;Protein: 9.8g;Carbs: 16.1g.

Pea & Carrot Noodles

Servings:4 | Cooking Time:25 Minutes

Ingredients:
- 2 tbsp olive oil
- 4 carrots, spiralized
- 1 sweet onion, chopped
- 2 cups peas
- 2 garlic cloves, minced
- ¼ cup chopped fresh parsley
- Salt and black pepper to taste

Directions:
1. Warm 2 tbsp of olive oil in a pot over medium heat and sauté the onion and garlic for 3 minutes until just tender and fragrant. Add in spiralized carrots and cook for 4 minutes. Mix in peas, salt, and pepper and cook for 4 minutes. Drizzle with the remaining olive oil and sprinkle with parsley.

Nutrition Info:
- Per Serving: Calories: 157;Fat: 7g;Protein: 4.8g;Carbs: 19.6g.

Vegetable And Tofu Scramble

Servings:2 | Cooking Time: 10 Minutes

Ingredients:
- 2 tablespoons extra-virgin olive oil
- ½ red onion, finely chopped
- 1 cup chopped kale
- 8 ounces mushrooms, sliced
- 8 ounces tofu, cut into pieces
- 2 garlic cloves, minced
- Pinch red pepper flakes
- ½ teaspoon sea salt
- ⅛ teaspoon freshly ground black pepper

Directions:
1. Heat the olive oil in a medium nonstick skillet over medium-high heat until shimmering.
2. Add the onion, kale, and mushrooms to the skillet and cook for about 5 minutes, stirring occasionally, or until the vegetables start to brown.
3. Add the tofu and stir-fry for 3 to 4 minutes until softened.
4. Stir in the garlic, red pepper flakes, salt, and black pepper and cook for 30 seconds.

5. Let the mixture cool for 5 minutes before serving.

Nutrition Info:
- Per Serving: Calories: 233;Fat: 15.9g;Protein: 13.4g;Carbs: 11.9g.

Roasted Celery Root With Yogurt Sauce

Servings:6 | Cooking Time:50 Minutes

Ingredients:
- 3 tbsp olive oil
- 3 celery roots, sliced
- Salt and black pepper to taste
- ¼ cup plain yogurt
- ¼ tsp grated lemon zest
- 1 tsp lemon juice
- 1 tsp sesame seeds, toasted
- 1 tsp coriander seeds, crushed
- ¼ tsp dried thyme
- ¼ tsp chili powder
- ¼ cup fresh cilantro, chopped

Directions:
1. Preheat oven to 425ºF. Place the celery slices on a baking sheet. Sprinkle them with olive oil, salt, and pepper. Roast for 25-30 minutes. Flip each piece and continue to roast for 10-15 minutes until celery root is very tender and sides touching sheet are browned. Transfer celery to a serving platter.
2. Whisk yogurt, lemon zest and juice, and salt together in a bowl. In a separate bowl, combine sesame seeds, coriander seeds, thyme, chili powder, and salt. Drizzle celery root with yogurt sauce and sprinkle with seed mixture and cilantro.

Nutrition Info:
- Per Serving: Calories: 75;Fat: 7.5g;Protein: 0.7g;Carbs: 1.8g.

Baked Honey Acorn Squash

Servings:4 | Cooking Time:35 Minutes

Ingredients:
- 1 acorn squash, cut into wedges
- 2 tbsp olive oil
- 2 tbsp honey
- 2 tbsp rosemary, chopped
- 2 tbsp walnuts, chopped

Directions:
1. Preheat oven to 400°F. In a bowl, mix honey, rosemary, and olive oil. Lay the squash wedges on a baking sheet and drizzle with the honey mixture. Bake for 30 minutes until squash is tender and slightly caramelized, turning each slice over halfway through. Serve cooled sprinkled with walnuts.

Nutrition Info:
- Per Serving: Calories: 136;Fat: 6g;Protein: 0.9g;Carbs: 20g.

Cheesy Sweet Potato Burgers

Servings:4 | Cooking Time: 19 To 20 Minutes

Ingredients:
- 1 large sweet potato
- 2 tablespoons extra-virgin olive oil, divided
- 1 cup chopped onion
- 1 large egg
- 1 garlic clove
- 1 cup old-fashioned rolled oats
- 1 tablespoon dried oregano
- 1 tablespoon balsamic vinegar
- ¼ teaspoon kosher salt
- ½ cup crumbled Gorgonzola cheese

Directions:
1. Using a fork, pierce the sweet potato all over and microwave on high for 4 to 5 minutes, until softened in the center. Cool slightly before slicing in half.
2. Meanwhile, in a large skillet over medium-high heat, heat 1 tablespoon of the olive oil. Add the onion and sauté for 5 minutes.
3. Spoon the sweet potato flesh out of the skin and put the flesh in

a food processor. Add the cooked onion, egg, garlic, oats, oregano, vinegar and salt. Pulse until smooth. Add the cheese and pulse four times to barely combine.

4. Form the mixture into four burgers. Place the burgers on a plate, and press to flatten each to about ¾-inch thick.

5. Wipe out the skillet with a paper towel. Heat the remaining 1 tablespoon of the oil over medium-high heat for about 2 minutes. Add the burgers to the hot oil, then reduce the heat to medium. Cook the burgers for 5 minutes per side.

6. Transfer the burgers to a plate and serve.

Nutrition Info:
- Per Serving: Calories: 290;Fat: 12.0g;Protein: 12.0g;Carbs: 43.0g.

Cauliflower Hash With Carrots

Servings:4 | Cooking Time: 10 Minutes

Ingredients:
- 3 tablespoons extra-virgin olive oil
- 1 large onion, chopped
- 1 tablespoon minced garlic
- 2 cups diced carrots
- 4 cups cauliflower florets
- ½ teaspoon ground cumin
- 1 teaspoon salt

Directions:
1. In a large skillet, heat the olive oil over medium heat.
2. Add the onion and garlic and sauté for 1 minute. Stir in the carrots and stir-fry for 3 minutes.
3. Add the cauliflower florets, cumin, and salt and toss to combine.
4. Cover and cook for 3 minutes until lightly browned. Stir well and cook, uncovered, for 3 to 4 minutes, until softened.
5. Remove from the heat and serve warm.

Nutrition Info:
- Per Serving: Calories: 158;Fat: 10.8g;Protein: 3.1g;Carbs: 14.9g.

Baked Tomatoes And Chickpeas

Servings:4 | Cooking Time: 40 To 45 Minutes

Ingredients:
- 1 tablespoon extra-virgin olive oil
- ½ medium onion, chopped
- 3 garlic cloves, chopped
- ¼ teaspoon ground cumin
- 2 teaspoons smoked paprika
- 2 cans chickpeas, drained and rinsed
- 4 cups halved cherry tomatoes
- ½ cup plain Greek yogurt, for serving
- 1 cup crumbled feta cheese, for serving

Directions:
1. Preheat the oven to 425ºF.
2. Heat the olive oil in an ovenproof skillet over medium heat.
3. Add the onion and garlic and sauté for about 5 minutes, stirring occasionally, or until tender and fragrant.
4. Add the paprika and cumin and cook for 2 minutes. Stir in the chickpeas and tomatoes and allow to simmer for 5 to 10 minutes.
5. Transfer the skillet to the preheated oven and roast for 25 to 30 minutes, or until the mixture bubbles and thickens.
6. Remove from the oven and serve topped with yogurt and crumbled feta cheese.

Nutrition Info:
- Per Serving: Calories: 411;Fat: 14.9g;Protein: 20.2g;Carbs: 50.7g.

Baby Kale And Cabbage Salad

Servings:6 | Cooking Time: 0 Minutes

Ingredients:
- 2 bunches baby kale, thinly sliced
- ½ head green savoy cabbage, cored and thinly sliced
- 1 medium red bell pepper, thinly sliced
- 1 garlic clove, thinly sliced
- 1 cup toasted peanuts
- Dressing:
- Juice of 1 lemon
- ¼ cup apple cider vinegar
- 1 teaspoon ground cumin
- ¼ teaspoon smoked paprika

Directions:
1. In a large mixing bowl, toss together the kale and cabbage.
2. Make the dressing: Whisk together the lemon juice, vinegar, cumin and paprika in a small bowl.
3. Pour the dressing over the greens and gently massage with your hands.
4. Add the pepper, garlic and peanuts to the mixing bowl. Toss to combine.
5. Serve immediately.

Nutrition Info:
- Per Serving: Calories: 199;Fat: 12.0g;Protein: 10.0g;Carbs: 17.0g.

Sautéed Spinach And Leeks

Servings:2 | Cooking Time: 8 Minutes

Ingredients:
- 3 tablespoons olive oil
- 2 garlic cloves, crushed
- 2 leeks, chopped
- 2 red onions, chopped
- 9 ounces fresh spinach
- 1 teaspoon kosher salt
- ½ cup crumbled goat cheese

Directions:
1. Coat the bottom of the Instant Pot with the olive oil.
2. Add the garlic, leek, and onions and stir-fry for about 5 minutes, on Sauté mode.
3. Stir in the spinach. Sprinkle with the salt and sauté for an additional 3 minutes, stirring constantly.
4. Transfer to a plate and scatter with the goat cheese before serving.

Nutrition Info:
- Per Serving: Calories: 447;Fat: 31.2g;Protein: 14.6g;Carbs: 28.7g.

Celery And Mustard Greens

Servings:4 | Cooking Time: 15 Minutes

Ingredients:
- ½ cup low-sodium vegetable broth
- 1 celery stalk, roughly chopped
- ½ sweet onion, chopped
- ½ large red bell pepper, thinly sliced
- 2 garlic cloves, minced
- 1 bunch mustard greens, roughly chopped

Directions:
1. Pour the vegetable broth into a large cast iron pan and bring it to a simmer over medium heat.
2. Stir in the celery, onion, bell pepper, and garlic. Cook uncovered for about 3 to 5 minutes, or until the onion is softened.
3. Add the mustard greens to the pan and stir well. Cover, reduce the heat to low, and cook for an additional 10 minutes, or until the liquid is evaporated and the greens are wilted.
4. Remove from the heat and serve warm.

Nutrition Info:
• Per Serving: Calories: 39;Fat: 0g;Protein: 3.1g;Carbs: 6.8g.

Zucchini And Artichokes Bowl With Farro

Servings:4 | Cooking Time: 10 Minutes

Ingredients:
• ⅓ cup extra-virgin olive oil
• ⅓ cup chopped red onions
• ½ cup chopped red bell pepper
• 2 garlic cloves, minced
• 1 cup zucchini, cut into ½-inch-thick slices
• ½ cup coarsely chopped artichokes
• ½ cup canned chickpeas, drained and rinsed
• 3 cups cooked farro
• Salt and freshly ground black pepper, to taste
• ½ cup crumbled feta cheese, for serving (optional)
• ¼ cup sliced olives, for serving (optional)
• 2 tablespoons fresh basil, chiffonade, for serving (optional)
• 3 tablespoons balsamic vinegar, for serving (optional)

Directions:
1. Heat the olive oil in a large skillet over medium heat until it shimmers.
2. Add the onions, bell pepper, and garlic and sauté for 5 minutes, stirring occasionally, until softened.
3. Stir in the zucchini slices, artichokes, and chickpeas and sauté for about 5 minutes until slightly tender.
4. Add the cooked farro and toss to combine until heated through. Sprinkle the salt and pepper to season.
5. Divide the mixture into bowls. Top each bowl evenly with feta cheese, olive slices, and basil and sprinkle with the balsamic vinegar, if desired.

Nutrition Info:
• Per Serving: Calories: 366;Fat: 19.9g;Protein: 9.3g;Carbs: 50.7g.

Sautéed Mushrooms With Garlic & Parsley

Servings:6 | Cooking Time:15 Minutes

Ingredients:
• 3 tbsp butter
• 2 lb cremini mushrooms, sliced
• 2 tbsp garlic, minced
• Salt and black pepper to taste
• 1 tbsp fresh parsley, chopped

Directions:
1. Melt the butter in a skillet over medium heat. Cook the garlic for 1-2 minutes until soft. Stir in the mushrooms and season with salt. Sauté for 7-8 minutes, stirring often. Remove to a serving dish. Top with pepper and parsley to serve.

Nutrition Info:
• Per Serving: Calories: 183;Fat: 9g;Protein: 8.9g;Carbs: 10.1g.

Sautéed Cabbage With Parsley

Servings:4 | Cooking Time: 12 To 14 Minutes

Ingredients:
• 1 small head green cabbage, cored and sliced thin
• 2 tablespoons extra-virgin olive oil, divided
• 1 onion, halved and sliced thin
• ¾ teaspoon salt, divided
• ¼ teaspoon black pepper
• ¼ cup chopped fresh parsley
• 1½ teaspoons lemon juice

Directions:
1. Place the cabbage in a large bowl with cold water. Let sit for 3 minutes. Drain well.
2. Heat 1 tablespoon of the oil in a skillet over medium-high heat until shimmering. Add the onion and ¼ teaspoon of the salt and cook for 5 to 7 minutes, or until softened and lightly browned. Transfer to a bowl.
3. Heat the remaining 1 tablespoon of the oil in now-empty skillet over medium-high heat until shimmering. Add the cabbage and sprinkle with the remaining ½ teaspoon of the salt and black pepper. Cover and cook for about 3 minutes, without stirring, or until cabbage is wilted and lightly browned on bottom.
4. Stir and continue to cook for about 4 minutes, uncovered, or until the cabbage is crisp-tender and lightly browned in places, stirring once halfway through cooking. Off heat, stir in the cooked onion, parsley and lemon juice.
5. Transfer to a plate and serve.

Nutrition Info:
• Per Serving: Calories: 117;Fat: 7.0g;Protein: 2.7g;Carbs: 13.4g.

Moroccan Tagine With Vegetables

Servings:2 | Cooking Time: 40 Minutes

Ingredients:
• 2 tablespoons olive oil
• ½ onion, diced
• 1 garlic clove, minced
• 2 cups cauliflower florets
• 1 medium carrot, cut into 1-inch pieces
• 1 cup diced eggplant
• 1 can whole tomatoes with their juices
• 1 can chickpeas, drained and rinsed
• 2 small red potatoes, cut into 1-inch pieces
• 1 cup water
• 1 teaspoon pure maple syrup
• ½ teaspoon cinnamon
• ½ teaspoon turmeric
• 1 teaspoon cumin
• ½ teaspoon salt
• 1 to 2 teaspoons harissa paste

Directions:
1. In a Dutch oven, heat the olive oil over medium-high heat. Sauté the onion for 5 minutes, stirring occasionally, or until the onion is translucent.
2. Stir in the garlic, cauliflower florets, carrot, eggplant, tomatoes, and potatoes. Using a wooden spoon or spatula to break up the tomatoes into smaller pieces.
3. Add the chickpeas, water, maple syrup, cinnamon, turmeric, cumin, and salt and stir to incorporate. Bring the mixture to a boil.
4. Once it starts to boil, reduce the heat to medium-low. Stir in the harissa paste, cover, allow to simmer for about 40 minutes, or until the vegetables are softened. Taste and adjust seasoning as needed.
5. Let the mixture cool for 5 minutes before serving.

Nutrition Info:
• Per Serving: Calories: 293;Fat: 9.9g;Protein: 11.2g;Carbs: 45.5g.

Tahini & Feta Butternut Squash

Servings:6 | Cooking Time:50 Minutes

Ingredients:
• 3 lb butternut squash, peeled, halved lengthwise, and seeded
• 3 tbsp olive oil
• Salt and black pepper to taste
• 2 tbsp fresh thyme, chopped
• 1 tbsp tahini
• 1 ½ tsp lemon juice
• 1 tsp honey
• 1 oz feta cheese, crumbled
• ¼ cup pistachios, chopped

Directions:
1. Preheat oven to 425°F. Slice the squash halves crosswise into ½-inch-thick pieces. Toss them with 2 tablespoons of olive oil, salt, and pepper and arrange them on a greased baking sheet in an

even layer. Roast for 45-50 minutes or until golden and tender. Transfer squash to a serving platter. Whisk tahini, lemon juice, honey, remaining oil, and salt together in a bowl. Drizzle squash with tahini dressing and sprinkle with feta, pistachios, and thyme. Serve and enjoy!

Nutrition Info:
• Per Serving: Calories: 212;Fat: 12g;Protein: 4.1g;Carbs: 27g.

Garlicky Broccoli Rabe

Servings:4 | Cooking Time: 5 To 6 Minutes

Ingredients:
• 14 ounces broccoli rabe, trimmed and cut into 1-inch pieces
• 2 teaspoons salt, plus more for seasoning
• Black pepper, to taste
• 2 tablespoons extra-virgin olive oil
• 3 garlic cloves, minced
• ¼ teaspoon red pepper flakes

Directions:
1. Bring 3 quarts water to a boil in a large saucepan. Add the broccoli rabe and 2 teaspoons of the salt to the boiling water and cook for 2 to 3 minutes, or until wilted and tender.
2. Drain the broccoli rabe. Transfer to ice water and let sit until chilled. Drain again and pat dry.
3. In a skillet over medium heat, heat the oil and add the garlic and red pepper flakes. Sauté for about 2 minutes, or until the garlic begins to sizzle.
4. Increase the heat to medium-high. Stir in the broccoli rabe and cook for about 1 minute, or until heated through, stirring constantly. Season with salt and pepper.
5. Serve immediately.

Nutrition Info:
• Per Serving: Calories: 87;Fat: 7.3g;Protein: 3.4g;Carbs: 4.0g.

Parmesan Stuffed Zucchini Boats

Servings:4 | Cooking Time: 15 Minutes

Ingredients:
• 1 cup canned low-sodium chickpeas, drained and rinsed
• 1 cup no-sugar-added spaghetti sauce
• 2 zucchinis
• ¼ cup shredded Parmesan cheese

Directions:
1. Preheat the oven to 425ºF.
2. In a medium bowl, stir together the chickpeas and spaghetti sauce.
3. Cut the zucchini in half lengthwise and scrape a spoon gently down the length of each half to remove the seeds.
4. Fill each zucchini half with the chickpea sauce and top with one-quarter of the Parmesan cheese.
5. Place the zucchini halves on a baking sheet and roast in the oven for 15 minutes.
6. Transfer to a plate. Let rest for 5 minutes before serving.

Nutrition Info:
• Per Serving: Calories: 139;Fat: 4.0g;Protein: 8.0g;Carbs: 20.0g.

Steamed Beetroot With Nutty Yogurt

Servings:4 | Cooking Time:30 Min + Chilling Time

Ingredients:
• ¼ cup extra virgin olive oil
• 1 lb beetroots, cut into wedges
• 1 cup Greek yogurt
• 3 spring onions, sliced
• 5 dill pickles, finely chopped
• 2 garlic cloves, minced
• 2 tbsp fresh parsley, chopped
• 1 oz mixed nuts, crushed
• Salt to taste

Directions:
1. In a pot over medium heat, insert a steamer basket and pour in 1 cup of water. Place in the beetroots and steam for 10-15 minutes until tender. Remove to a plate and let cool. In a bowl, combine the pickles, spring onions, garlic, salt, 3 tbsp of olive oil, Greek yogurt, and nuts and mix well. Spread the yogurt mixture on a serving plate and arrange the beetroot wedges on top. Drizzle with the remaining olive oil and top with parsley. Serve and enjoy!

Nutrition Info:
• Per Serving: Calories: 271;Fat: 18g;Protein: 9.6g;Carbs: 22g.

Parmesan Asparagus With Tomatoes

Servings:6 | Cooking Time:30 Minutes

Ingredients:
• 3 tbsp olive oil
• 2 garlic cloves, minced
• 12 oz cherry tomatoes, halved
• 1 tsp dried oregano
• 10 Kalamata olives, chopped
• 2 lb asparagus, trimmed
• 2 tbsp fresh basil, chopped
• ¼ cup Parmesan cheese, grated
• Salt and black pepper to taste

Directions:
1. Warm 2 tbsp of olive oil in a skillet over medium heat sauté the garlic for 1-2 minutes, stirring often, until golden. Add tomatoes, olives, and oregano and cook until tomatoes begin to break down, about 3 minutes; transfer to a bowl.
2. Coat the asparagus with the remaining olive oil and cook in a grill pan over medium heat for about 5 minutes, turning once until crisp-tender. Sprinkle with salt and pepper. Transfer asparagus to a serving platter, top with tomato mixture, and sprinkle with basil and Parmesan cheese. Serve and enjoy!

Nutrition Info:
• Per Serving: Calories: 157;Fat: 7g;Protein: 7.3g;Carbs: 19g.

Garlic-butter Asparagus With Parmesan

Servings:2 | Cooking Time: 8 Minutes

Ingredients:
• 1 cup water
• 1 pound asparagus, trimmed
• 2 cloves garlic, chopped
• 3 tablespoons almond butter
• Salt and ground black pepper, to taste
• 3 tablespoons grated Parmesan cheese

Directions:
1. Pour the water into the Instant Pot and insert a trivet.
2. Put the asparagus on a tin foil add the butter and garlic. Season to taste with salt and pepper.
3. Fold over the foil and seal the asparagus inside so the foil doesn't come open. Arrange the asparagus on the trivet.
4. Secure the lid. Select the Manual mode and set the cooking time for 8 minutes at High Pressure.
5. Once cooking is complete, do a quick pressure release. Carefully open the lid.
6. Unwrap the foil packet and serve sprinkled with the Parmesan cheese.

Nutrition Info:
• Per Serving: Calories: 243;Fat: 15.7g;Protein: 12.3g;Carbs: 15.3g.

Balsamic Grilled Vegetables

Servings:4 | Cooking Time:20 Minutes

Ingredients:
- ¼ cup olive oil
- 4 carrots, cut in half
- 2 onions, quartered
- 1 zucchini, cut into rounds
- 1 eggplant, cut into rounds
- 1 red bell pepper, chopped
- Salt and black pepper to taste
- Balsamic vinegar to taste

Directions:
1. Heat your grill to medium-high. Brush the vegetables lightly with olive oil, and season with salt and pepper. Grill the vegetables for 3–4 minutes per side. Transfer to a serving dish and drizzle with balsamic vinegar. Serve and enjoy!

Nutrition Info:
- Per Serving: Calories: 184;Fat: 14g;Protein: 2.1g;Carbs: 14g.

Greek-style Eggplants

Servings:4 | Cooking Time:25 Minutes

Ingredients:
- 1 ½ lb eggplants, sliced into rounds
- ¼ cup olive oil
- Salt and black pepper to taste
- 4 tsp balsamic vinegar
- 1 tbsp capers, minced
- 1 garlic clove, minced
- ½ tsp lemon zest
- ½ tsp fresh oregano, minced
- 3 tbsp fresh mint, minced

Directions:
1. Preheat oven to 420ºF. Arrange the eggplant rounds on a greased baking dish and drizzle with some olive oil. Sprinkle with salt and pepper. Bake for 10-12 per side until mahogany lightly charred. Whisk remaining olive oil, balsamic vinegar, capers, garlic, lemon zest, oregano, salt, and pepper together in a bowl. Drizzle the mixture all over the eggplants and sprinkle with mint. Serve and enjoy!

Nutrition Info:
- Per Serving: Calories: 111;Fat: 9.2g;Protein: 1.2g;Carbs: 7g.

Sweet Potato Chickpea Buddha Bowl

Servings:2 | Cooking Time: 10 To 15 Minutes

Ingredients:
- Sauce:
- 1 tablespoon tahini
- 2 tablespoons plain Greek yogurt
- 2 tablespoons hemp seeds
- 1 garlic clove, minced
- Pinch salt
- Freshly ground black pepper, to taste
- Bowl:
- 1 small sweet potato, peeled and finely diced
- 1 teaspoon extra-virgin olive oil
- 1 cup from 1 can low-sodium chickpeas, drained and rinsed
- 2 cups baby kale

Directions:
1. Make the Sauce
2. Whisk together the tahini and yogurt in a small bowl.
3. Stir in the hemp seeds and minced garlic. Season with salt pepper. Add 2 to 3 tablespoons water to create a creamy yet pourable consistency and set aside.
4. Make the Bowl
5. Preheat the oven to 425ºF. Line a baking sheet with parchment paper.
6. Place the sweet potato on the prepared baking sheet and drizzle with the olive oil. Toss well
7. Roast in the preheated oven for 10 to 15 minutes, stirring once during cooking, or until fork-tender and browned.
8. In each of 2 bowls, place ½ cup of chickpeas, 1 cup of baby kale, and half of the cooked sweet potato. Serve drizzled with half of the prepared sauce.

Nutrition Info:
- Per Serving: Calories: 323;Fat: 14.1g;Protein: 17.0g;Carbs: 36.0g.

Feta & Zucchini Rosti Cakes

Servings:4 | Cooking Time:25 Minutes

Ingredients:
- 5 tbsp olive oil
- 1 lb zucchini, shredded
- 4 spring onions, chopped
- Salt and black pepper to taste
- 4 oz feta cheese, crumbled
- 1 egg, lightly beaten
- 2 tbsp minced fresh dill
- 1 garlic clove, minced
- ¼ cup flour
- Lemon wedges for serving

Directions:
1. Preheat oven to 380ºF. In a large bowl, mix the zucchini, spring onions, feta cheese, egg, dill, garlic, salt, and pepper. Sprinkle flour over the mixture and stir to incorporate.
2. Warm the oil in a skillet over medium heat. Cook the rosti mixture in small flat fritters for about 4 minutes per side until crisp and golden on both sides, pressing with a fish slice as they cook. Serve with lemon wedges.

Nutrition Info:
- Per Serving: Calories: 239;Fat: 19.8g;Protein: 7.8g;Carbs: 9g.

Cauliflower Rice Risotto With Mushrooms

Servings:4 | Cooking Time: 10 Minutes

Ingredients:
- 1 teaspoon extra-virgin olive oil
- ½ cup chopped portobello mushrooms
- 4 cups cauliflower rice
- ½ cup half-and-half
- ¼ cup low-sodium vegetable broth
- 1 cup shredded Parmesan cheese

Directions:
1. In a medium skillet, heat the olive oil over medium-low heat until shimmering.
2. Add the mushrooms and stir-fry for 3 minutes.
3. Stir in the cauliflower rice, half-and-half, and vegetable broth. Cover and bring to a boil over high heat for 5 minutes, stirring occasionally.
4. Add the Parmesan cheese and stir to combine. Continue cooking for an additional 3 minutes until the cheese is melted.
5. Divide the mixture into four bowls and serve warm.

Nutrition Info:
- Per Serving: Calories: 167;Fat: 10.7g;Protein: 12.1g;Carbs: 8.1g.

Balsamic Cherry Tomatoes

Servings:4 | Cooking Time:10 Minutes

Ingredients:
- 2 tbsp olive oil
- 2 lb cherry tomatoes, halved
- 2 tbsp balsamic glaze
- Salt and black pepper to taste
- 1 garlic clove, minced
- 2 tbsp fresh basil, torn

Directions:
1. Warm the olive oil in a skillet over medium heat. Add the cherry tomatoes and cook for 1-2 minutes, stirring occasionally. Stir in garlic, salt, and pepper and cook until fragrant, about 30 seconds. Drizzle with balsamic glaze and decorate with basil. Serve and enjoy!

Nutrition Info:
- Per Serving: Calories: 45;Fat: 2.5g;Protein: 1.1g;Carbs: 5.6g.

Chapter 4 Beans , Grains, And Pastas Recipes

Chapter 4 Beans , Grains, And Pastas Recipes

Simple Green Rice

Servings:4 | Cooking Time:35 Minutes

Ingredients:
- 2 tbsp butter
- 4 spring onions, sliced
- 1 leek, sliced
- 1 medium zucchini, chopped
- 5 oz broccoli florets
- 2 oz curly kale
- ½ cup frozen green peas
- 2 cloves garlic, minced
- 1 thyme sprig, chopped
- 1 rosemary sprig, chopped
- 1 cup white rice
- 2 cups vegetable broth
- 1 large tomato, chopped
- 2 oz Kalamata olives, sliced

Directions:
1. Melt the butter in a saucepan over medium heat. Cook the spring onions, leek, and zucchini for about 4-5 minutes or until tender. Add in the garlic, thyme, and rosemary and continue to sauté for about 1 minute or until aromatic. Add in the rice, broth, and tomato. Bring to a boil, turn the heat to a gentle simmer, and cook for about 10-12 minutes. Stir in broccoli, kale, and green peas, and continue cooking for 5 minutes. Fluff the rice with a fork and garnish with olives.

Nutrition Info:
- Per Serving: Calories: 403;Fat: 11g;Protein: 9g;Carbs: 64g.

Bulgur Pilaf With Garbanzo

Servings:4 | Cooking Time: 20 Minutes

Ingredients:
- 3 tablespoons extra-virgin olive oil
- 1 large onion, chopped
- 1 can garbanzo beans, rinsed and drained
- 2 cups bulgur wheat, rinsed and drained
- 1½ teaspoons salt
- ½ teaspoon cinnamon
- 4 cups water

Directions:
1. In a large pot over medium heat, heat the olive oil. Add the onion and cook for 5 minutes.
2. Add the garbanzo beans and cook for an additional 5 minutes.
3. Stir in the remaining ingredients.
4. Reduce the heat to low. Cover and cook for 10 minutes.
5. When done, fluff the pilaf with a fork. Cover and let sit for another 5 minutes before serving.

Nutrition Info:
- Per Serving: Calories: 462;Fat: 13.0g;Protein: 15.0g;Carbs: 76.0g.

Rigatoni With Peppers & Mozzarella

Servings:4 | Cooking Time:30 Min + Marinating Time

Ingredients:
- 1 lb fresh mozzarella cheese, cubed
- 3 tbsp olive oil
- ¼ cup chopped fresh chives
- ¼ cup basil, chopped
- ½ tsp red pepper flakes
- 1 tsp apple cider vinegar
- Salt and black pepper to taste
- 3 garlic cloves, minced
- 2 cups sliced onions
- 3 cups bell peppers, sliced
- 2 cups tomato sauce
- 8 oz rigatoni
- 1 tbsp butter
- ¼ cup grated Parmesan cheese

Directions:

1. Bring to a boil salted water in a pot over high heat. Add the rigatoni and cook according to package directions. Drain and set aside, reserving 1 cup of the cooking water. Combine the mozzarella, 1 tablespoon of olive oil, chives, basil, pepper flakes, apple cider vinegar, salt, and pepper. Let the cheese marinate for 30 minutes at room temperature.
2. Warm the remaining olive oil in a large skillet over medium heat. Stir-fry the garlic for 10 seconds and add the onions and peppers. Cook for 3-4 minutes, stirring occasionally until the onions are translucent. Pour in the tomato sauce, and reduce the heat to a simmer. Add the rigatoni and reserved cooking water and toss to coat. Heat off and adjust the seasoning with salt and pepper. Toss with marinated mozzarella cheese and butter. Sprinkle with Parmesan cheese and serve.

Nutrition Info:
- Per Serving: Calories: 434;Fat: 18g;Protein: 44g;Carbs: 27g.

Hot Zucchini Millet

Servings:4 | Cooking Time:30 Minutes

Ingredients:
- 3 tbsp olive oil
- 2 tomatoes, chopped
- 2 zucchinis, chopped
- 1 cup millet
- 2 spring onions, chopped
- ½ cup cilantro, chopped
- 1 tsp chili paste
- ½ cup lemon juice
- Salt and black pepper to taste

Directions:
1. Warm the olive oil in a skillet over medium heat and sauté millet for 1-2 minutes. Pour in 2 cups of water, salt, and pepper and bring to a simmer. Cook for 15 minutes. Mix in spring onions, tomatoes, zucchini, chili paste, and lemon juice. Serve topped with cilantro.

Nutrition Info:
- Per Serving: Calories: 230;Fat: 11g;Protein: 3g;Carbs: 15g.

Friday Night Penne In Tomato Sauce

Servings:6 | Cooking Time:60 Minutes

Ingredients:
- ¼ cup olive oil
- 1 shallot, sliced thin
- 2 lb cherry tomatoes, halved
- 3 garlic cloves, sliced thin
- 1 tbsp balsamic vinegar
- 1 tbsp sugar
- Salt and black pepper to taste
- ¼ tsp red pepper flakes
- 1 lb penne
- ¼ cup oregano, chopped
- Grated Pecorino cheese

Directions:
1. Preheat oven to 350°F. In a bowl, drizzle shallot with some olive oil and mix well. In a separate bowl, gently add the tomatoes, remaining oil, garlic, vinegar, sugar, red pepper flakes, salt, and pepper. Spread tomato mixture in even layer in a rimmed baking sheet, spread shallot over the tomatoes, and roast until edges of the shallot begin to brown and tomato skins are slightly shriveled, 33-38 minutes; do not stir. Let cool for 5 to 10 minutes.
2. Meanwhile, fill a large pot with water and bring to a boil. Add the pasta and a pinch of salt and cook until al dente. Reserve ½ cup of cooking liquid, drain pasta and return it to the pot. Using a spatula, scrape tomato mixture onto the pasta. Add oregano and

toss to combine. Season to taste and adjust consistency with the cooking water. Serve topped with Pecorino cheese.

Nutrition Info:
- Per Serving: Calories: 423;Fat: 16g;Protein: 15g;Carbs: 45g.

Freekeh Pilaf With Dates And Pistachios

Servings:4 | Cooking Time: 10 Minutes

Ingredients:
- 2 tablespoons extra-virgin olive oil, plus extra for drizzling
- 1 shallot, minced
- 1½ teaspoons grated fresh ginger
- ¼ teaspoon ground coriander
- ¼ teaspoon ground cumin
- Salt and pepper, to taste
- 1¾ cups water
- 1½ cups cracked freekeh, rinsed
- 3 ounces pitted dates, chopped
- ¼ cup shelled pistachios, toasted and coarsely chopped
- 1½ tablespoons lemon juice
- ¼ cup chopped fresh mint

Directions:
1. Set the Instant Pot to Sauté mode and heat the olive oil until shimmering.
2. Add the shallot, ginger, coriander, cumin, salt, and pepper to the pot and cook for about 2 minutes, or until the shallot is softened. Stir in the water and freekeh.
3. Secure the lid. Select the Manual mode and set the cooking time for 4 minutes at High Pressure. Once cooking is complete, do a quick pressure release. Carefully open the lid.
4. Add the dates, pistachios and lemon juice and gently fluff the freekeh with a fork to combine. Season to taste with salt and pepper.
5. Transfer to a serving dish and sprinkle with the mint. Serve drizzled with extra olive oil.

Nutrition Info:
- Per Serving: Calories: 280;Fat: 8.0g;Protein: 8.0g;Carbs: 46.0g.

Macaroni & Cauliflower Gratin

Servings:4 | Cooking Time:45 Minutes

Ingredients:
- 16 oz elbow pasta
- 20 oz cauliflower florets
- 1 cup heavy cream
- 1 cup grated mozzarella
- 1 tsp dried thyme
- 1 tsp smoked paprika
- Salt to taste
- ½ tsp red chili flakes

Directions:
1. In a pot of boiling water, cook the macaroni for 8-10 minutes until al dente. Drain and set aside.
2. Preheat the oven to 350° F. Grease a baking dish with cooking spray. Set aside. Bring 4 cups of water to a boil in a large pot and blanch the cauliflower for 4 minutes. Drain through a colander. In a large bowl, mix the cauliflower, macaroni, heavy cream, half of the mozzarella cheese, thyme, paprika, salt, and red chili flakes until well-combined. Transfer the mixture to the baking dish and top with the remaining cheese. Bake for 30 minutes. Allow cooling for 2 minutes and serve afterwards.

Nutrition Info:
- Per Serving: Calories: 301;Fat: 21g;Protein: 11g;Carbs: 13g.

Vegetarian Brown Rice Bowl

Servings:4 | Cooking Time:25 Minutes

Ingredients:
- ½ lb broccoli rabe, halved lengthways
- 2 tbsp olive oil
- 1 onion, sliced
- 1 red bell pepper, cut into strips
- ½ cup green peas
- 1 carrot, chopped
- 1 celery stalk, chopped
- 1 garlic clove, minced
- ½ cup brown rice
- 2 cups vegetable broth
- Salt and black pepper to taste
- ½ tsp dried thyme
- ¾ tsp paprika
- 2 green onions, chopped

Directions:
1. Warm the olive oil in a skillet over medium heat and sauté onion, garlic, carrot, celery, and bell pepper for 10 minutes. Stir in rice, vegetable broth, salt, pepper, thyme, paprika, and green onions and bring to a simmer. Cook for 15 minutes. Add in broccoli rabe and green peas and cook for 5 minutes.

Nutrition Info:
- Per Serving: Calories: 320;Fat: 5g;Protein: 5g;Carbs: 23g.

Smoky Paprika Chickpeas

Servings:4 | Cooking Time:30 Minutes

Ingredients:
- ¼ cup extra-virgin olive oil
- 4 garlic cloves, sliced thin
- ½ tsp red pepper flakes
- 1 onion, chopped fine
- Salt and black pepper to taste
- 1 tsp smoked paprika
- 2 cans chickpeas
- 1 cup chicken broth
- 2 tbsp minced fresh parsley
- 2 tsp lemon juice

Directions:
1. Warm 3 tbsp of olive oil in a skillet over medium heat. Cook garlic and pepper flakes until the garlic turns golden but not brown, about 3 minutes. Stir in onion and salt and cook until softened and lightly browned, 5 minutes. Stir in smoked paprika, chickpeas, and broth and bring to a boil. Simmer covered for 7 minutes until chickpeas are heated through.
2. Uncover, increase the heat to high, and continue to cook until nearly all liquid has evaporated, about 3 minutes. Remove and stir in parsley and lemon juice. Season with salt and pepper and drizzle with remaining olive oil. Serve warm.

Nutrition Info:
- Per Serving: Calories: 223;Fat: 11.4g;Protein: 7g;Carbs: 25g.

Papaya, Jicama, And Peas Rice Bowl

Servings:4 | Cooking Time: 45 Minutes

Ingredients:
- Sauce:
- Juice of ¼ lemon
- 2 teaspoons chopped fresh basil
- 1 tablespoon raw honey
- 1 tablespoon extra-virgin olive oil
- Sea salt, to taste
- Rice:
- 1½ cups wild rice
- 2 papayas, peeled, seeded, and diced
- 1 jicama, peeled and shredded
- 1 cup snow peas, julienned
- 2 cups shredded cabbage
- 1 scallion, white and green parts, chopped

Directions:
1. Combine the ingredients for the sauce in a bowl. Stir to mix well. Set aside until ready to use.
2. Pour the wild rice in a saucepan, then pour in enough water to cover. Bring to a boil.

3. Reduce the heat to low, then simmer for 45 minutes or until the wild rice is soft and plump. Drain and transfer to a large serving bowl.

4. Top the rice with papayas, jicama, peas, cabbage, and scallion. Pour the sauce over and stir to mix well before serving.

Nutrition Info:
- Per Serving: Calories: 446;Fat: 7.9g;Protein: 13.1g;Carbs: 85.8g.

Bell Pepper & Bean Salad

Servings:6 | Cooking Time:30 Minutes

Ingredients:
- ¼ cup extra-virgin olive oil
- 3 garlic cloves, minced
- 2 cans cannellini beans
- Salt and black pepper to taste
- 2 tsp sherry vinegar
- 1 red onion, sliced
- 1 red bell pepper, chopped
- ¼ cup chopped fresh parsley
- 2 tsp chopped fresh chives
- ¼ tsp crushed red pepper

Directions:
1. Warm 1 tbsp of olive oil in a saucepan over medium heat. Sauté the garlic until it turns golden but not brown, about 3 minutes. Add beans, 2 cups of water, and salt, and pepper, and bring to a simmer. Heat off. Let sit for 20 minutes.

2. Mix well the vinegar and red onion in a salad bowl. Drain the beans and remove the garlic. Add beans, remaining olive oil, bell pepper, parsley, crushed red pepper, chives, salt, and pepper to the onion mixture and gently toss to combine.

Nutrition Info:
- Per Serving: Calories: 131;Fat: 7.7g;Protein: 6g;Carbs: 13.5g.

Stewed Borlotti Beans

Servings:6 | Cooking Time:25 Minutes

Ingredients:
- 3 tbsp olive oil
- 1 onion, chopped
- 1 can tomato paste
- ¼ cup red wine vinegar
- 8 fresh sage leaves, chopped
- 2 garlic cloves, minced
- ½ cup water
- 2 cans borlotti beans

Directions:
1. Warm the olive oil in a saucepan over medium heat. Sauté the onion and garlic for 5 minutes, stirring frequently. Add the tomato paste, vinegar, and 1 cup of water, and mix well. Turn the heat to low. Drain and rinse one can of the beans in a colander and add to the saucepan. Pour the entire second can of beans (including the liquid) into the saucepan. Simmer for 10 minutes, stirring occasionally. Serve warm sprinkled with sage.

Nutrition Info:
- Per Serving: Calories: 434;Fat: 2g;Protein: 26g;Carbs: 80g.

Chickpea Salad With Tomatoes And Basil

Servings:2 | Cooking Time: 45 Minutes

Ingredients:
- 1 cup dried chickpeas, rinsed
- 1 quart water, or enough to cover the chickpeas by 3 to 4 inches
- 1½ cups halved grape tomatoes
- 1 cup chopped fresh basil
leaves
- 2 to 3 tablespoons balsamic vinegar
- ½ teaspoon garlic powder
- ½ teaspoon salt, plus more as needed

Directions:
1. In your Instant Pot, combine the chickpeas and water.

2. Secure the lid. Select the Manual mode and set the cooking time for 45 minutes at High Pressure.

3. Once cooking is complete, do a natural pressure release for 20 minutes, then release any remaining pressure. Carefully open the lid and drain the chickpeas. Refrigerate to cool (unless you want to serve this warm, which is good, too).

4. While the chickpeas cool, in a large bowl, stir together the basil, tomatoes, vinegar, garlic powder, and salt. Add the beans, stir to combine, and serve.

Nutrition Info:
- Per Serving: Calories: 395;Fat: 6.0g;Protein: 19.8g;Carbs: 67.1g.

Cherry, Apricot, And Pecan Brown Rice Bowl

Servings:2 | Cooking Time: 1 Hour 1 Minutes

Ingredients:
- 2 tablespoons olive oil
- 2 green onions, sliced
- ½ cup brown rice
- 1 cup low -sodium chicken stock
- 2 tablespoons dried cherries
- 4 dried apricots, chopped
- 2 tablespoons pecans, toasted and chopped
- Sea salt and freshly ground pepper, to taste

Directions:
1. Heat the olive oil in a medium saucepan over medium-high heat until shimmering.

2. Add the green onions and sauté for 1 minutes or until fragrant.

3. Add the rice. Stir to mix well, then pour in the chicken stock.

4. Bring to a boil. Reduce the heat to low. Cover and simmer for 50 minutes or until the brown rice is soft.

5. Add the cherries, apricots, and pecans, and simmer for 10 more minutes or until the fruits are tender.

6. Pour them in a large serving bowl. Fluff with a fork. Sprinkle with sea salt and freshly ground pepper. Serve immediately.

Nutrition Info:
- Per Serving: Calories: 451;Fat: 25.9g;Protein: 8.2g;Carbs: 50.4g.

Creamy Saffron Chicken With Ziti

Servings:4 | Cooking Time:35 Minutes

Ingredients:
- 3 tbsp butter
- 16 oz ziti
- 4 chicken breasts, cut into strips
- ½ tsp ground saffron threads
- 1 yellow onion, chopped
- 2 garlic cloves, minced
- 1 tbsp almond flour
- 1 pinch cardamom powder
- 1 pinch cinnamon powder
- 1 cup heavy cream
- 1 cup chicken stock
- ¼ cup chopped scallions
- 3 tbsp chopped parsley
- Salt and black pepper to taste

Directions:
1. In a pot of boiling water, cook the ziti pasta for 8-10 minutes until al dente. Drain and set aside.

2. Melt the butter in a large skillet, season the chicken with salt, black pepper, and cook in the oil until golden brown on the outside, 5 minutes. Stir in the saffron, onion, garlic and cook until the onion softens and the garlic and saffron are fragrant, 3 minutes. Stir in the almond flour, cardamom powder, and cinnamon powder, and cook for 1 minute to exude some fragrance. Add the heavy cream, chicken stock and cook for 2 to 3 minutes. Adjust the taste with salt, pepper and mix in the ziti and scallions. Allow

warming for 1-2 minutes and turn the heat off. Garnish with parsley.

Nutrition Info:
• Per Serving: Calories: 775;Fat: 48g;Protein: 73g;Carbs: 3g.

Minestrone Chickpeas And Macaroni Casserole

Servings:5 | Cooking Time: 7 Hours 20 Minutes

Ingredients:
• 1 can chickpeas, drained and rinsed
• 1 can diced tomatoes, with the juice
• 1 can no-salt-added tomato paste
• 3 medium carrots, sliced
• 3 cloves garlic, minced
• 1 medium yellow onion, chopped
• 1 cup low-sodium vegetable soup
• ½ teaspoon dried rosemary
• 1 teaspoon dried oregano
• 2 teaspoons maple syrup
• ½ teaspoon sea salt
• ¼ teaspoon ground black pepper
• ½ pound fresh green beans, trimmed and cut into bite-size pieces
• 1 cup macaroni pasta
• 2 ounces Parmesan cheese, grated

Directions:
1. Except for the green beans, pasta, and Parmesan cheese, combine all the ingredients in the slow cooker and stir to mix well.
2. Put the slow cooker lid on and cook on low for 7 hours.
3. Fold in the pasta and green beans. Put the lid on and cook on high for 20 minutes or until the vegetable are soft and the pasta is al dente.
4. Pour them in a large serving bowl and spread with Parmesan cheese before serving.

Nutrition Info:
• Per Serving: Calories: 349;Fat: 6.7g;Protein: 16.5g;Carbs: 59.9g.

Herby Fusilli In Chickpea Sauce

Servings:4 | Cooking Time:35 Minutes

Ingredients:
• 1 can chickpeas, drained, liquid reserved
• ¼ cup olive oil
• ½ large shallot, chopped
• 5 garlic cloves, thinly sliced
• 1 cup whole-grain fusilli
• Salt and black pepper to taste
• ¼ cup Parmesan, shaved
• 2 tsp dried parsley
• 1 tsp dried oregano
• A pinch of red pepper flakes

Directions:
1. Heat the oil in a skillet over medium heat and sauté the shallot and garlic for 3-5 minutes until the garlic is golden. Add ¾ of the chickpeas and 2 tbsp of the water from the can; bring to a simmer. Remove from the heat, transfer to a blender, and pulse until smooth. Add the remaining chickpeas and some more of the reserved liquid if it's too thick.
2. Bring a large pot of salted water to a boil and cook pasta until al dente, 7-8 minutes. Reserve ½ cup of the pasta liquid, drain the pasta and return it to the pot. Add the chickpea sauce to the hot pasta and keep adding ¼ cup of the pasta liquid until your desired consistency is reached. Place the pasta pot over medium heat and mix occasionally until the sauce thickens. Season with salt and pepper. Sprinkle with freshly grated Parmesan cheese, parsley, oregano, and red pepper flakes. Serve and enjoy!

Nutrition Info:
• Per Serving: Calories: 322;Fat: 18g;Protein: 12g;Carbs: 36g.

Catalan Sherry Fennel Millet

Servings:6 | Cooking Time:40 Minutes

Ingredients:
• 1 fennel bulb, stalks discarded, cored, and finely chopped
• 3 tbsp olive oil
• 1 ½ cups millet
• Salt and black pepper to taste
• 1 onion, chopped fine
• 3 garlic cloves, minced
• ¼ tsp dried thyme
• 1 oz Parmesan cheese, grated
• ¼ cup minced fresh parsley
• 2 tsp sherry vinegar

Directions:
1. Bring 4 quarts of salted water to boil in a pot. Add millet and cook until tender, 15-20 minutes. Drain millet, return to now-empty pot, and cover to keep warm.
2. Heat 2 tablespoons oil in a skillet over medium heat until shimmering. Add onion, fennel, and salt and cook, stirring occasionally, until softened, 8-10 minutes. Add garlic and thyme and cook until fragrant, 30 seconds. Add the remaining oil and millet and cook, stirring frequently until heated through, 2 minutes. Off heat, stir in Parmesan, parsley, and vinegar. Season with salt and pepper to taste.

Nutrition Info:
• Per Serving: Calories: 312;Fat: 16g;Protein: 11g;Carbs: 29g.

Quick Pesto Pasta

Servings:4 | Cooking Time:20 Minutes

Ingredients:
• 1 lb linguine
• 2 tomatoes, chopped
• 10 oz basil pesto
• ½ cup pine nuts, toasted
• ½ cup Parmesan cheese, grated
• 1 lemon, zested

Directions:
1. Bring to a boil salted water in a pot over high heat. Add the linguine and cook according to package directions, 9-11 minutes. Drain and transfer to a serving bowl. Add the tomatoes, pesto, and lemon zest toss gently to coat the pasta. Sprinkle with Parmesan cheese and pine nuts and serve.

Nutrition Info:
• Per Serving: Calories: 617;Fat: 17g;Protein: 23g;Carbs: 94g.

Jalapeño Veggie Rice Stew

Servings:4 | Cooking Time:45 Minutes

Ingredients:
• 2 tbsp olive oil
• 1 cup rice
• 1 lb green beans, chopped
• 2 zucchinis, sliced
• 1 bell pepper, sliced
• 1 jalapeño pepper, chopped
• 1 carrot, chopped
• 2 spring onions, chopped
• 2 cloves garlic, minced
• 2 tomatoes, pureed
• 1 cup vegetable broth
• ½ tsp dried sage
• 1 tsp paprika
• Salt and black pepper to taste

Directions:
1. Cook the rice in a pot with 2 cups of water for about 20 minutes. Using a fork, fluff the rice and set aside. Heat the olive oil in a pot over medium heat. Add in the zucchinis, green beans, bell pepper, jalapeño pepper, carrot, spring onions, tomatoes, and garlic and stir-fry for 10 minutes or until the veggies are softened. Pour in vegetable broth, sage, paprika, salt, and black pepper. Cook covered for 7 minutes. Distribute the rice across bowls and top with the veggie mixture. Serve hot.

Nutrition Info:

- Per Serving: Calories: 153;Fat: 7.9g;Protein: 5.7g;Carbs: 19g.

Bulgur Pilaf With Kale And Tomatoes

Servings:2 | Cooking Time: 10 Minutes

Ingredients:
- 2 tablespoons olive oil
- 2 cloves garlic, minced
- 1 bunch kale, trimmed and cut into bite-sized pieces
- Juice of 1 lemon
- 2 cups cooked bulgur wheat
- 1 pint cherry tomatoes, halved
- Sea salt and freshly ground pepper, to taste

Directions:
1. Heat the olive oil in a large skillet over medium heat. Add the garlic and sauté for 1 minute.
2. Add the kale leaves and stir to coat. Cook for 5 minutes until leaves are cooked through and thoroughly wilted.
3. Add the lemon juice, bulgur and tomatoes. Season with sea salt and freshly ground pepper to taste, then serve.

Nutrition Info:
- Per Serving: Calories: 300;Fat: 14.0g;Protein: 6.2g;Carbs: 37.8g.

Old-fashioned Pasta Primavera

Servings:4 | Cooking Time:25 Minutes

Ingredients:
- ½ cup grated Pecorino Romano cheese
- 2 cups cauliflower florets, cut into matchsticks
- ¼ cup olive oil
- 16 oz tortiglioni
- ½ cup chopped green onions
- 1 red bell pepper, sliced
- 4 garlic cloves, minced
- 1 cup grape tomatoes, halved
- 2 tsp dried Italian seasoning
- ½ lemon, juiced

Directions:
1. In a pot of boiling water, cook the tortiglioni pasta for 8-10 minutes until al dente. Drain and set aside.
2. Heat olive oil in a skillet and sauté onion, cauliflower, and bell pepper for 7 minutes. Mix in garlic and cook until fragrant, 30 seconds. Stir in the tomatoes and Italian seasoning; cook until the tomatoes soften, 5 minutes. Mix in the lemon juice and tortiglioni. Garnish with cheese.

Nutrition Info:
- Per Serving: Calories: 283;Fat: 18g;Protein: 15g;Carbs: 5g.

Pasta In Dilly Walnut Sauce

Servings:4 | Cooking Time:10 Minutes

Ingredients:
- 3 tbsp extra-virgin olive oil
- 8 oz whole-wheat pasta
- ¼ cup walnuts, chopped
- 3 garlic cloves, finely minced
- ½ cup fresh dill, chopped
- ¼ cup grated Parmesan cheese

Directions:
1. Cook the whole-wheat pasta according to pack instructions, drain and let it cool. Place the olive oil, dill, garlic, Parmesan cheese, and walnuts in a food processor and blend for 15 seconds or until paste forms. Pour over the cooled pasta and toss to combine. Serve immediately.

Nutrition Info:
- Per Serving: Calories: 559;Fat: 17g;Protein: 21g;Carbs: 91g.

Mint & Lemon Cranberry Beans

Servings:6 | Cooking Time:1 Hour 45 Minutes

Ingredients:
- ¼ cup olive oil
- Salt and black pepper to taste
- 1 lb cranberry beans, soaked
- 1 onion, chopped
- 2 carrots, chopped
- 4 garlic cloves, sliced thin
- 1 tbsp tomato paste
- 2 tomatoes, chopped
- ½ tsp paprika
- ½ cup dry white wine
- 4 cups vegetable broth
- 2 tbsp lemon juice
- 2 tbsp minced fresh mint

Directions:
1. Preheat oven to 350° F. Warm the olive oil in a pot over medium heat. Sauté the onion and carrots until softened, about 5 minutes. Stir in garlic, tomato paste, tomatoes, paprika, salt, and pepper and cook until fragrant, about 1 minute. Stir in wine, scraping up any browned bits. Stir in broth, ½ cup of water, and beans and bring to boil. Place in the oven and cook covered for about 1 ½ hours, stirring every 30 minutes until the beans are tender. Sprinkle with lemon juice and mint. Serve.

Nutrition Info:
- Per Serving: Calories: 248;Fat: 8.6g;Protein: 3g;Carbs: 9.5g.

Creamy Shrimp With Tie Pasta

Servings:4 | Cooking Time:25 Minutes

Ingredients:
- 1 lb shrimp, peeled and deveined
- 1 tbsp olive oil
- 2 tbsp unsalted butter
- Salt and black pepper to taste
- 6 garlic cloves, minced
- ½ cup dry white wine
- 1 ½ cups heavy cream
- ½ cup grated Asiago cheese
- 2 tbsp chopped fresh parsley
- 16 oz bow tie pasta
- Salt to taste

Directions:
1. In a pot of boiling salted water, cook the tie pasta for 8-10 minutes until al dente. Drain and set aside.
2. Heat the olive oil in a large skillet, season the shrimp with salt and black pepper, and cook in the oil on both sides until pink and opaque, 2 minutes. Set aside. Melt the butter in the skillet and sauté the garlic until fragrant. Stir in the white wine and cook until reduced by half, scraping the bottom of the pan to deglaze. Reduce the heat to low and stir in the heavy cream. Allow simmering for 1 minute and stir in the Asiago cheese to melt. Return the shrimp to the sauce and sprinkle the parsley on top. Adjust the taste with salt and black pepper, if needed. Top the pasta with sauce and serve.

Nutrition Info:
- Per Serving: Calories: 493;Fat: 32g;Protein: 34g;Carbs: 16g.

Herb Bean Stew

Servings:4 | Cooking Time:70 Minutes

Ingredients:
- 2 tbsp olive oil
- 3 tomatoes, cubed
- 1 yellow onion, chopped
- 1 celery stalk, chopped
- 2 tbsp parsley, chopped
- 2 garlic cloves, minced
- 1 cup lima beans, soaked
- 1 tsp paprika
- 1 tsp dried oregano
- ½ tsp dried thyme
- Salt and black pepper to taste

Directions:
1. Cover the lima beans with water in a pot and place over medium heat. Bring to a boil and cook for 30 minutes. Drain and set

aside. Warm olive oil in the pot over medium heat and cook onion and garlic for 3 minutes. Stir in tomatoes, celery, oregano, thyme, and paprika and cook for 5 minutes. Pour in 3 cups of water and return the lima beans; season with salt and pepper. Simmer for 30 minutes. Top with parsley.

Nutrition Info:
• Per Serving: Calories: 310;Fat: 16g;Protein: 16g;Carbs: 30g.

Valencian-style Mussel Rice

Servings:4 | Cooking Time:40 Minutes

Ingredients:
• 1 lb mussels, cleaned and debearded
• 2 tbsp olive oil
• 2 garlic cloves, minced
• 1 yellow onion, chopped
• 2 tomatoes, chopped
• 2 cups fish stock
• 1 cup white rice
• 1 bunch parsley, chopped
• Salt and white pepper to taste

Directions:
1. Warm the olive oil in a pot over medium heat and cook onion and garlic for 5 minutes. Stir in rice for 1 minute. Pour in tomatoes and fish stock and bring to a boil. Add in the mussels and simmer for 20 minutes. Discard any unopened mussels. Adjust the taste with salt and white pepper. Serve topped with parsley.

Nutrition Info:
• Per Serving: Calories: 310;Fat: 15g;Protein: 12g;Carbs: 17g.

Swoodles With Almond Butter Sauce

Servings:4 | Cooking Time: 20 Minutes

Ingredients:
• Sauce:
• 1 garlic clove
• 1-inch piece fresh ginger, peeled and sliced
• ¼ cup chopped yellow onion
• ¾ cup almond butter
• 1 tablespoon tamari
• 1 tablespoon raw honey
• 1 teaspoon paprika
• 1 tablespoon fresh lemon juice
• ⅛ teaspoon ground red pepper
• Sea salt and ground black pepper, to taste
• ¼ cup water
• Swoodles:
• 2 large sweet potatoes, spiralized
• 2 tablespoons coconut oil, melted
• Sea salt and ground black pepper, to taste
• For Serving:
• ½ cup fresh parsley, chopped
• ½ cup thinly sliced scallions

Directions:
1. Make the Sauce
2. Put the garlic, ginger, and onion in a food processor, then pulse to combine well.
3. Add the almond butter, tamari, honey, paprika, lemon juice, ground red pepper, salt, and black pepper to the food processor. Pulse to combine well. Pour in the water during the pulsing until the mixture is thick and smooth.
4. Make the Swoodles:
5. Preheat the oven to 425ºF. Line a baking sheet with parchment paper.
6. Put the spiralized sweet potato in a bowl, then drizzle with olive oil. Toss to coat well. Transfer them on the baking sheet. Sprinkle with salt and pepper.
7. Bake in the preheated oven for 20 minutes or until lightly browned and al dente. Check the doneness during the baking and remove any well-cooked swoodles.
8. Transfer the swoodles on a large plate and spread with sauce, parsley, and scallions. Toss to serve.

Nutrition Info:
• Per Serving: Calories: 441;Fat: 33.6g;Protein: 12.0g;Carbs: 29.6g.

Ricotta & Olive Rigatoni

Servings:4 | Cooking Time:25 Minutes

Ingredients:
• 2 tbsp extra-virgin olive oil
• 1 lb rigatoni
• ½ lb Ricotta cheese, crumbled
• 3⁄4 cup black olives, chopped
• 10 sun-dried tomatoes, sliced
• 1 tbsp dried oregano
• Black pepper to taste

Directions:
1. Bring to a boil salted water in a pot over high heat. Add the rigatoni and cook according to package directions; drain. Heat the olive oil in a large saucepan over medium heat. Add the rigatoni, ricotta, olives, and sun-dried tomatoes. Toss mixture to combine and cook 2–3 minutes or until cheese just starts to melt. Season with oregano and pepper.

Nutrition Info:
• Per Serving: Calories: 383;Fat: 28g;Protein: 15g;Carbs: 21g.

Caprese Pasta With Roasted Asparagus

Servings:6 | Cooking Time: 25 Minutes

Ingredients:
• 8 ounces uncooked small pasta, like orecchiette (little ears) or farfalle (bow ties)
• 1½ pounds fresh asparagus, ends trimmed and stalks chopped into 1-inch pieces
• 1½ cups grape tomatoes, halved
• 2 tablespoons extra-virgin olive oil
• ¼ teaspoon kosher salt
• ¼ teaspoon freshly ground black pepper
• 2 cups fresh Mozzarella, drained and cut into bite-size pieces
• ⅓ cup torn fresh basil leaves
• 2 tablespoons balsamic vinegar

Directions:
1. Preheat the oven to 400ºF.
2. In a large stockpot of salted water, cook the pasta for about 8 to 10 minutes. Drain and reserve about ¼ cup of the cooking liquid.
3. Meanwhile, in a large bowl, toss together the asparagus, tomatoes, oil, salt and pepper. Spread the mixture onto a large, rimmed baking sheet and bake in the oven for 15 minutes, stirring twice during cooking.
4. Remove the vegetables from the oven and add the cooked pasta to the baking sheet. Mix with a few tablespoons of cooking liquid to help the sauce become smoother and the saucy vegetables stick to the pasta.
5. Gently mix in the Mozzarella and basil. Drizzle with the balsamic vinegar. Serve from the baking sheet or pour the pasta into a large bowl.

Nutrition Info:
• Per Serving: Calories: 147;Fat: 3.0g;Protein: 16.0g;Carbs: 17.0g.

Arugula & Cheese Pasta With Red Sauce

Servings:6 | Cooking Time:60 Minutes

Ingredients:
- ¼ cup olive oil
- 1 shallot, sliced thin
- 2 lb cherry tomatoes, halved
- 3 large garlic cloves, sliced
- 1 tbsp red wine vinegar
- 3 oz ricotta cheese, crumbled
- 1 tsp sugar
- Salt and black pepper to taste
- ¼ tsp red pepper flakes
- 1 lb penne
- 4 oz baby arugula

Directions:
1. Preheat oven to 350° F. Toss shallot with 1 tsp of oil in a bowl. In a separate bowl, toss tomatoes with remaining oil, garlic, vinegar, sugar, salt, pepper, and flakes. Spread tomato mixture in even layer in rimmed baking sheet, scatter shallot over tomatoes, and roast until edges of shallot begin to brown and tomato skins are slightly charred, 35-40 minutes; do not stir. Let cool for 5 to 10 minutes.
2. Meanwhile, bring a pot filled with salted water to a boil and add pasta. Cook, stirring often until al dente. Reserve ½ cup cooking water, then drain pasta and return it to pot. Add arugula to pasta and toss until wilted. Using a spatula, scrape tomato mixture onto pasta and toss to combine. Season to taste and adjust consistency with reserved cooking water as needed. Serve, passing ricotta cheese separately.

Nutrition Info:
- Per Serving: Calories: 444;Fat: 19g;Protein: 18g;Carbs: 44g.

Ziti Marinara Bake

Servings:4 | Cooking Time:60 Minutes

Ingredients:
- For the Marinara Sauce:
- 2 tbsp olive oil
- ¼ onion, diced
- 3 cloves garlic, chopped
- 1 can tomatoes, diced
- Sprig of fresh thyme
- ½ bunch fresh basil
- Salt and pepper to taste
- For the Ziti:
- 1 lb ziti
- 3 ½ cups marinara sauce
- 1 cup cottage cheese
- 1 cup grated Mozzarella
- ¾ cup grated Pecorino cheese

Directions:
1. In a saucepan, warm the olive oil over medium heat. Stir-fry onion and garlic until lightly browned, 3 minutes. Add the tomatoes and herbs, and bring to a boil, then simmer for 7 minutes, covered. Set aside. Discard the herb sprigs and stir in sea salt and black pepper to taste.
2. Preheat the oven to 375°F. Prepare the pasta according to package directions. Drain and mix the pasta in a bowl along with 2 cups of marinara sauce, cottage cheese, and half the Mozzarella and Pecorino cheeses. Transfer the mixture to a baking dish, and top with the remaining marinara sauce and cheese. Bake for 25 to 35 minutes, or until bubbly and golden brown. Serve warm.

Nutrition Info:
- Per Serving: Calories: 455;Fat: 17g;Protein: 19g;Carbs: 62g.

Lentil And Mushroom Pasta

Servings:2 | Cooking Time: 50 Minutes

Ingredients:
- 2 tablespoons olive oil
- 1 large yellow onion, finely diced
- 2 portobello mushrooms, trimmed and chopped finely
- 2 tablespoons tomato paste
- 3 garlic cloves, chopped
- 1 teaspoon oregano
- 2½ cups water
- 1 cup brown lentils
- 1 can diced tomatoes with basil (with juice if diced)
- 1 tablespoon balsamic vinegar
- 8 ounces pasta of choice, cooked
- Salt and black pepper, to taste
- Chopped basil, for garnish

Directions:
1. Place a large stockpot over medium heat. Add the oil. Once the oil is hot, add the onion and mushrooms. Cover and cook until both are soft, about 5 minutes. Add the tomato paste, garlic, and oregano and cook 2 minutes, stirring constantly.
2. Stir in the water and lentils. Bring to a boil, then reduce the heat to medium-low and cook for 5 minutes, covered.
3. Add the tomatoes (and juice if using diced) and vinegar. Replace the lid, reduce the heat to low and cook until the lentils are tender, about 30 minutes.
4. Remove the sauce from the heat and season with salt and pepper to taste. Garnish with the basil and serve over the cooked pasta.

Nutrition Info:
- Per Serving: Calories: 463;Fat: 15.9g;Protein: 12.5g;Carbs: 70.8g.

Moroccan Rice Pilaf

Servings:4 | Cooking Time:40 Minutes

Ingredients:
- 2 tbsp olive oil
- ¼ cup pine nuts
- 1 ¼ cups brown rice
- 1 onion, diced
- 2 cups chicken stock
- 1 cinnamon stick
- ¼ cup dried apricots, chopped
- Salt and black pepper to taste

Directions:
1. Warm the olive oil in a large saucepan over medium heat.
2. Sauté the onions and pine nuts for 5-7 minutes, or until the pine nuts are golden and the onion is translucent. Add the rice and sauté for 2 minutes until lightly browned. Pour the stock and bring it to a boil. Add the cinnamon and apricots.
3. Lower the heat, cover the pan, and simmer for 17-20 minutes or until the rice is tender and the liquid is mostly absorbed. When ready, remove from the heat and fluff with a fork. Season to taste and serve warm.

Nutrition Info:
- Per Serving: Calories: 510;Fat: 24g;Protein: 13g;Carbs: 62g.

Spinach Farfalle With Ricotta Cheese

Servings:4 | Cooking Time:25 Minutes

Ingredients:
- ¼ cup extra-virgin olive oil
- ½ cup crumbled ricotta cheese
- 2 tbsp black olives, halved
- 4 cups fresh baby spinach, chopped
- 2 tbsp scallions, chopped
- 16 oz farfalle pasta
- ¼ cup red wine vinegar
- 2 tsp lemon juice
- Salt and black pepper to taste

Directions:
1. Cook the farfalle pasta to pack instructions, drain and let it to cool. Mix the scallions, spinach, and cooled pasta in a bowl. Top with ricotta and olives. Combine the vinegar, olive oil, lemon juice, salt, and pepper in another bowl. Pour over the pasta mixture and toss to combine. Serve chilled.

Nutrition Info:
- Per Serving: Calories: 377;Fat: 16g;Protein: 12g;Carbs: 44g.

Israeli Couscous With Asparagus

Servings:6 | Cooking Time: 25 Minutes

Ingredients:
- 1½ pounds asparagus spears, ends trimmed and stalks chopped into 1-inch pieces
- 1 garlic clove, minced
- 1 tablespoon extra-virgin olive oil
- ¼ teaspoon freshly ground
- black pepper
- 1¾ cups water
- 1 box uncooked whole-wheat or regular Israeli couscous
- ¼ teaspoon kosher salt
- 1 cup garlic-and-herb goat cheese, at room temperature

Directions:
1. Preheat the oven to 425ºF.
2. In a large bowl, stir together the asparagus, garlic, oil, and pepper. Spread the asparagus on a large, rimmed baking sheet and roast for 10 minutes, stirring a few times. Remove the pan from the oven, and spoon the asparagus into a large serving bowl. Set aside.
3. While the asparagus is roasting, bring the water to a boil in a medium saucepan. Add the couscous and season with salt, stirring well.
4. Reduce the heat to medium-low. Cover and cook for 12 minutes, or until the water is absorbed.
5. Pour the hot couscous into the bowl with the asparagus. Add the goat cheese and mix thoroughly until completely melted.
6. Serve immediately.

Nutrition Info:
- Per Serving: Calories: 103;Fat: 2.0g;Protein: 6.0g;Carbs: 18.0g.

Wild Rice With Cheese & Mushrooms

Servings:4 | Cooking Time:30 Minutes

Ingredients:
- 2 cups chicken stock
- 1 cup wild rice
- 1 onion, chopped
- ½ lb wild mushrooms, sliced
- 2 garlic cloves, minced
- 1 lemon, juiced and zested
- 1 tbsp chives, chopped
- ½ cup mozzarella, grated
- Salt and black pepper to taste

Directions:
1. Warm chicken stock in a pot over medium heat and add in wild rice, onion, mushrooms, garlic, lemon juice, lemon zest, salt, and pepper. Bring to a simmer and cook for 20 minutes. Transfer to a baking tray and top with mozzarella cheese. Place the tray under the broiler for 4 minutes until the cheese is melted. Sprinkle with chives and serve.

Nutrition Info:
- Per Serving: Calories: 230;Fat: 6g;Protein: 6g;Carbs: 13g.

Spicy Farfalle With Zucchini & Tomatoes

Servings:6 | Cooking Time:30 Minutes

Ingredients:
- 2 lb zucchini, halved lengthwise cut into ½ inch
- 2 tbsp Pecorino-Romano cheese, grated
- 5 tbsp extra-virgin olive oil
- Salt and black pepper to taste
- 3 garlic cloves, minced
- ½ tsp red pepper flakes
- 1 lb farfalle
- 12 oz grape tomatoes, halved
- ½ cup fresh basil, chopped
- ¼ cup pine nuts, toasted
- 2 tbsp balsamic vinegar

Directions:
1. Sprinkle zucchini with 1 tablespoon salt and let drain in a colander for 30 minutes; pat dry. Heat 1 tbsp of oil in a large skillet.

Add half of the zucchini and cook until golden brown and slightly charred, 5-7 minutes, reducing the heat if the skillet begins to scorch; transfer to plate. Repeat with 1 tbsp of oil and remaining zucchini; set aside. Heat 1 tbsp of oil in the same skillet and stir-fry garlic and pepper flakes for 30 seconds. Add in squash and stir-fry for 40 seconds.
2. Meanwhile, bring a large pot filled with water to a boil. Add pasta, a pinch of salt and cook until al dente. Reserve ½ cup of cooking liquid, drain pasta and return it to pot. Add the zucchini mixture, tomatoes, basil, pine nuts, vinegar, and remaining oil and toss to combine. Season to taste and adjust consistency with the reserved cooking liquid as needed. Serve with freshly grated Pecorino-Romano cheese.

Nutrition Info:
- Per Serving: Calories: 422;Fat: 13g;Protein: 14g;Carbs: 41g.

Chicken Farfalle In Mustard Sauce

Servings:4 | Cooking Time:40 Minutes

Ingredients:
- 1 tbsp olive oil
- 16 oz farfalle
- 4 chicken breasts, cut into strips
- Salt and black pepper to taste
- 1 yellow onion, finely sliced
- 1 yellow bell pepper, sliced
- 1 garlic clove, minced
- 1 tbsp wholegrain mustard
- 5 tbsp heavy cream
- 1 cup minced mustard greens
- 1 tbsp chopped parsley

Directions:
1. In a pot of boiling water, cook the farfalle pasta for 8-10 minutes until al dente. Drain and set aside.
2. Heat the olive oil in a large skillet, season the chicken with salt, black pepper, and cook in the oil until golden brown, 10 minutes. Set aside. Stir in the onion, bell pepper and cook until softened, 5 minutes. Mix in the garlic and cook until fragrant, 30 seconds. Mix in the mustard and heavy cream; simmer for 2 minutes and mix in the chicken and mustard greens. Allow wilting for 2 minutes and adjust the taste with salt and black pepper. Stir in the farfalle pasta, allow warming for 1 minute and dish the food onto serving plates. Garnish with the parsley and serve warm.

Nutrition Info:
- Per Serving: Calories: 692;Fat: 38g;Protein: 65g;Carbs: 16g.

Ribollita (tuscan Bean Soup)

Servings:6 | Cooking Time:1 Hour 45 Minutes

Ingredients:
- 3 tbsp olive oil
- Salt and black pepper to taste
- 2 cups canned cannellini beans
- 6 oz pancetta, chopped
- ¼ tsp red pepper flakes
- 1 onion, chopped
- 2 carrots, chopped
- 1 celery rib, chopped
- 3 garlic cloves, minced
- 4 cups chicken broth
- 1 lb lacinato kale, chopped
- 1 can diced tomatoes
- 1 rosemary sprig, chopped
- Crusty bread for serving

Directions:
1. Warm the olive oil in a skillet over medium heat and add the pancetta. Cook, stirring occasionally, until pancetta is lightly browned and fat has rendered, 5-6 minutes. Add onion, carrots, and celery and cook, stirring occasionally, until softened and lightly browned, 4-6 minutes. Stir in garlic and red pepper flakes and cook until fragrant, 1 minute.
2. Stir in broth, 2 cups of water, and beans and bring to a boil. Cover and simmer for 15 minutes. Stir in lacinato kale and toma-

...nkle with rosemary and ...sty bread.

Serving: Calories: 385;Fat: 18g;Protein: 36g;Carbs: 25g.

Quinoa & Watercress Salad With Nuts

Servings:4 | Cooking Time:5 Minutes

Ingredients:
- 2 boiled eggs, cut into wedges
- 2 cups watercress
- 2 cups cherry tomatoes, halved
- 1 cucumber, sliced
- 1 cup quinoa, cooked
- 1 cup almonds, chopped
- 2 tbsp olive oil
- 1 avocado, peeled and sliced
- 2 tbsp fresh cilantro, chopped
- Salt to taste
- 1 lemon, juiced

Directions:
1. Place watercress, cherry tomatoes, cucumber, quinoa, almonds, olive oil, cilantro, salt, and lemon juice in a bowl and toss to combine. Top with egg wedges and avocado slices and serve immediately.

Nutrition Info:
- Per Serving: Calories: 530;Fat: 35g;Protein: 20g;Carbs: 45g.

Raspberry & Nut Quinoa

Servings:4 | Cooking Time:5 Minutes

Ingredients:
- 1 tbsp honey
- 2 cups almond milk
- 2 cups quinoa, cooked
- ½ tsp cinnamon powder
- 1 cup raspberries
- ¼ cup walnuts, chopped

Directions:
1. Combine quinoa, milk, cinnamon powder, honey, raspberries, and walnuts in a bowl. Serve in individual bowls.

Nutrition Info:
- Per Serving: Calories: 300;Fat: 15g;Protein: 5g;Carbs: 15g.

Rosemary Fava Bean Purée

Servings:4 | Cooking Time:20 Minutes

Ingredients:
- 3 tbsp olive oil
- 4 garlic cloves, minced
- 1 tsp ground cumin
- 2 cans fava beans
- 3 tbsp tahini
- 2 tbsp lemon juice
- 4 lemon wedges
- Salt and black pepper to taste
- 1 tomato, chopped
- 1 small onion, chopped
- 2 hard-cooked eggs, chopped
- 1 tbsp rosemary, chopped

Directions:
1. Warm 2 tbsp of olive oil in a saucepan over medium heat. Cook garlic cumin until fragrant, about 2 minutes. Stir in beans and their liquid and tahini. Bring to a simmer and cook until liquid thickens slightly, 8-10 minutes. Heat off.
2. Mash beans to a coarse consistency using a potato masher. Stir in lemon juice. Season with salt and pepper. Top with tomato, onion, rosemary, and eggs, and drizzle with the remaining oil. Serve with lemon wedges.

Nutrition Info:
- Per Serving: Calories: 173;Fat: 8.8g;Protein: 9g;Carbs: 9.8g.

Cumin Rice Stuffed Bell Peppers

Servings:4 | Cooking Time:35 Minutes

Ingredients:
- 1 tbsp olive oil
- 2 lb mixed bell peppers, halved
- 1 cup white rice, rinsed
- ½ cup ricotta cheese, crumbled
- 2 tomatoes, pureed
- 1 onion, chopped
- 1 tsp ground cumin
- 1 tsp ground fennel seeds
- Salt and black pepper to taste

Directions:
1. Blanch the peppers in a pot with salted water over medium heat for 1-2 minutes, drain and set aside. Add the rice to the pot, bring to a boil and simmer for 15 minutes. Drain and remove to a bowl. Add in olive oil, cumin, ground fennel seeds, onion, tomatoes, salt, and pepper and stir to combine. Divide the mixture between the pepper halves and top with ricotta cheese. Bake for 8-10 minutes. Serve right away.

Nutrition Info:
- Per Serving: Calories: 285;Fat: 6.7g;Protein: 8g;Carbs: 48.3g.

Baked Pesto Penne With Broccoli

Servings:4 | Cooking Time:40 Minutes

Ingredients:
- 1 lb broccoli florets
- 16 oz penne pasta
- 1 cup vegetable stock
- Salt and black pepper
- 2 tbsp basil pesto
- 2 cups mozzarella, shredded
- 3 tbsp Parmesan cheese, grated
- 2 green onions, chopped

Directions:
1. Bring to a bowl salted water over medium heat and add in the pasta. Cook for 7-9 minutes until al dente. Drain and set aside. Preheat the oven to 380° F. Place pasta, vegetable stock, salt, pepper, basil pesto, broccoli, and green onions in a greased baking pan and combine. Scatter with mozzarella and parmesan cheeses and bake for 30 minutes. Serve.

Nutrition Info:
- Per Serving: Calories: 190;Fat: 4g;Protein: 8g;Carbs: 9g.

Lemon Couscous With Broccoli

Servings:4 | Cooking Time:20 Minutes

Ingredients:
- 2 tsp olive oil
- Salt and black pepper to taste
- 1 small red onion, sliced
- 1 lemon, zested
- 1 head broccoli, cut into florets
- 1 cup couscous

Directions:
1. Heat a pot filled with salted water over medium heat; bring to a boil. Add in the broccoli and cook for 4-6 minutes until tender. Remove to a boil with a slotted spoon. In another bowl, place the couscous and cover with boiling broccoli water. Cover and let sit for 3-4 minutes until the water is absorbrd. Fluff the couscous with a fork and season with lemon zest, salt. and pepper. Stir in broccoli and top with red onion to serve.

Nutrition Info:
- Per Serving: Calories: 620;Fat: 45g;Protein: 11g;Carbs: 51g.

Parmesan Zucchini Farfalle

Servings:4 | Cooking Time:42 Minutes

Ingredients:
- 3 tbsp olive oil
- 2 garlic cloves, minced
- 4 medium zucchini, diced
- Salt and black pepper to taste
- ½ cup milk
- ¼ tsp ground nutmeg
- 8 oz bow ties
- ½ cup Romano cheese, grated
- 1 tbsp lemon juice

Directions:
1. Heat the oil in a large skillet over medium heat. Stir-fry garlic for 1 minute. Add zucchini, pepper, and salt, stir and cook for 15 minutes, stirring once or twice. In a microwave-safe bowl, warm the milk in the microwave on high for 30 seconds. Stir the milk and nutmeg into the skillet and cook for another 5 minutes, stirring occasionally.
2. Meanwhile, in a large pot, cook the pasta according to the package directions. Drain the pasta in a colander, saving ¼ cup of the pasta liquid. Add the pasta and liquid to the skillet. Mix everything together and remove from the heat. Stir in the grated cheese and lemon juice and serve immediately.

Nutrition Info:
- Per Serving: Calories: 277;Fat: 8g;Protein: 8g;Carbs: 32g.

Sweet Potatoes Stuffed With Beans

Servings:4 | Cooking Time:50 Minutes

Ingredients:
- 4 sweet potatoes, pierced with a fork
- 2 tbsp olive oil
- 1 cup canned cannellini beans
- 1 small red pepper, chopped
- 1 tbsp lemon zest
- 2 tbsp lemon juice
- 1 garlic clove, minced
- 1 tbsp oregano, chopped
- 1 tbsp parsley, chopped
- Salt and black pepper to taste
- 1 avocado, mashed
- 1 tbsp tahini paste

Directions:
1. Preheat oven to 360° F. Line a baking sheet with parchment paper and place in the sweet potatoes. Bake for 40 minutes. Let cool and cut in half. Using a spoon, remove some flesh of the potatoes and place it in a bowl. Mix in beans, red pepper, lemon zest, half of the lemon juice, half of the oil, half of the garlic, oregano, half of the parsley, salt, and pepper.
2. Divide the mixture between the potato halves. In another bowl, combine avocado, 2 tbsp of water, tahini, remaining lemon juice, remaining oil, remaining garlic, and remaining parsley and scatter over stuffed potatoes. Serve chilled.

Nutrition Info:
- Per Serving: Calories: 303;Fat: 3g;Protein: 8g;Carbs: 40g.

Veggie & Beef Ragu

Servings:4 | Cooking Time:20 Minutes

Ingredients:
- 2 tbsp butter
- 16 oz tagliatelle pasta
- 1 lb ground beef
- Salt and black pepper to taste
- ¼ cup tomato sauce
- 1 green bell pepper, chopped
- 1 red bell pepper, chopped
- 1 small red onion, chopped
- 1 cup grated Parmesan cheese

Directions:
1. In a pot of boiling water, cook the tagliatelle pasta for 8-10 minutes until al dente. Drain and set aside.
2. Heat half of the butter in a medium skillet and cook the beef until brown, 5 minutes. in the tomato sauce and cook for reduces by a quarter. Stir in the bell peppers 1 minute and turn the heat off. Adjust the taste with salt pepper and mix in the tagliatelle. Dish the food onto serving plates. Garnish with Parmesan.

Nutrition Info:
- Per Serving: Calories: 451;Fat: 26g;Protein: 39g;Carbs: 6g.

Quinoa With Baby Potatoes And Broccoli

Servings:4 | Cooking Time: 10 Minutes

Ingredients:
- 2 tablespoons olive oil
- 1 cup baby potatoes, cut in half
- 1 cup broccoli florets
- 2 cups cooked quinoa
- Zest of 1 lemon
- Sea salt and freshly ground pepper, to taste

Directions:
1. Heat the olive oil in a large skillet over medium heat until shimmering.
2. Add the potatoes and cook for about 6 to 7 minutes, or until softened and golden brown. Add the broccoli and cook for about 3 minutes, or until tender.
3. Remove from the heat and add the quinoa and lemon zest. Season with salt and pepper to taste, then serve.

Nutrition Info:
- Per Serving: Calories: 205;Fat: 8.6g;Protein: 5.1g;Carbs: 27.3g.

Spinach & Salmon Fettuccine In White Sauce

Servings:4 | Cooking Time:35 Minutes

Ingredients:
- 5 tbsp butter
- 16 oz fettuccine
- 4 salmon fillets, cubed
- Salt and black pepper to taste
- 3 garlic cloves, minced
- 1 ¼ cups heavy cream
- ½ cup dry white wine
- 1 tsp grated lemon zest
- 1 cup baby spinach
- Lemon wedges for garnishing

Directions:
1. In a pot of boiling water, cook the fettuccine pasta for 8-10 minutes until al dente. Drain and set aside.
2. Melt half of the butter in a large skillet; season the salmon with salt, black pepper, and cook in the butter until golden brown on all sides and flaky within, 8 minutes. Transfer to a plate and set aside.
3. Add the remaining butter to the skillet to melt and stir in the garlic. Cook until fragrant, 1 minute. Mix in heavy cream, white wine, lemon zest, salt, and pepper. Allow boiling over low heat for 5 minutes. Stir in spinach, allow wilting for 2 minutes and stir in fettuccine and salmon until well-coated in the sauce. Garnish with lemon wedges.

Nutrition Info:
- Per Serving: Calories: 795;Fat: 46g;Protein: 72g;Carbs: 20g.

Sardine & Caper Tagliatelle

Servings:4 | Cooking Time:20 Minutes

Ingredients:
- 1 tbsp olive oil
- 8 oz tagliatelle
- ¼ cup chopped onion
- 2 garlic cloves, minced
- 1 tsp tomato paste
- 16 canned sardines in olive oil
- 1 tbsp capers

• 1 tbsp chopped parsley
• 1 tsp chopped oregano
• pepper to taste

Directions:
1. Boil water in a pot over medium heat and place in the pasta. Cook for 8-10 minutes for al dente. Drain and set aside; reserve ½ cup of the cooking liquid. Warm the olive oil in a pan over medium heat. Place in onion, garlic, and oregano and cook for 5 minutes until soft. Stir in salt, tomato paste, pepper, and ½ cup of reserved liquid for 1 minute. Mix in cooked pasta, capers, and sardines and toss to coat. Serve topped with Parmesan cheese and parsley.

Nutrition Info:
• Per Serving: Calories: 412;Fat: 13g;Protein: 23g;Carbs: 47g.

Cheesy Chicken Pasta

Servings:4 | Cooking Time:35 Minutes

Ingredients:
• 16 oz whole-wheat pasta
• 2 tbsp olive oil
• 2 chicken breasts, cubed
• 1 yellow onion, minced
• 3 garlic cloves, minced
• 1 tsp Italian seasoning
• ¼ tsp red chili flakes
• ¼ tsp cayenne pepper
• 1 cup marinara sauce
• 2 tbsp grated mozzarella
• 2 tbsp grated Parmesan cheese
• Salt and black pepper to taste

Directions:
1. In a pot of boiling water, cook the whole-wheat pasta according to the package directions. Drain and set aside.
2. Heat the olive oil in a large pot, season the chicken with salt, black pepper, and cook in the oil until golden brown on both sides and cooked within, 10 minutes. Transfer to a plate, cut into cubes and set aside. Add the onion and garlic to the pan and cook until softened and fragrant, 3 minutes.
3. Season with Italian seasoning, garlic powder, chili flakes, and cayenne pepper. Cook for 1 minute. Stir in marinara sauce and simmer for 5 minutes. Adjust the taste with salt and black pepper. Reduce heat to low and return the chicken to the sauce and pasta, mozzarella and Parmesan cheeses. Stir until the cheese melts. Serve.

Nutrition Info:
• Per Serving: Calories: 763;Fat: 34g;Protein: 83g;Carbs: 18g.

Quinoa And Chickpea Vegetable Bowls

Servings:4 | Cooking Time: 15 Minutes

Ingredients:
• 1 cup red dry quinoa, rinsed and drained
• 2 cups low-sodium vegetable soup
• 2 cups fresh spinach
• 2 cups finely shredded red cabbage
• 1 can chickpeas, drained and rinsed
• 1 ripe avocado, thinly sliced
• 1 cup shredded carrots
• 1 red bell pepper, thinly sliced
• 4 tablespoons Mango Sauce
• ½ cup fresh cilantro, chopped
• Mango Sauce:
• 1 mango, diced
• ¼ cup fresh lime juice
• ½ teaspoon ground turmeric
• 1 teaspoon finely minced fresh ginger
• ¼ teaspoon sea salt
• Pinch of ground red pepper
• 1 teaspoon pure maple syrup
• 2 tablespoons extra-virgin olive oil

Directions:
1. Pour the quinoa and vegetable soup in a saucepan. Bring to a boil. Reduce the heat to low. Cover and cook for 15 minutes or until tender. Fluffy with a fork.
2. Meanwhile, combine the ingredients for the mango sauce in a food processor. Pulse until smooth.
3. Divide the quinoa, spinach, and cabbage into 4 serving bowls, then top with chickpeas, avocado, carrots, and bell pepper. Dress them with the mango sauce and spread with cilantro. Serve immediately.

Nutrition Info:
• Per Serving: Calories: 366;Fat: 11.1g;Protein: 15.5g;Carbs: 55.6g.

Black Bean & Chickpea Burgers

Servings:4 | Cooking Time:35 Minutes

Ingredients:
• 1 tsp olive oil
• 1 can black beans
• 1 can chickpeas
• ½ white onion, chopped
• 2 garlic cloves, minced
• 2 free-range eggs
• 1 tsp ground cumin
• Salt and black pepper to taste
• 1 cup panko breadcrumbs
• ½ cup old-fashioned rolled oats
• 6 hamburger buns, halved
• 2 avocados
• 2 tbsp lemon juice
• 6 large lettuce leaves

Directions:
1. Preheat oven to 380° F. Blitz the black beans, chickpeas, eggs, cumin, salt, and pepper in a food processor until smooth. Transfer the mixture to a bowl and add the onion and garlic and mix well. Stir in the bread crumbs and oats. Shape the mixture into 6 balls, flatten them with your hands to make patties. Brush both sides of the burgers with oil. Arrange them on a parchment-lined baking sheet. Bake for 30 minutes, flippingonce until slightly crispy on the edges.
2. Meanwhile, mash the avocado with the lemon juice and a pinch of salt with a fork until smooth; set aside. Toast the buns for 2-3 minutes. Spread the avocado mixture onto the base of each bun, then top with the burgers and lettuce leaves. Finish with the bun tops. Serve and enjoy!

Nutrition Info:
• Per Serving: Calories: 867;Fat: 22g;Protein: 39g;Carbs: 133g.

Florentine Bean & Vegetable Gratin

Servings:4 | Cooking Time:50 Minutes

Ingredients:
• ½ cup Parmigiano Reggiano cheese, grated
• 4 pancetta slices
• 2 tbsp olive oil
• 4 garlic cloves, minced
• 1 onion, chopped
• ½ fennel bulb, chopped
• 1 tbsp brown rice flour
• 2 cans white beans
• 1 can tomatoes, diced
• 1 medium zucchini, chopped
• 1 tsp porcini powder
• 1 tbsp fresh basil, chopped
• ½ tsp dried oregano
• 1 tsp red pepper flakes
• Salt to taste
• 2 tbsp butter, cubed

Directions:
1. Heat the olive in a skillet over medium heat. Fry the pancetta for 5 minutes until crispy. Drain on paper towels, chop, and reserve. Add garlic, onion, and fennel to the skillet and sauté for 5 minutes until softened. Stir in rice flour for 3 minutes.
2. Preheat oven to 350° F. Add the beans, tomatoes, and zucchini to a casserole dish and pour in the sautéed vegetable and chopped pancetta; mix well. Sprinkle with porcini powder, oregano, red

pepper flakes, and salt. Top with Parmigiano Reggiano cheese and butter and bake for 25 minutes or until the cheese is lightly browned. Garnish with basil and serve.

Nutrition Info:
- Per Serving: Calories: 483;Fat: 28g;Protein: 19g;Carbs: 42g.

Spicy Bean Rolls

Servings:4 | Cooking Time:25 Minutes

Ingredients:
- 1 tbsp olive oil
- 1 red onion, chopped
- 2 garlic cloves, minced
- 1 green bell pepper, sliced
- 2 cups canned cannellini beans
- 1 red chili pepper, chopped
- 1 tbsp cilantro, chopped
- 1 tsp cumin, ground
- Salt and black pepper to taste
- 4 whole-wheat tortillas
- 1 cup mozzarella, shredded

Directions:
1. Warm the olive oil in a skillet over medium heat and sauté onion for 3 minutes. Stir in garlic, bell pepper, cannellini beans, red chili pepper, cilantro, cumin, salt, and pepper and cook for 15 minutes. Spoon bean mixture on each tortilla and top with cheese. Roll up and serve right away.

Nutrition Info:
- Per Serving: Calories: 680;Fat: 15g;Protein: 38g;Carbs: 75g.

Greek-style Shrimp & Feta Macaroni

Servings:6 | Cooking Time:50 Minutes

Ingredients:
- 10 Kalamata olives
- 1 ½ lb elbow macaroni
- 2 red chili peppers, minced
- 1 garlic clove, minced
- 2 whole garlic cloves
- 2 tbsp fresh parsley, chopped
- 1 ¼ cups fresh basil, sliced
- ½ cup extra-virgin olive oil
- ½ tsp honey
- ½ lemon, juiced and zested
- ¼ cup butter
- 1 small red onion, chopped
- 1 lb button mushrooms,
- sliced
- 1 tsp sweet paprika
- 6 ripe plum tomatoes, puréed
- ¼ cup dry white wine
- 1 oz ouzo
- 1 cup heavy cream
- 1 cup feta cheese, crumbled
- 24 shrimp, peeled and deveined
- 1 cup feta cheese, cubed
- 1 tsp dried Greek oregano
- Salt and black pepper to taste

Directions:
1. Bring to a boil salted water in a pot over high heat. Add the macaroni and cook for 6-8 minutes until al dente. Drain. Set aside. Preheat your broiler. Place the chilies, whole garlic, parsley, ¼ cup of basil, ¼ cup of oil, honey, lemon juice, lemon zest, and salt in a food processor and blend until all the ingredients are well incorporated. Set aside.
2. Warm the remaining olive oil and butter in a large skillet over medium heat. Sauté the onion, minced garlic, mushrooms, and paprika for 5 minutes until tender. Pour in the tomatoes, wine, and ouzo and season with salt and pepper. Simmer for 6–7 minutes until most of the liquid evaporates, 5 minutes.
3. Stir in the heavy cream and crumbled feta cheese for 3 minutes until the sauce is thickened. Add in remaining basil and pasta and stir to combine. Pour the mixture into a baking dish and top with shrimp and cubed feta cheese. Broil 5 minutes or until the shrimp turn pink and cheese melts. Drizzle with reserved parsley-basil sauce and sprinkle with oregano. Let cool for 5 minutes. Serve topped with olives.

Nutrition Info:

Parsley Beef Fusilli

Servings:4 | Cooking Time:30 Minutes

Ingredients:
- 1 cup grated Pecorino Romano cheese
- 1 lb thick-cut New York strip steaks, cut into 1-inch cubes
- 4 tbsp butter
- 16 oz fusilli pasta
- Salt and black pepper to taste
- 4 garlic cloves, minced
- 2 tbsp chopped fresh parsley

Directions:
1. In a pot of boiling water, cook the fusilli pasta for 8-10 minutes until al dente. Drain and set aside.
2. Melt the butter in a large skillet, season the steaks with salt, black pepper and cook in the butter until brown, and cooked through, 10 minutes. Stir in the garlic and cook until fragrant, 1 minute. Mix in the parsley and fusilli pasta; toss well and season with salt and black pepper. Dish the food, top with the Pecorino Romano cheese and serve immediately.

Nutrition Info:
- Per Serving: Calories: 422;Fat: 22g;Protein: 36g;Carbs: 17g.

Spicy Chicken Lentils

Servings:4 | Cooking Time:1 Hour 20 Minutes

Ingredients:
- 2 tbsp olive oil
- 1 lb chicken thighs, skinless, boneless, and cubed
- 1 tbsp coriander seeds
- 1 bay leaf
- 1 tbsp tomato paste
- 2 carrots, chopped
- 1 onion, chopped
- 2 garlic cloves, chopped
- ½ tsp red chili flakes
- ½ tsp paprika
- 4 cups chicken stock
- 1 cup brown lentils
- Salt and black pepper to taste

Directions:
1. Warm the olive oil in a pot over medium heat and cook chicken, onion, and garlic for 6-8 minutes. Stir in carrots, tomato paste, coriander seeds, bay leaf, red chili pepper, and paprika for 3 minutes. Pour in the chicken stock and bring to a boil. Simmer for 25 minutes. Add in lentils, season with salt and pepper and cook for another 15 minutes. Discard bay leaf and serve right away.

Nutrition Info:
- Per Serving: Calories: 320;Fat: 14g;Protein: 14g;Carbs: 18g.

Triple-green Pasta With Cheese

Servings:4 | Cooking Time: 14 To 16 Minutes

Ingredients:
- 8 ounces uncooked penne
- 1 tablespoon extra-virgin olive oil
- 2 garlic cloves, minced
- ¼ teaspoon crushed red pepper
- 2 cups chopped fresh flat-leaf parsley, including stems
- 5 cups loosely packed baby
- spinach
- ¼ teaspoon ground nutmeg
- ¼ teaspoon kosher salt
- ¼ teaspoon freshly ground black pepper
- ⅓ cup Castelvetrano olives, pitted and sliced
- ⅓ cup grated Parmesan cheese

Directions:
1. In a large stockpot of salted water, cook the pasta for about 8 to 10 minutes. Drain the pasta and reserve ¼ cup of the cooking liquid.
2. Meanwhile, heat the olive oil in a large skillet over medium

heat. Add the garlic and red pepper and cook for 30 seconds, stirring constantly.

3. Add the parsley and cook for 1 minute, stirring constantly. Add the spinach, nutmeg, salt, and pepper, and cook for 3 minutes, stirring occasionally, or until the spinach is wilted.

4. Add the cooked pasta and the reserved ¼ cup cooking liquid to the skillet. Stir in the olives and cook for about 2 minutes, or until most of the pasta water has been absorbed.

5. Remove from the heat and stir in the cheese before serving.

Nutrition Info:
• Per Serving: Calories: 262;Fat: 4.0g;Protein: 15.0g;Carbs: 51.0g.

Leftover Pasta & Mushroom Frittata

Servings:4 | Cooking Time:25 Minutes

Ingredients:
• 2 tbsp olive oil
• 4 oz leftover spaghetti, cooked
• 8 large eggs, beaten
• ¼ cup heavy cream
• ½ tsp Italian seasoning
• ½ tsp garlic salt
• 1/8 tsp garlic pepper
• 1 cup chopped mushrooms
• 1 cup Pecorino cheese, grated

Directions:
1. Preheat your broiler. Warm the olive oil in a large skillet over medium heat. Add mushrooms and cook for 3–4 minutes, until almost tender. In a large bowl, beat the eggs with cream, Italian seasoning, garlic salt, and garlic pepper. Stir in the leftover spaghetti. Pour the egg mixture over the mushrooms and level with a spatula. Cook for 5–7 minutes until the eggs are almost set. Sprinkle with cheese and place under broiler for 3–5 minutes, until the cheese melts. Serve.

Nutrition Info:
• Per Serving: Calories: 400;Fat: 30g;Protein: 23g;Carbs: 11g.

Mushroom Bulgur Pilaf With Almonds

Servings:2 | Cooking Time:45 Minutes

Ingredients:
• 3 scallions, minced
• 2 oz mushrooms, sliced
• 1 tbsp olive oil
• 1 garlic clove, minced
• ¼ cup almonds, sliced
• ½ cup bulgur
• 1 ½ cups chicken stock
• ½ tsp dried thyme
• 1 tbsp parsley, chopped
• Salt to taste

Directions:
1. Warm the olive oil in a saucepan over medium heat. Add garlic, scallions, mushrooms, and almonds, and sauté for 3 minutes. Pour the bulgur and cook, stirring, for 1 minute to toast it. Add the stock and thyme and bring the mixture to a boil. Cover and reduce the heat to low. Simmer the bulgur for 25 minutes or until the liquid is absorbed and the bulgur is tender. Sprinkle with parsley and season with salt to serve.

Nutrition Info:
• Per Serving: Calories: 342;Fat: 15g;Protein: 11g;Carbs: 48g.

Chickpea & Asparagus Sautée

Servings:4 | Cooking Time:25 Minutes

Ingredients:
• 2 tbsp olive oil
• 2 garlic cloves, minced
• 2 potatoes, cubed
• 1 yellow onion, chopped
• 1 cup canned chickpeas
• Salt and black pepper to taste
• 1 lb asparagus, chopped
• 1 tsp sweet paprika
• 1 tsp ground coriander
• 2 tomatoes, chopped
• 2 tbsp parsley, chopped
• ½ cup ricotta cheese, crumbled

Directions:
1. Warm the olive oil in a skillet over medium heat and sauté potatoes, onion, garlic, salt, and pepper for 7 minutes, stirring occasionally. Add in chickpeas, salt, pepper, asparagus, paprika, and coriander and sauté another 6-7 minutes. Remove to a bowl. Mix in tomatoes, parsley, and ricotta cheese and serve right away.

Nutrition Info:
• Per Serving: Calories: 540;Fat: 22g;Protein: 30g;Carbs: 36g.

Pea & Mint Tortellini

Servings:4 | Cooking Time:30 Minutes

Ingredients:
• 1 package frozen cheese tortellini
• 2 tbsp olive oil
• 3 garlic cloves, minced
• ½ cup vegetable broth
• 2 cups frozen baby peas
• 1 lemon, zested
• 2 tbsp mint leaves, chopped

Directions:
1. Bring to a boil salted water in a pot over high heat. Add the tortellini and cook according to package directions. Drain and transfer to a bowl. Warm the olive oil in a large saucepan over medium and sauté the garlic for 2 minutes until golden. Pour in the broth and peas and bring to a simmer. Add in the tortellini and cook for 4–5 minutes until the mixture is slightly thickened. Stir in lemon zest, top with mint, and serve.

Nutrition Info:
• Per Serving: Calories: 272;Fat: 11g;Protein: 11g;Carbs: 34g.

Kale Chicken With Pappardelle

Servings:4 | Cooking Time:30 Min + Chilling Time

Ingredients:
• 1 cup grated Parmigiano-Reggiano cheese
• 4 chicken thighs, cut into 1-inch pieces
• 3 tbsp olive oil
• 16 oz pappardelle pasta
• Salt and black pepper to taste
• 1 yellow onion, chopped
• 4 garlic cloves, minced
• 12 cherry tomatoes, halved
• ½ cup chicken broth
• 2 cups baby kale, chopped
• 2 tbsp pine nuts for topping

Directions:
1. In a pot of boiling water, cook the pappardelle pasta for 8-10 minutes until al dente. Drain and set aside.
2. Heat the olive oil in a medium pot. Season the chicken with salt and pepper and sear in the oil until golden brown on the outside. Transfer to a plate and set aside. Add the onion and garlic to the oil and cook until softened and fragrant, 3 minutes. Mix in tomatoes and chicken broth and cook over low heat until the tomatoes soften and the liquid reduces by half. Season with salt and pepper. Return the chicken to the pot and stir in kale. Allow wilting for 2 minutes. Spoon the pappardelle onto serving plates, top with kale sauce and Parmigianino-Reggiano cheese. Garnish with pine nuts.

Nutrition Info:
• Per Serving: Calories: 740;Fat: 53g;Protein: 50g;Carbs: 15g.

Feta & Garbanzo Bowl

Servings:4 | Cooking Time:10 Minutes

Ingredients:
- 2 cups canned garbanzo beans
- 2 tomatoes, diced
- 1 cucumber, thinly sliced
- 1 tsp garlic, minced
- 1 red onion, chopped
- 2 green hot peppers, chopped
- 1 red bell pepper, sliced
- 2 tbsp fresh parsley, chopped
- 1 fresh lemon, juiced
- 1 cup feta cheese, crumbled
- 1 tsp harissa
- ¼ tsp chili flakes
- Salt and black pepper to taste
- Fresh mint leaves, chopped

Directions:
1. In a bowl, combine the garbanzo beans with cucumber, garlic, onion, hot peppers, tomatoes, bell pepper, parsley, lemon juice, chili flakes, harissa, salt, and black pepper. Adjust the seasonings. Serve topped with crumbled feta cheese and freshly chopped mint leaves.

Nutrition Info:
- Per Serving: Calories: 330;Fat: 11g;Protein: 17g;Carbs: 43g.

Tomato Basil Pasta

Servings:2 | Cooking Time: 2 Minutes

Ingredients:
- 2 cups dried campanelle or similar pasta
- 1¾ cups vegetable stock
- ½ teaspoon salt, plus more as needed
- 2 tomatoes, cut into large dices
- 1 or 2 pinches red pepper
- flakes
- ½ teaspoon garlic powder
- ½ teaspoon dried oregano
- 10 to 12 fresh sweet basil leaves
- Freshly ground black pepper, to taste

Directions:
1. In your Instant Pot, stir together the pasta, stock, and salt. Scatter the tomatoes on top (do not stir).
2. Secure the lid. Select the Manual mode and set the cooking time for 2 minutes at High Pressure.
3. Once cooking is complete, do a quick pressure release. Carefully open the lid.
4. Stir in the red pepper flakes, oregano, and garlic powder. If there's more than a few tablespoons of liquid in the bottom, select Sauté and cook for 2 to 3 minutes until it evaporates.
5. When ready to serve, chiffonade the basil and stir it in. Taste and season with more salt and pepper, as needed. Serve warm.

Nutrition Info:
- Per Serving: Calories: 415;Fat: 2.0g;Protein: 15.2g;Carbs: 84.2g.

Apricot & Almond Couscous

Servings:4 | Cooking Time:25 Minutes

Ingredients:
- 2 tbsp olive oil
- 1 small onion, diced
- 1 cup couscous
- 2 cups water
- ½ cup dried apricots, soaked
- ½ cup slivered hazelnuts
- ½ tsp dried mint
- ½ tsp dried thyme

Directions:
1. In a skillet, heat the olive and stir-fry the onion until translucent and soft. Stir in the couscous and cook for 2-3 minutes. Add the water, cover, and cook for 8-10 minutes until the water is mostly absorbed. Remove from the heat and let sit for a few

minutes. Fluff with a fork and fold in the apricots, nuts, mint, and thyme.

Nutrition Info:
- Per Serving: Calories: 388;Fat: 8g;Protein: 14g;Carbs: 36g.

Moroccan-style Vegetable Bean Stew

Servings:6 | Cooking Time:50 Minutes

Ingredients:
- 3 tbsp olive oil
- 1 onion, chopped
- 8 oz Swiss chard, torn
- 4 garlic cloves, minced
- 1 tsp ground cumin
- ½ tsp paprika
- ½ tsp ground coriander
- ¼ tsp ground cinnamon
- 2 tbsp tomato paste
- 2 tbsp cornstarch
- 4 cups vegetable broth
- 2 carrots, chopped
- 1 can chickpeas
- 1 can butter beans
- 3 tbsp minced fresh parsley
- 3 tbsp harissa sauce
- Salt and black pepper to taste

Directions:
1. Warm the olive oil in a saucepan over medium heat. Sauté the onion until softened, about 3 minutes. Stir in garlic, cumin, paprika, coriander, and cinnamon and cook until fragrant, about 30 seconds. Stir in tomato paste and cornstarch and cook for 1 minute. Pour in broth and carrots, scraping up any browned bits, smoothing out any lumps, and bringing to boil. Reduce to a gentle simmer and cook for 10 minutes. Stir in chard, chickpeas, beans, salt, and pepper and simmer until vegetables are tender, 10-15 minutes. Sprinkle with parsley and some harissa sauce. Serve with the remaining sauce harissa on the side.

Nutrition Info:
- Per Serving: Calories: 387;Fat: 3.2g;Protein: 7g;Carbs: 28.7g.

Lentil And Vegetable Curry Stew

Servings:8 | Cooking Time: 4 Hours 7 Minutes

Ingredients:
- 1 tablespoon coconut oil
- 1 yellow onion, diced
- ¼ cup yellow Thai curry paste
- 2 cups unsweetened coconut milk
- 2 cups dry red lentils, rinsed well and drained
- 3 cups bite-sized cauliflower florets
- 2 golden potatoes, cut into
- chunks
- 2 carrots, peeled and diced
- 8 cups low-sodium vegetable soup, divided
- 1 bunch kale, stems removed and roughly chopped
- Sea salt, to taste
- ½ cup fresh cilantro, chopped
- Pinch crushed red pepper flakes

Directions:
1. Heat the coconut oil in a nonstick skillet over medium-high heat until melted.
2. Add the onion and sauté for 5 minutes or until translucent.
3. Pour in the curry paste and sauté for another 2 minutes, then fold in the coconut milk and stir to combine well. Bring to a simmer and turn off the heat.
4. Put the lentils, cauliflower, potatoes, and carrot in the slow cooker. Pour in 6 cups of vegetable soup and the curry mixture. Stir to combine well.
5. Cover and cook on high for 4 hours or until the lentils and vegetables are soft. Stir periodically.
6. During the last 30 minutes, fold the kale in the slow cooker and pour in the remaining vegetable soup. Sprinkle with salt.
7. Pour the stew in a large serving bowl and spread the cilantro

and red pepper flakes on top before serving hot.

Nutrition Info:
• Per Serving: Calories: 530;Fat: 19.2g;Protein: 20.3g;Carbs: 75.2g.

Roasted Butternut Squash And Zucchini With Penne

Servings:6 | Cooking Time: 30 Minutes

Ingredients:
• 1 large zucchini, diced
• 1 large butternut squash, peeled and diced
• 1 large yellow onion, chopped
• 2 tablespoons extra-virgin olive oil
• 1 teaspoon paprika
• ½ teaspoon garlic powder
• ½ teaspoon sea salt
• ½ teaspoon freshly ground black pepper
• 1 pound whole-grain penne
• ½ cup dry white wine
• 2 tablespoons grated Parmesan cheese

Directions:
1. Preheat the oven to 400ºF. Line a baking sheet with aluminum foil.
2. Combine the zucchini, butternut squash, and onion in a large bowl. Drizzle with olive oil and sprinkle with paprika, garlic powder, salt, and ground black pepper. Toss to coat well.
3. Spread the vegetables in the single layer on the baking sheet, then roast in the preheated oven for 25 minutes or until the vegetables are tender.
4. Meanwhile, bring a pot of water to a boil, then add the penne and cook for 14 minutes or until al dente. Drain the penne through a colander.
5. Transfer ½ cup of roasted vegetables in a food processor, then pour in the dry white wine. Pulse until smooth.
6. Pour the puréed vegetables in a nonstick skillet and cook with penne over medium-high heat for a few minutes to heat through.
7. Transfer the penne with the purée on a large serving plate, then spread the remaining roasted vegetables and Parmesan on top before serving.

Nutrition Info:
• Per Serving: Calories: 340;Fat: 6.2g;Protein: 8.0g;Carbs: 66.8g.

Cranberry & Walnut Freekeh Pilaf

Servings:4 | Cooking Time:30 Minutes

Ingredients:
• 2 tbsp olive oil
• 2 ½ cups freekeh, soaked
• 2 medium onions, diced
• ¼ tsp ground cinnamon
• ¼ tsp ground allspice
• ¼ tsp ground nutmeg
• 5 cups chicken stock
• ⅓ cup walnuts, chopped
• Salt and black pepper to taste
• ½ cup Greek yogurt
• 1 ½ tsp lemon juice
• ½ tsp garlic powder
• 1 tbsp dried cranberries

Directions:
1. Warm the olive oil in a large skillet over medium heat and sauté the onions and cook until fragrant. Add the freekeh, cinnamon, nutmeg, and allspice. Stir for 1 minute. Pour in the stock, cranberries, and walnuts and season with salt and pepper. Bring to a simmer. Cover and reduce the heat to low.
2. Simmer for 15 minutes until the freekeh is tender. Remove from the heat and leave to sit for 5 minutes. In a small bowl, mix the yogurt, lemon juice, and garlic powder. Add the yogurt mixture to the freekeh and serve immediately.

Nutrition Info:

• Per Serving: Calories: 650;Fat: 25g;Protein: 12g;Carbs: 91g.

Lebanese Flavor Broken Thin Noodles

Servings:6 | Cooking Time: 25 Minutes

Ingredients:
• 1 tablespoon extra-virgin olive oil
• 1 cup vermicelli, broken into 1- to 1½-inch pieces
• 3 cups shredded cabbage
• 1 cup brown rice
• 3 cups low-sodium vegetable soup
• ½ cup water
• 2 garlic cloves, mashed
• ¼ teaspoon sea salt
• ⅛ teaspoon crushed red pepper flakes
• ½ cup coarsely chopped cilantro
• Fresh lemon slices, for serving

Directions:
1. Heat the olive oil in a saucepan over medium-high heat until shimmering.
2. Add the vermicelli and sauté for 3 minutes or until toasted.
3. Add the cabbage and sauté for 4 minutes or until tender.
4. Pour in the brown rice, vegetable soup, and water. Add the garlic and sprinkle with salt and red pepper flakes.
5. Bring to a boil over high heat. Reduce the heat to medium low. Put the lid on and simmer for another 10 minutes.
6. Turn off the heat, then let sit for 5 minutes without opening the lid.
7. Pour them on a large serving platter and spread with cilantro. Squeeze the lemon slices over and serve warm.

Nutrition Info:
• Per Serving: Calories: 127;Fat: 3.1g;Protein: 4.2g;Carbs: 22.9g.

Carrot & Caper Chickpeas

Servings:4 | Cooking Time:35 Minutes

Ingredients:
• 3 tbsp olive oil
• 3 tbsp capers, drained
• 1 lemon, juiced and zested
• 1 red onion, chopped
• 14 oz canned chickpeas
• 4 carrots, peeled and cubed
• 1 tbsp parsley, chopped
• Salt and black pepper to taste

Directions:
1. Warm the olive oil in a skillet over medium heat and cook onion, lemon zest, lemon juice, and capers for 5 minutes. Stir in chickpeas, carrots, parsley, salt, and pepper and cook for another 20 minutes. Serve and enjoy!

Nutrition Info:
• Per Serving: Calories: 210;Fat: 5g;Protein: 4g;Carbs: 7g.

Genovese Mussel Linguine

Servings:4 | Cooking Time:40 Minutes

Ingredients:
• 1 lb mussels, scrubbed and debearded
• 1 tbsp olive oil
• ½ cup Pinot Grigio wine
• 2 garlic cloves, minced
• ½ tsp red pepper flakes
• ½ lemon, zested and juiced
• 1 lb linguine
• Salt and black pepper to taste
• 2 tbsp parsley, finely chopped

Directions:
1. In a saucepan, bring mussels and wine to a boil, cover, and cook, shaking pan occasionally, until mussels open, 5-7 minutes. As they open, remove them with a slotted spoon into a bowl. Discard all closed mussels. Drain steaming liquid through fine-mesh strainer into a bowl, avoiding any gritty sediment that has settled

on the bottom of the pan.

2. Wipe the pan clean. Warm the olive oil in the pan and stir-fry garlic and pepper flake until the garlic turn golden, 3 minutes. Stir in reserved mussel liquid and lemon zest and juice, bring to a simmer and cook for 3-4 minutes. Stir in mussels and cook until heated through, 3 minutes.

3. Bring a large pot filled with salted water to a boil. Add pasta and cook until al dente. Reserve ½ cup of cooking liquid, drain pasta and return it to pot. Add the sauce and parsley and toss to combine and season to taste. Adjust consistency with the reserved cooking liquid as needed and serve.

Nutrition Info:
• Per Serving: Calories: 423;Fat: 9g;Protein: 16g;Carbs: 37g.

Authentic Fava Bean & Garbanzo Fül

Servings:6 | Cooking Time:20 Minutes

Ingredients:
• 3 tbsp extra-virgin olive oil
• 1 can garbanzo beans
• 1 can fava beans
• ½ tsp lemon zest
• ½ tsp dried oregano
• ½ cup lemon juice
• 3 cloves garlic, minced
• Salt to taste

Directions:
1. Place the garbanzo beans, fava beans, and 3 cups of water in a pot over medium heat. Cook for 10 minutes. Drain the beans Reserving 1 cup of the liquid, and put them in a bowl. Mix the reserved liquid, lemon juice, lemon zest, oregano, minced garlic, and salt together and add to the beans in the bowl. With a potato masher, mash up about half the beans in the bowl. Stir the mixture to combine. Drizzle the olive oil over the top. Serve with pita bread if desired.

Nutrition Info:
• Per Serving: Calories: 199;Fat: 9g;Protein: 10g;Carbs: 25g.

Turkish Canned Pinto Bean Salad

Servings:4 | Cooking Time: 3 Minutes

Ingredients:
• ¼ cup extra-virgin olive oil, divided
• 3 garlic cloves, lightly crushed and peeled
• 2 cans pinto beans, rinsed
• 2 cups plus 1 tablespoon water
• Salt and pepper, to taste
• ¼ cup tahini
• 3 tablespoons lemon juice
• 1 tablespoon ground dried
Aleppo pepper, plus extra for serving
• 8 ounces cherry tomatoes, halved
• ¼ red onion, sliced thinly
• ½ cup fresh parsley leaves
• 2 hard-cooked large eggs, quartered
• 1 tablespoon toasted sesame seeds

Directions:
1. Add 1 tablespoon of the olive oil and garlic to a medium saucepan over medium heat. Cook for about 3 minutes, stirring constantly, or until the garlic turns golden but not brown.

2. Add the beans, 2 cups of the water and 1 teaspoon salt and bring to a simmer. Remove from the heat, cover and let sit for 20 minutes. Drain the beans and discard the garlic.

3. In a large bowl, whisk together the remaining 3 tablespoons of the oil, tahini, lemon juice, Aleppo, the remaining 1 tablespoon of the water and ¼ teaspoon salt. Stir in the beans, tomatoes, onion and parsley. Season with salt and pepper to taste.

4. Transfer to a serving platter and top with the eggs. Sprinkle with the sesame seeds and extra Aleppo before serving.

Nutrition Info:
• Per Serving: Calories: 402;Fat: 18.9g;Protein: 16.2g;Carbs: 44.4g.

Lemony Farro And Avocado Bowl

Servings:4 | Cooking Time: 25 Minutes

Ingredients:
• 1 tablespoon plus 2 teaspoons extra-virgin olive oil, divided
• ½ medium onion, chopped
• 1 carrot, shredded
• 2 garlic cloves, minced
• 1 cup pearled farro
• 2 cups low-sodium vegetable
soup
• 2 avocados, peeled, pitted, and sliced
• Zest and juice of 1 small lemon
• ¼ teaspoon sea salt

Directions:
1. Heat 1 tablespoon of olive oil in a saucepan over medium-high heat until shimmering.
2. Add the onion and sauté for 5 minutes or until translucent.
3. Add the carrot and garlic and sauté for 1 minute or until fragrant.
4. Add the farro and pour in the vegetable soup. Bring to a boil over high heat. Reduce the heat to low. Put the lid on and simmer for 20 minutes or until the farro is al dente.
5. Transfer the farro in a large serving bowl, then fold in the avocado slices. Sprinkle with lemon zest and salt, then drizzle with lemon juice and 2 teaspoons of olive oil.
6. Stir to mix well and serve immediately.

Nutrition Info:
• Per Serving: Calories: 210;Fat: 11.1g;Protein: 4.2g;Carbs: 27.9g.

Classic Falafel

Servings:6 | Cooking Time:20 Minutes

Ingredients:
• 2 cups olive oil
• Salt and black pepper to taste
• 1 cup chickpeas, soaked
• 5 scallions, chopped
• ¼ cup fresh parsley leaves
• ¼ cup fresh cilantro leaves
• ¼ cup fresh dill
• 6 garlic cloves, minced
• ½ tsp ground cumin
• ½ tsp ground coriander

Directions:
1. Pat dry chickpeas with paper towels and place them in your food processor. Add in scallions, parsley, cilantro, dill, garlic, salt, pepper, cumin, and ground coriander and pulse, scraping down sides of the bowl as needed. Shape the chickpea mixture into 2-tablespoon-size disks, about 1 ½ inches wide and 1 inch thick, and place on a parchment paper–lined baking sheet.
2. Warm the olive oil in a skillet over medium heat. Fry the falafel until deep golden brown, 2-3 minutes per side. With a slotted spoon, transfer falafel to a paper towel-lined plate to drain. Serve hot.

Nutrition Info:
• Per Serving: Calories: 349;Fat: 26.3g;Protein: 19g;Carbs: 9g.

Bean And Veggie Pasta

Servings:2 | Cooking Time: 15 Minutes

Ingredients:

- 16 ounces small whole wheat pasta, such as penne, farfalle, or macaroni
- 5 cups water
- 1 can cannellini beans, drained and rinsed
- 1 can diced (with juice) or crushed tomatoes
- 1 yellow onion, chopped
- 1 red or yellow bell pepper, chopped
- 2 tablespoons tomato paste
- 1 tablespoon olive oil
- 3 garlic cloves, minced
- ¼ teaspoon crushed red pepper (optional)
- 1 bunch kale, stemmed and chopped
- 1 cup sliced basil
- ½ cup pitted Kalamata olives, chopped

Directions:

1. Add the pasta, water, beans, tomatoes (with juice if using diced), onion, bell pepper, tomato paste, oil, garlic, and crushed red pepper (if desired), to a large stockpot or deep skillet with a lid. Bring to a boil over high heat, stirring often.
2. Reduce the heat to medium-high, add the kale, and cook, continuing to stir often, until the pasta is al dente, about 10 minutes.
3. Remove from the heat and let sit for 5 minutes. Garnish with the basil and olives and serve.

Nutrition Info:

- Per Serving: Calories: 565;Fat: 17.7g;Protein: 18.0g;Carbs: 85.5g.

Portuguese Thyme & Mushroom Millet

Servings:6 | Cooking Time:35 Minutes

Ingredients:

- 10 oz cremini mushrooms, chopped
- 3 tbsp olive oil
- 1 ½ cups millet
- Salt and black pepper to taste
- 1 shallot, minced
- ½ tsp dried thyme
- 3 tbsp dry sherry
- 3 tbsp parsley, minced
- 1 ½ tsp Port wine

Directions:

1. In a large pot, bring 4 quarts of water to a boil. Add millet and a pinch of salt, return to a boil and cook until tender, 15-20 minutes. Drain millet and cover to keep warm.
2. Warm 2 tablespoons of oil in a large skillet over medium heat. Add mushrooms, shallot, thyme, and salt and stir occasionally, until moisture has evaporated and vegetables start to brown, 10 minutes. Stir in wine, scraping off any browned bits from the bottom until the skillet is almost dry. Add the remaining oil and farro and keep stirring for 2 minutes. Stir in parsley and wine. Season with salt and pepper and serve.

Nutrition Info:

- Per Serving: Calories: 323;Fat: 18g;Protein: 10g;Carbs: 27g.

Broccoli And Carrot Pasta Salad

Servings:2 | Cooking Time: 10 Minutes

Ingredients:

- 8 ounces whole-wheat pasta
- 2 cups broccoli florets
- 1 cup peeled and shredded carrots
- ¼ cup plain Greek yogurt
- Juice of 1 lemon
- 1 teaspoon red pepper flakes
- Sea salt and freshly ground pepper, to taste

Directions:

1. Bring a large pot of lightly salted water to a boil. Add the pasta

to the boiling water and cook until al dente. Drain and let rest for a few minutes.
2. When cooled, combine the pasta with the veggies, yogurt, lemon juice, and red pepper flakes in a large bowl, and stir thoroughly to combine.
3. Taste and season to taste with salt and pepper. Serve immediately.

Nutrition Info:

- Per Serving: Calories: 428;Fat: 2.9g;Protein: 15.9g;Carbs: 84.6g.

Greek-style Chickpea Salad

Servings:6 | Cooking Time:15 Minutes

Ingredients:

- ¼ cup extra-virgin olive oil
- 2 cans chickpeas
- 1 cucumber, sliced
- 2 tbsp lemon juice
- Salt and black pepper to taste
- 2 tomatoes, chopped
- 1 cup baby arugula
- 12 Kalamata olives, chopped

Directions:

1. Whish the olive oil, lemon juice, salt, and pepperin a salad bowl. Add the tomatoes, cucumber, arugula, and olives and toss to combine. Serve immediately or refrigerate in an airtight glass container for up to 1 day.

Nutrition Info:

- Per Serving: Calories: 222;Fat: 12.7g;Protein: 6g;Carbs: 22g.

Mushroom & Green Onion Rice Pilaf

Servings:4 | Cooking Time:30 Minutes

Ingredients:

- 2 tbsp olive oil
- 1 cup rice, rinsed
- 2 greens onions, chopped
- 2 cups chicken stock
- 1 cup mushrooms, sliced
- 1 garlic clove, minced
- Salt and black pepper to taste
- ½ cup Parmesan cheese, grated
- 2 tbsp cilantro, chopped

Directions:

1. Warm the olive oil in a skillet over medium heat and cook onion, garlic, and mushrooms for 5 minutes until tender. Stir in rice, salt, and pepper for 1 minute. Pour in chicken stock and cook for 15-18 minutes. Transfer to a platter, scatter Parmesan cheese all over, and sprinkle with cilantro to serve.

Nutrition Info:

- Per Serving: Calories: 250;Fat: 10g;Protein: 13g;Carbs: 28g.

Israeli Style Eggplant And Chickpea Salad

Servings:6 | Cooking Time: 20 Minutes

Ingredients:

- 2 tablespoons balsamic vinegar
- 2 tablespoons freshly squeezed lemon juice
- 1 teaspoon ground cumin
- ¼ teaspoon sea salt
- 2 tablespoons olive oil, divided
- 1 medium globe eggplant,
- stem removed, cut into flat cubes (about ½ inch thick)
- 1 can chickpeas, drained and rinsed
- ¼ cup chopped mint leaves
- 1 cup sliced sweet onion
- 1 garlic clove, finely minced
- 1 tablespoon sesame seeds, toasted

Directions:

1. Preheat the oven to 550ºF or the highest level of your oven or broiler. Grease a baking sheet with 1 tablespoon of olive oil.
2. Combine the balsamic vinegar, lemon juice, cumin, salt, and 1

tablespoon of olive oil in a small bowl. Stir to mix well.

3. Arrange the eggplant cubes on the baking sheet, then brush with 2 tablespoons of the balsamic vinegar mixture on both sides.

4. Broil in the preheated oven for 8 minutes or until lightly browned. Flip the cubes halfway through the cooking time.

5. Meanwhile, combine the chickpeas, mint, onion, garlic, and sesame seeds in a large serving bowl. Drizzle with remaining balsamic vinegar mixture. Stir to mix well.

6. Remove the eggplant from the oven. Allow to cool for 5 minutes, then slice them into ½-inch strips on a clean work surface.

7. Add the eggplant strips in the serving bowl, then toss to combine well before serving.

Nutrition Info:
- Per Serving: Calories: 125;Fat: 2.9g;Protein: 5.2g;Carbs: 20.9g.

Power Green Barley Pilaf

Servings:6 | Cooking Time:25 Minutes

Ingredients:
- 3 tbsp olive oil
- 1 small onion, chopped fine
- Salt and black pepper to taste
- 1 ½ cups pearl barley, rinsed
- 2 garlic cloves, minced
- ½ tsp dried thyme
- 2 ½ cups water
- ¼ cup parsley, minced
- 2 tbsp cilantro, chopped
- 1 ½ tsp lemon juice

Directions:
1. Warm the olive oil in a saucepan over medium heat. Stir-fry onion for 5 minutes until soft. Stir in barley, garlic, and thyme and cook, stirring frequently, until barley is lightly toasted and fragrant, 3-4 minutes. Stir in water and bring to a simmer. Reduce heat to low, cover, and simmer until barley is tender and water is absorbed, 25-35 minutes. Lay clean dish towel underneath the lid and let pilaf sit for 10 minutes. Add parsley, cilantro, and lemon juice and fluff gently with a fork to mix. Season with salt and pepper and serve warm.

Nutrition Info:
- Per Serving: Calories: 275;Fat: 21g;Protein: 12g;Carbs: 32g.

Mozzarella & Asparagus Pasta

Servings:6 | Cooking Time:40 Minutes

Ingredients:
- 1 ½ lb asparagus, trimmed, cut into 1-inch
- 2 tbsp olive oil
- 8 oz orecchiette
- 2 cups cherry tomatoes, halved
- Salt and black pepper to taste
- 2 cups fresh mozzarella, drained and chopped
- ⅓ cup torn basil leaves
- 2 tbsp balsamic vinegar

Directions:
1. Preheat oven to 390° F. In a large pot, cook the pasta according to the directions. Drain, reserving ¼ cup of cooking water.

2. In the meantime, in a large bowl, toss in asparagus, cherry tomatoes, oil, pepper, and salt. Spread the mixture onto a rimmed baking sheet and bake for 15 minutes, stirring twice throughout cooking. Remove the veggies from the oven, and add the cooked pasta to the baking sheet. Mix with a few tbsp of pasta water to smooth the sauce and veggies. Slowly mix in the mozzarella and basil. Drizzle with the balsamic vinegar and serve in bowls.

Nutrition Info:
- Per Serving: Calories: 188;Fat: 11g;Protein: 14g;Carbs: 23g.

Hummus & Bean Lettuce Rolls

Servings:4 | Cooking Time:20 Minutes

Ingredients:
- 2 tbsp extra-virgin olive oil
- ½ cup diced red onion
- 2 chopped fresh tomatoes
- 1 tsp paprika
- ¼ tsp ground nutmeg
- Salt and black pepper to taste
- 1 can cannellini beans
- ¼ cup chopped fresh parsley
- ½ cup hummus
- 8 romaine lettuce leaves

Directions:
1. Warm the olive oil in a skillet over medium heat. Add the onion and cook for 3 minutes, stirring occasionally. Add the tomatoes and paprika and cook for 3 more minutes, stirring occasionally. Add the beans and cook for 3 more minutes, stirring occasionally. Remove from the heat and sprinkle with salt, pepper, cumin, nutmeg, and parsley. Stir well.

2. Spread the hummus on the lettuce leaves. Spoon the warm bean mixture down the center of each leaf. Fold one side of the lettuce leaf over the filling lengthwise, then fold over the other side to make a wrap and serve.

Nutrition Info:
- Per Serving: Calories: 188;Fat: 5g;Protein: 10g;Carbs: 28g.

Eggplant & Chickpea Casserole

Servings:6 | Cooking Time:75 Minutes

Ingredients:
- ¼ cup olive oil
- 2 onions, chopped
- 1 green bell pepper, chopped
- Salt and black pepper to taste
- 3 garlic cloves, minced
- 1 tsp dried oregano
- ½ tsp ground cumin
- 1 lb eggplants, cubed
- 1 can tomatoes, diced
- 2 cans chickpeas

Directions:
1. Preheat oven to 400° F. Warm the olive oil in a skillet over medium heat. Add the onions, bell pepper, salt, and pepper.

2. Cook for about 5 minutes until softened. Stir in garlic, oregano, and cumin for about 30 seconds until fragrant. Transfer to a baking dish and add the eggplants, tomatoes, and chickpeas and stir. Place in the oven and bake for 45-60 minutes, shaking the dish twice during cooking. Serve.

Nutrition Info:
- Per Serving: Calories: 260;Fat: 12g;Protein: 8g;Carbs: 33.4g.

Black-eyed Pea And Vegetable Stew

Servings:2 | Cooking Time: 40 Minutes

Ingredients:
- ½ cup black-eyed peas, soaked in water overnight
- 3 cups water, plus more as needed
- 1 large carrot, peeled and cut into ½-inch pieces (about ¾ cup)
- 1 large beet, peeled and cut into ½-inch pieces (about ¾ cup)
- ¼ teaspoon turmeric
- ¼ teaspoon cayenne pepper
- ¼ teaspoon ground cumin seeds, toasted
- ¼ cup finely chopped parsley
- ¼ teaspoon salt (optional)
- ½ teaspoon fresh lime juice

Directions:
1. Pour the black-eyed peas and water into a large pot, then cook over medium heat for 25 minutes.

2. Add the carrot and beet to the pot and cook for 10 minutes more, adding more water as needed.

3. Add the turmeric, cayenne pepper, cumin, and parsley to the

pot and cook for another 6 minutes, or until the vegetables are softened. Stir the mixture periodically. Season with salt, if desired.

4. Serve drizzled with the fresh lime juice.

Nutrition Info:
- Per Serving: Calories: 89;Fat: 0.7g;Protein: 4.1g;Carbs: 16.6g.

Bolognese Penne Bake

Servings:6 | Cooking Time:55 Minutes

Ingredients:
- 1 lb penne pasta
- 1 lb ground beef
- A pinch of two salt
- 1 basil-tomato sauce
- 1 lb baby spinach, washed
- 3 cups mozzarella, shredded

Directions:
1. Bring a pot of salted water to a boil, add the pasta, and cook until al dente. Reserve 1 cup of the pasta water; drain the pasta.
2. Preheat the oven to 350°F. In a skillet over medium heat, stir-fry the ground beef along with a pinch of salt until browned, 5 minutes. Stir in basil-tomato sauce and 2 cups of pasta water and let simmer for 5 minutes. Add a handful of spinach, one at a time, into the sauce, and cook for 3 minutes.
3. In a large baking dish, add the pasta and pour the sauce over it. Stir in 1 ½ cups of mozzarella cheese, cover the dish with aluminum foil and bake for 20 minutes. After 20 minutes, remove the foil, top with the remaining mozzarella, and bake for another 8-12 minutes until golden brown. Serve.

Nutrition Info:
- Per Serving: Calories: 445;Fat: 21g;Protein: 29g;Carbs: 43g.

Rosemary Barley With Walnuts

Servings:4 | Cooking Time:45 Minutes

Ingredients:
- 2 tbsp olive oil
- ½ cup diced onion
- ½ cup diced celery
- 1 carrot, peeled and diced
- 3 cups water
- 1 cup barley
- ½ tsp thyme
- ½ tsp rosemary
- ¼ cup pine nuts
- Salt and black pepper to taste

Directions:
1. Warm the olive oil in a medium saucepan over medium heat. Sauté the onion, celery, and carrot over medium heat until tender. Add the water, barley, and seasonings, and bring to a boil. Reduce the heat and simmer for 23 minutes or until tender. Stir in the pine nuts and season to taste. Serve warm.

Nutrition Info:
- Per Serving: Calories: 276;Fat: 9g;Protein: 7g;Carbs: 41g.

Mashed Beans With Cumin

Servings:4 | Cooking Time: 10 To 12 Minutes

Ingredients:
- 1 tablespoon extra-virgin olive oil, plus extra for serving
- 4 garlic cloves, minced
- 1 teaspoon ground cumin
- 2 cans fava beans
- 3 tablespoons tahini
- 2 tablespoons lemon juice, plus lemon wedges for serving
- Salt and pepper, to taste
- 1 tomato, cored and cut into ½-inch pieces
- 1 small onion, chopped finely
- 2 hard-cooked large eggs, chopped
- 2 tablespoons minced fresh parsley

Directions:
1. Add the olive oil, garlic and cumin to a medium saucepan over

medium heat. Cook for about 2 minutes, or until fragrant.
2. Stir in the beans with their liquid and tahini. Bring to a simmer and cook for 8 to 10 minutes, or until the liquid thickens slightly.
3. Turn off the heat, mash the beans to a coarse consistency with a potato masher. Stir in the lemon juice and 1 teaspoon pepper. Season with salt and pepper.
4. Transfer the mashed beans to a serving dish. Top with the tomato, onion, eggs and parsley. Drizzle with the extra olive oil.
5. Serve with the lemon wedges.

Nutrition Info:
- Per Serving: Calories: 125;Fat: 8.6g;Protein: 4.9g;Carbs: 9.1g.

Creamy Garlic Parmesan Chicken Pasta

Servings:4 | Cooking Time: 15 Minutes

Ingredients:
- 3 tablespoons extra-virgin olive oil
- 2 boneless, skinless chicken breasts, cut into thin strips
- 1 large onion, thinly sliced
- 3 tablespoons garlic, minced
- 1½ teaspoons salt
- 1 pound fettuccine pasta
- 1 cup heavy whipping cream
- ¾ cup freshly grated Parmesan cheese, divided
- ½ teaspoon freshly ground black pepper

Directions:
1. In a large skillet over medium heat, heat the olive oil. Add the chicken and cook for 3 minutes.
2. Add the onion, garlic and salt to the skillet. Cook for 7 minutes, stirring occasionally.
3. Meanwhile, bring a large pot of salted water to a boil and add the pasta, then cook for 7 minutes.
4. While the pasta is cooking, add the heavy cream, ½ cup of the Parmesan cheese and black pepper to the chicken. Simmer for 3 minutes.
5. Reserve ½ cup of the pasta water. Drain the pasta and add it to the chicken cream sauce.
6. Add the reserved pasta water to the pasta and toss together. Simmer for 2 minutes. Top with the remaining ¼ cup of the Parmesan cheese and serve warm.

Nutrition Info:
- Per Serving: Calories: 879;Fat: 42.0g;Protein: 35.0g;Carbs: 90.0g.

Baked Rolled Oat With Pears And Pecans

Servings:6 | Cooking Time: 30 Minutes

Ingredients:
- 2 tablespoons coconut oil, melted, plus more for greasing the pan
- 3 ripe pears, cored and diced
- 2 cups unsweetened almond milk
- 1 tablespoon pure vanilla extract
- ¼ cup pure maple syrup
- 2 cups gluten-free rolled oats
- ½ cup raisins
- ¾ cup chopped pecans
- ¼ teaspoon ground nutmeg
- 1 teaspoon ground cinnamon
- ½ teaspoon ground ginger
- ¼ teaspoon sea salt

Directions:
1. Preheat the oven to 350°F. Grease a baking dish with melted coconut oil, then spread the pears in a single layer on the baking dish evenly.
2. Combine the almond milk, vanilla extract, maple syrup, and coconut oil in a bowl. Stir to mix well.
3. Combine the remaining ingredients in a separate large bowl. Stir to mix well. Fold the almond milk mixture in the bowl, then

pour the mixture over the pears.

4. Place the baking dish in the preheated oven and bake for 30 minutes or until lightly browned and set.

5. Serve immediately.

Nutrition Info:
- Per Serving: Calories: 479;Fat: 34.9g;Protein: 8.8g;Carbs: 50.1g.

Lemon-basil Spaghetti

Servings:6 | Cooking Time:30 Minutes

Ingredients:
- ½ cup extra-virgin olive oil
- Zest and juice from 1 lemon
- 1 garlic clove, minced
- Salt and black pepper to taste
- 2 oz ricotta cheese, chopped
- 1 lb spaghetti
- 6 tbsp shredded fresh basil

Directions:
1. In a bowl, whisk oil, grated lemon zest, juice, garlic, salt, and pepper. Stir in ricotta cheese and mix well. Meanwhile, bring a pot filled with salted water to a boil. Cook the pasta until al dente. Reserve ½ cup of the cooking liquid, then drain pasta and return it to the pot. Add oil mixture and basil and toss to combine. Season to taste and adjust consistency with reserved cooking water as needed. Serve warm.

Nutrition Info:
- Per Serving: Calories: 395;Fat: 11g;Protein: 10g;Carbs: 37g.

Tortellini & Cannellini With Meatballs

Servings:4 | Cooking Time:30 Minutes

Ingredients:
- 2 tbsp parsley, chopped
- 12 oz fresh tortellini
- 3 tbsp olive oil
- 5 cloves garlic, minced
- ½ lb meatballs
- 1 can cannellini beans
- 1 can roasted tomatoes
- Salt and black pepper to taste

Directions:
1. Bring to a boil salted water in a pot over high heat. Add the tortellini and cook according to package directions. Drain and set aside. Warm the olive oil in a large skillet over medium heat and sauté the garlic for 1 minute. Stir in meatballs and brown for 4–5 minutes on all sides. Add the tomatoes and cannellini and continue to cook for 5 minutes or until heated through. Adjust the seasoning with salt and pepper. Stir in tortellini. Sprinkle with parsley and serve.

Nutrition Info:
- Per Serving: Calories: 578;Fat: 30g;Protein: 25g;Carbs: 58g.

Two-bean Cassoulet

Servings:4 | Cooking Time:40 Minutes

Ingredients:
- 2 tbsp olive oil
- 1 cup canned pinto beans
- 1 cup canned can kidney beans
- 2 red bell peppers, chopped
- 1 onion, chopped
- 1 celery stalk, chopped
- 2 garlic cloves, minced
- 1 can diced tomatoes
- 1 tbsp red pepper flakes
- 1 tsp ground cumin
- Salt and black pepper to taste
- ¼ tsp ground coriander

Directions:
1. Warm olive oil in a pot over medium heat and sauté bell peppers, celery, garlic, and onion for 5 minutes until tender. Stir in ground cumin, ground coriander, salt, and pepper for 1 minute. Pour in beans, tomatoes, and red pepper flakes. Bring to a boil, then decrease the heat and simmer for another 20 minutes. Serve immediately.

Nutrition Info:
- Per Serving: Calories: 361;Fat: 8.4g;Protein: 17g;Carbs: 56g.

Tomato Bean & Sausage Casserole

Servings:4 | Cooking Time:45 Minutes

Ingredients:
- 2 tbsp olive oil
- 1 lb Italian sausages
- 1 can cannellini beans
- 1 carrot, chopped
- 1 onion, chopped
- 2 garlic cloves, minced
- 1 tsp paprika
- 1 can tomatoes, diced
- 1 celery stalk, chopped
- Salt and black pepper to taste

Directions:
1. Preheat oven to 350° F. Warm olive oil in a pot over medium heat. Sauté onion, garlic, celery, and carrot for 3-4 minutes, stirring often until softened. Add in sausages and cook for another 3 minutes, turning occasionally. Stir in paprika for 30 seconds. Heat off. Mix in tomatoes, beans, salt, and pepper. Pour into a baking dish and bake for 30 minutes.

Nutrition Info:
- Per Serving: Calories: 862;Fat: 44g;Protein: 43g;Carbs: 76g.

Chapter 5 Poultry And Meats Recipes

Chapter 5 Poultry And Meats Recipes

Smooth Chicken Breasts With Nuts

Servings:4 | Cooking Time:40 Minutes

Ingredients:
- 2 tbsp olive oil
- 1 ½ lb chicken breasts, cubed
- 4 spring onions, chopped
- 2 carrots, peeled and sliced
- ¼ cup mayonnaise
- ½ cup Greek yogurt
- 1 cup toasted cashews, chopped
- Salt and black pepper to taste

Directions:
1. Warm the olive oil in a skillet over medium heat and brown chicken for 8 minutes on all sides. Stir in spring onions, carrots, mayonnaise, yogurt, salt, and pepper and bring to a simmer. Cook for 20 minutes. Top with cashews to serve.

Nutrition Info:
- Per Serving: Calories: 310;Fat: 15g;Protein: 16g;Carbs: 20g.

Chermoula Roasted Pork Tenderloin

Servings:2 | Cooking Time: 20 Minutes

Ingredients:
- ½ cup fresh cilantro
- ½ cup fresh parsley
- 6 small garlic cloves
- 3 tablespoons olive oil, divided
- 3 tablespoons freshly squeezed lemon juice
- 2 teaspoons cumin
- 1 teaspoon smoked paprika
- ½ teaspoon salt, divided
- Pinch freshly ground black pepper
- 1 pork tenderloin

Directions:
1. Preheat the oven to 425ºF.
2. In a food processor, combine the cilantro, parsley, garlic, 2 tablespoons of olive oil, lemon juice, cumin, paprika, and ¼ teaspoon of salt. Pulse 15 to 20 times, or until the mixture is fairly smooth. Scrape the sides down as needed to incorporate all the ingredients. Transfer the sauce to a small bowl and set aside.
3. Season the pork tenderloin on all sides with the remaining ¼ teaspoon of salt and a generous pinch of black pepper.
4. Heat the remaining 1 tablespoon of olive oil in a sauté pan.
5. Sear the pork for 3 minutes, turning often, until golden brown on all sides.
6. Transfer the pork to a baking dish and roast in the preheated oven for 15 minutes, or until the internal temperature registers 145ºF.
7. Cool for 5 minutes before serving.

Nutrition Info:
- Per Serving: Calories: 169;Fat: 13.1g;Protein: 11.0g;Carbs: 2.9g.

Homemade Pizza Burgers

Servings:4 | Cooking Time:20 Minutes

Ingredients:
- ¼ tsp mustard powder
- ¼ tsp cumin
- 1 ¼ lb ground beef
- ½ tsp garlic salt
- ¼ tsp red pepper flakes
- ½ tsp Italian seasoning
- 1 cup passata
- 8 mozzarella cheese slices

Directions:
1. Preheat your grill to medium. In a large bowl, lightly mix with your hands the ground beef, mustard powder, cumin, garlic salt, pepper flakes, and Italian seasoning. Shape the mixture into 4 patties. Grill the burgers for about 10 minutes, turning them occasionally to ensure even cooking. In the last 2 minutes of cooking, top each burger with a generous tablespoon of passata and 2 slices of cheese per burger. Remove and let sit for 1–2 minutes before serving.

Nutrition Info:
- Per Serving: Calories: 556;Fat: 39g;Protein: 41g;Carbs: 8g.

Exotic Pork Chops

Servings:4 | Cooking Time:35 Minutes

Ingredients:
- 2 tbsp olive oil
- 2 cups chicken stock
- 2 garlic cloves, minced
- 4 pork loin chops, boneless
- 2 spring onions, chopped
- 2 mangos, peeled and cubed
- 1 tsp sweet paprika
- Salt and black pepper to taste
- ½ tsp dried oregano

Directions:
1. Warm the olive oil in a skillet over medium heat and sear pork chops for 4 minutes on both sides. Put in onions and garlic and cook for another 3 minutes. Stir in mangos, paprika, salt, pepper, oregano, and chicken stock and cook for 15 minutes, stirring often. Serve immediately.

Nutrition Info:
- Per Serving: Calories: 310;Fat: 15g;Protein: 25g;Carbs: 13g.

Pork Chops In Tomato Olive Sauce

Servings:4 | Cooking Time:20 Minutes

Ingredients:
- 2 tbsp olive oil
- 4 pork loin chops, boneless
- 6 tomatoes, crushed
- 3 tbsp basil, chopped
- 10 black olives, halved
- 1 yellow onion, chopped
- 1 garlic clove, minced

Directions:
1. Warm the olive oil in a skillet over medium heat and brown pork chops for 6 minutes on all sides. Share into plates. In the same skillet, stir tomatoes, basil, olives, onion, and garlic and simmer for 4 minutes. Drizzle tomato sauce over.

Nutrition Info:
- Per Serving: Calories: 340;Fat: 18g;Protein: 35g;Carbs: 13g.

Vegetable Pork Loin

Servings:4 | Cooking Time:30 Minutes

Ingredients:
- 2 tbsp canola oil
- 2 carrots, chopped
- 2 garlic cloves, minced
- 1 lb pork loin, cubed
- 4 oz snow peas
- ¾ cup beef stock
- 1 onion, chopped
- Salt and white pepper to taste

Directions:
1. Warm the oil in a skillet over medium heat and sear pork for 5 minutes. Stir in snow peas, carrots, garlic, stock, onion, salt, and pepper and bring to a boil; cook for 15 minutes.

Nutrition Info:
• Per Serving: Calories: 340;Fat: 18g;Protein: 28g;Carbs: 21g.

Baked Beef With Kale Slaw & Bell Peppers

Servings:4 | Cooking Time:35 Minutes

Ingredients:
• 2 tsp olive oil
• 1 lb skirt steak
• 4 cups kale slaw
• 1 tbsp garlic powder
• Salt and black pepper to taste
• 1 small red onion, sliced
• 10 sundried tomatoes, halved
• ½ red bell pepper, sliced

Directions:
1. Preheat the broiler. Brush steak with olive oil, salt, garlic powder, and pepper and place under the broiler for 10 minutes, turning once. Remove to a cutting board and let rest for 10 minutes, then cut the steak diagonally.
2. In the meantime, place sun-dried tomatoes, kale slaw, onion, and bell pepper in a bowl and mix to combine. Transfer to a serving plate and top with steak slices to serve.

Nutrition Info:
• Per Serving: Calories: 359;Fat: 16g;Protein: 38g;Carbs: 22g.

Chili Beef Stew

Servings:4 | Cooking Time:35 Minutes

Ingredients:
• 2 tbsp olive oil
• 1 lb beef stew, ground
• Salt and black pepper to taste
• 1 onion, chopped
• 2 garlic cloves, minced
• 1 tbsp chili paste
• 2 tbsp balsamic vinegar
• ¼ cup chicken stock
• ¼ cup mint, chopped

Directions:
1. Warm the olive oil in a skillet over medium heat and cook onion for 3 minutes. Put in beef stew and cook for another 3 minutes. Stir in salt, pepper, garlic, chili paste, vinegar, stock, and mint and cook for an additional 20-25 minutes.

Nutrition Info:
• Per Serving: Calories: 310;Fat: 14g;Protein: 20g;Carbs: 16g.

Roasted Herby Chicken

Servings:4 | Cooking Time:80 Minutes

Ingredients:
• 2 tbsp butter, melted
• 1 chicken
• 2 lemons, halved
• 4 rosemary sprigs
• 1 bay leaf
• 6 thyme sprigs
• 1 tsp lemon juice
• Salt and black pepper to taste

Directions:
1. Preheat oven to 420° F and fit a rack into a roasting tray. Brush the chicken with butter on all sides. Put the lemons, herbs, and bay leaf inside the cavity. Drizzle with lemon juice and sprinkle with salt and pepper. Roast for 60-65 minutes. Let rest for 10 minutes before carving.

Nutrition Info:
• Per Serving: Calories: 235;Fat: 7g;Protein: 32g;Carbs: 2g.

Herby Turkey Stew

Servings:4 | Cooking Time:60 Minutes

Ingredients:
• 1 skinless, boneless turkey breast, cubed
• 2 tbsp olive oil
• Salt and black pepper to taste

• 1 tbsp sweet paprika
• ½ cup chicken stock
• 1 lb pearl onions
• 2 garlic cloves, minced
• 1 carrot, sliced
• 1 tsp cumin, ground
• 1 tbsp basil, chopped
• 1 tbsp cilantro, chopped

Directions:
1. Warm the olive oil in a pot over medium heat and sear turkey for 8 minutes, stirring occasionally. Stir in pearl onions, carrot, and garlic and cook for another 3 minutes. Season with salt, pepper, cumin, and paprika. Pour in the stock and bring to a boil; cook for 40 minutes. Top with basil and cilantro.

Nutrition Info:
• Per Serving: Calories: 260;Fat: 12g;Protein: 19g;Carbs: 24g.

Cilantro Turkey Penne With Asparagus

Servings:4 | Cooking Time:40 Minutes

Ingredients:
• 3 tbsp olive oil
• 16 oz penne pasta
• 1 lb turkey breast strips
• 1 lb asparagus, chopped
• 1 tsp basil, chopped
• Salt and black pepper to taste
• ½ cup tomato sauce
• 2 tbsp cilantro, chopped

Directions:
1. Bring to a boil salted water in a pot over medium heat and cook penne until "al dente", 8-10 minutes. Drain and set aside; reserve 1 cup of the cooking water.
2. Warm the olive oil in a skillet over medium heat and sear turkey for 4 minutes, stirring periodically. Add in asparagus and sauté for 3-4 more minutes. Pour in the tomato sauce and reserved pasta liquid and bring to a boil; simmer for 20 minutes. Stir in cooked penne, season with salt and pepper, and top with the basil and cilantro to serve.

Nutrition Info:
• Per Serving: Calories: 350;Fat: 22g;Protein: 19g;Carbs: 23g.

Mushroom & Sausage With Orecchiette

Servings:2 | Cooking Time:30 Minutes

Ingredients:
• ½ cup cremini mushrooms, sliced
• 1 tbsp olive oil
• ½ medium onion, diced
• 2 garlic cloves, minced
• 4 oz Italian sausage
• ½ tsp Italian seasoning
• 8 oz dry orecchiette pasta
• 2 cups chicken stock
• 1 cup baby spinach
• ¼ cup heavy cream
• 1 tbsp basil, chopped

Directions:
1. Warm the olive oil in a pan over medium heat. Add the onion, garlic, and mushrooms and sauté for 5 minutes until tender. Remove the sausage from its casing and add it to the pan, breaking it up well. Stir-fry for 5 more minutes or until the sausage is no longer pink. Season with Italian seasoning and add the pasta and chicken stock; bring the mixture to a boil. Lower the heat to medium-low and t simmer for 9-11 minutes or until the pasta is cooked. Remove from the heat. Add the spinach and stir until it wilts, 3 minutes. Stir in the heavy cream. Serve topped with basil, and enjoy!

Nutrition Info:
• Per Serving: Calories: 531;Fat: 19g;Protein: 23g;Carbs: 69g.

Cream Zucchini & Chicken Dish

Servings:4 | Cooking Time:70 Minutes

Ingredients:
- 3 tbsp canola oil
- 1 lb turkey breast, sliced
- Salt and black pepper to taste
- 3 garlic cloves, minced
- 2 zucchinis, sliced
- 1 cup chicken stock
- ¼ cup heavy cream
- 2 tbsp parsley, chopped

Directions:
1. Warm the olive oil in a pot over medium heat. Cook the turkey for 10 minutes on both sides. Put in garlic and cook for 1 minute. Season with salt and pepper. Stir in zucchinis for 3-4 minutes and pour in the chicken stock. Bring to a boil and cook for 40 minutes. Stir in heavy cream and parsley.

Nutrition Info:
- Per Serving: Calories: 270;Fat: 11g;Protein: 16g;Carbs: 27g.

Parsley-dijon Chicken And Potatoes

Servings:6 | Cooking Time: 22 Minutes

Ingredients:
- 1 tablespoon extra-virgin olive oil
- 1½ pounds boneless, skinless chicken thighs, cut into 1-inch cubes, patted dry
- 1½ pounds Yukon Gold potatoes, unpeeled, cut into ½-inch cubes
- 2 garlic cloves, minced
- ¼ cup dry white wine
- 1 cup low-sodium or no-salt-added chicken broth
- 1 tablespoon Dijon mustard
- ¼ teaspoon freshly ground black pepper
- ¼ teaspoon kosher or sea salt
- 1 cup chopped fresh flat-leaf (Italian) parsley, including stems
- 1 tablespoon freshly squeezed lemon juice

Directions:
1. In a large skillet over medium-high heat, heat the oil. Add the chicken and cook for 5 minutes, stirring only after the chicken has browned on one side. Remove the chicken and reserve on a plate.
2. Add the potatoes to the skillet and cook for 5 minutes, stirring only after the potatoes have become golden and crispy on one side. Push the potatoes to the side of the skillet, add the garlic, and cook, stirring constantly, for 1 minute. Add the wine and cook for 1 minute, until nearly evaporated. Add the chicken broth, mustard, salt, pepper, and reserved chicken. Turn the heat to high and bring to a boil.
3. Once boiling, cover, reduce the heat to medium-low, and cook for 10 to 12 minutes, until the potatoes are tender and the internal temperature of the chicken measures 165ºF on a meat thermometer and any juices run clear.
4. During the last minute of cooking, stir in the parsley. Remove from the heat, stir in the lemon juice, and serve.

Nutrition Info:
- Per Serving: Calories: 324;Fat: 9.0g;Protein: 16.0g;Carbs: 45.0g.

Baked Teriyaki Turkey Meatballs

Servings:6 | Cooking Time: 20 Minutes

Ingredients:
- 1 pound lean ground turkey
- 1 egg, whisked
- ¼ cup finely chopped scallions, both white and green parts
- 2 garlic cloves, minced
- 2 tablespoons reduced-sodium tamari or gluten-free soy sauce
- 1 teaspoon grated fresh gin-ger
- 1 tablespoon honey
- 2 teaspoons mirin
- 1 teaspoon olive oil

Directions:
1. Preheat the oven to 400ºF. Line a baking sheet with parchment paper and set aside.
2. Mix together the ground turkey, whisked egg, scallions, garlic, tamari, ginger, honey, mirin, and olive oil in a large bowl, and stir until well blended.
3. Using a tablespoon to scoop out rounded heaps of the turkey mixture, and then roll them into balls with your hands. Transfer the balls to the prepared baking sheet.
4. Bake in the preheated oven for 20 minutes, flipping the balls with a spatula halfway through, or until the meatballs are browned and cooked through.
5. Serve warm.

Nutrition Info:
- Per Serving: Calories: 158;Fat: 8.6g;Protein: 16.2g;Carbs: 4.0g.

Roasted Pork Tenderloin With Apple Sauce

Servings:4 | Cooking Time:35 Minutes

Ingredients:
- 2 tbsp olive oil
- 1 lb pork tenderloin
- Salt and black pepper to taste
- ¼ cup apple jelly
- ¼ cup apple juice
- 2 tbsp wholegrain mustard
- 3 sprigs fresh thyme
- ½ tbsp cornstarch
- ½ tbsp heavy cream

Directions:
1. Preheat oven to 330° F. Warm the oil in a skillet over medium heat. Season the pork with salt and pepper. Sear it for 6-8 minutes on all sides. Transfer to a baking sheet. To the same skillet, add the apple jelly, juice, and mustard and stir for 5 minutes over low heat, stirring often. Top with the pork and thyme sprigs. Place the skillet in the oven and bake for 15-18 minutes, brushing the pork with the apple-mustard sauce every 5 minutes. Remove the pork and let it rest for 15 minutes. Place a small pot over low heat. Blend the cornstarch with heavy cream and cooking juices and pour the mixture into the pot. Stir for 2 minutes until thickens. Drizzle the sauce over the pork. Serve sliced and enjoy!

Nutrition Info:
- Per Serving: Calories: 146;Fat: 7g;Protein: 13g;Carbs: 8g.

Chicken Thighs With Roasted Artichokes

Servings:4 | Cooking Time:25 Minutes

Ingredients:
- 2 artichoke hearts, halved lengthwise
- 2 tbsp butter, melted
- 3 tbsp olive oil
- 2 lemons, zested and juiced
- ½ tsp salt
- 4 chicken thighs

Directions:
1. Preheat oven to 450° F. Place a large, rimmed baking sheet in the oven. Whisk the olive oil, lemon zest, and lemon juice in a bowl. Add the artichoke hearts and turn them to coat on all sides. Lay the artichoke halves flat-side down in the center of 4 aluminum foil sheets and close up loosely to create packets. Put the chicken in the remaining lemon mixture and toss to coat. Carefully remove the hot baking sheet from the oven and pour on the butter; tilt the pan to coat.
2. Arrange the chicken thighs, skin-side down, on the sheet, add the artichoke packets. Roast for about 20 minutes or until the chicken is cooked through and the skin is slightly charred. Check

the artichokes for doneness and bake for another 5 minutes if needed. Serve and enjoy!

Nutrition Info:
- Per Serving: Calories: 832;Fat: 80g;Protein: 19g;Carbs: 11g.

Provençal Flank Steak Au Pistou
Servings:4 | Cooking Time:25 Minutes

Ingredients:
- 8 tbsp olive oil
- 1 lb flank steak
- Salt and black pepper to taste
- ½ cup parsley, chopped
- ¼ cup fresh basil, chopped
- 2 garlic cloves, minced
- ½ tsp celery seeds
- 1 orange, zested and juiced
- 1 tsp red pepper flakes
- 1 tbsp red wine vinegar

Directions:
1. Place the parsley, basil, garlic, orange zest and juice, celery seeds, salt, pepper, and red pepper flakes, and pulse until finely chopped in your food processor. With the processor running, stream in the red wine vinegar and 6 tbsp of olive oil until well combined. Set aside until ready to serve.
2. Preheat your grill. Rub the steak with the remaining olive oil, salt, and pepper. Place the steak on the grill and cook for 6-8 minutes on each side. Remove and leave to sit for 10 minutes. Slice the steak and drizzle with pistou. Serve.

Nutrition Info:
- Per Serving: Calories: 441;Fat: 36g;Protein: 25g;Carbs: 3g.

Baked Root Veggie & Chicken
Servings:6 | Cooking Time:50 Minutes

Ingredients:
- 2 sweet potatoes, peeled and cubed
- ½ cup green olives, pitted and smashed
- ¼ cup olive oil
- 2 lb chicken breasts, sliced
- 2 tbsp harissa seasoning
- 1 lemon, zested and juiced
- Salt and black pepper to taste
- 2 carrots, chopped
- 1 onion, chopped
- ½ cup feta cheese, crumbled
- ½ cup parsley, chopped

Directions:
1. Preheat the oven to 390° F. Place chicken, harissa seasoning, lemon juice, lemon zest, olive oil, salt, pepper, carrots, sweet potatoes, and onion in a roasting pan and mix well. Bake for 40 minutes. Combine feta cheese and green olives in a bowl. Share chicken mixture into plates and top with olive mixture. Top with parsley and parsley and serve immediately.

Nutrition Info:
- Per Serving: Calories: 310;Fat: 10g;Protein: 15g;Carbs: 23g.

Harissa Turkey With Couscous
Servings:4 | Cooking Time:20 Min + Marinating Time

Ingredients:
- 1 lb skinless turkey breast slices
- 2 tbsp olive oil
- 1 tsp garlic powder
- ½ tsp ground coriander
- 1 tbsp harissa seasoning
- 1 cup couscous
- 2 tbsp raisins, soaked
- 2 tbsp chopped parsley
- Salt and black pepper to taste

Directions:
1. Whisk the olive oil, garlic powder, ground coriander, harissa, salt, and pepper in a bowl. Add the turkey slices and toss to coat. Marinate covered for 30 minutes. Place the couscous in a large bowl and pour 1 ½ cups of salted boiling water. Cover and leave

to sit for 5 minutes. Fluff with a fork and stir in raisins and parsley. Keep warm until ready to serve.
2. Preheat your grill to high. Place the turkey slices on the grill and cook for 3 minutes per side until cooked through with no pink showing. Serve with the couscous.

Nutrition Info:
- Per Serving: Calories: 350;Fat: 7g;Protein: 47g;Carbs: 19g.

Rich Beef Meal
Servings:4 | Cooking Time:40 Minutes

Ingredients:
- 1 tbsp olive oil
- 1 lb beef meat, cubed
- 1 red onion, chopped
- 1 garlic clove, minced
- 1 celery stalk, chopped
- Salt and black pepper to taste
- 14 oz canned tomatoes, diced
- 1 cup vegetable stock
- ½ tsp ground nutmeg
- 2 tsp dill, chopped

Directions:
1. Warm the olive oil in a skillet over medium heat and cook onion and garlic for 5 minutes. Put in beef and cook for 5 more minutes. Stir in celery, salt, pepper, tomatoes, stock, nutmeg, and dill and bring to a boil. Cook for 20 minutes.

Nutrition Info:
- Per Serving: Calories: 300;Fat: 14g;Protein: 19g;Carbs: 16g.

Easy Pork Souvlaki
Servings:6 | Cooking Time:20 Min + Marinating Time

Ingredients:
- 3 tbsp olive oil
- 1 onion, grated
- 3 garlic cloves, minced
- 1 tsp ground cumin
- Salt and black pepper to taste
- 2 tsp dried oregano
- 2 lb boneless pork butt, cubed
- 2 lemons, cut into wedges

Directions:
1. In a large bowl, whisk the olive oil, onion, garlic, cumin, salt, pepper, and oregano. Add pork and toss to coat. Cover and place in the refrigerator for at least 2 hours or overnight.
2. Preheat your grill to medium-high. Thread the pork cubes onto bamboo skewers. Place the pork on the grill and cook for about 10 minutes on all sides or until the pork is cooked through. Serve with lemon wedges.

Nutrition Info:
- Per Serving: Calories: 279;Fat: 16g;Protein: 29g;Carbs: 5g.

Rosemary Pork Chops With Cabbage Mix
Servings:4 | Cooking Time:35 Minutes

Ingredients:
- ½ green cabbage head, shredded
- 2 tsp olive oil
- 4 pork chops
- 4 bell peppers, chopped
- 1 tsp rosemary
- 2 tbsp wine vinegar
- 2 spring onions, chopped
- Salt and black pepper to taste

Directions:
1. Warm half of oil in a skillet over medium heat. Cook spring onions for 3 minutes. Stir in vinegar, cabbage, bell peppers, salt, and pepper and simmer for 10 minutes. Heat off.
2. Preheat the grill over medium heat. Sprinkle pork chops with remaining oil, salt, pepper, and rosemary and grill for 10 minutes on both sides. Share chops into plates with cabbage mixture on the side. Serve immediately.

Nutrition Info:

- Per Serving: Calories: 230;Fat: 19g;Protein: 13g;Carbs: 18g.

Paprika Chicken With Caper Dressing
Servings:4 | Cooking Time:35 Minutes

Ingredients:
- 2 tbsp canola oil
- 4 chicken breast halves
- Salt and black pepper to taste
- 1 tbsp sweet paprika
- 1 onion, chopped
- 1 tbsp balsamic vinegar
- 2 tbsp parsley, chopped
- 1 avocado, peeled and cubed
- 2 tbsp capers

Directions:
1. Preheat the grill over medium heat. Rub chicken halves with half of the canola oil, paprika, salt, and pepper and grill them for 14 minutes on both sides. Share into plates. Combine onion, remaining oil, vinegar, parsley, avocado, and capers in a bowl. Pour the sauce over the chicken and serve.

Nutrition Info:
- Per Serving: Calories: 300;Fat: 13g;Protein: 15g;Carbs: 25g.

Apricot-glazed Pork Skewers
Servings:6 | Cooking Time:50 Minutes

Ingredients:
- 2 lb pork tenderloin, cubed
- 1 cup apricot jam
- ½ cup apricot nectar
- 1 cup dried whole apricots
- 2 onions, cut into wedges
- ½ tsp dried rosemary

Directions:
1. Coat the pork cubes with apricot jam, cover, and set aside for 10-15 minutes. Bring to a boil the apricot nectar, rosemary, and dried apricots in a saucepan over medium heat. Lower the heat and simmer for 2-3 minutes. Remove the apricots with a perforated spoon and pour the hot liquid over the pork. Stir and drain the pork, reserving the marinade.
2. Preheat your grill to medium-high. Alternate pork cubes, onion wedges, and apricots onto 6 metal skewers. Brush them with some marinade and grill for 10-12 minutes, turning and brushing with some more marinade until the pork is slightly pink and onions are crisp-tender. Simmer the remaining marinade for 3-5 minutes. Serve the skewers with marinade on the side.

Nutrition Info:
- Per Serving: Calories: 393;Fat: 4g;Protein: 34g;Carbs: 59g.

Chicken & Spinach Dish
Servings:4 | Cooking Time:60 Minutes

Ingredients:
- 2 tbsp olive oil
- 2 cups baby spinach
- 1 lb chicken sausage, sliced
- 1 red bell pepper, chopped
- 1 onion, sliced
- 2 tbsp garlic, minced
- Salt and black pepper to taste
- ½ cup chicken stock
- 1 tbsp balsamic vinegar

Directions:
1. Preheat oven to 380° F. Warm olive oil in a skillet over medium heat. Cook sausages for 6 minutes on all sides. Remove to a bowl. Add the bell pepper, onion, garlic, salt, pepper to the skillet and sauté for 5 minutes. Pour in stock and vinegar and return the sausages. Bring to a boil and cook for 10 minutes. Add in the spinach and cook until wilts, about 4 minutes. Serve and enjoy!

Nutrition Info:
- Per Serving: Calories: 300;Fat: 15g;Protein: 27g;Carbs: 18g.

Smoky Turkey Bake
Servings:4 | Cooking Time:50 Minutes

Ingredients:
- 1 skinless, boneless turkey breast, roughly cubed
- 2 tbsp olive oil
- 1 shallot, sliced
- 1 tbsp smoked paprika
- 2 chili peppers, chopped
- Salt and black pepper to taste
- ½ cup chicken stock
- 1 tbsp parsley, chopped

Directions:
1. Preheat the oven to 390° F. Grease a roasting pan with oil. Toss turkey, shallot, paprika, chili peppers, salt, pepper, stock, and parsley on the pan and bake for 40 minutes. Serve.

Nutrition Info:
- Per Serving: Calories: 320;Fat: 19g;Protein: 35g;Carbs: 24g.

Mustardy Steak In Mushroom Sauce
Servings:4 | Cooking Time:30 Min + Marinating Time

Ingredients:
- For the steak
- 2 tbsp olive oil
- 1 lb beef skirt steak
- 1 cup red wine
- 2 garlic cloves, minced
- 1 tbsp Worcestershire sauce
- 1 tbsp dried thyme
- 1 tsp yellow mustard
- For the mushroom sauce
- 1 lb mushrooms, sliced
- 1 tsp dried dill
- 2 garlic cloves, minced
- 1 cup dry red wine
- Salt and black pepper to taste

Directions:
1. Combine wine, garlic, Worcestershire sauce, 2 tbsp of olive oil, thyme, and mustard in a bowl. Place in the steak, cover with plastic wrap and let it marinate for at least 3 hours in the refrigerator. Remove the steak and pat dry with paper towels.
2. Warm olive oil in a pan over medium heat and sear steak for 8 minutes on all sides; set aside. In the same pan, sauté mushrooms, dill, salt, and pepper for 6 minutes, stirring periodically. Add in garlic and sauté for 30 seconds. Pour in the wine and scrape off any bits from the bottom. Simmer for 5 minutes until the liquid reduces. Slice the steak and top with the mushroom sauce. Serve hot.

Nutrition Info:
- Per Serving: Calories: 424;Fat: 24g;Protein: 29g;Carbs: 8g.

Dragon Pork Chops With Pickle Topping
Servings:4 | Cooking Time:30 Minutes

Ingredients:
- ½ cup roasted bell peppers, chopped
- 6 dill pickles, sliced
- 1 cup dill pickle juice
- 6 pork chops, boneless
- Salt and black pepper to taste
- 1 tsp hot pepper sauce
- 1 ½ cups tomatoes, cubed
- 1 jalapeno pepper, chopped
- 10 black olives, sliced

Directions:
1. Place pork chops, hot sauce, and pickle juice in a bowl and marinate in the fridge for 15 minutes. Preheat your grill to High. Remove the chops from the fridge and grill them for 14 minutes on both sides. Combine dill pickles, tomatoes, jalapeño pepper, roasted peppers, and black olives in a bowl. Serve chops topped with the pickle mixture.

Nutrition Info:
- Per Serving: Calories: 230;Fat: 7g;Protein: 36g;Carbs: 7g.

Grilled Pork Chops With Apricot Chutney

Servings:4 | Cooking Time:40 Minutes

Ingredients:

- 1 tbsp olive oil
- ½ tsp garlic powder
- 4 pork loin chops, boneless
- Salt and black pepper to taste
- ¼ tsp ground cumin
- ½ tsp sage, dried
- 1 tsp chili powder
- For the chutney
- 3 cups apricots, peeled and
- chopped
- ½ cup red sweet pepper, chopped
- 1 tsp olive oil
- ¼ cup shallot, minced
- ½ jalapeno pepper, minced
- 1 tbsp balsamic vinegar
- 2 tbsp cilantro, chopped

Directions:

1. Warm the olive oil in a skillet over medium heat and cook the shallot for 5 minutes. Stir in sweet pepper, apricots, jalapeño pepper, vinegar, and cilantro and cook for 10 minutes. Remove from heat.
2. In the meantime, sprinkle pork chops with olive oil, salt, pepper, garlic powder, cumin, sage, and chili powder. Preheat the grill to medium heat. Grill pork chops for 12-14 minutes on both sides. Serve topped with apricot chutney.

Nutrition Info:

- Per Serving: Calories: 300;Fat: 11g;Protein: 39g;Carbs: 14g.

Chicken Sausage & Zucchini Soup

Servings:4 | Cooking Time:30 Minutes

Ingredients:

- 2 tbsp olive oil
- 2 chicken sausage, chopped
- 4 cups chicken stock
- 3 garlic cloves, minced
- 1 yellow onion, chopped
- 4 zucchinis, cubed
- 1 lemon, zested
- ½ cup basil, chopped
- Salt and black pepper to taste

Directions:

1. Warm the olive oil in a pot over medium heat and brown the sausages for 5 minutes; reserve. Add zucchini, onion, and garlic to the pot and sauté for 5 minutes. Add in the chicken stock, lemon zest, salt, and pepper and bring to a boil. Simmer for 10 minutes. Return the sausages and cook for another 5 minutes. Top with basil and serve right away.

Nutrition Info:

- Per Serving: Calories: 280;Fat: 12g;Protein: 5g;Carbs: 17g.

Cocktail Meatballs In Almond Sauce

Servings:4 | Cooking Time:30 Minutes

Ingredients:

- 3 tbsp olive oil
- 8 oz ground pork
- 8 oz ground beef
- ½ cup finely minced onions
- 1 large egg, beaten
- 1 potato, shredded
- Salt and black pepper to taste
- 1 tsp garlic powder
- ½ tsp oregano
- 2 tbsp chopped parsley
- ¼ cup ground almonds
- 1 cup chicken broth
- ¼ cup butter

Directions:

1. Place the ground meat, onions, egg, potato, salt, garlic powder, pepper, and oregano in a large bowl. Shape the mixture into small meatballs, about 1 inch in diameter, and place on a plate. Let sit for 10 minutes at room temperature.
2. Warm the olive oil in a skillet over medium heat. Add the meatballs and brown them for 6-8 minutes on all sides; reserve.

In the hot skillet, melt the butter and add the almonds and broth. Cook for 3-5 minutes. Add the meatballs to the skillet, cover, and cook for 8-10 minutes. Top with parsley.

Nutrition Info:

- Per Serving: Calories: 449;Fat: 42g;Protein: 16g;Carbs: 3g.

Greek-style Lamb Burgers

Servings:4 | Cooking Time: 10 Minutes

Ingredients:

- 1 pound ground lamb
- ½ teaspoon salt
- ½ teaspoon freshly ground black pepper
- 4 tablespoons crumbled feta cheese
- Buns, toppings, and tzatziki, for serving (optional)

Directions:

1. Preheat the grill to high heat.
2. In a large bowl, using your hands, combine the lamb with the salt and pepper.
3. Divide the meat into 4 portions. Divide each portion in half to make a top and a bottom. Flatten each half into a 3-inch circle. Make a dent in the center of one of the halves and place 1 tablespoon of the feta cheese in the center. Place the second half of the patty on top of the feta cheese and press down to close the 2 halves together, making it resemble a round burger.
4. Grill each side for 3 minutes, for medium-well. Serve on a bun with your favorite toppings and tzatziki sauce, if desired.

Nutrition Info:

- Per Serving: Calories: 345;Fat: 29.0g;Protein: 20.0g;Carbs: 1.0g.

Rosemary Pork Loin With Green Onions

Servings:4 | Cooking Time:50 Minutes

Ingredients:

- 2 lb pork loin roast, boneless and cubed
- 2 tbsp olive oil
- 2 garlic cloves, minced
- Salt and black pepper to taste
- 1 cup tomato sauce
- 1 tsp rosemary, chopped
- 4 green onions, chopped

Directions:

1. Preheat the oven to 360° F. Heat olive oil in a skillet over medium heat and cook pork, garlic, and green onions for 6-7 minutes, stirring often. Add in tomato sauce, rosemary, and 1 cup of water. Season with salt and pepper. Transfer to a baking dish and bake for 40 minutes. Serve warm.

Nutrition Info:

- Per Serving: Calories: 280;Fat: 16g;Protein: 19g;Carbs: 18g.

Greek-style Chicken & Egg Bake

Servings:4 | Cooking Time:45 Minutes

Ingredients:

- ½ lb Halloumi cheese, grated
- 1 tbsp olive oil
- 1 lb chicken breasts, cubed
- 4 eggs, beaten
- 1 tsp dry mustard
- 2 cloves garlic, crushed
- 2 red bell peppers, sliced
- 1 red onion, sliced
- 2 tomatoes, chopped
- 1 tsp sweet paprika
- ½ tsp dried basil
- Salt to taste

Directions:

1. Preheat oven to 360° F. Warm the olive oil in a skillet over medium heat. Add the bell peppers, garlic, onion, and salt and cook for 3 minutes. Stir in tomatoes for an additional 5 minutes. Put in chicken breasts, paprika, dry mustard, and basil. Cook for

another 6-8 minutes. Transfer the mixture to a greased baking pan and pour over the beaten eggs; season with salt. Bake for 15-18 minutes. Remove and spread the cheese over the top. Let cool for a few minutes. Serve sliced.

Nutrition Info:
- Per Serving: Calories: 480;Fat: 31g;Protein: 39g;Carbs: 12g.

Lamb With Couscous & Chickpeas
Servings:6 | Cooking Time:50 Minutes

Ingredients:
- 1 lb lamb shoulder, halved
- 3 tbsp olive oil
- 1 cup couscous
- Salt and black pepper to taste
- 1 onion, finely chopped
- 10 strips orange zest
- 1 tsp ground coriander
- ¼ tsp ground cinnamon
- ½ tsp cayenne pepper
- ½ cup dry white wine
- 2 ½ cups chicken broth
- 1 can chickpeas
- ½ cup dates, chopped
- ½ cup sliced almonds, toasted

Directions:
1. Cover the couscous in a bowl with 1 ½ cups of boiling water and put a lid. Let stand for 5 minutes to absorb the water.
2. Preheat oven to 330° F. Heat 2 tablespoons oil in a pot over medium heat. Season the lamb with salt and pepper and brown it for 4 minutes per side; set aside.
3. Stir-fry onion into the fat left in the pot, 3 minutes. Stir in orange zest, coriander, cinnamon, cayenne, and pepper until fragrant, 30 seconds. Stir in wine, scraping off any browned bits. Stir in broth and chickpeas and bring to a boil.
4. Make a nestle of lamb into the pot along with any accumulated juices. Cover, transfer the pot in the oven, and cook until fork slips easily in and out of the lamb, 1 hour.
5. Transfer the lamb to cutting board, let cool slightly, then shred using 2 forks, discarding excess fat and bones. Strain cooking liquid through a fine mesh strainer set over the bowl. Return solids and 1 ½ cups of cooking liquid to the pot and bring to a simmer over medium heat; discard the remaining liquid. Stir in couscous and dates. Add shredded lamb and almonds. Season to taste and serve.

Nutrition Info:
- Per Serving: Calories: 555;Fat: 31g;Protein: 37g;Carbs: 42g.

Chicken Bake With Cottage Cheese
Servings:4 | Cooking Time:40 Minutes

Ingredients:
- ¼ cup cottage cheese, crumbled
- 2 tbsp olive oil
- 1 lb chicken breasts, sliced
- 2 garlic cloves, minced
- ½ tsp onion powder
- Salt and black pepper to taste
- 4 red onions, sliced
- ¼ tsp dried oregano

Directions:
1. Preheat the oven to 360° F. Toss chicken, olive oil, garlic, dried oregano, onion powder, salt, pepper, and onions in a roasting pan and bake for 30 minutes. Top with cottage cheese.

Nutrition Info:
- Per Serving: Calories: 290;Fat: 16g;Protein: 25g;Carbs: 16g.

Holiday Leg Of Lamb
Servings:4 | Cooking Time:2 Hours 20 Minutes

Ingredients:
- ½ cup butter
- 2 lb leg of lamb, boneless
- 2 tbsp tomato paste
- 2 tbsp yellow mustard
- 2 tbsp basil, chopped
- 2 garlic cloves, minced
- Salt and black pepper to taste
- 1 cup white wine
- ½ cup sour cream

Directions:
1. Preheat oven to 360° F. Warm butter in a skillet over medium heat. Sear leg of lamb for 10 minutes on all sides. Stir in mustard, basil, tomato paste, garlic, salt, pepper, wine, and sour cream and bake for 2 hours. Serve right away.

Nutrition Info:
- Per Serving: Calories: 320;Fat: 13g;Protein: 15g;Carbs: 23g.

Slow Cooker Beef With Tomatoes
Servings:4 | Cooking Time:8 Hours 10 Minutes

Ingredients:
- 1 ½ lb beef shoulder, cubed
- ½ cup chicken stock
- 2 tomatoes, chopped
- 2 garlic cloves, minced
- 1 tbsp cinnamon powder
- Salt and black pepper to taste
- 2 tbsp cilantro, chopped

Directions:
1. Place the beef, tomatoes, garlic, cinnamon, salt, pepper, chicken stock, and cilantro in your slow cooker. Cover with the lid and cook for 8 hours on Low. Serve immediately.

Nutrition Info:
- Per Serving: Calories: 360;Fat: 16g;Protein: 16g;Carbs: 19g.

Greek Peachy Lamb
Servings:4 | Cooking Time:70 Minutes

Ingredients:
- 2 tbsp olive oil
- 1 lb lamb, cubed
- 2 cups Greek yogurt
- 2 peaches, peeled and cubed
- 1 onion, chopped
- 2 tbsp parsley, chopped
- ½ tsp red pepper flakes
- Salt and black pepper to taste

Directions:
1. Warm the olive oil in a skillet over medium heat and sear lamb for 5 minutes. Put in onion and cook for another 5 minutes. Stir in yogurt, peaches, parsley, red pepper flakes, salt, and pepper, and bring to a boil. Cook for 45 minutes.

Nutrition Info:
- Per Serving: Calories: 310;Fat: 16g;Protein: 16g;Carbs: 17g.

Chicken Souvlaki
Servings:4 | Cooking Time:20 Min + Cooling Time

Ingredients:
- 1 red bell pepper, cut into chunks
- 2 chicken breasts, cubed
- 2 tbsp olive oil
- 2 cloves garlic, minced
- 8 oz cipollini onions
- ½ cup lemon juice
- Salt and black pepper to taste
- 1 tsp rosemary, chopped
- 1 cup tzatziki sauce

Directions:
1. In a bowl, mix oil, garlic, salt, pepper, and lemon juice and add the chicken, cipollini, rosemary, and bell pepper. Refrigerate for 2 hours. Preheat your grill to high heat. Thread chicken, bell pepper, and cipollini onto skewers and grill them for 6 minutes per side. Serve with tzatziki sauce.

Nutrition Info:
- Per Serving: Calories: 363;Fat: 14.1g;Protein: 32g;Carbs: 8g.

Spanish Chicken Skillet

Servings:4 | Cooking Time:25 Minutes

Ingredients:
- 2 tbsp olive oil
- ½ cup chicken stock
- 4 chicken breasts
- 2 garlic cloves, minced
- 1 celery stalk, chopped
- 1 tbsp oregano, dried
- Salt and black pepper to taste
- 1 white onion, chopped
- 1 ½ cups tomatoes, cubed
- 10 green olives, sliced

Directions:
1. Warm the olive oil in a skillet over medium heat. Season the chicken with salt and pepper and cook for 4 minutes on both sides. Stir in garlic, oregano, stock, onion, celery, tomatoes, and olives and bring to a boil. Simmer for 13-15 minutes.

Nutrition Info:
- Per Serving: Calories: 140;Fat: 7g;Protein: 11g;Carbs: 13g.

Curried Green Bean & Chicken Breasts

Servings:4 | Cooking Time:8 Hours 10 Minutes

Ingredients:
- 12 oz green beans, chopped
- 1 lb chicken breasts, cubed
- 1 cup chicken stock
- 1 onion, chopped
- 1 tbsp white wine vinegar
- 1 cup Kalamata olives, chopped
- 1 tbsp curry powder
- 2 tsp basil, dried
- Salt and black pepper to taste

Directions:
1. Place chicken, green beans, chicken stock, onion, vinegar, olives, curry powder, basil, salt, and pepper in your slow cooker. Cover with the lid and cook for 8 hours on Low.

Nutrition Info:
- Per Serving: Calories: 290;Fat: 13g;Protein: 19g;Carbs: 20g.

Mushroom Chicken Piccata

Servings:4 | Cooking Time:25 Minutes

Ingredients:
- 3 tbsp olive oil
- 2 tbsp butter
- 1 lb chicken breasts, sliced
- Salt and black pepper to taste
- ¼ cup ground flaxseed
- 2 tbsp almond flour
- 2 cups mushrooms, sliced
- ½ cup white wine
- ¼ cup lemon juice
- ¼ cup capers, chopped
- ¼ cup parsley, chopped
- 16 oz cooked spaghetti

Directions:
1. Combine the ground flaxseed, almond flour, salt, and pepper in a bowl. Coat the chicken with the mixture.
2. Warm the olive oil in a large skillet over medium heat. Sear the chicken for 3-4 minutes per side until golden; reserve. Add the butter to the skillet and sauté the mushrooms and for 5-7 minutes. Pour in the white wine, lemon juice, capers, and salt and bring to a boil, whisking to incorporate any little browned bits that have stuck to the bottom of the skillet. Lower the heat to low and return the browned chicken. Cover and simmer 5-6 more minutes until the sauce thickens. Place the spaghetti in a serving platter and spoon the chicken and mushrooms on top. Garnish with parsley.

Nutrition Info:
- Per Serving: Calories: 538;Fat: 44g;Protein: 30g;Carbs: 8g.

Panko Grilled Chicken Patties

Servings:4 | Cooking Time: 8 To 10 Minutes

Ingredients:
- 1 pound ground chicken
- 3 tablespoons crumbled feta cheese
- 3 tablespoons finely chopped red pepper
- ¼ cup finely chopped red onion
- 3 tablespoons panko bread crumbs
- 1 garlic clove, minced
- 1 teaspoon chopped fresh oregano
- ¼ teaspoon salt
- ⅛ teaspoon freshly ground black pepper
- Cooking spray

Directions:
1. Mix together the ground chicken, feta cheese, red pepper, red onion, bread crumbs, garlic, oregano, salt, and black pepper in a large bowl, and stir to incorporate.
2. Divide the chicken mixture into 8 equal portions and form each portion into a patty with your hands.
3. Preheat a grill to medium-high heat and oil the grill grates with cooking spray.
4. Arrange the patties on the grill grates and grill each side for 4 to 5 minutes, or until the patties are cooked through.
5. Rest for 5 minutes before serving.

Nutrition Info:
- Per Serving: Calories: 241;Fat: 13.5g;Protein: 23.2g;Carbs: 6.7g.

Roasted Chicken Thighs With Basmati Rice

Servings:2 | Cooking Time: 50 To 55 Minutes

Ingredients:
- Chicken:
- ½ teaspoon cumin
- ½ teaspoon cinnamon
- ½ teaspoon paprika
- ¼ teaspoon ginger powder
- ¼ teaspoon garlic powder
- ¼ teaspoon coriander
- ¼ teaspoon salt
- ⅛ teaspoon cayenne pepper
- 10 ounces boneless, skinless
- chicken thighs
- Rice:
- 1 tablespoon olive oil
- ½ small onion, minced
- ½ cup basmati rice
- 2 pinches saffron
- 1 cup low-sodium chicken stock
- ¼ teaspoon salt

Directions:
1. Make the Chicken
2. Preheat the oven to 350°F.
3. Combine the cumin, cinnamon, paprika, ginger powder, garlic powder, coriander, salt, and cayenne pepper in a small bowl.
4. Using your hands to rub the spice mixture all over the chicken thighs.
5. Transfer the chicken thighs to a baking dish. Roast in the pre-heated oven for 35 to 40 minutes, or until the internal temperature reaches 165°F on a meat thermometer.
6. Make the Rice
7. Meanwhile, heat the olive oil in a skillet over medium-high heat.
8. Sauté the onion for 5 minutes until fragrant, stirring occasionally.
9. Stir in the basmati rice, saffron, chicken stock, and salt. Reduce the heat to low, cover, and bring to a simmer for 15 minutes, until light and fluffy.
10. Remove the chicken from the oven to a plate and serve with the rice.

Nutrition Info:

- Per Serving: Calories: 400;Fat: 9.6g;Protein: 37.2g;Carbs: 40.7g.

Shallot Beef

Servings:4 | Cooking Time:50 Minutes

Ingredients:
- 2 tbsp olive oil
- 1 lb beef meat, cubed
- 1 lb shallots, chopped
- 1 tbsp sweet paprika
- Salt and black pepper to taste
- 1 ½ cups chicken stock
- 4 garlic cloves, minced
- 1 cup balsamic vinegar

Directions:
1. Warm the olive oil in a pot over medium heat and sauté shallots, balsamic vinegar, salt, and pepper for 10 minutes. Stir in beef, paprika, chicken stock, and garlic and bring to a simmer. Cook for 30 minutes. Serve immediately.

Nutrition Info:
- Per Serving: Calories: 312;Fat: 13g;Protein: 18g;Carbs: 16g.

Hot Pork Meatballs

Servings:4 | Cooking Time:30 Minutes

Ingredients:
- 3 tbsp olive oil
- 1 lb ground pork
- 2 tbsp parsley, chopped
- 2 green onions, chopped
- 4 garlic cloves, minced
- 1 red chili, chopped
- 1 cup veggie stock
- 2 tbsp hot paprika

Directions:
1. Combine pork, parsley, green onions, garlic, and red chili in a bowl and form medium balls out of the mixture. Warm olive oil in a skillet over medium heat. Sear meatballs for 8 minutes on all sides. Stir in stock and hot paprika and simmer for another 12 minutes. Serve warm.

Nutrition Info:
- Per Serving: Calories: 240;Fat: 19g;Protein: 15g;Carbs: 12g.

Parsley Eggplant Lamb

Servings:4 | Cooking Time:70 Minutes

Ingredients:
- 2 tbsp olive oil
- 1 cup chicken stock
- 1 ½ lb lamb meat, cubed
- 2 eggplants, cubed
- 2 onions, chopped
- 2 tbsp tomato paste
- 2 tbsp parsley, chopped
- 4 garlic cloves, minced

Directions:
1. Warm the olive oil in a skillet over medium heat and cook onions and garlic for 4 minutes. Put in lamb and cook for 6 minutes. Stir in eggplants and tomato paste for 5 minutes. Pour in the stock and bring to a boil. Cook for another 50 minutes, stirring often. Serve garnished with parsley.

Nutrition Info:
- Per Serving: Calories: 310;Fat: 19g;Protein: 15g;Carbs: 23g.

Authentic Turkey Kofta

Servings:4 | Cooking Time:35 Minutes

Ingredients:
- 1 lb ground turkey
- ¼ cup breadcrumbs
- 1 egg
- 2 tbsp hot sauce
- ½ tsp celery seeds
- 2 garlic cloves, minced
- ¼ red onion, chopped
- 2 tbsp chopped fresh mint
- Salt and black pepper to taste

Directions:
1. Preheat oven to 350° F. In a bowl, place turkey, breadcrumbs, egg, garlic, red onion, mint, hot sauce, celery seeds, salt, and pepper. Make small balls out of the mixture and arrange them on a lined with parchment paper baking sheet. Bake for 25 minutes until brown. Serve and enjoy!

Nutrition Info:
- Per Serving: Calories: 270;Fat: 14g;Protein: 33.6g;Carbs: 6g.

Greek Beef Kebabs

Servings:2 | Cooking Time: 20 Minutes

Ingredients:
- 6 ounces beef sirloin tip, trimmed of fat and cut into 2-inch pieces
- 3 cups of any mixture of vegetables: mushrooms, summer squash, zucchini, onions, red peppers, cherry tomatoes
- ½ cup olive oil
- ¼ cup freshly squeezed lemon juice
- 2 tablespoons balsamic vinegar
- 2 teaspoons dried oregano
- 1 teaspoon garlic powder
- 1 teaspoon salt
- 1 teaspoon minced fresh rosemary
- Cooking spray

Directions:
1. Put the beef in a plastic freezer bag.
2. Slice the vegetables into similar-size pieces and put them in a second freezer bag.
3. Make the marinade: Mix the olive oil, lemon juice, balsamic vinegar, oregano, garlic powder, salt, and rosemary in a measuring cup. Whisk well to combine. Pour half of the marinade over the beef, and the other half over the vegetables.
4. Put the beef and vegetables in the refrigerator to marinate for 4 hours.
5. When ready, preheat the grill to medium-high heat and spray the grill grates with cooking spray.
6. Thread the meat onto skewers and the vegetables onto separate skewers.
7. Grill the meat for 3 minutes per side. They should only take 10 to 12 minutes to cook, depending on the thickness of the meat.
8. Grill the vegetables for about 3 minutes per side, or until they have grill marks and are softened. Serve hot.

Nutrition Info:
- Per Serving: Calories: 284;Fat: 18.2g;Protein: 21.0g;Carbs: 9.0g.

Herby Chicken With Asparagus Sauce

Servings:4 | Cooking Time:40 Minutes

Ingredients:
- 1 chicken legs
- 4 garlic cloves, minced
- 4 fresh thyme, minced
- 3 fresh rosemary, minced
- Salt and black pepper to taste
- 2 tbsp olive oil
- 8 oz asparagus, chopped
- 1 onion, chopped
- 1 cup chicken stock
- 1 tbsp soy sauce
- 1 fresh thyme sprig
- 1 tbsp flour
- 2 tbsp parsley, chopped

Directions:
1. Warm the olive oil on Sauté in your Instant Pot. Add in onion and asparagus and sauté for 5 minutes until softened. Pour in chicken stock, 1 thyme sprig, black pepper, soy sauce, and salt, and stir. Insert a trivet over the asparagus mixture. Rub all sides of the chicken with garlic, rosemary, black pepper, lemon zest, thyme, and salt. Arrange the chicken legs on the trivet. Seal the

lid, select Manual, and cook for 20 minutes on High Pressure. Do a quick release. Remove the chicken to a serving platter. In the inner pot, sprinkle flour over the asparagus mixture and blend the sauce with an immersion blender until desired consistency. Top the chicken with asparagus sauce and garnish with parsley. Serve and enjoy!

Nutrition Info:
- Per Serving: Calories: 193;Fat: 11g;Protein: 16g;Carbs: 10g.

Chicken Cacciatore

Servings:2 | Cooking Time: 1 Hour And 30 Minutes

Ingredients:
- 1½ pounds bone-in chicken thighs, skin removed and patted dry
- Salt, to taste
- 2 tablespoons olive oil
- ½ large onion, thinly sliced
- 4 ounces baby bella mushrooms, sliced
- 1 red sweet pepper, cut into 1-inch pieces
- 1 can crushed fire-roasted tomatoes
- 1 fresh rosemary sprig
- ½ cup dry red wine
- 1 teaspoon Italian herb seasoning
- ½ teaspoon garlic powder
- 3 tablespoons flour

Directions:
1. Season the chicken thighs with a generous pinch of salt.
2. Heat the olive oil in a Dutch oven over medium-high heat. Add the chicken and brown for 5 minutes per side.
3. Add the onion, mushrooms, and sweet pepper to the Dutch oven and sauté for another 5 minutes.
4. Add the tomatoes, rosemary, wine, Italian seasoning, garlic powder, and salt, stirring well.
5. Bring the mixture to a boil, then reduce the heat to low. Allow to simmer slowly for at least 1 hour, stirring occasionally, or until the chicken is tender and easily pulls away from the bone.
6. Measure out 1 cup of the sauce from the pot and put it into a bowl. Add the flour and whisk well to make a slurry.
7. Increase the heat to medium-high and slowly whisk the slurry into the pot. Stir until it comes to a boil and cook until the sauce is thickened.
8. Remove the chicken from the bones and shred it, and add it back to the sauce before serving, if desired.

Nutrition Info:
- Per Serving: Calories: 520;Fat: 23.1g;Protein: 31.8g;Carbs: 37.0g.

Baked Turkey With Veggies

Servings:4 | Cooking Time:70 Minutes

Ingredients:
- 2 tbsp olive oil
- 1 lb turkey breasts, sliced
- ¼ cup chicken stock
- 1 carrot, chopped
- 1 red onion, chopped
- 2 mixed bell peppers, chopped
- Salt and black pepper to taste
- 1 tbsp cilantro, chopped

Directions:
1. Preheat oven to 380° F. Grease a roasting pan with olive oil. Combine turkey, stock, carrots, bell peppers, onion, salt, and pepper in the pan and bake for 1 hour. Top with cilantro.

Nutrition Info:
- Per Serving: Calories: 510;Fat: 15g;Protein: 11g;Carbs: 16g.

Chicken Drumsticks With Peach Glaze

Servings:4 | Cooking Time:35 Minutes

Ingredients:
- 2 tbsp olive oil
- 8 chicken drumsticks, skinless
- 3 peaches, peeled and chopped
- ¼ cup honey
- ¼ cup cider vinegar
- 1 sweet onion, chopped
- 1 tsp minced fresh rosemary
- Salt to taste

Directions:
1. Warm the olive oil in a large skillet over medium heat. Sprinkle chicken with salt and pepper and brown it for about 7 minutes per side. Remove to a plate. Add onion and rosemary to the skillet and sauté for 1 minute or until lightly golden. Add honey, vinegar, salt, and peaches and cook for 10-12 minutes or until peaches are softened. Add the chicken back to the skillet and heat just until warm, brushing with the sauce. Serve chicken thighs with peach sauce. Enjoy!

Nutrition Info:
- Per Serving: Calories: 1492;Fat: 26g;Protein: 54g;Carbs: 27g.

Caprese Stuffed Chicken Breasts

Servings:4 | Cooking Time:40 Minutes

Ingredients:
- 4 oz fresh mozzarella cheese, shredded
- 5 tbsp olive oil
- 2 chicken breasts
- 1 cup spinach, torn
- ¼ cup fresh basil, chopped
- 6 sundried tomatoes, diced
- Salt and black pepper to taste
- 1 tbsp rosemary, chopped
- ½ tsp garlic powder
- 1 tbsp balsamic vinegar

Directions:
1. Preheat the oven to 375°F. In a bowl, mix the spinach, cheese, basil, sun-dried tomatoes, salt, pepper, rosemary, and garlic powder. Cut a pocket in each chicken breast and stuff with the filling. Press the opening together with your fingers.
2. Warm 2 tablespoons olive oil in a medium skillet over medium heat. Carefully sear the chicken breasts for 3-4 minutes on each side until lightly golden. Transfer to a greased baking dish, incision-side up. Cover with foil and bake for 30-40 minutes until the chicken is cooked through. Remove from the oven and let it sit covered for 10 minutes. In a small bowl, whisk together the remaining 3 tablespoons of olive oil, balsamic vinegar, salt, and pepper. Cut the chicken breasts in half. Serve drizzled with balsamic vinaigrette.

Nutrition Info:
- Per Serving: Calories: 434;Fat: 35g;Protein: 27g;Carbs: 3g.

Picante Beef Stew

Servings:4 | Cooking Time:35 Minutes

Ingredients:
- 2 tbsp olive oil
- 1 carrot, chopped
- 4 potatoes, diced
- 1 tsp ground nutmeg
- ½ tsp cinnamon
- 1 lb beef stew meat, cubed
- ½ cup sweet chili sauce
- ½ cup vegetable stock
- 1 tbsp cilantro, chopped
- Salt and black pepper to taste

Directions:
1. Warm the olive oil in a skillet over medium heat and sear beef for 5 minutes. Stir in chili sauce, carrot, potatoes, stock, nutmeg, cinnamon, cilantro, salt, and pepper and bring to a boil. Cook for another 20 minutes. Serve immediately.

Nutrition Info:
- Per Serving: Calories: 300;Fat: 22g;Protein: 20g;Carbs: 26g.

Beef, Tomato, And Lentils Stew

Servings:4 | Cooking Time: 10 Minutes

Ingredients:
- 1 tablespoon extra-virgin olive oil
- 1 pound extra-lean ground beef
- 1 onion, chopped
- 1 can chopped tomatoes with
- garlic and basil, drained
- 1 can lentils, drained
- ½ teaspoon sea salt
- ⅛ teaspoon freshly ground black pepper

Directions:
1. Heat the olive oil in a pot over medium-high heat until shimmering.
2. Add the beef and onion to the pot and sauté for 5 minutes or until the beef is lightly browned.
3. Add the remaining ingredients. Bring to a boil. Reduce the heat to medium and cook for 4 more minutes or until the lentils are tender. Keep stirring during the cooking.
4. Pour them in a large serving bowl and serve immediately.

Nutrition Info:
- Per Serving: Calories: 460;Fat: 14.8g;Protein: 44.2g;Carbs: 36.9g.

Honey Mustard Pork Chops

Servings:4 | Cooking Time:40 Minutes

Ingredients:
- 2 tbsp olive oil
- ½ cup vegetable stock
- 2 tbsp wholegrain mustard
- 1 tbsp honey
- 4 pork loin chops, boneless
- Salt and black pepper to taste

Directions:
1. Preheat oven to 380° F. Mix honey, mustard, salt, pepper, paprika, and olive oil in a bowl. Add in the pork and toss to coat. Transfer to a greased baking sheet and pour in the vegetable stock. Bake covered with foil for 30 minutes. Remove the foil and bake for 6-8 minutes until golden brown.

Nutrition Info:
- Per Serving: Calories: 180;Fat: 6g;Protein: 26g;Carbs: 3g.

Bell Pepper & Onion Pork Chops

Servings:4 | Cooking Time:30 Minutes

Ingredients:
- 2 tbsp olive oil
- 4 pork chops
- Salt and black pepper to taste
- 1 tsp fennel seeds
- 1 red bell pepper, sliced
- 1 green bell pepper, sliced
- 1 yellow onion, thinly sliced
- 2 tsp Italian seasoning
- 2 garlic cloves, minced
- 1 tbsp balsamic vinegar

Directions:
1. Warm the olive oil in a large skillet over medium heat. Season the pork chops with salt and pepper and add them to the skillet. Cook for 6-8 minutes on both sides or until golden brown; reserve. Sauté the garlic, sliced bell peppers, onions, fennel seeds, and herbs in the skillet for 6-8 minutes until tender, stirring occasionally. Return the pork, cover, and lower the heat to low. Cook for another 3 minutes or until the pork is cooked through. Transfer the pork and vegetables to a serving platter. Add the vinegar to the skillet and stir to combine for 1-2 minutes. Drizzle the sauce over the pork.

Nutrition Info:
- Per Serving: Calories: 508;Fat: 40g;Protein: 31g;Carbs: 8g.

Baked Garlicky Pork Chops

Servings:4 | Cooking Time:45 Minutes

Ingredients:
- 1 tbsp olive oil
- 4 pork loin chops, boneless
- Salt and black pepper to taste
- 4 garlic cloves, minced
- 1 tbsp thyme, chopped

Directions:
1. Preheat the oven to 390° F. Place pork chops, salt, pepper, garlic, thyme, and olive oil in a roasting pan and bake for 10 minutes. Decrease the heat to 360° F and bake for 25 minutes.

Nutrition Info:
- Per Serving: Calories: 170;Fat: 6g;Protein: 26g;Carbs: 2g.

Pork Chops In Wine Sauce

Servings:4 | Cooking Time:30 Minutes

Ingredients:
- 2 tbsp olive oil
- 4 pork chops
- 1 cup red onion, sliced
- 10 black peppercorns, crushed
- ¼ cup vegetable stock
- ¼ cup dry white wine
- 2 garlic cloves, minced
- Salt to taste

Directions:
1. Warm the olive oil in a skillet over medium heat and sear pork chops for 8 minutes on both sides. Put in onion and garlic and cook for another 2 minutes. Mix in stock, wine, salt, and peppercorns and cook for 10 minutes, stirring often.

Nutrition Info:
- Per Serving: Calories: 240;Fat: 10g;Protein: 25g;Carbs: 14g.

Baked Chicken & Veggie

Servings:4 | Cooking Time:50 Minutes

Ingredients:
- 4 fresh prunes, cored and quartered
- 2 tbsp olive oil
- 4 chicken legs
- 1 lb baby potatoes, halved
- 1 carrot, julienned
- 2 tbsp chopped fresh parsley
- Salt and black pepper to taste

Directions:
1. Preheat oven to 420° F. Combine potatoes, carrot, prunes, olive oil, salt, and pepper in a bowl. Transfer to a baking dish. Top with chicken. Season with salt and pepper. Roast for about 40-45 minutes. Serve topped with parsley.

Nutrition Info:
- Per Serving: Calories: 473;Fat: 23g;Protein: 21g;Carbs: 49g.

Sweet Chicken Stew

Servings:4 | Cooking Time:50 Minutes

Ingredients:
- 2 tbsp olive oil
- 3 garlic cloves, minced
- 3 tbsp cilantro, chopped
- Salt and black pepper to taste
- 2 cups chicken stock
- 2 shallots, thinly sliced
- 1 lb chicken breasts, cubed
- 5 oz dried pitted prunes, halved

Directions:
1. Warm the olive oil in a pot over medium heat and cook shallots and garlic for 3 minutes. Add in chicken breasts and cook for

another 5 minutes, stirring occasionally. Pour in chicken stock and prunes and season with salt and pepper. Cook for 30 minutes. Garnish with cilantro and serve.

Nutrition Info:
• Per Serving: Calories: 310;Fat: 26g;Protein: 7g;Carbs: 16g.

Coriander Pork Roast

Servings:4 | Cooking Time:2 Hours 10 Minutes

Ingredients:
• 2 tbsp olive oil
• 2 lb pork loin roast, boneless
• Salt and black pepper to taste
• 2 garlic cloves, minced
• 1 tsp ground coriander
• 1 tbsp coriander seeds
• 2 tsp red pepper, crushed

Directions:
1. Preheat the oven to 360° F. Toss pork, salt, pepper, garlic, ground coriander, coriander seeds, red pepper, and olive oil in a roasting pan and bake for 2 hours. Serve sliced.

Nutrition Info:
• Per Serving: Calories: 310;Fat: 5g;Protein: 16g;Carbs: 7g.

Chicken With Farro & Carrots

Servings:4 | Cooking Time:50 Minutes

Ingredients:
• 2 tbsp olive oil
• 3 carrots, chopped
• 1 cup farro, soaked
• 1 lb chicken breasts, cubed
• 1 red onion, chopped
• 4 garlic cloves, minced
• 2 tbsp dill, chopped
• 2 tbsp tomato paste
• 2 cups vegetable stock
• Salt and black pepper to taste

Directions:
1. Warm olive oil in your pressure cooker on Sauté and sear the chicken for 10 minutes on all sides, stirring occasionally. Remove to a plate. Add onion, garlic, and carrots to the cooker and sauté for 3 minutes. Stir in tomato paste, farro, and vegetable stock and return the chicken. Seal the lid, select Pressure Cook, and cook for 30 minutes on High. Do a natural pressure release for 10 minutes. Adjust the taste with salt and pepper. Sprinkle with dill and serve.

Nutrition Info:
• Per Serving: Calories: 317;Fat: 13g;Protein: 8g;Carbs: 18g.

Greek-style Veggie & Beef In Pita

Servings:2 | Cooking Time:30 Minutes

Ingredients:
• Beef
• 1 tbsp olive oil
• ½ medium onion, minced
• 2 garlic cloves, minced
• 6 oz lean ground beef
• 1 tsp dried oregano
• Yogurt Sauce
• ⅓ cup plain Greek yogurt
• 1 oz crumbled feta cheese
• 1 tbsp minced fresh dill
• 1 tbsp minced scallions
• 1 tbsp lemon juice
• Garlic salt to taste
• Sandwiches
• 2 Greek-style pitas, warm
• 6 cherry tomatoes, halved
• 1 cucumber, sliced
• Salt and black pepper to taste

Directions:
1. Warm the 1 tbsp olive oil in a pan over medium heat. Sauté the onion, garlic, and ground for 5-7 minutes, breaking up the meat well. When the meat is no longer pink, drain off any fat and stir in oregano. Turn off the heat.
2. In a small bowl, combine the yogurt, feta, dill, scallions, lemon juice, and garlic salt. Divide the yogurt sauce between the warm pitas. Top with ground beef, cherry tomatoes, and diced cucumber. Season with salt and pepper. Serve.

Nutrition Info:
• Per Serving: Calories: 541;Fat: 21g;Protein: 29g;Carbs: 57g.

Picante Green Pea & Chicken

Servings:4 | Cooking Time:35 Minutes

Ingredients:
• 2 tbsp olive oil
• 1 lb chicken breasts, halved
• 1 tsp chili powder
• Salt and black pepper to taste
• 1 tsp garlic powder
• 1 tbsp smoked paprika
• ½ cup chicken stock
• 2 tsp sherry vinegar
• 3 tsp hot sauce
• 2 tsp cumin, ground
• 1 cup green peas
• 1 carrot, chopped

Directions:
1. Warm the olive oil in a skillet over medium heat and cook chicken for 6 minutes on both sides. Sprinkle with chili powder, salt, pepper, garlic powder, and paprika. Pour in the chicken stock, vinegar, hot sauce, cumin, carrot, and green peas and bring to a boil; cook for an additional 15 minutes.

Nutrition Info:
• Per Serving: Calories: 240;Fat: 19g;Protein: 14g;Carbs: 16g.

Cheesy Bean & Chicken Bake

Servings:4 | Cooking Time:40 Minutes

Ingredients:
• 1 ½ lb skinless, boneless chicken thighs, cubed
• ½ cup canned artichokes, drained and chopped
• 2 tbsp olive oil
• 2 garlic cloves, minced
• 1 tbsp oregano, chopped
• 2 shallots, sliced
• 1 tsp paprika
• 1 cup canned white beans
• ½ cup parsley, chopped
• 1 cup mozzarella, shredded
• Salt and black pepper to taste

Directions:
1. Preheat the oven to 390° F. Warm the olive oil in a skillet over medium heat and sauté the chicken for 5 minutes. Transfer to a baking pan and garlic, oregano, artichokes, paprika, shallots, beans, parsley, salt, and pepper. Top with mozzarella cheese and bake for 25 minutes.

Nutrition Info:
• Per Serving: Calories: 200;Fat: 7g;Protein: 13g;Carbs: 13g.

Beef & Vegetable Stew

Servings:6 | Cooking Time:and Total Time: 35 Minutes

Ingredients:
• 2 sweet potatoes, cut into chunks
• 2 lb beef meat for stew
• ¾ cup red wine
• 1 tbsp butter
• 6 oz tomato paste
• 6 oz baby carrots, chopped
• 1 onion, finely chopped
• Salt to taste
• 4 cups beef broth
• ½ cup green peas
• 1 tsp dried thyme
• 3 garlic cloves, crushed

Directions:
1. Heat the butter on Sauté in your Instant pot. Add beef and brown for 5-6 minutes. Add onions and garlic, and keep stirring for 3 more minutes. Add the remaining ingredients and seal the lid. Cook on Meat/Stew for 20 minutes on High pressure. Do a quick release and serve immediately.

Nutrition Info:

• Per Serving: Calories: 470;Fat: 15g;Protein: 51g;Carbs: 27g.

Sausage & Herb Eggs
Servings:2 | Cooking Time:20 Minutes

Ingredients:
- 2 tbsp olive oil
- ½ cup leeks, chopped
- ½ lb pork sausage, crumbled
- 4 eggs, whisked
- 1 thyme sprig, chopped
- 1 tsp habanero pepper, minced
- ½ tsp dried marjoram
- 1 tsp garlic puree
- ½ cup green olives, sliced
- Salt and black pepper to taste

Directions:
1. Warm the olive oil in a skillet over medium heat. Sauté the leeks until they are just tender, about 4 minutes. Add the garlic, habanero pepper, salt, black pepper, and sausage; cook for 8 minutes, stirring frequently. Pour in the eggs and sprinkle with thyme and marjoram. Cook for an additional 4 minutes, stirring with a spoon. Garnish with olives. Serve.

Nutrition Info:
- Per Serving: Calories: 460;Fat: 41g;Protein: 16g;Carbs: 6g.

Chicken Lentils With Artichokes
Servings:4 | Cooking Time:50 Minutes

Ingredients:
- 2 tbsp olive oil
- 4 chicken breasts, halved
- 1 lemon, juiced and zested
- 2 garlic cloves, crushed
- 1 tbsp thyme, chopped
- 6 oz canned artichokes hearts
- 1 cup canned lentils, drained
- 1 cup chicken stock
- 1 tsp cayenne pepper
- Salt and black pepper to taste

Directions:
1. Warm the olive oil in a skillet over medium heat and cook chicken for 5-6 minutes until browned, flipping once. Mix in lemon zest, garlic, lemon juice, salt, pepper, thyme, artichokes, lentils, stock, and cayenne pepper and bring to a boil. Cook for 35 minutes. Serve immediately.

Nutrition Info:
- Per Serving: Calories: 300;Fat: 16g;Protein: 25g;Carbs: 25g.

Savory Tomato Chicken
Servings:4 | Cooking Time:90 Minutes

Ingredients:
- 3 tbsp olive oil
- 1 can diced tomatoes,
- 4 chicken breast halves
- 2 whole cloves
- ¼ cup chicken broth
- 2 tbsp tomato paste
- ¼ tsp chili flakes
- 1 tsp ground allspice
- ½ tsp dried mint
- 1 cinnamon stick
- Salt and black pepper to taste

Directions:
1. Place tomatoes, chicken broth, olive oil, tomato paste, chili flakes, mint, allspice, cloves, cinnamon stick, salt, and pepper in a pot over medium heat and bring just to a boil. Then, lower the heat and simmer for 30 minutes. Strain the sauce through a fine-mesh sieve and discard the cloves and cinnamon stick. Let it cool completely.
2. Preheat oven to 350° F. Lay the chicken on a baking dish and pour the sauce over. Bake covered with aluminum foil for 40-45 minutes. Uncover and continue baking for 5 more minutes.

Nutrition Info:
- Per Serving: Calories: 259;Fat: 14g;Protein: 24g;Carbs: 11g.

Syrupy Chicken Breasts
Servings:4 | Cooking Time:30 Minutes

Ingredients:
- 2 tbsp olive oil
- 2 cups peaches, cubed
- 1 tbsp smoked paprika
- 1 lb chicken breasts, cubed
- 2 cups chicken broth
- Salt and black pepper to taste
- 1 tbsp chives, chopped

Directions:
1. Warm the olive oil in a skillet over medium heat and sauté chicken, salt, and pepper for 8 minutes, stirring occasionally. Stir in peaches, paprika, and chicken broth and cook for another 15 minutes. Serve topped with chives.

Nutrition Info:
- Per Serving: Calories: 280;Fat: 14g;Protein: 17g;Carbs: 26g.

Coconut Chicken Tenders
Servings:6 | Cooking Time: 15 To 20 Minutes

Ingredients:
- 4 chicken breasts, each cut lengthwise into 3 strips
- ½ teaspoon salt
- ¼ teaspoon freshly ground black pepper
- ½ cup coconut flour
- 2 eggs
- 2 tablespoons unsweetened plain almond milk
- 1 cup unsweetened coconut flakes

Directions:
1. Preheat the oven to 400ºF. Line a baking sheet with parchment paper.
2. On a clean work surface, season the chicken with salt and pepper.
3. In a small bowl, add the coconut flour. In a separate bowl, whisk the eggs with almond milk until smooth. Place the coconut flakes on a plate.
4. One at a time, roll the chicken strips in the coconut flour, then dredge them in the egg mixture, shaking off any excess, and finally in the coconut flakes to coat.
5. Arrange the coated chicken pieces on the baking skeet. Bake in the preheated oven for 15 to 20 minutes, flipping the chicken halfway through, or until the chicken is golden brown and cooked through.
6. Remove from the oven and serve on plates.

Nutrition Info:
- Per Serving: Calories: 215;Fat: 12.6g;Protein: 20.2g;Carbs: 8.9g.

Easy Grilled Pork Chops
Servings:4 | Cooking Time: 10 Minutes

Ingredients:
- ¼ cup extra-virgin olive oil
- 2 tablespoons fresh thyme leaves
- 1 teaspoon smoked paprika
- 1 teaspoon salt
- 4 pork loin chops, ½-inch-thick

Directions:
1. In a small bowl, mix together the olive oil, thyme, paprika, and salt.
2. Put the pork chops in a plastic zip-top bag or a bowl and coat them with the spice mix. Let them marinate for 15 minutes.
3. Preheat the grill to high heat. Cook the pork chops for 4 minutes on each side until cooked through.
4. Serve warm.

Nutrition Info:
- Per Serving: Calories: 282;Fat: 23.0g;Protein: 21.0g;Carbs: 1.0g.

Grilled Lemon Chicken

Servings:2 | Cooking Time: 12 To 14 Minutes

Ingredients:
- Marinade:
- 4 tablespoons freshly squeezed lemon juice
- 2 tablespoons olive oil, plus more for greasing the grill grates
- 1 teaspoon dried basil
- 1 teaspoon paprika
- ½ teaspoon dried thyme
- ¼ teaspoon salt
- ¼ teaspoon garlic powder
- 2 boneless, skinless chicken breasts

Directions:
1. Make the marinade: Whisk together the lemon juice, olive oil, basil, paprika, thyme, salt, and garlic powder in a large bowl until well combined.
2. Add the chicken breasts to the bowl and let marinate for at least 30 minutes.
3. When ready to cook, preheat the grill to medium-high heat. Lightly grease the grill grates with the olive oil.
4. Discard the marinade and arrange the chicken breasts on the grill grates.
5. Grill for 12 to 14 minutes, flipping the chicken halfway through, or until a meat thermometer inserted in the center of the chicken reaches 165ºF.
6. Let the chicken cool for 5 minutes and serve warm.

Nutrition Info:
- Per Serving: Calories: 251;Fat: 15.5g;Protein: 27.3g;Carbs: 1.9g.

Chicken With Halloumi Cheese

Servings:4 | Cooking Time:40 Minutes

Ingredients:
- 2 tbsp butter
- 1 cup Halloumi cheese, cubed
- Salt and black pepper to taste
- 1 hard-boiled egg yolk
- ½ cup olive oil
- 6 black olives, halved
- 1 tbsp fresh cilantro, chopped
- 1 tbsp balsamic vinegar
- 1 tbsp garlic, finely minced
- 1 tbsp fresh lemon juice
- 1 ½ lb chicken wings

Directions:
1. Melt the butter in a saucepan over medium heat. Sear the chicken wings for 5 minutes per side. Season with salt and pepper to taste. Place the chicken wings on a parchment-lined baking pan. Mash the egg yolk with a fork and mix in the garlic, lemon juice, balsamic vinegar, olive oil, and salt until creamy, uniform, and smooth.
2. Preheat oven to 380° F. Spread the egg mixture over the chicken. Bake for 15-20 minutes. Top with the cheese and bake an additional 5 minutes until hot and bubbly. Scatter cilantro and olives on top of the chicken wings. Serve.

Nutrition Info:
- Per Serving: Calories: 560;Fat: 48g;Protein: 41g;Carbs: 2g.

Chicken Caprese

Servings:4 | Cooking Time:50 Minutes

Ingredients:
- 1 tsp garlic powder
- ½ cup basil pesto
- 4 chicken breast halves
- 3 tomatoes, sliced
- 1 cup mozzarella, shredded
- Salt and black pepper to taste

Directions:
1. Preheat the oven to 390° F. Line a baking dish with parchment paper and grease with cooking spray. Combine chicken, garlic powder, salt, pepper, and pesto in a bowl and arrange them on the sheet. Top with tomatoes and mozzarella and bake for 40 minutes. Serve hot.

Nutrition Info:
- Per Serving: Calories: 350;Fat: 21g;Protein: 33g;Carbs: 5g.

Spinach-cheese Stuffed Pork Loin

Servings:6 | Cooking Time:55 Minutes

Ingredients:
- 1 ½ lb pork tenderloin
- 6 slices pancetta, chopped
- 1 cup mushrooms, sliced
- 5 sundried tomatoes, diced
- Salt and black pepper to taste

Directions:
1. Place a skillet over medium heat and stir-fry the pancetta for 5 minutes until crispy. Add the mushrooms and sauté for another 4-5 minutes until tender, stirring occasionally. Stir in sundried tomatoes and season with salt and pepper; set aside. Preheat the oven to 350°F. Using a sharp knife, cut the pork tenderloin in half lengthwise, leaving about 1-inch border; be careful not to cut through to the other side. Open the tenderloin like a book to form a large rectangle.
2. Flatten it to about ¼-inch thickness with a meat tenderizer. Season the pork generously with salt and pepper. Top all over with pancetta filling. Roll up pork tenderloin and tightly secure with kitchen twine. Place on a greased baking sheet. Bake for 60-75 minutes until the pork is cooked through, depending on the thickness of the pork. Remove from the oven and let rest for 10 minutes at room temperature. Remove the twine and discard. Slice the pork into medallions and serve.

Nutrition Info:
- Per Serving: Calories: 270;Fat: 21g;Protein: 20g;Carbs: 2g.

Pork Chops In Italian Tomato Sauce

Servings:4 | Cooking Time:40 Minutes

Ingredients:
- 2 tbsp olive oil
- 4 pork chops
- ½ cup tomato puree
- Salt and black pepper to taste
- 1 tbsp Italian seasoning
- 1 tbsp rosemary, chopped

Directions:
1. Preheat the oven to 380° F. Warm olive oil in a skillet over medium heat. Sear pork. Stir in salt, pepper, tomato purée, Italian seasoning, and rosemary and bake for 20 minutes.

Nutrition Info:
- Per Serving: Calories: 230;Fat: 19g;Protein: 13g;Carbs: 12g.

Juicy Pork Chops

Servings:4 | Cooking Time:30 Minutes

Ingredients:

- 3 tbsp olive oil
- 4 pork chops
- Salt and black pepper to taste
- 5 tbsp chicken broth
- 6 garlic cloves, minced
- ¼ cup honey
- 2 tbsp apple cider vinegar
- 2 tbsp parsley, chopped

Directions:

1. Warm the olive oil in a large skillet over medium heat. Season the pork chops with salt and pepper and add them to the skillet. Cook for 10 minutes on both sides or until golden brown; reserve. Lower the heat and add 3 tablespoons of broth, scraping the bits and flavors from the bottom of the skillet; cook for 2 minutes until the broth evaporates. Add the garlic and cook for 30 seconds. Stir in honey, vinegar, and the remaining broth. Cook for 3-4 minutes until the sauce thickens slightly. Return the pork chops and cook for 2 minutes. Top with parsley and serve.

Nutrition Info:

- Per Serving: Calories: 302;Fat: 16g;Protein: 22g;Carbs: 19g.

Lemon Pesto Pork Shoulder

Servings:4 | Cooking Time:35 Minutes

Ingredients:

- ¼ cup olive oil
- 1 tsp red pepper flakes
- 2 garlic cloves, minced
- 2 lb pork shoulder, cubed
- 2 tsp dried marjoram
- ¼ cup lemon juice
- 2 tsp basil pesto
- Salt and black pepper to taste

Directions:

1. Warm the olive oil in a skillet over medium heat and sear pork for 5 minutes. Stir in marjoram, red pepper flakes, lemon juice, garlic, basil pesto, salt, and pepper and cook for another 20 minutes, stirring often. Serve immediately.

Nutrition Info:

- Per Serving: Calories: 310;Fat: 16g;Protein: 24g;Carbs: 18g.

Parmesan Chicken Breasts

Servings:4 | Cooking Time:35 Minutes

Ingredients:

- 1 tbsp olive oil
- 1 ½ lb chicken breasts, cubed
- 1 tsp ground coriander
- 1 tsp parsley flakes
- 2 garlic cloves, minced
- 1 cup heavy cream
- Salt and black pepper to taste
- ¼ cup Parmesan cheese, grated
- 1 tbsp basil, chopped

Directions:

1. Warm the olive oil in a skillet over medium heat and brown chicken, salt, and pepper for 6 minutes on all sides. Add in garlic and cook for another minute. Stir in coriander, parsley, and cream and cook for an additional 20 minutes. Serve scattered with basil and Parmesan cheese.

Nutrition Info:

- Per Serving: Calories: 260;Fat: 18g;Protein: 27g;Carbs: 26g.

Cardamon Chicken Breasts

Servings:4 | Cooking Time:8 Hours 10 Minutes

Ingredients:

- 2 tbsp olive oil
- 2 chicken breasts, halved
- Juice of ½ lemon
- Zest of ½ lemon, grated
- 2 tsp cardamom, ground
- Salt and black pepper to taste
- 2 spring onions, chopped
- 2 tbsp tomato paste
- 2 garlic cloves, minced
- 1 cup pineapple juice
- ½ cup chicken stock
- ¼ cup cilantro, chopped

Directions:

1. Place chicken, lemon juice, lemon zest, cardamom, salt, pepper, olive oil, spring onions, tomato paste, garlic, pineapple juice, and stock in your slow cooker. Cover with the lid and cook for 8 hours on Low. Garnish with cilantro.

Nutrition Info:

- Per Serving: Calories: 340;Fat: 13g;Protein: 18g;Carbs: 25g.

Spinach Chicken With Chickpeas

Servings:4 | Cooking Time:25 Minutes

Ingredients:

- 2 tbsp olive oil
- 1 lb chicken breasts, cubed
- 10 oz spinach, chopped
- 1 cup canned chickpeas
- 1 onion, chopped
- 2 garlic cloves, minced
- ½ cup chicken stock
- 2 tbsp Parmesan cheese, grated
- 1 tbsp parsley, chopped
- Salt and black pepper to taste

Directions:

1. Warm the olive oil in a skillet over medium heat and brown chicken for 5 minutes. Season with salt and pepper. Stir in onion and garlic for 3 minutes. Pour in stock and chickpeas and bring to a boil. Cook for 20 minutes. Mix in spinach and cook until wilted, about 5 minutes. Top with Parmesan cheese and parsley. Serve and enjoy!

Nutrition Info:

- Per Serving: Calories: 290;Fat: 10g;Protein: 35g;Carbs: 22g.

Grilled Chicken Breasts With Italian Sauce

Servings:4 | Cooking Time:25 Min + Marinating Time

Ingredients:

- ½ cup olive oil
- 2 tbsp rosemary, chopped
- 2 tbsp parsley, chopped
- 1 tsp minced garlic
- 1 lemon, zested and juiced
- Salt and black pepper to taste
- 4 chicken breasts
- 2 tsp basil, chopped

Directions:

1. Combine the olive oil, rosemary, garlic, lemon juice, lemon zest, parsley, salt, and pepper in a plastic bag. Add the chicken and shake to coat. Refrigerate for 2 hours.

2. Heat your grill to medium heat. Remove the chicken breasts from the marinade and grill them for 6-8 minutes per side. Pour the marinade into a saucepan, add 2 tbsp of water and simmer for 2-3 minutes until the sauce thickens. Sprinkle with basil and serve the grilled chicken. Enjoy!

Nutrition Info:

- Per Serving: Calories: 449;Fat: 32g;Protein: 38g;Carbs: 2.1g.

Beef Keftedes (greek Meatballs)

Servings:6 | Cooking Time:20 Min + Chilling Time

Ingredients:

- 2 bread slices, soaked in water, squeezed, and crumbled
- 4 tbsp olive oil
- 2 lb ground beef
- 2 medium onions, grated
- 1 tbsp minced garlic
- 2 large eggs, beaten
- 2 tsp dried Greek oregano
- 2 tbsp fresh parsley, chopped
- 1 tsp fresh mint, chopped
- 1/8 tsp ground cumin
- Salt and black pepper to taste

Directions:

1. Mix well all the ingredients, except for the olive oil, in a large bowl. Shape the mixture into balls and place them on a tray. Cover with plastic wrap and place in the fridge for at least 2 hours. Warm the olive oil in a skillet over medium heat and sear the keftedes 6-8 minutes until they are browned on all sides. Work in batches as needed. Serve immediately.

Nutrition Info:
- Per Serving: Calories: 567;Fat: 46g;Protein: 28g;Carbs: 8g.

Crispy Pork Chops

Servings:6 | Cooking Time:20 Minutes

Ingredients:
- 2 tbsp butter
- 3 tbsp olive oil
- 6 pork chops, boneless
- 2 fresh eggs
- 2 tbsp chicken stock
- ½ cup grated Parmesan cheese
- 1 cup panko bread crumbs
- 1 tsp Italian seasoning
- ½ tsp dried basil

Directions:
1. Flatten the chops with a meat tenderizer. In a bowl, beat the eggs with chicken stock. Mix the Parmesan cheese, crumbs, Italian seasoning, and basil on a shallow plate. Dip each pork chop into the egg mixture, then coat with the cheese mixture. Warm the butter and olive oil in a large skillet over medium heat. Sear the pork chops for 6-8 minutes on both sides until brown and crisp. Serve immediately.

Nutrition Info:
- Per Serving: Calories: 449;Fat: 22g;Protein: 46g;Carbs: 15g.

Pork Tenderloin With Caraway Seeds

Servings:4 | Cooking Time:30 Minutes

Ingredients:
- 2 tbsp olive oil
- 1 lb pork tenderloin, sliced
- Salt and black pepper to taste
- 3 tbsp ground caraway seeds
- 1/3 cup half-and-half
- ½ cup dill, chopped

Directions:
1. Warm the olive oil in a skillet over medium heat and sear pork for 8 minutes on all sides. Stir in salt, pepper, ground caraway seeds, half-and-half, and dill and bring to a boil. Cook for another 12 minutes. Serve warm.

Nutrition Info:
- Per Serving: Calories: 330;Fat: 15g;Protein: 18g;Carbs: 15g.

Crispy Pesto Chicken

Servings:2 | Cooking Time: 50 Minutes

Ingredients:
- 12 ounces small red potatoes, scrubbed and diced into 1-inch pieces
- 1 tablespoon olive oil
- ½ teaspoon garlic powder
- ¼ teaspoon salt
- 1 boneless, skinless chicken breast
- 3 tablespoons prepared pesto

Directions:
1. Preheat the oven to 425ºF. Line a baking sheet with parchment paper.
2. Combine the potatoes, olive oil, garlic powder, and salt in a medium bowl. Toss well to coat.
3. Arrange the potatoes on the parchment paper and roast for 10 minutes. Flip the potatoes and roast for an additional 10 minutes.
4. Meanwhile, put the chicken in the same bowl and toss with the pesto, coating the chicken evenly.

5. Check the potatoes to make sure they are golden brown on the top and bottom. Toss them again and add the chicken breast to the pan.
6. Turn the heat down to 350ºF and roast the chicken and potatoes for 30 minutes. Check to make sure the chicken reaches an internal temperature of 165ºF and the potatoes are fork-tender.
7. Let cool for 5 minutes before serving.

Nutrition Info:
- Per Serving: Calories: 378;Fat: 16.0g;Protein: 29.8g;Carbs: 30.1g.

Rich Pork In Cilantro Sauce

Servings:4 | Cooking Time:30 Minutes

Ingredients:
- ½ cup olive oil
- 1 lb pork stew meat, cubed
- 1 tbsp walnuts, chopped
- 2 tbsp cilantro, chopped
- 2 tbsp basil, chopped
- 2 garlic cloves, minced
- Salt and black pepper to taste
- 2 cups Greek yogurt

Directions:
1. In a food processor, blend cilantro, basil, garlic, walnuts, yogurt, salt, pepper, and half of the oil until smooth.
2. Warm the remaining oil in a skillet over medium heat. Brown pork meat for 5 minutes. Pour sauce over meat and bring to a boil. Cook for another 15 minutes. Serve.

Nutrition Info:
- Per Serving: Calories: 280;Fat: 12g;Protein: 19g;Carbs: 21g.

Beef Filet Mignon In Mushroom Sauce

Servings:2 | Cooking Time:25 Minutes

Ingredients:
- 8 oz cremini mushrooms, quartered
- 2 tbsp olive oil
- 2 filet mignon steaks
- 1 shallot, minced
- 2 tsp flour
- 2 tsp tomato paste
- ½ cup red wine
- 1 cup chicken stock
- ½ tsp dried thyme
- 1 fresh rosemary sprig
- 1 tsp herbes de Provence
- Salt and black pepper to taste
- ¼ tsp garlic powder
- ¼ tsp shallot powder
- ¼ tsp mustard powder

Directions:
1. Warm 1 tablespoon of olive oil in a saucepan over medium heat. Add the mushrooms and shallot and stir-fry for 5-8 minutes. Stir in the flour and tomato paste and cook for another 30 seconds. Pour in the wine and scrape up any browned bits from the sauté pan. Add the chicken stock, thyme, and rosemary. Bring it to a boil and cook until the sauce thickens, 2-4 minutes. In a small bowl, mix the herbes de Provence, salt, garlic powder, shallot powder, mustard powder, salt, and pepper. Rub the beef with the herb mixture on both sides. Warm the remaining olive oil in a sauté over medium heat. Sear the beef for 2-3 minutes on each side. Serve topped with mushroom sauce.

Nutrition Info:
- Per Serving: Calories: 385;Fat: 20g;Protein: 25g;Carbs: 15g.

Greek Wraps

Servings:2 | Cooking Time:10 Minutes

Ingredients:
- 2 cooked chicken breasts, shredded
- 2 tbsp roasted peppers, chopped
- 1 cup baby kale
- 2 whole-wheat tortillas

- 2 oz provolone cheese, grated
- 1 tomato, chopped
- 10 Kalamata olives, sliced
- 1 red onion, chopped

Directions:
1. In a bowl, mix all the ingredients except for the tortillas. Distribute the mixture across the tortillas and wrap them.

Nutrition Info:
- Per Serving: Calories: 200;Fat: 8g;Protein: 7g;Carbs: 16g.

Peach Pork Chops

Servings:4 | Cooking Time:30 Minutes

Ingredients:
- 2 tbsp olive oil
- ½ tsp cayenne powder
- 4 pork chops, boneless
- ¼ cup peach preserves
- 1 tbsp thyme, chopped

Directions:
1. In a bowl, mix peach preserves, olive oil, and cayenne powder. Preheat your grill to medium. Rub pork chops with some peach glaze and grill for 10 minutes. Turn the chops, rub more glaze and cook for 10 minutes. Top with thyme.

Nutrition Info:
- Per Serving: Calories: 240;Fat: 12g;Protein: 24g;Carbs: 7g.

Grilled Beef With Mint-jalapeño Vinaigrette

Servings:4 | Cooking Time:25 Minutes

Ingredients:
- 2 tbsp olive oil
- 1 lb beef steaks
- 3 jalapeños, chopped
- 2 tbsp balsamic vinegar
- 1 cup mint leaves, chopped
- Salt and black pepper to taste
- 1 tbsp sweet paprika

Directions:
1. Warm half of oil in a skillet over medium heat and sauté jalapeños, balsamic vinegar, mint, salt, pepper, and paprika for 5 minutes. Preheat the grill to high. Rub beef steaks with the remaining oil, salt, and pepper and grill for 6 minutes on both sides. Top with mint vinaigrette and serve.

Nutrition Info:
- Per Serving: Calories: 320;Fat: 13g;Protein: 18g;Carbs: 19g.

Thyme Zucchini & Chicken Stir-fry

Servings:4 | Cooking Time:40 Minutes

Ingredients:
- 2 tbsp olive oil
- 2 cups tomatoes, crushed
- 1 lb chicken breasts, cubed
- Salt and black pepper to taste
- 2 shallots, sliced
- 3 garlic cloves, minced
- 2 zucchinis, sliced
- 2 tbsp thyme, chopped
- 1 cup chicken stock

Directions:
1. Warm the olive oil in a skillet over medium heat. Sear chicken for 6 minutes, stirring occasionally. Add in shallots and garlic and cook for another 4 minutes. Stir in tomatoes, salt, pepper, zucchinis, and stock and bring to a boil; simmer for 20 minutes. Garnish with thyme and serve.

Nutrition Info:
- Per Serving: Calories: 240;Fat: 10g;Protein: 19g;Carbs: 17g.

Tasty Chicken Pot

Servings:4 | Cooking Time:35 Minutes

Ingredients:
- 1 lb chicken thighs, skinless and boneless
- 2 tbsp olive oil
- 1 onion, chopped
- 2 garlic cloves, minced
- 1 tsp smoked paprika
- 1 tsp chili powder
- ½ tsp fennel seeds, ground
- 2 tsp oregano, dried
- 14 oz canned tomatoes, diced
- ½ cup capers

Directions:
1. Warm the olive oil in a skillet over medium heat and sauté the onion, garlic, paprika, chili powder, fennel seeds, and oregano for 3 minutes. Put in chicken, tomatoes, 1 cup of water, and capers. Bring to a boil and simmer for 20-25 minutes.

Nutrition Info:
- Per Serving: Calories: 160;Fat: 9g;Protein: 13g;Carbs: 10g.

Lamb & Paprika Cannellini Beans

Servings:4 | Cooking Time:50 Minutes

Ingredients:
- 1 can Cannellini beans
- 2 tbsp olive oil, divided
- 1 lb lamb shoulder, cubed
- Salt and black pepper to taste
- 2 garlic cloves, minced
- 1 large onion, diced
- 1 celery stalk, chopped
- 1 cup tomatoes, chopped
- 1 carrot, chopped
- ⅓ cup tomato paste
- 1 tsp paprika
- 1 tsp dried oregano

Directions:
1. Warm the olive oil in a pot over medium heat. Season the lamb with salt and pepper and sauté for 3-4 minutes until brown, stirring occasionally. Stir in the onion, celery, tomatoes, and carrots and cook for 4-5 minutes.
2. Add the paprika and tomato paste and stir to combine. Pour in the beans and 2 cups water. Bring the mixture to a boil and simmer for 20-25 minutes until the lamb is cooked. Season with salt, pepper, and oregano and serve.

Nutrition Info:
- Per Serving: Calories: 520;Fat: 24g;Protein: 37g;Carbs: 42g.

Pork Chops With Green Vegetables

Servings:4 | Cooking Time:70 Minutes

Ingredients:
- 2 tbsp olive oil, divided
- ½ lb green beans, trimmed
- ½ lb asparagus spears
- ½ cup frozen peas, thawed
- 2 tomatoes, chopped
- 1 lb pork chops
- 1 tbsp tomato paste
- 1 onion, chopped
- Salt and black pepper to taste

Directions:
1. Warm olive oil in a saucepan over medium heat. Sprinkle the chops with salt and pepper. Place in the pan and brown for 8 minutes in total; set aside. In the same pan, sauté onion for 2 minutes until soft. In a bowl, whisk the tomato paste and 1 cup of water and pour in the saucepan. Bring to a simmer and scrape any bits from the bottom. Add the chops back and bring to a boil. Then lower the heat and simmer for 40 minutes. Add in green beans, asparagus, peas, tomatoes, salt, and pepper and cook for 10 minutes until the greens are soft.

Nutrition Info:
- Per Serving: Calories: 341;Fat: 16g;Protein: 36g;Carbs: 15g.

Chapter 6 Fish And Seafood Recipes

Chapter 6 Fish And Seafood Recipes

Pesto Shrimp Over Zoodles

Servings:4 | Cooking Time: 10 Minutes

Ingredients:
- 1 pound fresh shrimp, peeled and deveined
- Salt and freshly ground black pepper, to taste
- 2 tablespoons extra-virgin olive oil
- ½ small onion, slivered
- 8 ounces store-bought jarred pesto
- ¾ cup crumbled goat or feta cheese, plus additional for serving
- 2 large zucchini, spiralized, for serving
- ¼ cup chopped flat-leaf Italian parsley, for garnish

Directions:
1. In a bowl, season the shrimp with salt and pepper. Set aside.
2. In a large skillet, heat the olive oil over medium-high heat. Sauté the onion until just golden, 5 to 6 minutes.
3. Reduce the heat to low and add the pesto and cheese, whisking to combine and melt the cheese. Bring to a low simmer and add the shrimp. Reduce the heat back to low and cover. Cook until the shrimp is cooked through and pink, about 3 to 4 minutes.
4. Serve the shrimp warm over zoodles, garnishing with chopped parsley and additional crumbled cheese.

Nutrition Info:
- Per Serving: Calories: 491;Fat: 35.0g;Protein: 29.0g;Carbs: 15.0g.

Roasted Red Snapper With Citrus Topping

Servings:2 | Cooking Time:35 Minutes

Ingredients:
- 2 tbsp olive oil
- 1 tsp fresh cilantro, chopped
- ½ tsp grated lemon zest
- ½ tbsp lemon juice
- ½ tsp grated grapefruit zest
- ½ tbsp grapefruit juice
- ½ tsp grated orange zest
- ½ tbsp orange juice
- ½ shallot, minced
- ¼ tsp red pepper flakes
- Salt and black pepper to taste
- 1 whole red snapper, cleaned

Directions:
1. Preheat oven to 380°F. Whisk the olive oil, cilantro, lemon juice, orange juice, grapefruit juice, shallot, and pepper flakes together in a bowl. Season with salt and pepper. Set aside the citrus topping until ready to serve.
2. In a separate bowl, combine lemon zest, orange zest, grapefruit zest, salt, and pepper. With a sharp knife, make 3-4 shallow slashes, about 2 inches apart, on both sides of the snapper. Spoon the citrus mixture into the fish cavity and transfer to a greased baking sheet. Roast for 25 minutes until the fish flakes. Serve drizzled with citrus topping, and enjoy!

Nutrition Info:
- Per Serving: Calories: 257;Fat: 21g;Protein: 16g;Carbs: 1.6g.

Honey-mustard Roasted Salmon

Servings:4 | Cooking Time: 15 To 20 Minutes

Ingredients:
- 2 tablespoons whole-grain mustard
- 2 garlic cloves, minced
- 1 tablespoon honey
- ¼ teaspoon salt
- ¼ teaspoon freshly ground black pepper
- 1 pound salmon fillet
- Nonstick cooking spray

Directions:
1. Preheat the oven to 425ºF. Coat a baking sheet with nonstick cooking spray.
2. Stir together the mustard, garlic, honey, salt, and pepper in a small bowl.
3. Arrange the salmon fillet, skin-side down, on the coated baking sheet. Spread the mustard mixture evenly over the salmon fillet.
4. Roast in the preheated oven for 15 to 20 minutes, or until it flakes apart easily and reaches an internal temperature of 145ºF.
5. Serve hot.

Nutrition Info:
- Per Serving: Calories: 185;Fat: 7.0g;Protein: 23.2g;Carbs: 5.8g.

Rosemary Wine Poached Haddock

Servings:4 | Cooking Time:40 Minutes

Ingredients:
- 4 haddock fillets
- Salt and black pepper to taste
- 2 garlic cloves, minced
- ½ cup dry white wine
- ½ cup seafood stock
- 4 rosemary sprigs for garnish

Directions:
1. Preheat oven to 380 °F. Sprinkle haddock fillets with salt and black pepper and arrange them on a baking dish. Pour in the wine, garlic, and stock. Bake covered for 20 minutes until the fish is tender; remove to a serving plate. Pour the cooking liquid into a pot over high heat. Cook for 10 minutes until reduced by half. Place on serving dishes and top with the reduced poaching liquid. Serve garnished with rosemary.

Nutrition Info:
- Per Serving: Calories: 215;Fat: 4g;Protein: 35g;Carbs: 3g.

Parsley Salmon Bake

Servings:4 | Cooking Time:20 Minutes

Ingredients:
- 2 tbsp olive oil
- 1 lb salmon fillets
- ¼ fresh parsley, chopped
- 1 garlic clove, minced
- ¼ tsp dried dill
- ¼ tsp chili powder
- ¼ tsp garlic powder
- 1 lemon, grated
- Salt and black pepper to taste

Directions:
1. Preheat oven to 350 °F. Sprinkle the salmon with dill, chili powder, garlic powder, salt, and pepper.
2. Warm olive oil in a pan over medium heat and sear salmon skin-side down for 5 minutes. Transfer to the oven and bake for another 4-5 minutes. Combine parsley, lemon zest, garlic, and salt in a bowl. Serve salmon topped with the mixture.

Nutrition Info:
- Per Serving: Calories: 212;Fat: 14g;Protein: 22g;Carbs: 0.5g.

Lemon Rosemary Roasted Branzino

Servings:2 | Cooking Time: 30 Minutes

Ingredients:
- 4 tablespoons extra-virgin olive oil, divided
- 2 branzino fillets, preferably at least 1 inch thick
- 1 garlic clove, minced
- 1 bunch scallions (white part only), thinly sliced
- 10 to 12 small cherry tomatoes, halved
- 1 large carrot, cut into ¼-inch rounds
- ½ cup dry white wine
- 2 tablespoons paprika
- 2 teaspoons kosher salt
- ½ tablespoon ground chili pepper
- 2 rosemary sprigs or 1 tablespoon dried rosemary
- 1 small lemon, thinly sliced
- ½ cup sliced pitted kalamata olives

Directions:
1. Heat a large ovenproof skillet over high heat until hot, about 2 minutes. Add 1 tablespoon of olive oil and heat for 10 to 15 seconds until it shimmers.
2. Add the branzino fillets, skin-side up, and sear for 2 minutes. Flip the fillets and cook for an additional 2 minutes. Set aside.
3. Swirl 2 tablespoons of olive oil around the skillet to coat evenly.
4. Add the garlic, scallions, tomatoes, and carrot, and sauté for 5 minutes, or until softened.
5. Add the wine, stirring until all ingredients are well combined. Carefully place the fish over the sauce.
6. Preheat the oven to 450ºF.
7. Brush the fillets with the remaining 1 tablespoon of olive oil and season with paprika, salt, and chili pepper. Top each fillet with a rosemary sprig and lemon slices. Scatter the olives over fish and around the skillet.
8. Roast for about 10 minutes until the lemon slices are browned. Serve hot.

Nutrition Info:
- Per Serving: Calories: 724;Fat: 43.0g;Protein: 57.7g;Carbs: 25.0g.

Tuna Gyros With Tzatziki

Servings:4 | Cooking Time:15 Minutes

Ingredients:
- 4 oz tzatziki
- ½ lb canned tuna, drained
- ½ cup tahini
- 4 sundried tomatoes, diced
- 2 tbsp warm water
- 2 garlic cloves, minced
- 1 tbsp lemon juice
- 4 pita wraps
- 5 black olives, chopped
- Salt and black pepper to taste

Directions:
1. In a bowl, combine the tahini, water, garlic, lemon juice, salt, and black pepper. Warm the pita wraps in a grilled pan for a few minutes, turning once. Spread the tahini and tzatziki sauces over the warmed pitas and top with tuna, sundried tomatoes, and olives. Fold in half and serve immediately.

Nutrition Info:
- Per Serving: Calories: 334;Fat: 24g;Protein: 21.3g;Carbs: 9g.

Crunchy Pollock Fillets

Servings:4 | Cooking Time:25 Minutes

Ingredients:
- 4 pollock fillets, boneless
- 2 cups potato chips, crushed
- 2 tbsp mayonnaise

Directions:
1. Preheat the oven to 380ºF. Line a baking sheet with parchment paper. Rub each fillet with mayonnaise and dip them in the potato chips. Place fillets on the sheet and bake for 12 minutes. Serve with salad.

Nutrition Info:
- Per Serving: Calories: 240;Fat: 9g;Protein: 26g;Carbs: 10g.

Better-for-you Cod & Potatoes

Servings:4 | Cooking Time:35 Minutes

Ingredients:
- 1 tbsp olive oil
- 2 cod fillets
- 1 tbsp basil, chopped
- Salt and black pepper to taste
- 2 potatoes, peeled and sliced
- 2 tsp turmeric powder
- 1 garlic clove, minced

Directions:
1. Preheat the oven to 360ºF. Spread the potatoes on a greased baking dish and season with salt and pepper. Bake for 10 minutes. Arrange the cod fillets on top of the potatoes, sprinkle with salt and pepper, and drizzle with some olive oil. Bake for 10-12 more minutes until the fish flakes easily.
2. Warm the remaining olive oil in a skillet over medium heat and sauté garlic for 1 minute. Stir in basil, salt, pepper, turmeric powder, and 3-4 tbsp of water; cook for another 2-3 minutes. Pour the sauce over the cod fillets and serve warm.

Nutrition Info:
- Per Serving: Calories: 300;Fat: 15g;Protein: 33g;Carbs: 28g.

Hazelnut Crusted Sea Bass

Servings:2 | Cooking Time: 15 Minutes

Ingredients:
- 2 tablespoons almond butter
- 2 sea bass fillets
- ⅓ cup roasted hazelnuts
- A pinch of cayenne pepper

Directions:
1. Preheat the oven to 425ºF. Line a baking dish with waxed paper.
2. Brush the almond butter over the fillets.
3. Pulse the hazelnuts and cayenne in a food processor. Coat the sea bass with the hazelnut mixture, then transfer to the baking dish.
4. Bake in the preheated oven for about 15 minutes. Cool for 5 minutes before serving.

Nutrition Info:
- Per Serving: Calories: 468;Fat: 30.8g;Protein: 40.0g;Carbs: 8.8g.

White Wine Cod Fillets

Servings:4 | Cooking Time:40 Minutes

Ingredients:
- 4 cod fillets
- Salt and black pepper to taste
- ½ fennel seeds, ground
- 1 tbsp olive oil
- ½ cup dry white wine
- ½ cup vegetable stock
- 2 garlic cloves, minced
- 1 tsp chopped fresh sage

- 4 rosemary sprigs

Directions:

1. Preheat oven to 375 °F. Season the cod fillets with salt, pepper, and ground fennel seeds and place them in a greased baking dish. Add the wine, stock, garlic, and sage and drizzle with olive oil. Cover with foil and bake for 20 minutes until the fish flakes easily with a fork. Remove the fillets from the dish. Place the liquid in a saucepan over high heat and cook, stirring frequently, until reduced by half, about 10 minutes. Serve the fish topped with sauce and fresh rosemary sprigs.

Nutrition Info:

- Per Serving: Calories: 89;Fat: 0.6g;Protein: 18g;Carbs: 1.8g.

Hot Jumbo Shrimp

Servings:4 | Cooking Time:20 Minutes

Ingredients:

- 2 lb shell-on jumbo shrimp, deveined
- ¼ cup olive oil
- Salt and black pepper to taste
- 6 garlic cloves, minced
- 1 tsp anise seeds
- ½ tsp red pepper flakes
- 2 tbsp minced fresh cilantro
- 1 lemon, cut into wedges

Directions:

1. Combine the olive oil, garlic, anise seeds, pepper flakes, and black pepper in a large bowl. Add the shrimp and cilantro and toss well, making sure the oil mixture gets into the interior of the shrimp. Arrange shrimp in a single layer on a baking tray. Set under the preheated broiler for approximately 4 minutes. Flip shrimp and continue to broil until it is opaque and shells are beginning to brown, about 2 minutes, rotating sheet halfway through broiling. Serve with lemon wedges.

Nutrition Info:

- Per Serving: Calories: 218;Fat: 9g;Protein: 30.8g;Carbs: 2.3g.

Mediterranean Cod Stew

Servings:6 | Cooking Time: 20 Minutes

Ingredients:

- 2 tablespoons extra-virgin olive oil
- 2 cups chopped onion
- 2 garlic cloves, minced
- ¾ teaspoon smoked paprika
- 1 can diced tomatoes, undrained
- 1 jar roasted red peppers, drained and chopped
- 1 cup sliced olives, green or black
- ⅓ cup dry red wine
- ¼ teaspoon kosher or sea salt
- ¼ teaspoon freshly ground black pepper
- 1½ pounds cod fillets, cut into 1-inch pieces
- 3 cups sliced mushrooms

Directions:

1. In a large stockpot over medium heat, heat the oil. Add the onion and cook for 4 minutes, stirring occasionally. Add the garlic and smoked paprika and cook for 1 minute, stirring often.
2. Mix in the tomatoes with their juices, roasted peppers, olives, wine, pepper, and salt, and turn the heat to medium-high. Bring the mixture to a boil. Add the cod fillets and mushrooms, and reduce the heat to medium.
3. Cover and cook for about 10 minutes, stirring a few times, until the cod is cooked through and flakes easily, and serve.

Nutrition Info:

- Per Serving: Calories: 167;Fat: 5.0g;Protein: 19.0g;Carbs: 11.0g.

Anchovy Spread With Avocado

Servings:2 | Cooking Time:5 Minutes

Ingredients:

- 1 avocado, peeled and pitted
- 1 tsp lemon juice
- ¼ celery stalk, chopped
- ¼ cup chopped shallots
- 2 anchovy fillets in olive oil
- Salt and black pepper to taste

Directions:

1. Combine lemon juice, avocado, celery, shallots, and anchovy fillets (with their olive oil) in a food processor. Blitz until smooth. Season with salt and black pepper. Serve.

Nutrition Info:

- Per Serving: Calories: 271;Fat: 20g;Protein: 15g;Carbs: 12g.

Canned Sardine Donburi (rice Bowl)

Servings:4 | Cooking Time: 40 To 50 Minutes

Ingredients:

- 4 cups water
- 2 cups brown rice, rinsed well
- ½ teaspoon salt
- 3 cans sardines packed in
- water, drained
- 3 scallions, sliced thin
- 1-inch piece fresh ginger, grated
- 4 tablespoons sesame oil

Directions:

1. Place the water, brown rice, and salt to a large saucepan and stir to combine. Allow the mixture to boil over high heat.
2. Once boiling, reduce the heat to low, and cook covered for 45 to 50 minutes, or until the rice is tender.
3. Meanwhile, roughly mash the sardines with a fork in a medium bowl.
4. When the rice is done, stir in the mashed sardines, scallions, and ginger.
5. Divide the mixture into four bowls. Top each bowl with a drizzle of sesame oil. Serve warm.

Nutrition Info:

- Per Serving: Calories: 603;Fat: 23.6g;Protein: 25.2g;Carbs: 73.8g.

Classic Prawn Scampi

Servings:4 | Cooking Time:25 Minutes

Ingredients:

- 1 lb prawns, peeled and deveined
- 2 tbsp olive oil
- 1 onion, chopped
- 6 garlic cloves, minced
- 1 lemon, juiced and zested
- ½ cup dry white wine
- Salt and black pepper to taste
- 2 cups fusilli, cooked
- ½ tsp red pepper flakes

Directions:

1. Warm olive oil in a pan over medium heat and sauté onion and garlic for 3 minutes, stirring often, until fragrant. Stir in prawns and cook for 3-4 minutes. Mix in lemon juice, lemon zest, salt, pepper, wine, and red flakes. Bring to a boil, then decrease the heat, and simmer for 2 minutes until the liquid is reduced by half. Turn the heat off. Stir in pasta and serve.

Nutrition Info:

- Per Serving: Calories: 388;Fat: 9g;Protein: 32g;Carbs: 38.2g.

Easy Breaded Shrimp

Servings:4 | Cooking Time: 4 To 6 Minutes

Ingredients:
- 2 large eggs
- 1 tablespoon water
- 2 cups seasoned Italian bread crumbs
- 1 teaspoon salt
- 1 cup flour
- 1 pound large shrimp, peeled and deveined
- Extra-virgin olive oil, as needed

Directions:
1. In a small bowl, beat the eggs with the water, then transfer to a shallow dish.
2. Add the bread crumbs and salt to a separate shallow dish, then mix well.
3. Place the flour into a third shallow dish.
4. Coat the shrimp in the flour, then the beaten egg, and finally the bread crumbs. Place on a plate and repeat with all of the shrimp.
5. Heat a skillet over high heat. Pour in enough olive oil to coat the bottom of the skillet. Cook the shrimp in the hot skillet for 2 to 3 minutes on each side. Remove and drain on a paper towel. Serve warm.

Nutrition Info:
- Per Serving: Calories: 714;Fat: 34.0g;Protein: 37.0g;Carbs: 63.0g.

Baked Lemon Salmon

Servings:4 | Cooking Time: 20 Minutes

Ingredients:
- ¼ teaspoon dried thyme
- Zest and juice of ½ lemon
- ¼ teaspoon salt
- ½ teaspoon freshly ground
- black pepper
- 1 pound salmon fillet
- Nonstick cooking spray

Directions:
1. Preheat the oven to 425ºF. Coat a baking sheet with nonstick cooking spray.
2. Mix together the thyme, lemon zest and juice, salt, and pepper in a small bowl and stir to incorporate.
3. Arrange the salmon, skin-side down, on the coated baking sheet. Spoon the thyme mixture over the salmon and spread it all over.
4. Bake in the preheated oven for about 15 to 20 minutes, or until the fish flakes apart easily. Serve warm.

Nutrition Info:
- Per Serving: Calories: 162;Fat: 7.0g;Protein: 23.1g;Carbs: 1.0g.

Pan-fried Tuna With Vegetables

Servings:4 | Cooking Time:25 Minutes

Ingredients:
- 2 tbsp olive oil
- 4 tuna fillets, boneless
- 1 red bell pepper, chopped
- 1 onion, chopped
- 4 garlic cloves, minced
- ½ cup fish stock
- 1 tsp basil, dried
- ½ cup cherry tomatoes, halved
- ½ cup black olives, halved
- Salt and black pepper to taste

Directions:
1. Warm the olive oil in a skillet over medium heat and fry tuna for 10 minutes on both sides. Divide the fish among plates. In the same skillet, cook onion, bell pepper, garlic, and cherry tomatoes for 3 minutes. Stir in salt, pepper, fish stock, basil, and olives and

cook for another 3 minutes. Top the tuna with the mixture and serve immediately.

Nutrition Info:
- Per Serving: Calories: 260;Fat: 9g;Protein: 29g;Carbs: 6g.

Parsley Littleneck Clams In Sherry Sauce

Servings:4 | Cooking Time:20 Minutes

Ingredients:
- 2 tbsp olive oil
- 1 cup dry sherry
- 3 shallots, minced
- 4 garlic cloves, minced
- 4 lb littleneck clams,
- scrubbed
- 2 tbsp minced fresh parsley
- ½ tsp cayenne pepper
- 1 Lemon, cut into wedges

Directions:
1. Bring the sherry wine, shallots, and garlic to a simmer in a large saucepan and cook for 3 minutes. Add clams, cover, and cook, stirring twice, until clams open, about 7 minutes. With a slotted spoon, transfer clams to a serving bowl, discarding any that refuse to open. Stir in olive oil, parsley, and cayenne pepper. Pour sauce over clams and serve with lemon wedges.

Nutrition Info:
- Per Serving: Calories: 333;Fat: 9g;Protein: 44.9g;Carbs: 14g.

Garlic Skillet Salmon

Servings:4 | Cooking Time: 14 To 16 Minutes

Ingredients:
- 1 tablespoon extra-virgin olive oil
- 2 garlic cloves, minced
- 1 teaspoon smoked paprika
- 1½ cups grape or cherry tomatoes, quartered
- 1 jar roasted red peppers, drained and chopped
- 1 tablespoon water
- ¼ teaspoon freshly ground black pepper
- ¼ teaspoon kosher or sea salt
- 1 pound salmon fillets, skin removed and cut into 8 pieces
- 1 tablespoon freshly squeezed lemon juice

Directions:
1. In a large skillet over medium heat, heat the oil. Add the garlic and smoked paprika and cook for 1 minute, stirring often. Add the tomatoes, roasted peppers, water, black pepper, and salt. Turn up the heat to medium-high, bring to a simmer, and cook for 3 minutes, stirring occasionally and smashing the tomatoes with a wooden spoon toward the end of the cooking time.
2. Add the salmon to the skillet, and spoon some of the sauce over the top. Cover and cook for 10 to 12 minutes, or until the salmon is cooked through and just starts to flake.
3. Remove the skillet from the heat, and drizzle lemon juice over the top of the fish. Stir the sauce, then break up the salmon into chunks with a fork. Serve hot.

Nutrition Info:
- Per Serving: Calories: 255;Fat: 11.7g;Protein: 24.2g;Carbs: 5.9g.

Grilled Lemon Pesto Salmon

Servings:2 | Cooking Time: 6 To 10 Minutes

Ingredients:
- 10 ounces salmon fillet
- Salt and freshly ground black pepper, to taste
- 2 tablespoons prepared pesto
- sauce
- 1 large fresh lemon, sliced
- Cooking spray

Directions:

1. Preheat the grill to medium-high heat. Spray the grill grates with cooking spray.
2. Season the salmon with salt and black pepper. Spread the pesto sauce on top.
3. Make a bed of fresh lemon slices about the same size as the salmon fillet on the hot grill, and place the salmon on top of the lemon slices. Put any additional lemon slices on top of the salmon.
4. Grill the salmon for 6 to 10 minutes, or until the fish is opaque and flakes apart easily.
5. Serve hot.

Nutrition Info:
- Per Serving: Calories: 316;Fat: 21.1g;Protein: 29.0g;Carbs: 1.0g.

Salmon Baked In Foil

Servings:4 | Cooking Time: 25 Minutes

Ingredients:
- 2 cups cherry tomatoes
- 3 tablespoons extra-virgin olive oil
- 3 tablespoons lemon juice
- 3 tablespoons almond butter
- 1 teaspoon oregano
- ½ teaspoon salt
- 4 salmon fillets

Directions:
1. Preheat the oven to 400ºF.
2. Cut the tomatoes in half and put them in a bowl.
3. Add the olive oil, lemon juice, butter, oregano, and salt to the tomatoes and gently toss to combine.
4. Cut 4 pieces of foil, about 12-by-12 inches each.
5. Place the salmon fillets in the middle of each piece of foil.
6. Divide the tomato mixture evenly over the 4 pieces of salmon. Bring the ends of the foil together and seal to form a closed pocket.
7. Place the 4 pockets on a baking sheet. Bake in the preheated oven for 25 minutes.
8. Remove from the oven and serve on a plate.

Nutrition Info:
- Per Serving: Calories: 410;Fat: 32.0g;Protein: 30.0g;Carbs: 4.0g.

Salmon Stuffed Peppers

Servings:4 | Cooking Time:25 Minutes

Ingredients:
- 4 bell peppers
- 10 oz canned salmon, drained
- 12 black olives, chopped
- 1 red onion, finely chopped
- ½ tsp garlic, minced
- 1/3 cup mayonnaise
- 1 cup cream cheese
- 1 tsp Mediterranean seasoning
- Salt and pepper flakes to taste

Directions:
1. Preheat oven to 390 °F. Cut the peppers into halves and remove the seeds. In a mixing bowl, combine the salmon, onion, garlic, mayonnaise, olives, salt, red pepper, Mediterranean spice mix, and cream cheese. Divide the mixture between the peppers and bake them in the oven for 10-12 minutes or until cooked through. Serve and enjoy!

Nutrition Info:
- Per Serving: Calories: 272;Fat: 14g;Protein: 29g;Carbs: 5g.

Wine-steamed Clams

Servings:4 | Cooking Time:30 Minutes

Ingredients:
- 4 lb clams, scrubbed and debearded
- 3 tbsp butter
- 3 garlic cloves, minced
- ¼ tsp red pepper flakes
- 1 cup dry white wine
- 3 sprigs fresh thyme
- 2 tbsp fresh dill, minced

Directions:
1. Melt the butter in a large saucepan over medium heat and cook garlic and pepper flakes, stirring constantly, until fragrant, about 30 seconds. Stir in wine and thyme sprigs, bring to a boil and cook until wine is slightly reduced, about 1 minute. Stir in clams. Cover the saucepan and simmer for 15-18 minutes. Remove, discard thyme sprigs and any clams that refuse to open. Sprinkle with dill and serve.

Nutrition Info:
- Per Serving: Calories: 326;Fat: 14g;Protein: 36g;Carbs: 12g.

Slow Cooker Salmon In Foil

Servings:2 | Cooking Time: 2 Hours

Ingredients:
- 2 salmon fillets
- 1 tablespoon olive oil
- 2 cloves garlic, minced
- ½ tablespoon lime juice
- 1 teaspoon finely chopped fresh parsley
- ¼ teaspoon black pepper

Directions:
1. Spread a length of foil onto a work surface and place the salmon fillets in the middle.
2. Mix together the olive oil, garlic, lime juice, parsley, and black pepper in a small bowl. Brush the mixture over the fillets. Fold the foil over and crimp the sides to make a packet.
3. Place the packet into the slow cooker, cover, and cook on High for 2 hours, or until the fish flakes easily with a fork.
4. Serve hot.

Nutrition Info:
- Per Serving: Calories: 446;Fat: 20.7g;Protein: 65.4g;Carbs: 1.5g.

Crispy Sole Fillets

Servings:4 | Cooking Time:10 Minutes

Ingredients:
- ¼ cup olive oil
- ½ cup flour
- ½ tsp paprika
- 8 skinless sole fillets
- Salt and black pepper to taste
- 4 lemon wedges

Directions:
1. Warm the olive oil in a skillet over medium heat. Mix the flour with paprika in a shallow dish. Coat the fish with the flour, shaking off any excess. Sear the sole fillets for 2-3 minutes per side until lightly browned. Serve with lemon wedges.

Nutrition Info:
- Per Serving: Calories: 219;Fat: 15g;Protein: 8.7g;Carbs: 13g.

Baked Cod With Vegetables

Servings:2 | Cooking Time: 25 Minutes

Ingredients:
- 1 pound thick cod fillet, cut into 4 even portions
- ¼ teaspoon onion powder (optional)
- ¼ teaspoon paprika
- 3 tablespoons extra-virgin olive oil
- 4 medium scallions
- ½ cup fresh chopped basil, divided
- 3 tablespoons minced garlic (optional)
- 2 teaspoons salt
- 2 teaspoons freshly ground
- black pepper
- ¼ teaspoon dry marjoram (optional)
- 6 sun-dried tomato slices
- ½ cup dry white wine
- ½ cup crumbled feta cheese
- 1 can oil-packed artichoke hearts, drained
- 1 lemon, sliced
- 1 cup pitted kalamata olives
- 1 teaspoon capers (optional)
- 4 small red potatoes, quartered

Directions:
1. Preheat the oven to 375ºF.
2. Season the fish with paprika and onion powder (if desired).
3. Heat an ovenproof skillet over medium heat and sear the top side of the cod for about 1 minute until golden. Set aside.
4. Heat the olive oil in the same skillet over medium heat. Add the scallions, ¼ cup of basil, garlic (if desired), salt, pepper, marjoram (if desired), tomato slices, and white wine and stir to combine. Bring to a boil and remove from heat.
5. Evenly spread the sauce on the bottom of skillet. Place the cod on top of the tomato basil sauce and scatter with feta cheese. Place the artichokes in the skillet and top with the lemon slices.
6. Scatter with the olives, capers (if desired), and the remaining ¼ cup of basil. Remove from the heat and transfer to the preheated oven. Bake for 15 to 20 minutes, or until it flakes easily with a fork.
7. Meanwhile, place the quartered potatoes on a baking sheet or wrapped in aluminum foil. Bake in the oven for 15 minutes until fork-tender.
8. Cool for 5 minutes before serving.

Nutrition Info:
- Per Serving: Calories: 1168;Fat: 60.0g;Protein: 63.8g;Carbs: 94.0g.

Avocado & Onion Tilapia

Servings:4 | Cooking Time:10 Minutes

Ingredients:
- 1 tbsp olive oil
- 1 tbsp orange juice
- ¼ tsp kosher salt
- ½ tsp ground coriander seeds
- 4 tilapia fillets, skin-on
- ¼ cup chopped red onions
- 1 avocado, skinned and sliced

Directions:
1. In a bowl, mix together the olive oil, orange juice, ground coriander seeds, and salt. Add the fish and turn to coat on all sides. Arrange the fillets on a greased microwave-safe dish. Top with onion and cover the dish with plastic wrap, leaving a small part open at the edge to vent the steam. Microwave on high for about 3 minutes. The fish is done when it just begins to separate into chunks when pressed gently with a fork. Top the fillets with the avocado and serve.

Nutrition Info:
- Per Serving: Calories: 210;Fat: 11g;Protein: 25g;Carbs: 5g.

Mustard Sardine Cakes

Servings:4 | Cooking Time:20 Minutes

Ingredients:
- 3 tbsp olive oil
- 1 tsp mustard powder
- 1 tsp chili powder
- 20 oz canned sardines, mashed
- 2 garlic cloves, minced
- 2 tbsp dill, chopped
- 1 onion, chopped
- 1 cup panko breadcrumbs
- 1 egg, whisked
- Salt and black pepper to taste
- 2 tbsp lemon juice

Directions:
1. Combine sardines, garlic, dill, onion, breadcrumbs, egg, mustard powder, chili powder, salt, pepper, and lemon juice in a bowl and form medium patties out of the mixture. Warm the olive oil in a skillet over medium heat and fry the cakes for 10 minutes on both sides. Serve with aioli.

Nutrition Info:
- Per Serving: Calories: 300;Fat: 14g;Protein: 7g;Carbs: 23g.

Fried Scallops With Bean Mash

Servings:2 | Cooking Time:20 Minutes

Ingredients:
- 4 tbsp olive oil
- 2 garlic cloves
- 2 tsp fresh thyme, minced
- 1 can cannellini beans
- ½ cup chicken stock
- Salt and black pepper to taste
- 10 oz sea scallops

Directions:
1. Warm 2 tablespoons of olive oil in a saucepan over medium heat. Sauté the garlic for 30 seconds or just until it's fragrant. Stir in the beans and stock and bring to a boil. Simmer for 5 minutes. Remove the beans to a bowl and mash them with a potato mash. Season with thyme, salt, and pepper.
2. Warm the remaining oil in a large sauté pan. Add the scallops, flat-side down, and cook for 2 minutes or until they're golden on the bottom. Flip over and cook for another 1-2 minutes or until opaque and slightly firm. Divide the bean mash between plates and top with scallops.

Nutrition Info:
- Per Serving: Calories: 465;Fat: 29g;Protein: 30g;Carbs: 21g.

Date & Hazelnut Crusted Barramundi

Servings:2 | Cooking Time:25 Minutes

Ingredients:
- 2 tbsp olive oil
- 2 barramundi fillets, boneless
- 1 shallot, sliced
- 4 lemon slices
- ½ lemon, zested and juiced
- 1 cup baby spinach
- ¼ cup hazelnuts, chopped
- 4 dates, pitted and chopped
- Salt and black pepper to taste

Directions:
1. Preheat oven to 380°F. Sprinkle barramundi with salt and pepper and place on 2 parchment paper pieces. Top each fillet with lemon slices, lemon juice, shallot, lemon zest, spinach, hazelnuts, dates, and parsley. Sprinkle each fillet with 1 tbsp of oil and fold the paper around it. Place them on a baking sheet and bake for 12 minutes. Serve and enjoy!

Nutrition Info:
- Per Serving: Calories: 240;Fat: 17g;Protein: 7g;Carbs: 26g.

Lemon Cioppino

Servings:6 | Cooking Time:6 Minutes

Ingredients:

- 1 lb mussels, scrubbed, de-bearded
- 1 lb large shrimp, peeled and deveined
- 1 ½ lb haddock fillets, cut into chunks
- 3 tbsp olive oil
- 1 fennel bulb, thinly sliced
- 1 onion, chopped
- 3 large shallots, chopped
- Salt to taste
- 4 garlic cloves, minced
- ¼ tsp red pepper flakes
- ¼ cup tomato paste
- 1 can diced tomatoes
- 1 ½ cups dry white wine
- 5 cups vegetable stock
- 1 bay leaf
- 1 lb clams, scrubbed
- 2 tbsp basil, chopped

Directions:

1. Warm the olive oil in a large pot over medium heat. Sauté the fennel, onion, garlic, and shallots for 8-10 minutes until tender. Add the red pepper flakes and sauté for 2 minutes. Stir in the tomato paste, tomatoes with their juices, wine, stock, salt, and bay leaf. Cover and bring to a simmer. Lower the heat to low and simmer for 30 minutes until the flavors blend.
2. Pour in the clams and mussels and cook for about 5 minutes. Add the shrimp and fish. Simmer gently until the fish and shrimp are just cooked through, 5 minutes. Discard any clams and mussels that refuse to open and bay leaf. Top with basil.

Nutrition Info:

- Per Serving: Calories: 163;Fat: 4.1g;Protein: 22g;Carbs: 8.3g.

Haddock With Cucumber Sauce

Servings:4 | Cooking Time: 10 Minutes

Ingredients:

- ¼ cup plain Greek yogurt
- ½ scallion, white and green parts, finely chopped
- ½ English cucumber, grated, liquid squeezed out
- 2 teaspoons chopped fresh
- mint
- 1 teaspoon honey
- Sea salt and freshly ground black pepper, to taste
- 4 haddock fillets, patted dry
- Nonstick cooking spray

Directions:

1. In a small bowl, stir together the yogurt, cucumber, scallion, mint, honey, and a pinch of salt. Set aside.
2. Season the fillets lightly with salt and pepper.
3. Place a large skillet over medium-high heat and spray lightly with cooking spray.
4. Cook the haddock, turning once, until it is just cooked through, about 5 minutes per side.
5. Remove the fish from the heat and transfer to plates.
6. Serve topped with the cucumber sauce.

Nutrition Info:

- Per Serving: Calories: 164;Fat: 2.0g;Protein: 27.0g;Carbs: 4.0g.

Saucy Cod With Calamari Rings

Servings:4 | Cooking Time:20 Minutes

Ingredients:

- 1 lb cod, skinless and cubed
- 2 tbsp olive oil
- 1 mango, peeled and cubed
- ½ lb calamari rings
- 1 tbsp garlic chili sauce
- ¼ cup lime juice
- ½ tsp smoked paprika
- ½ tsp cumin, ground
- 2 garlic cloves, minced
- Salt and black pepper to taste

Directions:

1. Warm the olive oil in a skillet over medium heat and cook chili sauce, lime juice, paprika, cumin, garlic, salt, pepper, and mango for 3 minutes. Stir in cod and calamari and cook for another 7 minutes. Serve warm.

Nutrition Info:

- Per Serving: Calories: 290;Fat: 13g;Protein: 16g;Carbs: 12g.

Vegetable & Shrimp Roast

Servings:4 | Cooking Time:30 Minutes

Ingredients:

- 2 lb shrimp, peeled and deveined
- 4 tbsp olive oil
- 2 bell peppers, cut into chunks
- 2 fennel bulbs, cut into wedges
- 2 red onions, cut into wedges
- 4 garlic cloves, unpeeled
- 8 Kalamata olives, halved
- 1 tsp lemon zest, grated
- 2 tsp oregano, dried
- 2 tbsp parsley, chopped
- Salt and black pepper to taste

Directions:

1. Preheat the oven to 390 °F. Place bell peppers, garlic, fennel, red onions, and olives in a roasting tray. Add in the lemon zest, oregano, half of the olive oil, salt, and pepper and toss to coat; roast for 15 minutes. Coat the shrimp with the remaining olive oil and pour over the veggies; roast for another 7 minutes. Serve topped with parsley.

Nutrition Info:

- Per Serving: Calories: 350;Fat: 20g;Protein: 11g;Carbs: 35g.

Dilly Haddock In Tomato Sauce

Servings:4 | Cooking Time:20 Minutes

Ingredients:

- 4 haddock fillets, boneless
- 1 cup vegetable stock
- 2 garlic cloves, minced
- 2 cups cherry tomatoes,
- halved
- Salt and black pepper to taste
- 2 tbsp dill, chopped

Directions:

1. In a skillet over medium heat, cook cherry tomatoes, garlic, salt, and pepper for 5 minutes. Stir in haddock fillets and vegetable stock and bring to a simmer. Cook covered for 10-12 minutes. Serve topped with dill.

Nutrition Info:

- Per Serving: Calories: 190;Fat: 2g;Protein: 35g;Carbs: 6g.

Balsamic-honey Glazed Salmon

Servings:4 | Cooking Time: 8 Minutes

Ingredients:

- ½ cup balsamic vinegar
- 1 tablespoon honey
- 4 salmon fillets
- Sea salt and freshly ground pepper, to taste
- 1 tablespoon olive oil

Directions:

1. Heat a skillet over medium-high heat. Combine the vinegar and honey in a small bowl.
2. Season the salmon fillets with the sea salt and freshly ground pepper; brush with the honey-balsamic glaze.
3. Add olive oil to the skillet, and sear the salmon fillets, cooking for 3 to 4 minutes on each side until lightly browned and medium rare in the center.
4. Let sit for 5 minutes before serving.

Nutrition Info:

- Per Serving: Calories: 454;Fat: 17.3g;Protein: 65.3g;Carbs: 9.7g.

Parsley Tomato Tilapia

Servings:4 | Cooking Time:20 Minutes

Ingredients:
- 2 tbsp olive oil
- 4 tilapia fillets, boneless
- ½ cup tomato sauce
- 2 tbsp parsley, chopped
- Salt and black pepper to taste

Directions:
1. Warm olive oil in a skillet over medium heat. Sprinkle tilapia with salt and pepper and cook until golden brown, flipping once, about 6 minutes. Pour in the tomato sauce and parsley and cook for an additional 4 minutes. Serve immediately.

Nutrition Info:
- Per Serving: Calories: 308;Fat: 17g;Protein: 16g;Carbs: 3g.

Roasted Trout Stuffed With Veggies

Servings:2 | Cooking Time: 25 Minutes

Ingredients:
- 2 whole trout fillets, dressed (cleaned but with bones and skin intact)
- 1 tablespoon extra-virgin olive oil
- ¼ teaspoon salt
- ⅛ teaspoon freshly ground black pepper
- 1 small onion, thinly sliced
- ½ red bell pepper, seeded and thinly sliced
- 1 poblano pepper, seeded and thinly sliced
- 2 or 3 shiitake mushrooms, sliced
- 1 lemon, sliced
- Nonstick cooking spray

Directions:
1. Preheat the oven to 425°F. Spray a baking sheet with nonstick cooking spray.
2. Rub both trout fillets, inside and out, with the olive oil. Season with salt and pepper.
3. Mix together the onion, bell pepper, poblano pepper, and mushrooms in a large bowl. Stuff half of this mixture into the cavity of each fillet. Top the mixture with 2 or 3 lemon slices inside each fillet.
4. Place the fish on the prepared baking sheet side by side. Roast in the preheated oven for 25 minutes, or until the fish is cooked through and the vegetables are tender.
5. Remove from the oven and serve on a plate.

Nutrition Info:
- Per Serving: Calories: 453;Fat: 22.1g;Protein: 49.0g;Carbs: 13.8g.

Garlic Shrimp With Arugula Pesto

Servings:2 | Cooking Time: 5 Minutes

Ingredients:
- 3 cups lightly packed arugula
- ½ cup lightly packed basil leaves
- ¼ cup walnuts
- 3 tablespoons olive oil
- 3 medium garlic cloves
- 2 tablespoons grated Parmesan cheese
- 1 tablespoon freshly squeezed lemon juice
- Salt and freshly ground black pepper, to taste
- 1 package zucchini noodles
- 8 ounces cooked, shelled shrimp
- 2 Roma tomatoes, diced

Directions:
1. Process the arugula, basil, walnuts, olive oil, garlic, Parmesan cheese, and lemon juice in a food processor until smooth, scraping down the sides as needed. Season with salt and pepper to taste.
2. Heat a skillet over medium heat. Add the pesto, zucchini noodles, and cooked shrimp. Toss to combine the sauce over the noodles and shrimp, and cook until heated through.
3. Taste and season with more salt and pepper as needed. Serve topped with the diced tomatoes.

Nutrition Info:
- Per Serving: Calories: 435;Fat: 30.2g;Protein: 33.0g;Carbs: 15.1g.

Shrimp & Spinach A La Puttanesca

Servings:4 | Cooking Time:20 Minutes

Ingredients:
- 1 lb fresh shrimp, shells and tails removed
- 1 cup baby spinach
- 16 oz cooked spaghetti
- 2 tbsp olive oil
- 3 anchovy fillets, chopped
- 3 garlic cloves, minced
- ½ tsp crushed red pepper
- 1 can tomatoes, diced
- 12 black olives, sliced
- 2 tbsp capers
- 1 tsp dried oregano

Directions:
1. Warm the olive oil in a large skillet over medium heat. Add in the anchovies, garlic, and crushed red peppers and cook for 3 minutes, stirring frequently and mashing up the anchovies with a wooden spoon until they have melted into the oil. Pour in the tomatoes with their juices, olives, capers, and oregano. Simmer until the sauce is lightly bubbling, about 3-4 minutes. Stir in the shrimp. Cook for 6-8 minutes or until they turn pink and white, stirring occasionally. Add the baby spinach and spaghetti and stir for 2 minutes until the spinach wilts. Serve and enjoy!

Nutrition Info:
- Per Serving: Calories: 362;Fat: 13g;Protein: 30g;Carbs: 31g.

Tuna And Zucchini Patties

Servings:4 | Cooking Time: 12 Minutes

Ingredients:
- 3 slices whole-wheat sandwich bread, toasted
- 2 cans tuna in olive oil, drained
- 1 cup shredded zucchini
- 1 large egg, lightly beaten
- ¼ cup diced red bell pepper
- 1 tablespoon dried oregano
- 1 teaspoon lemon zest
- ¼ teaspoon freshly ground black pepper
- ¼ teaspoon kosher or sea salt
- 1 tablespoon extra-virgin olive oil
- Salad greens or 4 whole-wheat rolls, for serving (optional)

Directions:
1. Crumble the toast into bread crumbs with your fingers (or use a knife to cut into ¼-inch cubes) until you have 1 cup of loosely packed crumbs. Pour the crumbs into a large bowl. Add the tuna, zucchini, beaten egg, bell pepper, oregano, lemon zest, black pepper, and salt. Mix well with a fork. With your hands, form the mixture into four (½-cup-size) patties. Place them on a plate, and press each patty flat to about ¾-inch thick.
2. In a large skillet over medium-high heat, heat the oil until it's very hot, about 2 minutes.
3. Add the patties to the hot oil, then reduce the heat down to medium. Cook the patties for 5 minutes, flip with a spatula, and cook for an additional 5 minutes. Serve the patties on salad greens or whole-wheat rolls, if desired.

Nutrition Info:
- Per Serving: Calories: 757;Fat: 72.0g;Protein: 5.0g;Carbs: 26.0g.

Peppercorn-seared Tuna Steaks

Servings:2 | Cooking Time: 10 Minutes

Ingredients:
- 2 ahi tuna steaks
- 1 teaspoon kosher salt
- ¼ teaspoon cayenne pepper
- 2 tablespoons olive oil
- 1 teaspoon whole peppercorns

Directions:
1. On a plate, Season the tuna steaks on both sides with salt and cayenne pepper.
2. In a skillet, heat the olive oil over medium-high heat until it shimmers.
3. Add the peppercorns and cook for about 5 minutes, or until they soften and pop.
4. Carefully put the tuna steaks in the skillet and sear for 1 to 2 minutes per side, depending on the thickness of the tuna steaks, or until the fish is cooked to the desired level of doneness.
5. Cool for 5 minutes before serving.

Nutrition Info:
- Per Serving: Calories: 260;Fat: 14.3g;Protein: 33.4g;Carbs: 0.2g.

Hot Tomato & Caper Squid Stew

Servings:4 | Cooking Time:50 Minutes

Ingredients:
- 1 cans whole peeled tomatoes, diced
- ¼ cup olive oil
- 1 onion, chopped
- 1 celery rib, sliced
- 3 garlic cloves, minced
- ¼ tsp red pepper flakes
- 1 red chili, minced
- ½ cup dry white wine
- 2 lb squid, sliced into rings
- Salt and black pepper to taste
- ⅓ cup green olives, chopped
- 1 tbsp capers
- 2 tbsp fresh parsley, chopped

Directions:
1. Warm the olive oil in a pot over medium heat. Sauté the onion, garlic, red chili, and celery until softened, about 5 minutes. Stir in pepper flakes and cook for about 30 seconds. Stir in wine, scraping up any browned bits, and cook until nearly evaporated, about 1 minute. Add 1 cup of water and season with salt and pepper. Stir the squid in the pot. Reduce heat to low, cover, and simmer until squid has released its liquid, about 15 minutes. Pour in tomatoes, olives, and capers, and continue to cook until squid is very tender, 30-35 minutes. Top with parsley. Serve and enjoy!

Nutrition Info:
- Per Serving: Calories: 334;Fat: 12g;Protein: 28g;Carbs: 30g.

Seafood Stew

Servings:4 | Cooking Time:25 Minutes

Ingredients:
- ½ lb skinless trout, cubed
- 2 tbsp olive oil
- ½ lb clams
- ½ lb cod, cubed
- 1 onion, chopped
- ½ fennel bulb, chopped
- 2 garlic cloves, minced
- ¼ cup dry white wine
- 2 tbsp chopped fresh parsley
- 1 can tomato sauce
- 1 cup fish broth
- 1 tbsp Italian seasoning
- ⅛ tsp red pepper flakes
- Salt and black pepper to taste

Directions:
1. Warm olive oil in a pot over medium heat and sauté onion and fennel for 5 minutes. Add in garlic and cook for 30 seconds. Pour in the wine and cook for 1 minute. Stir in tomato sauce, clams, broth, cod, trout, salt, Italian seasoning, red pepper flakes, and pepper. Bring just a boil and simmer for 5 minutes. Discard any unopened clams. Top with parsley.

Nutrition Info:
- Per Serving: Calories: 372;Fat: 15g;Protein: 34g;Carbs: 25g.

Lemony Shrimp With Orzo Salad

Servings:4 | Cooking Time: 22 Minutes

Ingredients:
- 1 cup orzo
- 1 hothouse cucumber, deseeded and chopped
- ½ cup finely diced red onion
- 2 tablespoons extra-virgin olive oil
- 2 pounds shrimp, peeled and deveined
- 3 lemons, juiced
- Salt and freshly ground black pepper, to taste
- ¾ cup crumbled feta cheese
- 2 tablespoons dried dill
- 1 cup chopped fresh flat-leaf parsley

Directions:
1. Bring a large pot of water to a boil. Add the orzo and cook covered for 15 to 18 minutes, or until the orzo is tender. Transfer to a colander to drain and set aside to cool.
2. Mix the cucumber and red onion in a bowl. Set aside.
3. Heat the olive oil in a medium skillet over medium heat until it shimmers.
4. Reduce the heat, add the shrimp, and cook each side for 2 minutes until cooked through.
5. Add the cooked shrimp to the bowl of cucumber and red onion. Mix in the cooked orzo and lemon juice and toss to combine. Sprinkle with salt and pepper. Scatter the top with the feta cheese and dill. Garnish with the parsley and serve immediately.

Nutrition Info:
- Per Serving: Calories: 565;Fat: 17.8g;Protein: 63.3g;Carbs: 43.9g.

Spicy Haddock Stew

Servings:6 | Cooking Time: 35 Minutes

Ingredients:
- ¼ cup coconut oil
- 1 tablespoon minced garlic
- 1 onion, chopped
- 2 celery stalks, chopped
- ½ fennel bulb, thinly sliced
- 1 carrot, diced
- 1 sweet potato, diced
- 1 can low-sodium diced tomatoes
- 1 cup coconut milk
- 1 cup low-sodium chicken broth
- ¼ teaspoon red pepper flakes
- 12 ounces haddock, cut into 1-inch chunks
- 2 tablespoons chopped fresh cilantro, for garnish

Directions:
1. In a large saucepan, heat the coconut oil over medium-high heat.
2. Add the garlic, onion, and celery and sauté for about 4 minutes, stirring occasionally, or until they are tender.
3. Stir in the fennel bulb, carrot, and sweet potato and sauté for 4 minutes more.
4. Add the diced tomatoes, coconut milk, chicken broth, and red pepper flakes and stir to incorporate, then bring the mixture to a boil.
5. Once it starts to boil, reduce the heat to low, and bring to a simmer for about 15 minutes, or until the vegetables are fork-tender.
6. Add the haddock chunks and continue simmering for about 10 minutes, or until the fish is cooked through.

7. Sprinkle the cilantro on top for garnish before serving.

Nutrition Info:
• Per Serving: Calories: 276;Fat: 20.9g;Protein: 14.2g;Carbs: 6.8g.

Baked Salmon With Tarragon Mustard Sauce

Servings:4 | Cooking Time: 12 Minutes

Ingredients:
• 1¼ pounds salmon fillet (skin on or removed), cut into 4 equal pieces
• ¼ cup Dijon mustard
• ¼ cup avocado oil mayonnaise
• Zest and juice of ½ lemon
• 2 tablespoons chopped fresh tarragon
• ½ teaspoon salt
• ¼ teaspoon freshly ground black pepper
• 4 tablespoons extra-virgin olive oil, for serving

Directions:
1. Preheat the oven to 425ºF. Line a baking sheet with parchment paper.
2. Arrange the salmon pieces on the prepared baking sheet, skin-side down.
3. Stir together the mustard, avocado oil mayonnaise, lemon zest and juice, tarragon, salt, and pepper in a small bowl. Spoon the mustard mixture over the salmon.
4. Bake for 10 to 12 minutes, or until the top is golden and salmon is opaque in the center.
5. Divide the salmon among four plates and drizzle each top with 1 tablespoon of olive oil before serving.

Nutrition Info:
• Per Serving: Calories: 386;Fat: 27.7g;Protein: 29.3g;Carbs: 3.8g.

Salmon Packets

Servings:4 | Cooking Time:25 Minutes

Ingredients:
• 2 tbsp olive oil
• ½ cup apple juice
• 4 salmon fillets
• 4 tsp lemon zest
• 4 tbsp chopped parsley
• Salt and black pepper to taste

Directions:
1. Preheat oven to 380°F. Brush salmon with olive oil and season with salt and pepper. Cut four pieces of nonstick baking paper and divide the salmon between them. Top each one with apple juice, lemon zest, and parsley.
2. Wrap the paper to make packets and arrange them on a baking sheet. Cook for 15 minutes until the salmon is cooked through. Remove the packets to a serving plate, open them, and drizzle with cooking juices to serve.

Nutrition Info:
• Per Serving: Calories: 495;Fat: 21g;Protein: 55g;Carbs: 5g.

Seafood Paella

Servings:4 | Cooking Time:22 Minutes

Ingredients:
• 2 tbsp olive oil
• 1 onion, finely chopped
• 3 garlic cloves, minced
• 1 red bell pepper, chopped
• ½ lb squid rings
• 1 tsp saffron
• 1 tsp paprika
• 1 cup Spanish rice
• 1 cup peeled shrimp
• 1 lb mussels, cleaned
• ½ cup green peas
• 2 tbsp parsley, chopped

• 1 lemon, cut into wedges
• Salt and black pepper to taste

Directions:
1. Warm the olive oil in a saucepan over medium heat. Sauté the onion, bell pepper, and garlic for 3 minutes. Add squid and fry for 5-6 minutes until golden. Stir in paprika, rice, saffron, and 2 cups of water. Bring to a boil and simmer for 15-18 minutes. Stir in shrimp, mussels, and green peas for 5-8 minutes. Season with salt and pepper. Sprinkle with parsley and serve with lemon wedges.

Nutrition Info:
• Per Serving: Calories: 507;Fat: 11g;Protein: 49g;Carbs: 51g.

Air-fried Flounder Fillets

Servings:4 | Cooking Time: 12 Minutes

Ingredients:
• 2 cups unsweetened almond milk
• ½ teaspoon onion powder
• ½ teaspoon garlic powder
• 4 flounder fillets
• ½ cup chickpea flour
• ½ cup plain yellow cornmeal
• ¼ teaspoon cayenne pepper
• Freshly ground black pepper, to taste

Directions:
1. Whisk together the almond milk, onion powder, and garlic powder in a large bowl until smooth.
2. Add the flounder, coating well on both sides, and let marinate for about 20 minutes.
3. Meanwhile, combine the chickpea flour, cornmeal, cayenne, and pepper in a shallow dish.
4. Dredge each piece of flounder fillets in the flour mixture until completely coated.
5. Preheat the air fryer to 380ºF.
6. Arrange the coated flounder fillets in the basket and cook for 12 minutes, flipping them halfway through.
7. Remove from the basket and serve on a plate.

Nutrition Info:
• Per Serving: Calories: 228;Fat: 5.7g;Protein: 28.2g;Carbs: 15.5g.

Hake Fillet In Herby Tomato Sauce

Servings:4 | Cooking Time:30 Minutes

Ingredients:
• 2 tbsp olive oil
• 1 onion, sliced thin
• 1 fennel bulb, sliced
• Salt and black pepper to taste
• 4 garlic cloves, minced
• 1 tsp fresh thyme, chopped
• 1 can diced tomatoes,
• ½ cup dry white wine
• 4 skinless hake fillets
• 2 tbsp fresh basil, chopped

Directions:
1. Warm the olive oil in a skillet over medium heat. Sauté the onion and fennel for about 5 minutes until softened. Stir in garlic and thyme and cook for about 30 seconds until fragrant. Pour in tomatoes and wine and bring to simmer.
2. Season the hake with salt and pepper. Nestle hake skinned side down into the tomato sauce and spoon some sauce over the top. Bring to simmer. Cook for 10-12 minutes until hake easily flakes with a fork. Sprinkle with basil and serve.

Nutrition Info:
• Per Serving: Calories: 452;Fat: 9.9g;Protein: 78g;Carbs: 9.7g.

Lemon-garlic Sea Bass

Servings:2 | Cooking Time:25 Minutes

Ingredients:
- 2 tbsp olive oil
- 2 sea bass fillets
- 1 lemon, juiced
- 4 garlic cloves, minced
- Salt and black pepper to taste

Directions:
1. Preheat the oven to 380°F. Line a baking sheet with parchment paper. Brush sea bass fillets with lemon juice, olive oil, garlic, salt, and pepper and arrange them on the sheet. Bake for 15 minutes. Serve with salad.

Nutrition Info:
- Per Serving: Calories: 530;Fat: 30g;Protein: 54g;Carbs: 15g.

Pan-seared Trout With Tzatziki

Servings:4 | Cooking Time:20 Minutes

Ingredients:
- 1 cucumber, grated and squeezed
- 3 tbsp olive oil
- 4 trout fillets, boneless
- ½ lime, juiced
- Salt and black pepper to taste
- 1 garlic clove, minced
- 1 tsp sweet paprika
- 4 garlic cloves, minced
- 2 cups Greek yogurt
- 1 tbsp dill, chopped

Directions:
1. Warm 2 tbsp of the olive oil in a skillet over medium heat. Sprinkle the trout with salt, pepper, lime juice, garlic, and paprika and sear for 8 minutes on all sides. Remove to a paper towel–lined plate. Combine cucumber, garlic, remaining olive oil, yogurt, salt, and dill in a bowl. Share trout into plates and serve with tzatziki.

Nutrition Info:
- Per Serving: Calories: 400;Fat: 19g;Protein: 41g;Carbs: 19g.

Cod Fillets In Mushroom Sauce

Servings:4 | Cooking Time:45 Minutes

Ingredients:
- 2 cups cremini mushrooms, sliced
- ¼ cup olive oil
- 4 cod fillets
- ½ cup shallots, chopped
- 2 garlic cloves, minced
- 2 cups canned diced tomatoes
- ½ cup clam juice
- ¼ tsp chili flakes
- ¼ tsp sweet paprika
- 1 tbsp capers
- ¼ cup raisins, soaked
- 1 lemon, cut into wedges
- Salt to taste

Directions:
1. Heat the oil in a skillet over medium heat. Sauté shallots and garlic for 2-3 minutes. Add in mushrooms and cook for another 4 minutes. Stir in tomatoes, clam juice, chili flakes, paprika, capers, and salt. Bring to a boil and simmer for 15 minutes.
2. Preheat oven to 380°F. Arrange the cod fillets on a greased baking pan. Cover with the mushroom mixture and top with the soaked raisins. Bake for 18-20 minutes. Serve garnished with lemon wedges.

Nutrition Info:
- Per Serving: Calories: 317;Fat: 13g;Protein: 25g;Carbs: 26g.

Shrimp And Pea Paella

Servings:2 | Cooking Time: 60 Minutes

Ingredients:
- 2 tablespoons olive oil
- 1 garlic clove, minced
- ½ large onion, minced
- 1 cup diced tomato
- ½ cup short-grain rice
- ½ teaspoon sweet paprika
- ½ cup dry white wine
- 1¼ cups low-sodium chicken stock
- 8 ounces large raw shrimp
- 1 cup frozen peas
- ¼ cup jarred roasted red peppers, cut into strips
- Salt, to taste

Directions:
1. Heat the olive oil in a large skillet over medium-high heat.
2. Add the garlic and onion and sauté for 3 minutes, or until the onion is softened.
3. Add the tomato, rice, and paprika and stir for 3 minutes to toast the rice.
4. Add the wine and chicken stock and stir to combine. Bring the mixture to a boil.
5. Cover and reduce the heat to medium-low, and simmer for 45 minutes, or until the rice is just about tender and most of the liquid has been absorbed.
6. Add the shrimp, peas, and roasted red peppers. Cover and cook for an additional 5 minutes. Season with salt to taste and serve.

Nutrition Info:
- Per Serving: Calories: 646;Fat: 27.1g;Protein: 42.0g;Carbs: 59.7g.

Garlic-butter Parmesan Salmon And Asparagus

Servings:2 | Cooking Time: 15 Minutes

Ingredients:
- 2 salmon fillets, skin on and patted dry
- Pink Himalayan salt
- Freshly ground black pepper, to taste
- 1 pound fresh asparagus, ends
- snapped off
- 3 tablespoons almond butter
- 2 garlic cloves, minced
- ¼ cup grated Parmesan cheese

Directions:
1. Preheat the oven to 400ºF. Line a baking sheet with aluminum foil.
2. Season both sides of the salmon fillets with salt and pepper.
3. Put the salmon in the middle of the baking sheet and arrange the asparagus around the salmon.
4. Heat the almond butter in a small saucepan over medium heat.
5. Add the minced garlic and cook for about 3 minutes, or until the garlic just begins to brown.
6. Drizzle the garlic-butter sauce over the salmon and asparagus and scatter the Parmesan cheese on top.
7. Bake in the preheated oven for about 12 minutes, or until the salmon is cooked through and the asparagus is crisp-tender. You can switch the oven to broil at the end of cooking time for about 3 minutes to get a nice char on the asparagus.
8. Let cool for 5 minutes before serving.

Nutrition Info:
- Per Serving: Calories: 435;Fat: 26.1g;Protein: 42.3g;Carbs: 10.0g.

10-minute Cod With Parsley Pistou

Servings:4 | Cooking Time: 10 Minutes

Ingredients:
- 1 cup packed roughly chopped fresh flat-leaf Italian parsley
- Zest and juice of 1 lemon
- 1 to 2 small garlic cloves, minced
- 1 teaspoon salt
- ½ teaspoon freshly ground black pepper
- 1 cup extra-virgin olive oil, divided
- 1 pound cod fillets, cut into 4 equal-sized pieces

Directions:
1. Make the pistou: Place the parsley, lemon zest and juice, garlic, salt, and pepper in a food processor until finely chopped.
2. With the food processor running, slowly drizzle in ¾ cup of olive oil until a thick sauce forms. Set aside.
3. Heat the remaining ¼ cup of olive oil in a large skillet over medium-high heat.
4. Add the cod fillets, cover, and cook each side for 4 to 5 minutes, until browned and cooked through.
5. Remove the cod fillets from the heat to a plate and top each with generous spoonfuls of the prepared pistou. Serve immediately.

Nutrition Info:
- Per Serving: Calories: 580;Fat: 54.6g;Protein: 21.1g;Carbs: 2.8g.

Salmon In Thyme Tomato Sauce

Servings:4 | Cooking Time:25 Minutes

Ingredients:
- 2 tbsp olive oil
- 4 salmon fillets, boneless
- 1 tsp thyme, chopped
- Salt and black pepper to taste
- 1 lb cherry tomatoes, halved

Directions:
1. Warm the olive oil in a skillet over medium heat and sear salmon for 6 minutes, turning once; set aside. In the same skillet, stir in cherry tomatoes for 3-4 minutes and sprinkle with thyme, salt, and pepper. Pour the sauce over the salmon.

Nutrition Info:
- Per Serving: Calories: 300;Fat: 18g;Protein: 26g;Carbs: 27g.

Baked Halibut Steaks With Vegetables

Servings:4 | Cooking Time: 20 Minutes

Ingredients:
- 2 teaspoon olive oil, divided
- 1 clove garlic, peeled and minced
- ½ cup minced onion
- 1 cup diced zucchini
- 2 cups diced fresh tomatoes
- 2 tablespoons chopped fresh basil
- ¼ teaspoon salt
- ¼ teaspoon ground black pepper
- 4 halibut steaks
- ⅓ cup crumbled feta cheese

Directions:
1. Preheat oven to 450ºF. Coat a shallow baking dish lightly with 1 teaspoon of olive oil.
2. In a medium saucepan, heat the remaining 1 teaspoon of olive oil.
3. Add the garlic, onion, and zucchini and mix well. Cook for 5 minutes, stirring occasionally, or until the zucchini is softened.
4. Remove the saucepan from the heat and stir in the tomatoes, basil, salt, and pepper.
5. Place the halibut steaks in the coated baking dish in a single layer. Spread the zucchini mixture evenly over the steaks. Scatter the top with feta cheese.
6. Bake in the preheated oven for about 15 minutes, or until the fish flakes when pressed lightly with a fork. Serve hot.

Nutrition Info:
- Per Serving: Calories: 258;Fat: 7.6g;Protein: 38.6g;Carbs: 6.5g.

Herby Mackerel Fillets In Red Sauce

Servings:2 | Cooking Time:15 Minutes

Ingredients:
- 1 tbsp butter
- 2 mackerel fillets
- ¼ cup white wine
- ½ cup spring onions, sliced
- 2 garlic cloves, minced
- ½ tsp dried thyme
- 1 tsp dried parsley
- Salt and black pepper to taste
- ½ cup vegetable broth
- ½ cup tomato sauce
- ½ tsp hot sauce
- 1 tbsp fresh mint, chopped

Directions:
1. In a pot over medium heat, melt the butter. Add in fish and cook for 6 minutes in total; set aside. Pour in the wine and scrape off any bits from the bottom. Add in spring onions and garlic; cook for 3 minutes until fragrant. Sprinkle with thyme, parsley, salt, and pepper. Stir in vegetable broth, tomato sauce, and add back the fillets. Cook for 3-4 minutes. Stir in hot sauce and top with mint. Serve and enjoy!

Nutrition Info:
- Per Serving: Calories: 334;Fat: 22g;Protein: 23.8g;Carbs: 7g.

Pancetta-wrapped Scallops

Servings:6 | Cooking Time:25 Minutes

Ingredients:
- 2 tsp olive oil
- 12 thin pancetta slices
- 12 medium scallops
- 2 tsp lemon juice
- 1 tsp chili powder

Directions:
1. Wrap pancetta around scallops and secure with toothpicks. Warm the olive oil in a skillet over medium heat and cook scallops for 6 minutes on all sides. Serve sprinkled with chili powder and lemon juice.

Nutrition Info:
- Per Serving: Calories: 310;Fat: 25g;Protein: 19g;Carbs: 24g.

Seafood Cakes With Radicchio Salad

Servings:4 | Cooking Time:30 Minutes

Ingredients:
- 2 tbsp butter
- 2 tbsp extra-virgin olive oil
- 1 lb lump crabmeat
- 4 scallions, sliced
- 1 garlic clove, minced
- ¼ cup cooked shrimp
- 2 tbsp heavy cream
- ¼ head radicchio, thinly sliced
- 1 green apple, shredded
- 2 tbsp lemon juice
- Salt and black pepper to taste

Directions:
1. In a food processor, place the shrimp, heavy cream, salt, and pepper. Blend until smooth. Mix crab meat and scallions in a bowl. Add in shrimp mixture and toss to combine. Make 4 patties out of the mixture. Transfer to the fridge for 10 minutes. Warm butter in a skillet over medium heat and brown patties for 8 minutes on all sides. Remove to a serving plate. Mix radicchio and apple in a bowl. Combine olive oil, lemon juice, garlic, and salt

in a small bowl and stir well. Pour over the salad and toss to combine. Serve and enjoy!

Nutrition Info:
• Per Serving: Calories: 238;Fat: 14.3g;Protein: 20g;Carbs: 8g.

Baked Cod With Lemony Rice

Servings:4 | Cooking Time:45 Minutes

Ingredients:
• 2 tbsp olive oil
• 1 cup rice
• 1 garlic clove, minced
• 1 tsp red pepper, crushed
• 2 shallots, chopped
• 1 tsp anchovy paste
• 1 tbsp oregano, chopped
• 6 black olives, chopped
• 2 tbsp capers, drained
• 1 tsp paprika
• 15 oz canned tomatoes, diced
• Salt and black pepper to taste
• 4 cod fillets, boneless
• 1 oz feta cheese, crumbled
• 1 tbsp parsley, chopped
• 2 cups chicken stock
• 1 lemon, zested

Directions:
1. Preheat the oven to 360ºF. Warm the olive oil in a skillet over medium heat. Sauté the garlic, red pepper, and shallot for 5 minutes. Stir in anchovy paste, paprika, oregano, olives, capers, tomatoes, salt, and pepper and cook for another 5 minutes. Put in cod fillets and top with the feta cheese and parsley. Bake for 15 minutes.
2. In the meantime, boil chicken stock in a pot over medium heat. Add in rice and lemon zest, bring to a simmer, and cook for 15-18 minutes. When ready, fluff with a fork. Share the rice into plates and top with cod mixture. Serve warm.

Nutrition Info:
• Per Serving: Calories: 410;Fat: 22g;Protein: 32g;Carbs: 22g.

Cioppino (seafood Tomato Stew)

Servings:2 | Cooking Time: 20 Minutes

Ingredients:
• 2 tablespoons olive oil
• ½ small onion, diced
• ½ green pepper, diced
• 2 teaspoons dried basil
• 2 teaspoons dried oregano
• ½ cup dry white wine
• 1 can diced tomatoes with basil
• 1 can no-salt-added tomato sauce
• 1 can minced clams with their juice
• 8 ounces peeled, deveined raw shrimp
• 4 ounces any white fish (a thick piece works best)
• 3 tablespoons fresh parsley
• Salt and freshly ground black pepper, to taste

Directions:
1. In a Dutch oven, heat the olive oil over medium heat.
2. Sauté the onion and green pepper for 5 minutes, or until tender.
3. Stir in the basil, oregano, wine, diced tomatoes, and tomato sauce and bring to a boil.
4. Once boiling, reduce the heat to low and bring to a simmer for 5 minutes.
5. Add the clams, shrimp, and fish and cook for about 10 minutes, or until the shrimp are pink and cooked through.
6. Scatter with the parsley and add the salt and black pepper to taste.
7. Remove from the heat and serve warm.

Nutrition Info:
• Per Serving: Calories: 221;Fat: 7.7g;Protein: 23.1g;Carbs: 10.9g.

Gluten-free Almond-crusted Salmon

Servings:4 | Cooking Time:20 Minutes

Ingredients:
• 1 tbsp olive oil
• ½ tsp lemon zest
• ¼ cup breadcrumbs
• ½ cup toasted almonds, ground
• ½ tsp dried thyme
• Salt and black pepper to taste
• 4 salmon steaks
• 1 lemon, cut into wedges

Directions:
1. Preheat oven to 350ºF. In a shallow dish, combine the lemon zest, breadcrumbs, almonds, thyme, salt, and pepper. Coat the salmon steaks with olive oil and arrange them on a baking sheet. Cover them with the almond mixture, pressing down lightly with your fingers to create a tightly packed crust. Bake for 10-12 minutes or until the almond crust is lightly browned and the fish is cooked through. Serve garnished with lemon wedges.

Nutrition Info:
• Per Serving: Calories: 568;Fat: 28g;Protein: 66g;Carbs: 9.6g.

Spiced Citrus Sole

Servings:4 | Cooking Time: 10 Minutes

Ingredients:
• 1 teaspoon garlic powder
• 1 teaspoon chili powder
• ½ teaspoon lemon zest
• ½ teaspoon lime zest
• ¼ teaspoon smoked paprika
• ¼ teaspoon freshly ground black pepper
• Pinch sea salt
• 4 sole fillets, patted dry
• 1 tablespoon extra-virgin olive oil
• 2 teaspoons freshly squeezed lime juice

Directions:
1. Preheat the oven to 450ºF. Line a baking sheet with aluminum foil and set aside.
2. Mix together the garlic powder, chili powder, lemon zest, lime zest, paprika, pepper, and salt in a small bowl until well combined.
3. Arrange the sole fillets on the prepared baking sheet and rub the spice mixture all over the fillets until well coated. Drizzle the olive oil and lime juice over the fillets.
4. Bake in the preheated oven for about 8 minutes until flaky.
5. Remove from the heat to a plate and serve.

Nutrition Info:
• Per Serving: Calories: 183;Fat: 5.0g;Protein: 32.1g;Carbs: 0g.

Mushroom & Shrimp Rice

Servings:4 | Cooking Time:40 Minutes

Ingredients:
• 2 tbsp olive oil
• 1 lb shrimp, peeled, deveined
• 1 cup white rice
• 4 garlic cloves, sliced
• ¼ tsp hot paprika
• 1 cup mushrooms, sliced
• ¼ cup green peas
• Juice of 1 lime
• Sea salt to taste
• ¼ cup chopped fresh chives

Directions:
1. Bring a pot of salted water to a boil. Cook the rice for 15-18 minutes, stirring occasionally. Drain and place in a bowl. Add in the green peas and mix to combine well. Taste and adjust the seasoning. Remove to a serving plate.
2. Heat the olive oil in a saucepan over medium heat and sauté garlic and hot paprika for 30-40 seconds until garlic is light golden brown. Remove the garlic with a slotted spoon. Add the mush-

rooms to the saucepan and sauté them for 5 minutes until tender. Put in the shrimp, lime juice, and salt and stir for 4 minutes. Turn the heat off. Add the chives and reserved garlic to the shrimp and pour over the rice. Serve and enjoy!

Nutrition Info:
- Per Serving: Calories: 342;Fat: 12g;Protein: 24g;Carbs: 33g.

Bell Pepper & Scallop Skillet

Servings:4 | Cooking Time:25 Minutes

Ingredients:
- 3 tbsp olive oil
- 2 celery stalks, sliced
- 2 lb sea scallops, halved
- 3 garlic cloves, minced
- Juice of 1 lime
- 1 red bell pepper, chopped
- 1 tbsp capers, chopped
- 1 tbsp mayonnaise
- 1 tbsp rosemary, chopped
- 1 cup chicken stock

Directions:
1. Warm olive oil in a skillet over medium heat and cook celery and garlic for 2 minutes. Stir in bell pepper, lime juice, capers, rosemary, and stock and bring to a boil. Simmer for 8 minutes. Mix in scallops and mayonnaise and cook for 5 minutes.

Nutrition Info:
- Per Serving: Calories: 310;Fat: 16g;Protein: 9g;Carbs: 33g.

Crispy Herb Crusted Halibut

Servings:4 | Cooking Time: 20 Minutes

Ingredients:
- 4 halibut fillets, patted dry
- Extra-virgin olive oil, for brushing
- ½ cup coarsely ground un-salted pistachios
- 1 tablespoon chopped fresh parsley
- 1 teaspoon chopped fresh basil
- 1 teaspoon chopped fresh thyme
- Pinch sea salt
- Pinch freshly ground black pepper

Directions:
1. Preheat the oven to 350°F. Line a baking sheet with parchment paper.
2. Place the fillets on the baking sheet and brush them generously with olive oil.
3. In a small bowl, stir together the pistachios, parsley, basil, thyme, salt, and pepper.
4. Spoon the nut mixture evenly on the fish, spreading it out so the tops of the fillets are covered.
5. Bake in the preheated oven until it flakes when pressed with a fork, about 20 minutes.
6. Serve immediately.

Nutrition Info:
- Per Serving: Calories: 262;Fat: 11.0g;Protein: 32.0g;Carbs: 4.0g.

Farro & Trout Bowls With Avocado

Servings:4 | Cooking Time:50 Minutes

Ingredients:
- 4 tbsp olive oil
- 8 trout fillets, boneless
- 1 cup farro
- Juice of 2 lemons
- Salt and black pepper to taste
- 1 avocado, chopped
- ¼ cup balsamic vinegar
- 1 garlic cloves, minced
- ¼ cup parsley, chopped
- ¼ cup mint, chopped
- 2 tbsp yellow mustard

Directions:

1. Boil salted water in a pot over medium heat and stir in farro. Simmer for 30 minutes and drain. Remove to a bowl and combine with lemon juice, mustard, garlic, salt, pepper, and half olive oil. Set aside. Mash the avocado with a fork in a bowl and mix with vinegar, salt, pepper, parsley, and mint.
2. Warm the remaining oil in a skillet over medium heat and brown trout fillets skin-side down for 10 minutes on both sides. Let cool and cut into pieces. Put over farro and stir in avocado dressing. Serve immediately.

Nutrition Info:
- Per Serving: Calories: 290;Fat: 13g;Protein: 37g;Carbs: 6g.

Steamed Trout With Lemon Herb Crust

Servings:2 | Cooking Time: 15 Minutes

Ingredients:
- 3 tablespoons olive oil
- 3 garlic cloves, chopped
- 2 tablespoons fresh lemon juice
- 1 tablespoon chopped fresh mint
- 1 tablespoon chopped fresh
- parsley
- ¼ teaspoon dried ground thyme
- 1 teaspoon sea salt
- 1 pound fresh trout
- 2 cups fish stock

Directions:
1. Stir together the olive oil, garlic, lemon juice, mint, parsley, thyme, and salt in a small bowl. Brush the marinade onto the fish.
2. Insert a trivet in the Instant Pot. Pour in the fish stock and place the fish on the trivet.
3. Secure the lid. Select the Steam mode and set the cooking time for 15 minutes at High Pressure.
4. Once cooking is complete, do a quick pressure release. Carefully open the lid. Serve warm.

Nutrition Info:
- Per Serving: Calories: 477;Fat: 29.6g;Protein: 51.7g;Carbs: 3.6g.

Dill Smoked Salmon & Eggplant Rolls

Servings:4 | Cooking Time:20 Minutes

Ingredients:
- 2 eggplants, lengthwise cut into thin slices
- 2 tbsp olive oil
- 1 cup ricotta cheese, soft
- 4 oz smoked salmon, chopped
- 2 tsp lemon zest, grated
- 1 small red onion, sliced
- Salt and pepper to the taste

Directions:
1. Mix salmon, cheese, lemon zest, onion, salt, and pepper in a bowl. Grease the eggplant with olive oil and grill them on a pre-heated grill pan for 3-4 minutes per side. Set aside to cool. Spread the cooled eggplant slices with the salmon mixture. Roll out and secure with toothpicks and serve.

Nutrition Info:
- Per Serving: Calories: 310;Fat: 25g;Protein: 12g;Carbs: 16g.

Sole Piccata With Capers

Servings:4 | Cooking Time: 17 Minutes

Ingredients:
- 1 teaspoon extra-virgin olive oil
- 4 sole fillets, patted dry
- 3 tablespoons almond butter
- 2 teaspoons minced garlic
- 2 tablespoons all-purpose flour
- 2 cups low-sodium chicken broth
- Juice and zest of ½ lemon

- 2 tablespoons capers

Directions:
1. Place a large skillet over medium-high heat and add the olive oil.
2. Sear the sole fillets until the fish flakes easily when tested with a fork, about 4 minutes on each side. Transfer the fish to a plate and set aside.
3. Return the skillet to the stove and add the butter.
4. Sauté the garlic until translucent, about 3 minutes.
5. Whisk in the flour to make a thick paste and cook, stirring constantly, until the mixture is golden brown, about 2 minutes.
6. Whisk in the chicken broth, lemon juice and zest.
7. Cook for about 4 minutes until the sauce is thickened.
8. Stir in the capers and serve the sauce over the fish.

Nutrition Info:
- Per Serving: Calories: 271;Fat: 13.0g;Protein: 30.0g;Carbs: 7.0g.

Grilled Sardines With Herby Sauce

Servings:4 | Cooking Time:15 Min + Marinating Time

Ingredients:
- 12 sardines, gutted and cleaned
- 1 lemon, cut into wedges
- 2 garlic cloves, minced
- 2 tbsp capers, finely chopped
- 1 tbsp whole capers
- 1 shallot, diced
- 1 tsp anchovy paste
- 1 lemon, zested and juiced
- 2 tbsp olive oil
- 1 tbsp parsley, finely chopped
- 1 tbsp basil, finely chopped

Directions:
1. In a bowl, blend garlic, chopped capers, shallot, anchovy paste, lemon zest, and olive oil. Add the sardines and toss to coat; let them sit to marinate for about 30 minutes.
2. Preheat your grill to high. Place the sardines on the grill. Cook for 3-4 minutes per side until the skin is browned and beginning to blister. Pour the marinade in a saucepan over medium heat and add the whole capers, parsley, basil, and lemon juice. Cook for 2-3 minutes until thickens. Pour the sauce over grilled sardines. Serve with lemon wedges.

Nutrition Info:
- Per Serving: Calories: 395;Fat: 21g;Protein: 46g;Carbs: 2.1g.

Fennel & Bell Pepper Salmon

Servings:4 | Cooking Time:30 Minutes

Ingredients:
- 2 tbsp olive oil
- 4 salmon fillets, boneless
- 1 fennel bulb, sliced
- Salt and black pepper to taste
- ½ tsp chili powder
- 1 yellow bell pepper, diced
- 1 red bell pepper, chopped
- 1 green bell pepper, chopped

Directions:
1. Warm olive oil in a skillet over medium heat. Season the salmon with chili powder, salt, and pepper and cook for 6-8 minutes, turning once. Remove to a serving plate. Add fennel and peppers to the skillet and cook for another 10 minutes until tender. Top the salmon with the mixture.

Nutrition Info:
- Per Serving: Calories: 580;Fat: 19g;Protein: 35g;Carbs: 73g.

Lemon Trout With Roasted Beets

Servings:4 | Cooking Time:45 Minutes

Ingredients:
- 1 lb medium beets, peeled and sliced
- 3 tbsp olive oil
- 4 trout fillets, boneless
- Salt and black pepper to taste
- 1 tbsp rosemary, chopped
- 2 spring onions, chopped
- 2 tbsp lemon juice
- ½ cup vegetable stock

Directions:
1. Preheat oven to 390°F. Line a baking sheet with parchment paper. Arrange the beets on the sheet, season with salt and pepper, and drizzle with some olive oil. Roast for 20 minutes.
2. Warm the remaining oil in a skillet over medium heat. Cook trout fillets for 8 minutes on all sides; reserve. Add spring onions to the skillet and sauté for 2 minutes. Stir in lemon juice and stock and cook for 5-6 minutes until the sauce thickens. Remove the beets to a plate and top with trout fillets. Pour the sauce all over and sprinkle with rosemary.

Nutrition Info:
- Per Serving: Calories: 240;Fat: 6g;Protein: 18g;Carbs: 22g.

Shrimp & Salmon In Tomato Sauce

Servings:4 | Cooking Time:30 Minutes

Ingredients:
- 1 lb shrimp, peeled and deveined
- 2 tbsp olive oil
- 1 lb salmon fillets
- Salt and black pepper to taste
- 1 cups tomatoes, chopped
- 1 onion, chopped
- 2 garlic cloves, minced
- ¼ tsp red pepper flakes
- 1 cup fish stock
- 1 tbsp cilantro, chopped

Directions:
1. Preheat the oven to 360°F. Line a baking sheet with parchment paper. Season the salmon with salt and pepper, drizzle with some olive oil, and arrange them on the sheet. Bake for 15 minutes. Remove to a serving plate.
2. Warm the remaining olive oil in a skillet over medium heat and sauté onion and garlic for 3 minutes until tender. Pour in tomatoes, fish stock, salt, pepper, and red pepper flakes and bring to a boil. Simmer for 10 minutes. Stir in shrimp and cook for another 8 minutes. Pour the sauce over the salmon and serve sprinkled with cilantro.

Nutrition Info:
- Per Serving: Calories: 240;Fat: 16g;Protein: 18g;Carbs: 22g.

Crispy Tilapia With Mango Salsa

Servings:2 | Cooking Time: 10 Minutes

Ingredients:
- Salsa:
- 1 cup chopped mango
- 2 tablespoons chopped fresh cilantro
- 2 tablespoons chopped red onion
- 2 tablespoons freshly squeezed lime juice
- ½ jalapeño pepper, seeded and minced
- Pinch salt
- Tilapia:
- 1 tablespoon paprika
- 1 teaspoon onion powder
- ½ teaspoon dried thyme
- ½ teaspoon freshly ground black pepper
- ¼ teaspoon cayenne pepper
- ½ teaspoon garlic powder
- ¼ teaspoon salt
- ½ pound boneless tilapia fillets
- 2 teaspoons extra-virgin olive oil

- 1 lime, cut into wedges, for	serving

Directions:
1. Make the salsa: Place the mango, cilantro, onion, lime juice, jalapeño, and salt in a medium bowl and toss to combine. Set aside.
2. Make the tilapia: Stir together the paprika, onion powder, thyme, black pepper, cayenne pepper, garlic powder, and salt in a small bowl until well mixed. Rub both sides of fillets generously with the mixture.
3. Heat the olive oil in a large skillet over medium heat.
4. Add the fish fillets and cook each side for 3 to 5 minutes until golden brown and cooked through.
5. Divide the fillets among two plates and spoon half of the prepared salsa onto each fillet. Serve the fish alongside the lime wedges.

Nutrition Info:
- Per Serving: Calories: 239;Fat: 7.8g;Protein: 25.0g;Carbs: 21.9g.

Steamed Mussels With Spaghetti

Servings:4 | Cooking Time:30 Minutes

Ingredients:
- 2 lb mussels, cleaned and beards removed
- 1 lb cooked spaghetti
- 3 tbsp butter
- 2 garlic cloves, minced
- 1 carrot, diced
- 1 onion, chopped
- 2 celery sticks, chopped
- 1 cup white wine
- 2 tbsp parsley, chopped
- ½ tsp red pepper flakes
- 1 lemon, juiced

Directions:
1. Melt butter in a saucepan over medium heat and sauté the garlic, carrot, onion, and celery for 4-5 minutes, stirring occasionally until softened. Add the mussels, white wine, and lemon juice, cover, and bring to a boil. Reduce the heat and steam the for 4-6 minutes. Discard any unopened mussels. Stir in spaghetti to coat. Sprinkle with parsley and red pepper flakes to serve.

Nutrition Info:
- Per Serving: Calories: 669;Fat: 16g;Protein: 41g;Carbs: 77g.

One-pot Shrimp With White Beans

Servings:4 | Cooking Time:23 Minutes

Ingredients:
- 1 lb large shrimp, peeled and deveined
- 3 tbsp olive oil
- Salt and black pepper to taste
- 1 red bell pepper, chopped
- 1 small red onion, chopped
- 2 garlic cloves, minced
- ¼ tsp red pepper flakes
- 2 cans cannellini beans
- 2 tbsp lemon zest

Directions:
1. Warm the olive oil in a skillet over medium heat. Add the shrimp and cook, without stirring, until spotty brown and edges turn pink, about 2 minutes. Remove the skillet from the heat, turn over the shrimp, and let sit until opaque throughout, about 30 seconds. Transfer shrimp to a bowl and cover with foil to keep warm.
2. Return the skillet to heat and reheat the olive oil. Sauté the bell pepper, garlic, and onion until softened, about 5 minutes. Stir in pepper flakes and salt for about 30 seconds. Pour in the beans and cook until heated through, 5 minutes. Add the shrimp with any accumulated juices back to the skillet cook for about 1 minute. Stir in lemon zest and serve.

Nutrition Info:
- Per Serving: Calories: 300;Fat: 18g;Protein: 25g;Carbs: 11g.

Leek & Olive Cod Casserole

Servings:4 | Cooking Time:30 Minutes

Ingredients:
- ½ cup olive oil
- 1 lb fresh cod fillets
- 1 cup black olives, chopped
- 4 leeks, trimmed and sliced
- 1 cup breadcrumbs
- ¾ cup chicken stock
- Salt and black pepper to taste

Directions:
1. Preheat oven to 350°F. Brush the cod with some olive oil, season with salt and pepper, and bake for 5-7 minutes. Let it cool, then cut it into 1-inch pieces.
2. Warm the remaining olive oil in a skillet over medium heat. Stir-fry the olives and leeks for 4 minutes until the leeks are tender. Add the breadcrumbs and chicken stock, stirring to mix. Fold in the pieces of cod. Pour the mixture into a greased baking dish and bake for 15 minutes or until cooked through.

Nutrition Info:
- Per Serving: Calories: 534;Fat: 33g;Protein: 24g;Carbs: 36g.

Tuna Burgers

Servings:4 | Cooking Time:20 Minutes

Ingredients:
- 2 tbsp olive oil
- 2 cans tuna, flaked
- 4 hamburger buns
- 3 green onions, chopped
- ¼ cup breadcrumbs
- 1 egg, beaten
- 2 tbsp chopped fresh parsley
- 1 tbsp Italian seasoning
- 1 lemon, zested
- ½ cup mayonnaise
- 1 tbsp chopped fresh dill
- 1 tbsp green olives, chopped
- Sea salt to taste

Directions:
1. Combine tuna, breadcrumbs, green onions, eggs, Italian seasoning, parsley, and lemon zest in a bowl. Shape the mixture into 6 patties. Warm olive oil in a skillet over medium heat and brown patties for 8 minutes on both sides. Mix mayonnaise, green olives, dill, and salt in a bowl. Spoon the mixture on the buns and top with the patties.

Nutrition Info:
- Per Serving: Calories: 423;Fat: 24g;Protein: 16g;Carbs: 35g.

Baked Haddock With Rosemary Gremolata

Servings:6 | Cooking Time:35 Min + Marinating Time

Ingredients:
- 1 cup milk
- Salt and black pepper to taste
- 2 tbsp rosemary, chopped
- 1 garlic clove, minced
- 1 lemon, zested
- 1 ½ lb haddock fillets

Directions:
1. In a large bowl, coat the fish with milk, salt, pepper, and 1 tablespoon of rosemary. Refrigerate for 2 hours.
2. Preheat oven to 380ºF. Carefully remove the haddock from the marinade, drain thoroughly, and place in a greased baking dish. Cover and bake 15–20 minutes until the fish is flaky. Remove fish from the oven and let it rest 5 minutes. To make the gremolata, mix the remaining rosemary, lemon zest, and garlic. Sprinkle the fish with gremolata and serve.

Nutrition Info:
- Per Serving: Calories: 112;Fat: 2g;Protein: 20g;Carbs: 3g.

Spicy Cod Fillets

Servings:4 | Cooking Time:35 Minutes

Ingredients:
- 2 tbsp olive oil
- 1 tsp lime juice
- Salt and black pepper to taste
- 1 tsp sweet paprika
- 1 tsp chili powder
- 1 onion, chopped
- 2 garlic cloves, minced
- 4 cod fillets, boneless
- 1 tsp ground coriander
- ½ cup fish stock
- ½ lb cherry tomatoes, cubed

Directions:
1. Warm olive oil in a skillet over medium heat. Season the cod with salt, pepper, and chili powder and cook in the skillet for 8 minutes on all sides; set aside. In the same skillet, cook onion and garlic for 3 minutes. Stir in lime juice, paprika, coriander, fish stock, and cherry tomatoes and bring to a boil. Simmer for 10 minutes. Serve topped with cod fillets.

Nutrition Info:
- Per Serving: Calories: 240;Fat: 17g;Protein: 17g;Carbs: 26g.

Drunken Mussels With Lemon-butter Sauce

Servings:4 | Cooking Time:15 Minutes

Ingredients:
- 4 lb mussels, cleaned
- 4 tbsp butter
- ½ cup chopped parsley
- 1 white onion, chopped
- 2 cups dry white wine
- ½ tsp sea salt
- 6 garlic cloves, minced
- Juice of ½ lemon

Directions:
1. Add wine, garlic, salt, onion, and ¼ cup of parsley in a pot over medium heat and let simmer. Put in mussels and simmer covered for 7-8 minutes. Divide mussels between four bowls. Stir butter and lemon juice into the pot and drizzle over the mussels. Top with parsley and serve.

Nutrition Info:
- Per Serving: Calories: 487;Fat: 18g;Protein: 37g;Carbs: 26g.

Baked Oysters With Vegetables

Servings:2 | Cooking Time: 15 To 17 Minutes

Ingredients:
- 2 cups coarse salt, for holding the oysters
- 1 dozen fresh oysters, scrubbed
- 1 tablespoon almond butter
- ¼ cup finely chopped scallions, both white and green parts
- ½ cup finely chopped artichoke hearts
- ¼ cup finely chopped red bell pepper
- 1 garlic clove, minced
- 1 tablespoon finely chopped fresh parsley
- Zest and juice of ½ lemon
- Pinch salt
- Freshly ground black pepper, to taste

Directions:
1. Pour the salt into a baking dish and spread to evenly fill the bottom of the dish.
2. Prepare a clean work surface to shuck the oysters. Using a shucking knife, insert the blade at the joint of the shell, where it hinges open and shut. Firmly apply pressure to pop the blade in, and work the knife around the shell to open. Discard the empty half of the shell. Using the knife, gently loosen the oyster, and remove any shell particles. Set the oysters in their shells on the salt, being careful not to spill the juices.
3. Preheat the oven to 425°F.
4. Heat the almond butter in a large skillet over medium heat. Add the scallions, artichoke hearts, and bell pepper, and cook for 5 to 7 minutes. Add the garlic and cook for 1 minute more.
5. Remove from the heat and stir in the parsley, lemon zest and juice, and season to taste with salt and pepper.
6. Divide the vegetable mixture evenly among the oysters. Bake in the preheated oven for 10 to 12 minutes, or until the vegetables are lightly browned. Serve warm.

Nutrition Info:
- Per Serving: Calories: 135;Fat: 7.2g;Protein: 6.0g;Carbs: 10.7g.

Balsamic Asparagus & Salmon Roast

Servings:4 | Cooking Time:20 Minutes

Ingredients:
- 2 tbsp olive oil
- 4 salmon fillets, skinless
- 2 tbsp balsamic vinegar
- 1 lb asparagus, trimmed
- Salt and black pepper to taste

Directions:
1. Preheat the oven to 380ºF. In a roasting pan, arrange the salmon fillets and asparagus spears. Season with salt and pepper and drizzle with olive oil and balsamic vinegar; roast for 12-15 minutes. Serve warm.

Nutrition Info:
- Per Serving: Calories: 310;Fat: 16g;Protein: 21g;Carbs: 19g.

Seared Salmon With Lemon Cream Sauce

Servings:4 | Cooking Time: 20 Minutes

Ingredients:
- 4 salmon fillets
- Sea salt and freshly ground black pepper, to taste
- 1 tablespoon extra-virgin olive oil
- ½ cup low-sodium vegetable broth
- Juice and zest of 1 lemon
- 1 teaspoon chopped fresh thyme
- ½ cup fat-free sour cream
- 1 teaspoon honey
- 1 tablespoon chopped fresh chives

Directions:
1. Preheat the oven to 400ºF.
2. Season the salmon lightly on both sides with salt and pepper.
3. Place a large ovenproof skillet over medium-high heat and add the olive oil.
4. Sear the salmon fillets on both sides until golden, about 3 minutes per side.
5. Transfer the salmon to a baking dish and bake in the preheated oven until just cooked through, about 10 minutes.
6. Meanwhile, whisk together the vegetable broth, lemon juice and zest, and thyme in a small saucepan over medium-high heat until the liquid reduces by about one-quarter, about 5 minutes.
7. Whisk in the sour cream and honey.
8. Stir in the chives and serve the sauce over the salmon.

Nutrition Info:
- Per Serving: Calories: 310;Fat: 18.0g;Protein: 29.0g;Carbs: 6.0g.

Crispy Fish Sticks

Servings:4 | Cooking Time:15 Minutes

Ingredients:
- 2 eggs, lightly beaten
- 1 tbsp milk
- 1 lb skinned tilapia fillet strips
- ½ cup yellow cornmeal
- ½ cup panko bread crumbs
- ¼ tsp smoked paprika
- 1 Spanish Padrón pepper, sliced
- Salt and black pepper to taste

Directions:
1. Put a large, rimmed baking sheet in your oven. Preheat the oven to 400 °F with the pan inside. In a large bowl, mix the eggs and milk. Add the fish strips to the egg mixture and stir gently to coat. Put the cornmeal, bread crumbs, smoked paprika, salt, and black pepper in a zip-top plastic bag. Transfer the fish to the bag, letting the excess egg wash drip off into the bowl before transferring. Seal the bag and shake gently to completely coat each fish stick.
2. Carefully remove the hot baking sheet with oven mitts from the oven and spray it with nonstick cooking spray. Remove the fish sticks from the bag and arrange them on the hot baking sheet. Top with Padrón pepper and bake for 6-8 minutes until gentle pressure with a fork causes the fish to flake.

Nutrition Info:
- Per Serving: Calories: 238;Fat: 3g;Protein: 22g;Carbs: 28g.

Baked Salmon With Basil And Tomato

Servings:2 | Cooking Time: 20 Minutes

Ingredients:
- 2 boneless salmon fillets
- 1 tablespoon dried basil
- 1 tomato, thinly sliced
- 1 tablespoon olive oil
- 2 tablespoons grated Parmesan cheese
- Nonstick cooking spray

Directions:
1. Preheat the oven to 375ºF. Line a baking sheet with a piece of aluminum foil and mist with nonstick cooking spray.
2. Arrange the salmon fillets onto the aluminum foil and scatter with basil. Place the tomato slices on top and drizzle with olive oil. Top with the grated Parmesan cheese.
3. Bake for about 20 minutes, or until the flesh is opaque and it flakes apart easily.
4. Remove from the oven and serve on a plate.

Nutrition Info:
- Per Serving: Calories: 403;Fat: 26.5g;Protein: 36.3g;Carbs: 3.8g.

Roasted Salmon With Tomatoes & Capers

Servings:4 | Cooking Time:25 Minutes

Ingredients:
- 1 tbsp olive oil
- 4 salmon steaks
- Salt and black pepper to taste
- ¼ mustard powder
- ½ tsp garlic powder
- 2 Roma tomatoes, chopped
- ¼ cup green olives, chopped
- 1 tsp capers
- ½ cup breadcrumbs
- 1 lemon, cut into wedges

Directions:
1. Preheat oven to 375 °F. Arrange the salmon fillets on a greased baking dish. Season with salt, pepper, garlic powder, and mustard powder and coat with the breadcrumbs. Drizzle with olive oil. Scatter the tomatoes, green olives, garlic, and capers around the fish fillets. Bake for 15 minutes until the salmon steaks flake easily with a fork. Serve with lemon wedges.

Nutrition Info:
- Per Serving: Calories: 504;Fat: 18g;Protein: 68g;Carbs: 14g.

Pan-fried Chili Sea Scallops

Servings:4 | Cooking Time:25 Minutes

Ingredients:
- 1 ½ lb large sea scallops, tendons removed
- 3 tbsp olive oil
- 1 garlic clove, finely chopped
- ½ red pepper flakes
- 2 tbsp chili sauce
- ¼ cup tomato sauce
- 1 small shallot, minced
- 1 tbsp minced fresh cilantro
- Salt and black pepper to taste

Directions:
1. Warm the olive oil in a skillet over medium heat. Add the scallops and cook for 2 minutes without moving them. Flip them and continue to cook for 2 more minutes, without moving them, until golden browned. Set aside. Add the shallot and garlic to the skillet and sauté for 3-5 minutes until softened. Pour in the chili sauce, tomato sauce, and red pepper flakes and stir for 3-4 minutes. Add the scallops back and warm through. Adjust the taste and top with cilantro.

Nutrition Info:
- Per Serving: Calories: 204;Fat: 14.1g;Protein: 14g;Carbs: 5g.

Juicy Basil-tomato Scallops

Servings:4 | Cooking Time:20 Minutes

Ingredients:
- 2 tbsp olive oil
- 1 tbsp basil, chopped
- 1 lb scallops, scrubbed
- 1 tbsp garlic, minced
- 1 onion, chopped
- 6 tomatoes, cubed
- 1 cup heavy cream
- 1 tbsp parsley, chopped

Directions:
1. Warm the olive oil in a skillet over medium heat and cook garlic and onion for 2 minutes. Stir in scallops, basil, tomatoes, heavy cream, and parsley and cook for an additional 7 minutes. Serve immediately.

Nutrition Info:
- Per Serving: Calories: 270;Fat: 12g;Protein: 11g;Carbs: 17g.

Oven-baked Spanish Salmon

Servings:4 | Cooking Time:30 Minutes

Ingredients:
- 15 green pimiento-stuffed olives
- 2 small red onions, sliced
- 1 cup fennel bulbs shaved
- 1 cup cherry tomatoes
- Salt and black pepper to taste
- 1 tsp cumin seeds
- ½ tsp smoked paprika
- 4 salmon fillets
- ½ cup chicken broth
- 3 tbsp olive oil
- 2 cups cooked farro

Directions:
1. Preheat oven to 375 °F. In a bowl, combine the onions, fennel, tomatoes, and olives. Season with salt, pepper, cumin, and paprika and mix well. Spread out on a greased baking dish. Arrange the fish fillets over the vegetables, season with salt, and gently pour the broth over. Drizzle with olive oil and bake for 20 minutes. Serve over farro.

Nutrition Info:
- Per Serving: Calories: 475;Fat: 18g;Protein: 50g;Carbs: 26g.

Shrimp & Squid Medley

Servings:4 | Cooking Time:25 Minutes

Ingredients:

- 2 tbsp butter
- ½ lb squid rings
- 1 lb shrimp, peeled, deveined
- Salt and black pepper to taste
- 2 garlic cloves, minced
- 1 tsp rosemary, dried
- 1 red onion, chopped
- 1 cup vegetable stock
- 1 lemon, juiced
- 1 tbsp parsley, chopped

Directions:

1. Melt butter in a skillet over medium heat and cook onion and garlic for 4 minutes. Stir in shrimp, salt, pepper, squid rings, rosemary, vegetable stock, and lemon juice and bring to a boil. Simmer for 8 minutes. Put in parsley and serve.

Nutrition Info:

- Per Serving: Calories: 300;Fat: 14g;Protein: 7g;Carbs: 23g.

Italian Tilapia Pilaf

Servings:2 | Cooking Time:45 Minutes

Ingredients:

- 3 tbsp olive oil
- 2 tilapia fillets, boneless
- ½ tsp Italian seasoning
- ½ cup brown rice
- ½ cup green bell pepper,
- diced
- ½ cup white onions, chopped
- ½ tsp garlic powder
- Salt and black pepper to taste

Directions:

1. Warm 1 tbsp of olive oil in a saucepan over medium heat. Cook onions, bell pepper, garlic powder, Italian seasoning, salt, and pepper for 3 minutes. Stir in brown rice and 2 cups of water and bring to a simmer. Cook for 18 minutes. Warm the remaining oil in a skillet over medium heat. Season the tilapia with salt and pepper. Fry for 10 minutes on both sides. Share the rice among plates and top with the tilapia fillets.

Nutrition Info:

- Per Serving: Calories: 270;Fat: 18g;Protein: 13g;Carbs: 26g.

Lemon Shrimp With Black Olives

Servings:4 | Cooking Time:25 Minutes

Ingredients:

- 1 lb shrimp, peeled and deveined
- 3 tbsp olive oil
- 1 lemon, juiced
- 1 tbsp flour
- 1 cup fish stock
- Salt and black pepper to taste
- 1 cup black olives, halved
- 1 tbsp rosemary, chopped

Directions:

1. Warm the olive oil in a skillet over medium heat and sear shrimp for 4 minutes on both sides; set aside. In the same skillet over low heat, stir in the flour for 2-3 minutes.
2. Gradually pour in the fish stock and lemon juice while stirring and simmer for 3-4 minutes until the sauce thickens. Adjust the seasoning with salt and pepper and mix in shrimp, olives, and rosemary. Serve immediately.

Nutrition Info:

- Per Serving: Calories: 240;Fat: 16g;Protein: 9g;Carbs: 16g.

Salmon Tartare With Avocado

Servings:4 | Cooking Time:10 Minutes + Chilling Time

Ingredients:

- 1 lb salmon, skinless, boneless and cubed
- 1 tbsp olive oil
- 4 tbsp scallions, chopped
- 2 tsp lemon juice
- 1 avocado, chopped
- Salt and black pepper to taste
- 1 tbsp parsley, chopped

Directions:

1. Mix scallions, lemon juice, olive oil, salmon, salt, pepper, and parsley in a bowl. Place in the fridge for 1 hour. Place a baking ring on a serving plate and pour in the salmon mixture. Top with avocado and gently press down. Serve.

Nutrition Info:

- Per Serving: Calories: 230;Fat: 15g;Protein: 6g;Carbs: 13g.

Chapter 7 Sides , Salads, And Soups Recipes

Chapter 7 Sides , Salads, And Soups Recipes

Sumptuous Greek Vegetable Salad

Servings:6 | Cooking Time: 0 Minutes

Ingredients:
- Salad:
- 1 can chickpeas, drained and rinsed
- 1 can artichoke hearts, drained and halved
- 1 head Bibb lettuce, chopped
- 1 cucumber, peeled deseeded, and chopped
- 1½ cups grape tomatoes, halved
- ¼ cup chopped basil leaves
- ½ cup sliced black olives
- ½ cup cubed feta cheese

- Dressing:
- 1 tablespoon freshly squeezed lemon juice (from about ½ small lemon)
- ¼ teaspoon freshly ground black pepper
- 1 tablespoon chopped fresh oregano
- 2 tablespoons extra-virgin olive oil
- 1 tablespoon red wine vinegar
- 1 teaspoon honey

Directions:
1. Combine the ingredients for the salad in a large salad bowl, then toss to combine well.
2. Combine the ingredients for the dressing in a small bowl, then stir to mix well.
3. Dressing the salad and serve immediately.

Nutrition Info:
- Per Serving: Calories: 165;Fat: 8.1g;Protein: 7.2g;Carbs: 17.9g.

Roasted Root Vegetable Soup

Servings:6 | Cooking Time: 35 Minutes

Ingredients:
- 2 parsnips, peeled and sliced
- 2 carrots, peeled and sliced
- 2 sweet potatoes, peeled and sliced
- 1 teaspoon chopped fresh rosemary
- 1 teaspoon chopped fresh thyme
- 1 teaspoon sea salt

- ½ teaspoon freshly ground black pepper
- 2 tablespoons extra-virgin olive oil
- 4 cups low-sodium vegetable soup
- ½ cup grated Parmesan cheese, for garnish (optional)

Directions:
1. Preheat the oven to 400ºF. Line a baking sheet with aluminum foil.
2. Combine the parsnips, carrots, and sweet potatoes in a large bowl, then sprinkle with rosemary, thyme, salt, and pepper, and drizzle with olive oil. Toss to coat the vegetables well.
3. Arrange the vegetables on the baking sheet, then roast in the preheated oven for 30 minutes or until lightly browned and soft. Flip the vegetables halfway through the roasting.
4. Pour the roasted vegetables with vegetable broth in a food processor, then pulse until creamy and smooth.
5. Pour the puréed vegetables in a saucepan, then warm over low heat until heated through.
6. Spoon the soup in a large serving bowl, then scatter with Parmesan cheese. Serve immediately.

Nutrition Info:
- Per Serving: Calories: 192;Fat: 5.7g;Protein: 4.8g;Carbs: 31.5g.

Moroccan Chicken & Chickpea Stew

Servings:6 | Cooking Time:40 Minutes

Ingredients:
- 1 lb boneless, skinless chicken legs
- 2 tsp ground cumin
- ½ tsp cayenne pepper
- 2 tbsp olive oil
- 1 onion, minced
- 2 jalapeño peppers, minced
- 3 garlic cloves, crushed

- 2 tsp freshly grated ginger
- ¼ cup chicken stock
- 1 can diced tomatoes
- 2 cans chickpeas
- Salt to taste
- ½ cup coconut milk
- ¼ cup fresh parsley, chopped
- 2 cups cooked basmati rice

Directions:
1. Season the chicken with salt, cayenne pepper, and cumin. Set on Sauté and warm the oil. Add in jalapeño peppers and onion, and cook for 5 minutes. Mix in ginger and garlic, and cook for 3 minutes until tender.
2. Add ¼ cup chicken stock into the cooker and scrape any browned bits of food. Mix the onion mixture with chickpeas, tomatoes, and salt. Stir in Seasoned chicken to coat in sauce.
3. Seal the lid and cook on High Pressure for 20 minutes. Release the pressure quickly. Remove the chicken and slice into chunks. Into the remaining sauce, mix in coconut milk; simmer for 5 minutes on Keep Warm. Split rice into 4 bowls. Top with chicken, then sauce and add cilantro for garnish.

Nutrition Info:
- Per Serving: Calories: 996;Fat: 24g;Protein: 55g;Carbs: 143g.

Spinach & Pea Salad With Rice

Servings:2 | Cooking Time:30 Minutes

Ingredients:
- 1 tbsp olive oil
- Salt and black pepper to taste
- ½ cup baby spinach
- ½ cup green peas, blanched
- 1 garlic clove, minced

- ½ cup white rice, rinsed
- 6 cherry tomatoes, halved
- 1 tbsp parsley, chopped
- 2 tbsp Italian salad dressing

Directions:
1. Bring a large pot of salted water to a boil over medium heat. Pour in the rice, cover, and simmer on low heat for 15-18 minutes or until the rice is al dente. Drain and let cool.
2. In a bowl, whisk the olive oil, garlic, salt, and black pepper. Toss the green peas, baby spinach, and rice together. Pour the dressing all over and gently stir to combine. Decorate with cherry tomatoes and parsley and serve. Enjoy!

Nutrition Info:
- Per Serving: Calories: 160;Fat: 14g;Protein: 4g;Carbs: 9g.

Homemade Lebanese Bulgur Salad

Servings:4 | Cooking Time:20 Min + Cooling Time

Ingredients:
- ½ cup olive oil
- 2 cups fresh parsley, chopped
- ¼ cup mint leaves, chopped
- ½ cup bulgur
- 4 tomatoes, chopped
- 4 spring onions, chopped

- 1 tbsp lemon juice
- 2 tsp sumac
- Salt and black pepper to taste

Directions:

1. Place 1 cup of water in a pot over medium heat and bring to a boil. Add in the bulgur and cook for 10-12 minutes. Let chill in a bowl. When cooled, stir in tomatoes, spring onions, sumac, black pepper, and salt. Drizzle with lemon juice and olive oil and toss to coat. Top with mint and parsley to serve.

Nutrition Info:

- Per Serving: Calories: 451;Fat: 27g;Protein: 11g;Carbs: 48g.

Zucchini & Green Bean Soup

Servings:4 | Cooking Time:30 Minutes

Ingredients:

- 1 ¼ lb green beans, cut into bite-sized chunks
- 2 tbsp olive oil
- 1 onion, chopped
- 1 celery with leaves, chopped
- 1 carrot, chopped
- 2 garlic cloves, minced
- 1 zucchini, chopped
- 5 cups vegetable broth
- 2 tomatoes, chopped
- Salt and black pepper to taste
- ½ tsp cayenne pepper
- 1 tsp oregano
- ½ tsp dried dill
- ½ cup black olives, sliced

Directions:

1. Warm the olive in a pot over medium heat. Sauté the onion, celery, and carrot for about 4 minutes or until the vegetables are just tender. Add in the garlic and zucchini and continue to sauté for 1 minute or until aromatic. Pour in the broth, green beans, tomatoes, salt, black pepper, cayenne pepper, oregano, and dried dill; bring to a boil. Reduce the heat to a simmer and let it cook for about 15 minutes. Serve in individual bowls with sliced olives.

Nutrition Info:

- Per Serving: Calories: 315;Fat: 24g;Protein: 16g;Carbs: 14g.

Pumpkin Soup With Crispy Sage Leaves

Servings:4 | Cooking Time: 10 Minutes

Ingredients:

- 1 tablespoon olive oil
- 2 garlic cloves, cut into ⅛-inch-thick slices
- 1 onion, chopped
- 2 cups freshly puréed pumpkin
- 4 cups low-sodium vegetable
- soup
- 2 teaspoons chipotle powder
- 1 teaspoon sea salt
- ½ teaspoon freshly ground black pepper
- ½ cup vegetable oil
- 12 sage leaves, stemmed

Directions:

1. Heat the olive oil in a stockpot over high heat until shimmering.
2. Add the garlic and onion, then sauté for 5 minutes or until the onion is translucent.
3. Pour in the puréed pumpkin and vegetable soup in the pot, then sprinkle with chipotle powder, salt, and ground black pepper. Stir to mix well.
4. Bring to a boil. Reduce the heat to low and simmer for 5 minutes.
5. Meanwhile, heat the vegetable oil in a nonstick skillet over high heat.
6. Add the sage leaf to the skillet and sauté for a minute or until crispy. Transfer the sage on paper towels to soak the excess oil.
7. Gently pour the soup in three serving bowls, then divide the crispy sage leaves in bowls for garnish. Serve immediately.

Nutrition Info:

- Per Serving: Calories: 380;Fat: 20.1g;Protein: 8.9g;Carbs: 45.2g.

Goat Cheese & Beet Salad With Nuts

Servings:4 | Cooking Time:10 Minutes

Ingredients:

- 3 steamed beets, cut into wedges
- 3 tbsp olive oil
- Salt and black pepper to taste
- 2 tbsp lime juice
- 4 oz goat cheese, crumbled
- 1/3 cup hazelnuts, chopped
- 1 tbsp chives, chopped

Directions:

1. Heat a pan over medium heat and toast the hazelnuts for 1-2 minutes, shaking the pan often. Remove and let cool.
2. In a bowl, mix olive oil, lime juice, salt, and pepper. Arrange beets on a serving platter. Drizzle with the dressing. Sprinkle with goat cheese, hazelnuts, and chives and serve.

Nutrition Info:

- Per Serving: Calories: 160;Fat: 5g;Protein: 5g;Carbs: 7g.

Greek-style Pasta Salad

Servings:4 | Cooking Time:10 Minutes

Ingredients:

- 2 tbsp olive oil
- 16 oz fusilli pasta
- 1 yellow bell pepper, cubed
- 1 green bell pepper, cubed
- Salt to taste
- 3 tomatoes, cubed
- 1 red onion, sliced
- 2 cups feta cheese, crumbled
- ¼ cup lemon juice
- 1 tbsp lemon zest, grated
- 1 cucumber, cubed
- 1 cup Kalamata olives, sliced

Directions:

1. Cook the fusilli pasta in boiling salted water until "al dente", 8-10 minutes. Drain and set aside to cool. In a bowl, whisk together olive oil, lemon zest, lemon juice, and salt. Add in bell peppers, tomatoes, onion, feta cheese, cucumber, olives, and pasta and toss to combine. Serve.

Nutrition Info:

- Per Serving: Calories: 420;Fat: 18g;Protein: 15g;Carbs: 50g.

Orange-honey Glazed Carrots

Servings:2 | Cooking Time: 15 To 20 Minutes

Ingredients:

- ½ pound rainbow carrots, peeled
- 2 tablespoons fresh orange juice
- 1 tablespoon honey
- ½ teaspoon coriander
- Pinch salt

Directions:

1. Preheat the oven to 400ºF.
2. Cut the carrots lengthwise into slices of even thickness and place in a large bowl.
3. Stir together the orange juice, honey, coriander, and salt in a small bowl. Pour the orange juice mixture over the carrots and toss until well coated.
4. Spread the carrots in a baking dish in a single layer. Roast for 15 to 20 minutes until fork-tender.
5. Let cool for 5 minutes before serving.

Nutrition Info:

- Per Serving: Calories: 85;Fat: 0g;Protein: 1.0g;Carbs: 21.0g.

Herby Tzatziki Sauce

Servings:2 | Cooking Time:10 Minutes

Ingredients:
- 1 medium cucumber, peeled and grated
- Salt to taste
- ½ cup Greek yogurt
- ½ lemon, juiced
- 1 tbsp fresh mint, chopped
- 1 tbsp fresh dill, chopped
- 1 garlic clove, minced

Directions:
1. Place the grated cucumber in a dishtowel and squeeze out the excess moisture. Transfer to a large bowl and add the lemon juice, salt, yogurt, lemon juice, mint, garlic, and dill and whisk the ingredients to combine. Store in an airtight container in the refrigerator for up to 2-3 days.

Nutrition Info:
- Per Serving: Calories: 179;Fat: 2.2g;Protein: 2.9g;Carbs: 7g.

Greek Salad With Dressing

Servings:4 | Cooking Time: 0 Minutes

Ingredients:
- 1 head iceberg lettuce
- 2 cups cherry tomatoes
- 1 large cucumber
- 1 medium onion
- ¼ cup lemon juice
- ½ cup extra-virgin olive oil
- 1 teaspoon salt
- 1 clove garlic, minced
- 1 cup Kalamata olives, pitted
- 1 package feta cheese, crumbled

Directions:
1. Cut the lettuce into 1-inch pieces and put them in a large salad bowl.
2. Cut the tomatoes in half and add them to the salad bowl.
3. Slice the cucumber into bite-sized pieces and add them to the salad bowl.
4. Thinly slice the onion and add it to the salad bowl.
5. In a separate bowl, whisk together the olive oil, lemon juice, salt, and garlic. Pour the dressing over the salad and gently toss to evenly coat.
6. Top the salad with the Kalamata olives and feta cheese and serve.

Nutrition Info:
- Per Serving: Calories: 539;Fat: 50.0g;Protein: 9.0g;Carbs: 18.0g.

Green Bean And Halloumi Salad

Servings:2 | Cooking Time: 5 Minutes

Ingredients:
- Dressing:
- ¼ cup unsweetened coconut milk
- 1 tablespoon olive oil
- 2 teaspoons freshly squeezed lemon juice
- ¼ teaspoon garlic powder
- ¼ teaspoon onion powder
- Pinch salt
- Pinch freshly ground black pepper
- Salad:
- ½ pound fresh green beans, trimmed
- 2 ounces Halloumi cheese, sliced into 2 (½-inch-thick) slices
- ½ cup halved cherry or grape tomatoes
- ¼ cup thinly sliced sweet onion

Directions:
1. Make the Dressing
2. Combine the coconut milk, olive oil, lemon juice, onion powder, garlic powder, salt, and pepper in a small bowl and whisk well. Set aside.
3. Make the Salad
4. Fill a medium-size pot with about 1 inch of water and add the green beans. Cover and steam them for about 3 to 4 minutes, or just until beans are tender. Do not overcook. Drain beans, rinse them immediately with cold water, and set them aside to cool.
5. Heat a nonstick skillet over medium-high heat and place the slices of Halloumi in the hot pan. After about 2 minutes, check to see if the cheese is golden on the bottom. If it is, flip the slices and cook for another minute or until the second side is golden.
6. Remove cheese from the pan and cut each piece into cubes.
7. Place the green beans, halloumi slices, tomatoes, and onion in a large bowl and toss to combine.
8. Drizzle the dressing over the salad and toss well to combine. Serve immediately.

Nutrition Info:
- Per Serving: Calories: 274;Fat: 18.1g;Protein: 8.0g;Carbs: 16.8g.

Chicken Salad With Mustard Dressing

Servings:4 | Cooking Time:15 Minutes

Ingredients:
- 2 cups chopped cooked chicken breasts
- 1 cup canned artichoke hearts, chopped
- 2 hard-boiled eggs, chopped
- ½ cup green olives, sliced
- 1 red bell pepper, chopped
- 8 cherry tomatoes, quartered
- 2 tbsp yellow mustard
- ½ cup extra-virgin olive oil
- 3 tbsp lemon juice
- 1green onion, chopped
- Salt and black pepper to taste
- ¼ tsp red pepper flakes

Directions:
1. In a salad bowl, whisk the mustard, oil, lemon juice, salt, pepper, and red pepper flakes. Add the chicken, eggs, green olives, bell pepper, artichoke hearts, green onion, and cherry tomatoes toss to coat. Serve.

Nutrition Info:
- Per Serving: Calories: 496;Fat: 36g;Protein: 28g;Carbs: 20g.

Mushroom & Bell Pepper Salad

Servings:4 | Cooking Time:15 Minutes

Ingredients:
- 2 tbsp olive oil
- ½ lb mushrooms, sliced
- 3 garlic cloves, minced
- Salt and black pepper to taste
- 1 tomato, diced
- 1 red bell pepper, sliced
- 3 tbsp lime juice
- ½ cup chicken stock
- 2 tbsp cilantro, chopped

Directions:
1. Warm the olive oil in a skillet over medium heat and sauté mushrooms for 4 minutes. Stir in garlic, salt, pepper, tomato, bell pepper, lime juice, and chicken stock and sauté for another 4 minutes. Top with cilantro and serve right away.

Nutrition Info:
- Per Serving: Calories: 89;Fat: 7.4g;Protein: 2.5g;Carbs: 5.6g.

The Ultimate Chicken Bean Soup

Servings:6 | Cooking Time:40 Minutes

Ingredients:
- 3 tbsp olive oil
- 3 garlic cloves, minced
- 1 onion, chopped
- 3 tomatoes, chopped
- 4 cups chicken stock
- 1 lb chicken breasts, cubed

- 1 red chili pepper, chopped
- 1 tbsp fennel seeds, crushed
- 14 oz canned white beans
- 1 lime, zested and juiced
- Salt and black pepper to taste
- 2 tbsp parsley, chopped

Directions:

1. Warm the olive oil in a pot over medium heat. Cook the onion and garlic, adding a splash of water, for 10 minutes until aromatic. Add in the chicken and chili pepper and sit-fry for another 6-8 minutes. Put in tomatoes, chicken stock, beans, lime zest, lime juice, salt, pepper, and fennel seeds and bring to a boil; cook for 30 minutes. Serve topped with parsley.

Nutrition Info:
- Per Serving: Calories: 670;Fat: 18g;Protein: 56g;Carbs: 74g.

Moroccan Lentil, Tomato, And Cauliflower Soup

Servings:6 | Cooking Time: 4 Hours

Ingredients:
- 1 cup chopped carrots
- 1 cup chopped onions
- 3 cloves garlic, minced
- ½ teaspoon ground coriander
- 1 teaspoon ground cumin
- 1 teaspoon ground turmeric
- ¼ teaspoon ground cinnamon
- ¼ teaspoon freshly ground black pepper
- 1 cup dry lentils
- 28 ounces tomatoes, diced, reserve the juice
- 1½ cups chopped cauliflower
- 4 cups low-sodium vegetable soup
- 1 tablespoon no-salt-added tomato paste
- 1 teaspoon extra-virgin olive oil
- 1 cup chopped fresh spinach
- ¼ cup chopped fresh cilantro
- 1 tablespoon red wine vinegar (optional)

Directions:

1. Put the carrots and onions in the slow cooker, then sprinkle with minced garlic, coriander, cumin, turmeric, cinnamon, and black pepper. Stir to combine well.
2. Add the lentils, tomatoes, and cauliflower, then pour in the vegetable soup and tomato paste. Drizzle with olive oil. Stir to combine well.
3. Put the slow cooker lid on and cook on high for 4 hours or until the vegetables are tender.
4. In the last 30 minutes during the cooking time, open the lid and stir the soup, then fold in the spinach.
5. Pour the cooked soup in a large serving bowl, then spread with cilantro and drizzle with vinegar. Serve immediately.

Nutrition Info:
- Per Serving: Calories: 131;Fat: 2.1g;Protein: 5.6g;Carbs: 25.0g.

Marinated Mushrooms And Olives

Servings:8 | Cooking Time: 0 Minutes

Ingredients:
- 1 pound white button mushrooms, rinsed and drained
- 1 pound fresh olives
- ½ tablespoon crushed fennel seeds
- 1 tablespoon white wine vinegar
- 2 tablespoons fresh thyme leaves
- Pinch chili flakes
- Sea salt and freshly ground pepper, to taste
- 2 tablespoons extra-virgin olive oil

Directions:

1. Combine all the ingredients in a large bowl. Toss to mix well.
2. Wrap the bowl in plastic and refrigerate for at least 1 hour to marinate.
3. Remove the bowl from the refrigerator and let sit under room temperature for 10 minutes, then serve.

Nutrition Info:
- Per Serving: Calories: 111;Fat: 9.7g;Protein: 2.4g;Carbs: 5.9g.

Kale & Bean Soup With Chorizo

Servings:4 | Cooking Time:45 Minutes

Ingredients:
- ½ cup Manchego cheese, grated
- 1 cup canned Borlotti beans, drained
- 2 tbsp olive oil
- 1 lb Spanish chorizo, sliced
- 1 carrot, chopped
- 1 yellow onion, chopped
- 1 celery stalk, chopped
- 2 garlic cloves, minced
- ½ lb kale, chopped
- 4 cups chicken stock
- 1 tsp rosemary, dried
- Salt and black pepper to taste

Directions:

1. Warm the olive oil in a large pot over medium heat and cook the chorizo for 5 minutes or until the fat is rendered and the chorizo is browned. Add in onion and continue to cook for another 3 minutes until soft and translucent. Stir in garlic and let it cook for 30-40 seconds until fragrant. Lastly, add the carrots and celery and cook for 4-5 minutes until tender.
2. Now, pour in the chicken stock, drained and washed beans, rosemary, salt, and pepper and bring to a boil. Reduce the heat to low, cover the pot and simmer for 30 minutes. Stir periodically, checking to make sure there is enough liquid. Five minutes before the end, add the kale. Adjust the seasoning. Ladle your soup into bowls and serve topped with Manchego cheese.

Nutrition Info:
- Per Serving: Calories: 580;Fat: 27g;Protein: 27g;Carbs: 38g.

Leek Cream Soup With Hazelnuts

Servings:4 | Cooking Time:25 Minutes

Ingredients:
- 2 tbsp olive oil
- 1 tbsp ground hazelnuts
- 4 leeks (white part), sliced
- 1 onion, chopped
- 2 garlic cloves, minced
- 4 cups chicken stock
- ¼ cup heavy cream
- 2 tbsp chopped chives

Directions:

1. Warm the olive oil in a medium saucepan. Add the leeks, garlic, and onion and sauté over low heat until tender, 3-5 minutes. Add ½ cup of chicken stock, then puree the mixture in a blender until smooth. Return the chicken stock mixture to the saucepan. Add the remaining chicken stock and simmer for 10 minutes. Stir in the heavy cream until combined. Pour into bowls and garnish with hazelnuts and chives. Serve and enjoy!

Nutrition Info:
- Per Serving: Calories: 395;Fat: 33.8g;Protein: 6g;Carbs: 22g.

Red Pollock & Tomato Stew

Servings:4 | Cooking Time:50 Minutes

Ingredients:
- 1 lb pollock fillet
- 4 garlic cloves, crushed
- 1 lb tomatoes, peeled and diced
- 2 bay leaves, whole
- 2 cups fish stock
- Salt and black pepper to taste
- 1 onion, finely chopped
- ½ cup olive oil

Directions:

1. Preheat your Instant Pot on Sauté mode and heat 2 tbsp olive oil. Add onion and sauté until translucent, stirring constantly, for

about 3-4 minutes. Add tomatoes and cook until soft. Press Cancel. Add the remaining ingredients and seal the lid. Cook on High Pressure for 15 minutes. When ready, do a quick release. Serve warm.

Nutrition Info:
- Per Serving: Calories: 370;Fat: 27g;Protein: 26.3g;Carbs: 7g.

Cucumber Salad With Goat Cheese

Servings:4 | Cooking Time:15 Minutes

Ingredients:
- 2 tbsp olive oil
- 4 oz goat cheese, crumbled
- 2 cucumbers, sliced
- 2 spring onions, chopped
- 2 garlic cloves, grated
- Salt and black pepper to taste

Directions:
1. Combine cucumbers, spring onions, olive oil, garlic, salt, pepper, and goat cheese in a bowl. Serve chilled.

Nutrition Info:
- Per Serving: Calories: 150;Fat: 6g;Protein: 6g;Carbs: 8g.

Cherry, Plum, Artichoke, And Cheese Board

Servings:4 | Cooking Time: 0 Minutes

Ingredients:
- 2 cups rinsed cherries
- 2 cups rinsed and sliced plums
- 2 cups rinsed carrots, cut into sticks
- 1 cup canned low-sodium artichoke hearts, rinsed and drained
- 1 cup cubed feta cheese

Directions:
1. Arrange all the ingredients in separated portions on a clean board or a large tray, then serve with spoons, knife, and forks.

Nutrition Info:
- Per Serving: Calories: 417;Fat: 13.8g;Protein: 20.1g;Carbs: 56.2g.

Olive Tapenade Flatbread With Cheese

Servings:4 | Cooking Time:35 Min + Chilling Time

Ingredients:
- For the flatbread
- 2 tbsp olive oil
- 2 ½ tsp dry yeast
- 1 ½ cups all-purpose flour
- ¾ tsp salt
- ½ cup lukewarm water
- ¼ tsp sugar
- For the tapenade
- 2 roasted red pepper slices, chopped
- ¼ cup extra-virgin olive oil
- 1 cup green olives, chopped
- 10 black olives, chopped
- 1 tbsp capers
- 1 garlic clove, minced
- 1 tbsp chopped basil leaves
- 1 tbsp chopped fresh oregano
- ¼ cup goat cheese, crumbled

Directions:
1. Combine lukewarm water, sugar, and yeast in a bowl. Set aside covered for 5 minutes. Mix the flour and salt in a bowl. Pour in the yeast mixture and mix. Knead until you obtain a ball. Place the dough onto a floured surface and knead for 5 minutes until soft. Leave the dough into an oiled bowl, covered to rise until it has doubled in size, about 40 minutes.
2. Preheat oven to 400° F. Cut the dough into 4 balls and roll each one out to a ½ inch thickness. Bake for 5 minutes. In a blender, mix black olives, roasted pepper, green olives, capers, garlic, oregano, basil, and olive oil for 20 seconds until coarsely chopped. Spread the olive tapenade on the flatbreads and top with goat cheese to serve.

Nutrition Info:
- Per Serving: Calories: 366;Fat: 19g;Protein: 7.3g;Carbs: 42g.

Cucumber Salad With Mustard Dressing

Servings:4 | Cooking Time:15 Minutes

Ingredients:
- 2 tbsp extra-virgin olive oil
- 2 cucumbers, chopped
- 1 red chili pepper, sliced
- 2 tbsp chives, chopped
- ¼ cup red wine vinegar
- 2 garlic cloves, minced
- 1 tsp yellow mustard
- ¼ tsp honey
- Salt and black pepper to taste

Directions:
1. Combine the cucumber, chili pepper, and chives in a bowl. Mix olive oil, honey, garlic, vinegar, mustard, salt, and pepper in another bowl. Pour over the salad and toss to combine.

Nutrition Info:
- Per Serving: Calories: 118;Fat: 7.5g;Protein: 2.5g;Carbs: 13g.

Warm Kale Salad With Red Bell Pepper

Servings:4 | Cooking Time:15 Minutes

Ingredients:
- 1 tbsp olive oil
- 4 cups kale, torn
- 2 cloves garlic, minced
- 1 red bell pepper, diced
- Salt and black pepper to taste
- ½ lemon, juiced

Directions:
1. Warm the olive oil in a large skillet over medium heat and add the garlic. Cook for 1 minute, and then add the bell pepper. Cook for 4-5 minutes until the pepper is tender. Stir in the kale. Cook for 3-4 minutes or just until wilted, then remove from heat. Place pepper and kale in a bowl and season with salt and black pepper. Drizzle with lemon juice.

Nutrition Info:
- Per Serving: Calories: 123;Fat: 4g;Protein: 6g;Carbs: 22g.

Moroccan Spinach & Lentil Soup

Servings:6 | Cooking Time:35 Minutes

Ingredients:
- 3 tsp olive oil
- 1 onion, chopped
- 1 large carrot, chopped
- 3 garlic cloves, sliced
- 1 ½ cups lentils
- 1 cup crushed tomatoes
- 12 oz spinach

Directions:
1. Warm the olive oil and sauté the onion, garlic, and carrot for 3 minutes. Add the lentils, tomatoes, and 6 cups of water and stir. Cook until the lentils are tender, about 15-20 minutes. Add the spinach and stir until wilted, 5 minutes. Serve hot.

Nutrition Info:
- Per Serving: Calories: 422;Fat: 17g;Protein: 22g;Carbs: 45g.

Three-bean Salad With Black Olives

Servings:6 | Cooking Time:15 Minutes

Ingredients:
- 1 lb green beans, trimmed
- 1 red onion, thinly sliced
- 2 tbsp marjoram, chopped
- ¼ cup black olives, chopped
- ½ cup canned cannellini beans
- ½ cup canned chickpeas
- 2 tbsp extra-virgin olive oil
- ½ cup balsamic vinegar
- ½ tsp dried oregano
- Salt and black pepper to taste

Directions:

1. Steam the green beans for about 2 minutes or until just tender. Drain and place them in an ice-water bath. Drain thoroughly and pat them dry with paper towels. Put them in a large bowl and toss with the remaining ingredients. Serve.

Nutrition Info:
- Per Serving: Calories: 187;Fat: 6g;Protein: 7g;Carbs: 27g.

Pepper & Cheese Stuffed Tomatoes

Servings:2 | Cooking Time:35 Minutes

Ingredients:
- ½ lb mixed bell peppers, chopped
- 1 tbsp olive oil
- 4 tomatoes
- 2 garlic cloves, minced
- ½ cup diced onion
- 1 tbsp chopped oregano
- 1 tbsp chopped basil
- 1 cup shredded mozzarella
- 1 tbsp grated Parmesan cheese
- Salt and black pepper to taste

Directions:

1. Preheat oven to 370° F. Cut the tops of the tomatoes and scoop out the pulp. Chop the pulp and set aside. Arrange the tomatoes on a lined with parchment paper baking sheet.

2. Warm the olive oil in a pan over medium heat. Add in garlic, onion, basil, bell peppers, and oregano, and cook for 5 minutes. Sprinkle with salt and pepper. Remove from the heat and mix in tomato pulp and mozzarella cheese. Divide the mixture between the tomatoes and top with Parmesan cheese. Bake for 20 minutes or until the cheese melts. Serve.

Nutrition Info:
- Per Serving: Calories: 285;Fat: 10g;Protein: 24g;Carbs: 28g.

Favorite Green Bean Stir-fry

Servings:4 | Cooking Time:15 Minutes

Ingredients:
- 1 tbsp olive oil
- 1 tbsp butter
- 1 fennel bulb, sliced
- 1 red onion, sliced
- 4 cloves garlic, pressed
- 1 lb green beans, steamed
- ½ tsp dried oregano
- 2 tbsp balsamic vinegar
- Salt and black pepper to taste

Directions:

1. Heat the butter and olive oil a saucepan over medium heat. Add in the onion and garlic and sauté for 3 minutes. Stir in oregano, fennel, balsamic vinegar, salt, and pepper. Stir-fry for another 6-8 minutes and add in the green beans; cook for 2-3 minutes. Adjust the seasoning and serve.

Nutrition Info:
- Per Serving: Calories: 126;Fat: 6g;Protein: 3.3g;Carbs: 16.6g.

Radicchio Salad With Sunflower Seeds

Servings:4 | Cooking Time:10 Minutes

Ingredients:
- 3 tbsp olive oil
- 1 cup radicchio, shredded
- 1 lettuce head, torn
- 1 cup raisins
- 2 tbsp lemon juice
- ¼ cup chives, chopped
- Salt and black pepper to taste
- 1 tbsp sunflower seeds, toasted

Directions:

1. Mix olive oil, raisins, lemon juice, chives, radicchio, salt, pepper, lettuce, and sunflower seeds in a bowl. Serve.

Nutrition Info:

- Per Serving: Calories: 70;Fat: 3g;Protein: 1g;Carbs: 3g.

Summer Fruit & Cheese Salad

Servings:6 | Cooking Time:10 Minutes

Ingredients:
- 1 cantaloupe, quartered and seeded
- 2 tbsp extra-virgin olive oil
- ½ small seedless watermelon
- 1 cup grape tomatoes
- 2 cups Goat cheese, crumbled
- ⅓ cup mint leaves, torn into small pieces
- 1 tbsp balsamic vinegar
- Salt and black pepper to taste

Directions:

1. Scoop balls out of the cantaloupe melon using a melon-baller. Put the balls in a shallow bowl. Repeat the process with the watermelon. Add the watermelon balls to the cantaloupe bowl. Add the tomatoes, Goat cheese, mint, olive oil, vinegar, pepper, and salt, and gently mix until everything is incorporated. Serve and enjoy!

Nutrition Info:
- Per Serving: Calories: 58;Fat: 2.2g;Protein: 1.1g;Carbs: 8.8g.

Party Summer Salad

Servings:4 | Cooking Time:10 Minutes

Ingredients:
- ½ cup extra virgin olive oil
- 2 cucumbers, sliced
- 2 mixed bell peppers, sliced
- 2 tomatoes, sliced
- 2 green onions, thinly sliced
- 2 gem lettuces, sliced
- 1 cup arugula
- 2 tbsp parsley, chopped
- Salt to taste
- 1 cup feta cheese, crumbled
- 3 tbsp lemon juice

Directions:

1. In a bowl, mix the cucumbers, bell peppers, green onions, gem lettuce, and arugula. In a small bowl, whisk the olive oil, lemon juice, and salt. Pour over the salad and toss to coat. Scatter the feta over and top with tomato and parsley.

Nutrition Info:
- Per Serving: Calories: 398;Fat: 34g;Protein: 19g;Carbs: 20g.

Lemon And Spinach Orzo

Servings:2 | Cooking Time: 10 Minutes

Ingredients:
- 1 cup dry orzo
- 1 bag baby spinach
- 1 cup halved grape tomatoes
- 2 tablespoons extra-virgin olive oil
- ¼ teaspoon salt
- Freshly ground black pepper
- ¾ cup crumbled feta cheese
- 1 lemon, juiced and zested

Directions:

1. Bring a medium pot of water to a boil. Stir in the orzo and cook uncovered for 8 minutes. Drain the water, then return the orzo to medium heat.

2. Add the spinach and tomatoes and cook until the spinach is wilted.

3. Sprinkle with the olive oil, salt, and pepper and mix well. Top with the feta cheese, lemon juice and zest, then toss one or two more times and serve.

Nutrition Info:
- Per Serving: Calories: 610;Fat: 27.0g;Protein: 21.0g;Carbs: 74.0g.

Mediterranean Diet Cookbook

Seafood Fideuà

Servings:4 | Cooking Time:35 Minutes

Ingredients:
- 2 tbsp olive oil
- ½ lb squid rings
- 1 lb mussels, cleaned
- ½ lb shrimp, deveined
- ½ tsp saffron
- 16 oz vermicelli pasta
- 1 yellow onion, chopped
- 1 tsp paprika
- 1 red bell pepper, chopped
- 3 garlic cloves, minced
- ½ cup tomatoes, crushed
- 4 cups fish stock
- 2 tbsp parsley, chopped
- 1 lemon cut into wedges
- Salt and black pepper to taste

Directions:
1. In a dry saucepan over medium heat, toast the vermicelli, shaking often until pale, 2 to 3 minutes; reserve. Warm the olive oil in the same saucepan and sauté onion, garlic, bell pepper for 5 minutes. Add in the squid and cook for 5 minutes. Stir in the tomatoes, paprika, and fish stock. Bring to a boil and add the saffron; stir. Lower the heat, cover, and simmer for 15 minutes. Add the vermicelli, shrimp, and mussels and simmer for 5 minutes. Discard any unopened mussels. Adjust the taste and sprinkle with parsley. Serve warm with lemon wedges.

Nutrition Info:
- Per Serving: Calories: 200;Fat: 9g;Protein: 27g;Carbs: 5g.

Cannellini Bean Stew With Spinach

Servings:4 | Cooking Time:45 Minutes

Ingredients:
- 2 tbsp olive oil
- 1 onion, chopped
- 2 cloves garlic, minced
- 2 carrots, peeled and chopped
- 1 cup celery, chopped
- 4 cups vegetable broth
- 1 cup cannellini beans,
- soaked
- 1 tsp dried thyme
- 1 tsp dried rosemary
- 1 bay leaf
- 1 cup spinach, torn
- Salt and black pepper to taste

Directions:
1. Preheat your Instant Pot on Sauté mode and warm olive oil. Stir in garlic and onion, and cook for 3 minutes until tender and fragrant. Mix in celery and carrots and cook for 2 to 3 minutes more until they start to soften. Add broth, bay leaf, thyme, rosemary, cannellini beans, and salt. Seal the lid and cook for 30 minutes on High Pressure. Do a quick pressure release. Stir in spinach and allow to sit for 2-4 minutes until the spinach wilts, and season with pepper and salt.

Nutrition Info:
- Per Serving: Calories: 285;Fat: 8.7g;Protein: 17g;Carbs: 36g.

Bell Pepper & Roasted Cabbage Salad

Servings:4 | Cooking Time:35 Minutes

Ingredients:
- 1 head green cabbage, shredded
- 4 tbsp olive oil
- 1 carrot, julienned
- ½ red bell pepper, seeded and julienned
- ½ green bell pepper, julienned
- 1 cucumber, shredded
- 1 shallot, sliced
- 2 tbsp parsley, chopped
- 1 tsp Dijon mustard
- 1 lemon, juiced
- 1 tsp mayonnaise
- Salt to taste

Directions:
1. Preheat the oven to 380° F. Season the green cabbage with salt and drizzle with some olive oil. Transfer to a baking dish and roast for 20-25 minutes, stirring often. Remove to a bowl and let cool for a few minutes. Stir in carrot, bell peppers, shallot, cucumber, and parsley. In another bowl, add the remaining olive oil, lemon juice, mustard, mayonnaise, and salt and whisk until well mixed. Drizzle over the cabbage mixture and toss to coat. Serve.

Nutrition Info:
- Per Serving: Calories: 195;Fat: 15g;Protein: 3.2g;Carbs: 16g.

Spinach & Cherry Tomato Salad

Servings:4 | Cooking Time:15 Minutes

Ingredients:
- ¼ cup olive oil
- 4 cups baby spinach leaves
- 10 cherry tomatoes, halved
- Salt and black pepper to taste
- ¼ cup pumpkin seeds
- ½ lemon, juiced

Directions:
1. Toast the pumpkin seeds in a dry sauté pan over medium heat for 2 minutes, shaking often. Let cool. In a small jar, add the olive oil, lemon juice, salt, and pepper. Place the baby spinach on a salad platter and top with cherry tomatoes. Drizzle with the vinaigrette and sprinkle with toasted pumpkin seeds. Serve immediately.

Nutrition Info:
- Per Serving: Calories: 199;Fat: 14g;Protein: 2g;Carbs: 36g.

Divine Fennel & Zucchini Salad

Servings:4 | Cooking Time:10 Minutes

Ingredients:
- 2 tbsp olive oil
- 1 cup fennel bulb, sliced
- 1 red onion, sliced
- 2 zucchinis, cut into ribbons
- Salt and black pepper to taste
- 2 tsp white wine vinegar
- 1 tsp lemon juice

Directions:
1. In a large bowl, combine fennel, zucchini, red onion, salt, pepper, olive oil, vinegar, and lemon juice and toss to coat.

Nutrition Info:
- Per Serving: Calories: 200;Fat: 4g;Protein: 3g;Carbs: 4g.

Vegetable Feta Bake

Servings:6 | Cooking Time:30 Minutes

Ingredients:
- 2 tbsp olive oil
- 1 medium onion, sliced
- 1 green bell pepper, chopped
- 1 red bell pepper, chopped
- ½ lb feta cheese slice
- 1 tsp dried oregano
- Black pepper to taste
- ½ lb cherry tomatoes, halved

Directions:
1. Preheat oven to 350° F. Warm the olive oil in a pan over medium heat. Add and sauté the onion and bell peppers for 6-8 minutes until soft. Place the feta in a small greased baking dish and top with sautéed vegetables. Top with oregano and black pepper. Arrange the cherry tomatoes around the cheese. Cover with foil and bake for 13-15 minutes.

Nutrition Info:
- Per Serving: Calories: 153;Fat: 13g;Protein: 6g;Carbs: 5g.

Greek Salad

Servings:4 | Cooking Time:10 Minutes

Ingredients:
- 2 tbsp extra-virgin olive oil
- 2 tomatoes, chopped
- ½ cup grated feta cheese
- 1 green bell pepper, chopped
- 10 Kalamata olives, chopped
- 1 red onion, thinly sliced
- 1 cucumber, chopped
- 2 tbsp apple cider vinegar
- 1 tbsp dried oregano
- Salt and black pepper to taste
- 2 tbsp fresh parsley, chopped

Directions:
1. In a salad bowl, combine bell pepper, red onion, tomatoes, cucumber, and olives. Mix the olive oil, apple cider vinegar, oregano, salt, and pepper in another bowl. Pour the dressing over the salad and toss to combine. Top with the feta cheese and sprinkle with parsley to serve.

Nutrition Info:
- Per Serving: Calories: 172;Fat: 13g;Protein: 4.4g;Carbs: 12g.

North African Tomato & Pepper Salad

Servings:6 | Cooking Time:20 Minutes

Ingredients:
- 4 tbsp olive oil
- 2 green bell peppers
- 1 jalapeño pepper
- 4 tomatoes, peeled and diced
- 1 cucumber, peeled and diced
- 1 tbsp dill, chopped
- 1 tbsp parsley, chopped
- 1 tsp ground cumin
- 1 lemon, juiced
- Salt and black pepper to taste

Directions:
1. Preheat oven to 360° F. Bake the bell peppers and jalapeño until the skin blackens and blisters. Combine the rest of the ingredients in a medium bowl and mix well. Remove the skins of the peppers. Seed and chop the peppers and add them to the salad. Season with salt and ground pepper. Toss to combine and serve.

Nutrition Info:
- Per Serving: Calories: 179;Fat: 10g;Protein: 4g;Carbs: 31g.

Anchovy Salad With Mustard Vinaigrette

Servings:6 | Cooking Time:10 Minutes

Ingredients:
- ½ cup olive oil
- ½ lemon, juiced
- 1 tsp Dijon mustard
- ¼ tsp honey
- Salt and black pepper to taste
- 4 tomatoes, diced
- 1 cucumber, peeled and diced
- 1 lb arugula
- 1 red onion, thinly sliced
- 2 tbsp parsley, chopped
- 4 anchovy filets, chopped

Directions:
1. In a bowl, whisk together the olive oil, lemon juice, honey, and mustard, and season with salt and pepper. Set aside. In a separate bowl, combine all the vegetables with the parsley and toss. Add the sardine fillets on top of the salad. Drizzle the dressing over the salad just before serving.

Nutrition Info:
- Per Serving: Calories: 168;Fat: 6g;Protein: 8g;Carbs: 29g.

Moroccan Spiced Couscous

Servings:2 | Cooking Time: 8 Minutes

Ingredients:
- 1 tablespoon olive oil
- ¾ cup couscous
- ¼ teaspoon cinnamon
- ¼ teaspoon garlic powder
- ¼ teaspoon salt, plus more as needed
- 1 cup water
- 2 tablespoons minced dried apricots
- 2 tablespoons raisins
- 2 teaspoons minced fresh parsley

Directions:
1. Heat the olive oil in a saucepan over medium-high heat until it shimmers.
2. Add the couscous, cinnamon, garlic powder, and salt. Stir for 1 minute to toast the couscous and spices.
3. Add the water, apricots, and raisins and bring the mixture to a boil.
4. Cover and turn off the heat. Allow the couscous to sit for 4 to 5 minutes and then fluff it with a fork. Sprinkle with the fresh parsley. Season with more salt as needed and serve.

Nutrition Info:
- Per Serving: Calories: 338;Fat: 8.0g;Protein: 9.0g;Carbs: 59.0g.

Cheese & Broccoli Quiche

Servings:4 | Cooking Time:45 Minutes

Ingredients:
- 1 tsp Mediterranean seasoning
- 3 eggs
- ½ cup heavy cream
- 3 tbsp olive oil
- 1 red onion, chopped
- 2 garlic cloves, minced
- 2 oz mozzarella, shredded
- 1 lb broccoli, cut into florets

Directions:
1. Preheat oven to 320° F. Warm the oil in a pan over medium heat. Sauté the onion and garlic until just tender and fragrant. Add in the broccoli and continue to cook until crisp-tender for about 4 minutes. Spoon the mixture into a greased casserole dish. Beat the eggs with heavy cream and Mediterranean seasoning. Spoon this mixture over the broccoli layer. Bake for 18-20 minutes. Top with the shredded cheese and broil for 5 to 6 minutes or until hot and bubbly on the top. Serve.

Nutrition Info:
- Per Serving: Calories: 198;Fat: 14g;Protein: 5g;Carbs: 12g.

Cheese & Pecan Salad With Orange Dressing

Servings:2 | Cooking Time:10 Minutes

Ingredients:
- Dressing
- 1 tbsp olive oil
- 2 tbsp orange juice
- 1 tbsp cider vinegar
- 1 tbsp honey
- Salt and black pepper to taste
- Salad
- 2 cups packed baby kale
- ½ small fennel bulb, sliced
- 3 tbsp toasted pecans, chopped
- 2 oz ricotta cheese, crumbled

Directions:
1. Mix the orange juice, olive oil, vinegar, and honey in a small bowl. Season with salt and pepper and set aside. Divide the baby kale, orange segments, fennel, pecans, and ricotta cheese evenly between two plates. Drizzle half of the dressing over each salad.

Nutrition Info:
- Per Serving: Calories: 502;Fat: 39g;Protein: 13g;Carbs: 31g.

Bell Pepper, Tomato & Egg Salad

Servings:4 | Cooking Time:15 Min + Chilling Time

Ingredients:
- 4 tbsp olive oil
- 2 hard-boiled eggs, chopped
- 2 cups Greek yogurt
- 1 cup tomatoes, chopped
- 2 mixed bell peppers, sliced
- 1 yellow onion, thinly sliced
- ½ tsp fresh garlic, minced
- 10 Kalamata olives, sliced
- 3 sun-dried tomatoes, chopped
- 1 tbsp fresh lemon juice
- 1 tsp dill, chopped
- 2 tbsp fresh parsley, chopped
- Salt and black pepper to taste

Directions:
1. In a bowl, combine the bell peppers, onion, garlic, Kalamata olives, chopped tomatoes, and sun-dried tomatoes. Stir in the chopped eggs. For the dressing, combine the lemon juice, olive oil, Greek yogurt, dill, salt, and black pepper in a bowl. Pour over the salad and transfer to the fridge to chill. Serve garnished with olives and parsley.

Nutrition Info:
- Per Serving: Calories: 279;Fat: 19g;Protein: 14g;Carbs: 14g.

Herby Grilled Mushroom Bruschetta

Servings:4 | Cooking Time:20 Minutes

Ingredients:
- 8 thick baguette slices
- 4 tsp aioli
- 12 oz mixed mushrooms
- 2 tbsp butter
- ¼ tsp dried thyme
- ¼ tsp dried oregano
- ½ tsp garlic powder
- ½ lemon, juiced and zested
- Salt and black pepper to taste
- 1 tbsp fresh parsley, chopped

Directions:
1. Melt the butter in a heavy skillet over medium heat. Add mushrooms and cook without stirring for 4–5 minutes. Stir in herbs, lemon zest and juice, and garlic powder and cook until accumulating liquid is mostly evaporated. Season with salt and pepper. Preheat a grill pan over medium heat. Grill the bread until dark brown marks decorate their faces, top, and bottom. Transfer to a serving plate. Spread the aioli onto the toasted bread slices. Spoon the mushrooms onto the bread and top with parsley.

Nutrition Info:
- Per Serving: Calories: 135;Fat: 7g;Protein: 8g;Carbs: 14g.

Authentic Marinara Sauce

Servings:6 | Cooking Time:46 Minutes

Ingredients:
- 2 cans crushed tomatoes with their juices
- 1 tsp dried oregano
- 2 tbsp + ¼ cup olive oil
- 2 tbsp butter
- 1 small onion, diced
- 1 red bell pepper, chopped
- 4 garlic cloves, minced
- Salt and black pepper to taste
- ½ cup thinly sliced basil
- 2 tbsp chopped rosemary
- 1 tsp red pepper flakes

Directions:
1. Warm 2 tablespoons olive oil and butter in a large skillet over medium heat. Add the onion, garlic, and red pepper and sauté for about 5 minutes until tender. Season with salt and pepper. Reduce the heat to low and add the tomatoes and their juices, remaining olive oil, oregano, half of the basil, rosemary, and red pepper flakes. Bring to a simmer and cover. Cook for 50-60 minutes. Blitz the sauce with an immersion blender and sprinkle with the remaining basil.

Nutrition Info:
- Per Serving: Calories: 265;Fat: 19g;Protein: 4.1g;Carbs: 18g.

Spanish Lentil Soup With Rice

Servings:4 | Cooking Time:30 Minutes

Ingredients:
- 2 tbsp olive oil
- ½ cup red lentils, rinsed
- ½ cup Spanish rice
- 4 cups vegetable stock
- Salt to taste
- 1 onion, finely chopped
- 2 garlic cloves, sliced
- 1 carrot, finely diced
- 1 tsp turmeric
- 4 sage leaves, chopped

Directions:
1. Heat the olive oil in a stockpot over medium heat. Sauté the onion, carrot, and garlic for 5 minutes until the onion and garlic are golden brown. Stir in the turmeric for 1 minute. Pour in stock, lentils, rice, and salt. Simmer for 15-20 minutes, stirring occasionally. Serve the soup garnished with chopped sage leaves.

Nutrition Info:
- Per Serving: Calories: 230;Fat: 7.2g;Protein: 9g;Carbs: 36.8g.

Green Beans With Tahini-lemon Sauce

Servings:2 | Cooking Time: 10 Minutes

Ingredients:
- 1 pound green beans, washed and trimmed
- 2 tablespoons tahini
- 1 garlic clove, minced
- Grated zest and juice of 1
- lemon
- Salt and black pepper, to taste
- 1 teaspoon toasted black or white sesame seeds (optional)

Directions:
1. Steam the beans in a medium saucepan fitted with a steamer basket (or by adding ¼ cup water to a covered saucepan) over medium-high heat. Drain, reserving the cooking water.
2. Mix the tahini, garlic, lemon zest and juice, and salt and pepper to taste. Use the reserved cooking water to thin the sauce as desired.
3. Toss the green beans with the sauce and garnish with the sesame seeds, if desired. Serve immediately.

Nutrition Info:
- Per Serving: Calories: 188;Fat: 8.4g;Protein: 7.2g;Carbs: 22.2g.

Potato Salad

Servings:6 | Cooking Time:20 Minutes

Ingredients:
- 4 russet potatoes, peeled and chopped
- 1 cup frozen mixed vegetables, thawed
- 3 hard-boiled eggs, chopped
- ½ cup Greek yogurt
- 10 pitted black olives
- ½ tsp dried mustard seeds
- ½ tsp lemon zest
- ½ tbsp lemon juice
- ½ tsp dried dill
- Salt and black pepper to taste

Directions:
1. Put the potatoes in a pot of salted water, bring to a boil, and cook for 5-7 minutes, until just fork-tender. Drain and set aside to cool. In a large bowl, mix the eggs, vegetables, yogurt, olives, pepper, mustard, lemon juice, lemon zest, and dill. Season with salt and pepper. Mix in potatoes. Serve.

Nutrition Info:
- Per Serving: Calories: 190;Fat: 4.8g;Protein: 9g;Carbs: 29.7g.

Quick Za´atar Spice

Servings:4 | Cooking Time:5 Minutes

Ingredients:
- 1 tsp ground cumin
- 1 tsp ground coriander
- ½ cup dried thyme
- 2 tbsp sesame seeds, toasted
- 1 ½ tbsp ground sumac
- ¼ tsp Aleppo chili flakes

Directions:
1. Mix all the ingredients in a bowl. Store in a glass jar at room temperature for up to 7-9 months.

Nutrition Info:
- Per Serving: Calories: 175;Fat: 13.9g;Protein: 5g;Carbs: 12g.

Kale & Chicken Soup With Vermicelli

Servings:4 | Cooking Time:25 Minutes

Ingredients:
- 2 tbsp olive oil
- 1 carrot, chopped
- 1 leek, chopped
- ½ cup vermicelli
- 4 cups chicken stock
- 2 cups kale, chopped
- 2 chicken breasts, cubed
- 1 cup orzo
- ¼ cup lemon juice
- 2 tbsp parsley, chopped
- Salt and black pepper to taste

Directions:
1. Warm the olive oil in a pot over medium heat and sauté leek and chicken for 6 minutes. Stir in carrot and chicken stock and bring to a boil. Cook for 10 minutes. Add in vermicelli, kale, orzo, and lemon juice and continue cooking for another 5 minutes. Adjust the seasoning with salt and pepper and sprinkle with parsley. Ladle into soup bowls and serve.

Nutrition Info:
- Per Serving: Calories: 310;Fat: 13g;Protein: 13g;Carbs: 17g.

Mustard Chicken Salad With Avocado

Servings:4 | Cooking Time:10 Minutes

Ingredients:
- 1 cup cooked chicken breasts, chopped
- ½ cup marinated artichoke hearts
- 2 tbsp olive oil
- 6 sundried tomatoes, chopped
- 1 cucumber, chopped
- 6 black olives, 6 sliced
- 2 cups Iceberg lettuce, torn
- 2 tbsp parsley, chopped
- 1 avocado, peeled and cubed
- ½ cup feta cheese, crumbled
- 4 tbsp red wine vinegar
- 2 tbsp Dijon mustard
- 1 tsp basil, dried
- 1 garlic clove, minced
- 2 tsp honey
- Salt and black pepper to taste
- 3 tbsp lemon juice

Directions:
1. Combine chicken, tomatoes, artichokes, cucumber, olives, lettuce, parsley, and avocado in a bowl. In a separate bowl, whisk vinegar, mustard, basil, garlic, honey, olive oil, salt, pepper, and lemon juice and pour over the salad. Mix well. Top with cheese and serve.

Nutrition Info:
- Per Serving: Calories: 340;Fat: 23g;Protein: 10g;Carbs: 26g.

Authentic Chicken Soup With Vegetables

Servings:4 | Cooking Time:35 Minutes

Ingredients:
- 2 tsp olive oil
- 1 cup mushrooms, chopped
- 1 large carrot, chopped
- 1 yellow onion, chopped
- 1 celery stalk, chopped
- 2 yellow squash, chopped
- 2 chicken breasts, cubed
- ½ cup chopped fresh parsley
- 4 cups chicken stock
- Salt and black pepper to taste

Directions:
1. Warm the oil in a skillet over medium heat. Place in carrot, onion, mushrooms, and celery and cook for 5 minutes. Stir in chicken and cook for 10 more minutes. Mix in squash, salt, and black pepper. Cook for 5 minutes, then lower the heat and pour in the stock. Cook covered for 10 more minutes. Divide between bowls and scatter with parsley.

Nutrition Info:
- Per Serving: Calories: 335;Fat: 9g;Protein: 33g;Carbs: 28g.

Horiatiki Salad (greek Salad)

Servings:4 | Cooking Time:10 Minutes

Ingredients:
- 1 green bell pepper, cut into chunks
- 1 head romaine lettuce, torn
- ½ red onion, cut into rings
- 2 tomatoes, cut into wedges
- 1 cucumber, thinly sliced
- 3 tbsp extra-virgin olive oil
- 2 tbsp lemon juice
- Garlic salt and pepper to taste
- ¼ tsp dried Greek oregano
- 1 cup feta cheese, cubed
- 1 handful of Kalamata olives

Directions:
1. In a salad bowl, whisk the olive oil, lemon juice, pepper, garlic salt, and oregano. Add in the lettuce, red onion, tomatoes, cucumber, and bell pepper and mix with your hands to coat. Top with feta and olives and serve immediately.

Nutrition Info:
- Per Serving: Calories: 226;Fat: 19g;Protein: 8g;Carbs: 9g.

Chili Lentil Soup

Servings:4 | Cooking Time:30 Minutes

Ingredients:
- 2 tbsp olive oil
- 1 cup lentils, rinsed
- 1 onion, chopped
- 2 carrots, chopped
- 1 potato, cubed
- 1 tomato, chopped
- 4 garlic cloves, minced
- 4 cups vegetable broth
- ½ tsp chili powder
- Salt and black pepper to taste
- 2 tbsp fresh parsley, chopped

Directions:
1. Warm the olive oil in a pot over medium heat. Add in onion, garlic, and carrots and sauté for 5-6 minutes until tender. Mix in lentils, broth, salt, pepper, chili powder, potato, and tomato. Bring to a boil, lower the heat and simmer for 15-18 minutes, stirring often. Top with parsley and serve.

Nutrition Info:
- Per Serving: Calories: 331;Fat: 9g;Protein: 19g;Carbs: 44.3g.

Chicken And Pastina Soup

Servings:6 | Cooking Time: 20 Minutes

Ingredients:
- 1 tablespoon extra-virgin olive oil
- 2 garlic cloves, minced
- 3 cups packed chopped kale, center ribs removed
- 1 cup minced carrots
- 8 cups no-salt-added chicken or vegetable broth
- ¼ teaspoon kosher or sea salt
- ¼ teaspoon freshly ground black pepper
- ¾ cup uncooked acini de pepe or pastina pasta
- 2 cups shredded cooked chicken
- 3 tablespoons grated Parmesan cheese

Directions:
1. In a large stockpot over medium heat, heat the oil. Add the garlic and cook for 30 seconds, stirring frequently. Add the kale and carrots and cook for 5 minutes, stirring occasionally.
2. Add the broth, salt, and pepper, and turn the heat to high. Bring the broth to a boil, and add the pasta. Reduce the heat to medium and cook for 10 minutes, or until the pasta is cooked through, stirring every few minutes so the pasta doesn't stick to the bottom. Add the chicken, and cook for another 2 minutes to warm through.
3. Ladle the soup into six bowls. Top each with ½ tablespoon of cheese and serve.

Nutrition Info:
- Per Serving: Calories: 275;Fat: 19.0g;Protein: 16.0g;Carbs: 11.0g.

Root Veggie Soup

Servings:4 | Cooking Time:40 Minutes

Ingredients:
- 3 cups chopped butternut squash
- 2 tbsp olive oil
- 1 carrot, chopped
- 1 leek, chopped
- 2 garlic cloves, minced
- 1 celery stalk, chopped
- 1 parsnip, chopped
- 1 potato, chopped
- 4 cups vegetable broth
- 1 tsp dried thyme
- Salt and black pepper to taste

Directions:
1. Warm olive oil in a pot over medium heat and sauté leek, garlic, parsnip, carrot, and celery for 5-6 minutes until the veggies start to brown. Throw in squash, potato, broth, thyme, salt, and pepper. Bring to a boil, then decrease the heat and simmer for 20-30 minutes until the veggies soften. Transfer to a food processor and blend until you get a smooth and homogeneous consistency.

Nutrition Info:
- Per Serving: Calories: 200;Fat: 9g;Protein: 7.2g;Carbs: 25.8g.

Veggie Cream Sauce

Servings:6 | Cooking Time:25 Minutes

Ingredients:
- 3 tbsp olive oil
- ½ zucchini, chopped
- 1 celery stalk, chopped
- 1 red bell pepper, sliced
- 2 tomatoes, chopped
- 3 garlic cloves, minced
- ½ tsp dried basil
- ½ cup baby spinach
- 1 cup heavy cream
- ¼ cup chopped fresh parsley

Directions:
1. Warm the olive oil in a large skillet over medium heat. Add the zucchini, celery, bell pepper, tomatoes, and garlic and sauté for 8-10 minutes until the vegetables are softened. Add the basil and

cook for 1 minute. Stir in spinach and cook until wilted, about 3 minutes. Add the cream and mix well and cook for about 4 minutes. Top with parsley and serve.

Nutrition Info:
- Per Serving: Calories: 149;Fat: 14g;Protein: 1.3g;Carbs: 5g.

Chilled Soup With Prawns

Servings:4 | Cooking Time:15 Minutes

Ingredients:
- 1 lb prawns, peeled and deveined
- 3 tbsp olive oil
- 1 cucumber, chopped
- 3 cups tomato juice
- 3 roasted red peppers, chopped
- 2 tbsp balsamic vinegar
- 1 garlic clove, minced
- Salt and black pepper to taste
- ½ tsp cumin
- 1 tsp thyme, chopped

Directions:
1. In a food processor, blitz tomato juice, cucumber, red peppers, 2 tbsp of olive oil, vinegar, cumin, salt, pepper, and garlic until smooth. Remove to a bowl and transfer to the fridge for 10 minutes. Warm the remaining oil in a pot over medium heat and sauté prawns, salt, pepper, and thyme for 4 minutes on all sides. Let cool. Ladle the soup into individual bowls and serve topped with prawns.

Nutrition Info:
- Per Serving: Calories: 270;Fat: 12g;Protein: 7g;Carbs: 13g.

Cucumber & Tomato Salad With Anchovies

Servings:4 | Cooking Time:10 Minutes

Ingredients:
- 2 tbsp extra virgin olive oil
- 1 tbsp lemon juice
- 4 canned anchovy fillets
- 6 black olives
- ½ head Romaine lettuce, torn
- Salt and black pepper to taste
- 1 cucumber, cubed
- 3 tomatoes, cubed
- 2 spring onions, chopped

Directions:
1. Whisk the olive oil, lemon juice, salt, and pepper in a bowl. Add the cucumber, tomatoes, and spring onions and toss to coat. Top with anchovies and black olives and serve.

Nutrition Info:
- Per Serving: Calories: 113;Fat: 8.5g;Protein: 2.9g;Carbs: 9g.

Tomato & Roasted Eggplant Soup

Servings:6 | Cooking Time:60 Minutes

Ingredients:
- 2 tbsp olive oil
- 3 eggplants, sliced lengthwise
- Salt to taste
- 1 red onion, chopped
- 2 tbsp garlic, minced
- 1 tsp dried thyme
- Salt and black pepper to taste
- 2 ripe tomatoes, halved
- 5 cups chicken broth
- ¼ cup heavy cream
- 2 tbsp fresh basil, chopped

Directions:
1. Preheat oven to 400° F. Place the eggplants on a greased sheet pan and drizzle with some olive oil. Roast for 45 minutes. Remove from oven and allow to cool. When cool, remove all of the insides, discarding the skins.
2. Warm the remaining olive oil in a large skillet over medium heat. Add the onions and garlic and cook for 5 minutes until soft and translucent. Add the thyme and season with salt and pepper. Put the eggplant, tomatoes, and onion in your food processor and

process until smooth. Pour the chicken broth into a pot and bring to a boil. Reduce heat to a simmer and add the eggplant mixture. Stir until well combined and fold in the heavy cream. Adjust to taste. Serve topped with basil.

Nutrition Info:
- Per Serving: Calories: 124;Fat: 5.1g;Protein: 3.5g;Carbs: 19g.

Mushroom & Spinach Orzo Soup

Servings:4 | Cooking Time:20 Minutes

Ingredients:
- 2 tbsp butter
- 3 cups spinach
- ½ cup orzo
- 4 cups chicken broth
- 1 cup feta cheese, crumbled
- Salt and black pepper to taste
- ½ tsp dried oregano
- 1 onion, chopped
- 2 garlic cloves, minced
- 1 cup mushrooms, sliced

Directions:
1. Melt butter in a pot over medium heat and sauté onion, garlic, and mushrooms for 5 minutes until tender. Add in chicken broth, orzo, salt, pepper, and oregano. Bring to a boil and reduce the heat to a low. Continue simmering for 10 minutes, partially covered. Stir in spinach and continue to cook until the spinach wilts, about 3-4 minutes. Ladle into individual bowls and serve garnished with feta cheese.

Nutrition Info:
- Per Serving: Calories: 370;Fat: 11g;Protein: 23g;Carbs: 44g.

Sweet Chickpea & Mushroom Stew

Servings:4 | Cooking Time:20 Minutes

Ingredients:
- ½ tbsp button mushrooms, chopped
- 1 cup chickpeas, cooked
- 1 onion, peeled, chopped
- 1 lb string beans, trimmed
- 1 apple, cut into 1-inch cubes
- ½ cup raisins
- 2 carrots, chopped
- 2 garlic cloves, crushed
- 4 cherry tomatoes
- 2 tbsp fresh mint, chopped
- 1 tsp grated ginger
- ½ cup orange juice
- ½ tsp salt

Directions:
1. Place all ingredients in the instant pot. Pour enough water to cover. Cook on High Pressure for 8 minutes. Do a natural release for 10 minutes.

Nutrition Info:
- Per Serving: Calories: 350;Fat: 3.7g;Protein: 14g;Carbs: 71g.

Cucumber Gazpacho

Servings:4 | Cooking Time: 0 Minutes

Ingredients:
- 2 cucumbers, peeled, deseeded, and cut into chunks
- ½ cup mint, finely chopped
- 2 cups plain Greek yogurt
- 2 garlic cloves, minced
- 2 cups low-sodium vegetable
- soup
- 1 tablespoon no-salt-added tomato paste
- 3 teaspoons fresh dill
- Sea salt and freshly ground pepper, to taste

Directions:
1. Put the cucumber, mint, yogurt, and garlic in a food processor, then pulse until creamy and smooth.
2. Transfer the puréed mixture in a large serving bowl, then add the vegetable soup, tomato paste, dill, salt, and ground black pepper. Stir to mix well.
3. Keep the soup in the refrigerator for at least 2 hours, then serve chilled.

Nutrition Info:
- Per Serving: Calories: 133;Fat: 1.5g;Protein: 14.2g;Carbs: 16.5g.

Classic Zuppa Toscana

Servings:4 | Cooking Time:25 Minutes

Ingredients:
- 2 tbsp olive oil
- 1 yellow onion, chopped
- 4 garlic cloves, minced
- 1 celery stalk, chopped
- 1 carrot, chopped
- 15 oz canned tomatoes, diced
- 1 zucchini, chopped
- 6 cups vegetable stock
- 2 tbsp tomato paste
- 15 oz canned white beans
- 5 oz Tuscan kale
- 1 tbsp basil, chopped
- Salt and black pepper to taste

Directions:
1. Warm the olive oil in a pot over medium heat. Cook garlic and onion for 3 minutes. Stir in celery, carrot, tomatoes, zucchini, stock, tomato paste, white beans, kale, salt, and pepper and bring to a simmer. Cook for 10 minutes. Top with basil.

Nutrition Info:
- Per Serving: Calories: 480;Fat: 9g;Protein: 28g;Carbs: 77g.

Arugula & Caper Green Salad

Servings:4 | Cooking Time:10 Minutes

Ingredients:
- 1 tbsp olive oil
- 10 green olives, sliced
- 4 cups baby arugula
- 1 tbsp capers, drained
- 1 tbsp balsamic vinegar
- 1 tsp lemon zest, grated
- 1 tbsp lemon juice
- 1 tsp parsley, chopped
- Salt and black pepper to taste

Directions:
1. Mix capers, olives, vinegar, lemon zest, lemon juice, oil, parsley, salt, pepper, and arugula in a bowl. Serve.

Nutrition Info:
- Per Serving: Calories: 160;Fat: 4g;Protein: 5g;Carbs: 4g.

Mushroom & Parmesan Risotto

Servings:4 | Cooking Time:25 Minutes

Ingredients:
- 1 ½ cups mixed mushrooms, sliced
- 3 tbsp olive oil
- 1 shallot, chopped
- 1 cup Arborio rice
- 4 cups vegetable stock
- 2 tbsp dry white wine
- 1 cup grated Parmesan cheese
- 2 tbsp butter
- 2 tbsp fresh parsley, chopped

Directions:
1. Pour the vegetable stock into a small saucepan over low heat and bring to a simmer; then turn the heat off.
2. Warm the olive oil in a large saucepan over medium heat. Sauté the mushrooms and shallot for 6 minutes until tender. Stir in rice for 3 minutes until opaque. Pour in the wine and stir. Gradually add the hot stock to the rice mixture, about 1 ladleful at a time, stirring until the liquid is absorbed. Remove the saucepan from the heat, stir in butter and 3 tbsp of Parmesan cheese. Cover and leave to rest for 5 minutes. Scatter the remaining cheese and parsley over the risotto and serve in bowls.

Nutrition Info:
- Per Serving: Calories: 354;Fat: 29g;Protein: 11g;Carbs: 22g.

Garbanzo & Arugula Salad With Blue Cheese

Servings:4 | Cooking Time:10 Minutes

Ingredients:
- 15 oz canned garbanzo beans, drained
- ½ cup Gorgonzola cheese, crumbled
- 3 tbsp olive oil
- 1 cucumber, cubed
- 3 oz black olives, sliced
- 1 Roma tomato, slivered
- ¼ cup red onion, chopped
- 5 cups arugula
- Salt to taste
- 1 tbsp lemon juice
- 2 tbsp parsley, chopped

Directions:
1. Place the arugula in a salad bowl. Add in garbanzo beans, cucumber, olives, tomato, and onion and mix to combine. In another small bowl, whisk the lemon juice, olive oil, and salt. Drizzle the dressing over the salad and sprinkle with gorgonzola cheese and parsley to serve.

Nutrition Info:
- Per Serving: Calories: 280;Fat: 17g;Protein: 10g;Carbs: 25g.

Spinach & Sundried Tomato Salad With Eggs

Servings:4 | Cooking Time:10 Minutes

Ingredients:
- 2 tbsp olive oil
- 10 oz baby spinach
- 6 eggs, at room temperature
- Juice of 1 lime
- 1 cup feta cheese, crumbled
- Salt and black pepper to taste
- 2 tbsp mustard
- 8 sundried tomatoes, chopped
- 1 cup walnuts, chopped

Directions:
1. Bring to a boil salted water in a pot over medium heat. Add in the eggs and cook for 10 minutes. Remove to a bowl with ice-cold water and let them cool; peel and chop.
2. Put the baby spinach on a large serving plate. Place olive oil, eggs, lime juice, feta cheese, salt, pepper, mustard, sun-dried tomatoes, and walnuts and toss to combine in a bowl. Pour the mixture over the spinach and serve.

Nutrition Info:
- Per Serving: Calories: 300;Fat: 9g;Protein: 7g;Carbs: 16g.

Basil Zucchini Marinara

Servings:4 | Cooking Time:25 Minutes

Ingredients:
- 2 tbsp olive oil
- 1 shallot, chopped
- 1 garlic clove, minced
- 1 zucchini, sliced into rounds
- Salt and black pepper to taste
- 1 cup marinara sauce
- ¼ cup mozzarella, shredded
- 2 tbsp fresh basil, chopped

Directions:
1. Warm the olive oil in a skillet over medium heat. Sauté the shallot and garlic for 3 minutes until just tender and fragrant. Add in the zucchini and season with salt and pepper; cook for 4 minutes until lightly browned. Add marinara sauce and bring to a simmer; cook until zucchini is tender, 5-8 minutes. Scatter the mozzarella cheese on top of the zucchini layer and cover; heat for about 3 minutes until the cheese is melted. Sprinkle with basil and serve immediately.

Nutrition Info:
- Per Serving: Calories: 93;Fat: 7g;Protein: 3g;Carbs: 5g.

Lemony Lamb Stew

Servings:4 | Cooking Time:60 Minutes

Ingredients:
- 2 potatoes, peeled, cut into bite-sized pieces
- 2 tbsp olive oil
- 1 onion, chopped
- 1 lb lamb neck, boneless
- 2 large carrots, chopped
- 1 tomato, diced
- 1 red bell pepper, chopped
- 2 garlic cloves, minced
- 2 tbsp parsley, chopped
- ¼ cup lemon juice
- Salt and black pepper to taste

Directions:
1. Warm the olive oil in your Instant Pot on Sauté. Add the meat and brown for 4-6 minutes, stirring occasionally. Stir in onion, carrot, and garlic and cook for 3 more minutes until softened. Pour in the tomato and 2 cups of water. Season with salt and pepper. Seal the lid and cook on High Pressure for 45 minutes. When ready, do a quick pressure release. Sprinkle with parsley. Serve into bowls and enjoy!

Nutrition Info:
- Per Serving: Calories: 251;Fat: 9.7g;Protein: 5g;Carbs: 34.2g.

Lamb & Spinach Soup

Servings:4 | Cooking Time:60 Minutes

Ingredients:
- ½ lb lamb shoulder, cut into bite-sized pieces
- 2 tbsp olive oil
- 1 onion, chopped
- 2 garlic cloves, minced
- 10 oz spinach, chopped
- 4 cups vegetable broth
- Salt and black pepper to taste

Directions:
1. Warm the olive oil on Sauté in your Instant Pot. Sauté the lamb, onion, and garlic for 6-8 minutes, stirring often. Pour in the broth and adjust the seasoning with salt and pepper. Seal the lid, press Soup/Broth, and cook for 30 minutes on High Pressure. Do a natural pressure release for 10 minutes. Press Sauté and add the spinach. Cook for 5 minutes. Serve.

Nutrition Info:
- Per Serving: Calories: 188;Fat: 12g;Protein: 14g;Carbs: 9g.

Sautéed White Beans With Rosemary

Servings:2 | Cooking Time: 12 Minutes

Ingredients:
- 1 tablespoon olive oil
- 2 garlic cloves, minced
- 1 can white cannellini beans, drained and rinsed
- 1 teaspoon minced fresh rosemary plus 1 whole fresh
- rosemary sprig
- ¼ teaspoon dried sage
- ½ cup low-sodium chicken stock
- Salt, to taste

Directions:
1. Heat the olive oil in a saucepan over medium-high heat.
2. Add the garlic and sauté for 30 seconds until fragrant.
3. Add the beans, minced and whole rosemary, sage, and chicken stock and bring the mixture to a boil.
4. Reduce the heat to medium and allow to simmer for 10 minutes, or until most of the liquid is evaporated. If desired, mash some of the beans with a fork to thicken them.
5. Season with salt to taste. Remove the rosemary sprig before serving.

Nutrition Info:
- Per Serving: Calories: 155;Fat: 7.0g;Protein: 6.0g;Carbs: 17.0g.

Mushroom Sauce

Servings:4 | Cooking Time:15 Minutes

Ingredients:
- 1 cup cremini mushrooms, chopped
- 2 tbsp olive oil
- 1 small onion, chopped
- 2 garlic cloves, minced
- 3 tbsp butter
- ½ cup white wine
- ½ cup vegetable broth
- 1 cup heavy cream
- 2 tbsp parsley, chopped

Directions:
1. Heat the olive oil in a pan over medium. Add the onion and garlic and sauté until the onion is translucent, 3 minutes. Add the butter and mushrooms and cook for 5-7 minutes until the mushrooms are tender. Pour in the wine and scrape up any browned bits from the bottom of the pan. Simmer for 3-4 minutes. Add the vegetable broth and simmer for 5 minutes until the sauce reduces by about three quarters. Add the heavy cream and simmer for 2-3 minutes. Sprinkle with parsley. Serve and enjoy!

Nutrition Info:
- Per Serving: Calories: 283;Fat: 27g;Protein: 2.1g;Carbs: 5g.

Dill Soup With Roasted Vegetables

Servings:4 | Cooking Time:45 Minutes

Ingredients:
- 3 tbsp olive oil
- 2 carrots, sliced
- 3 sweet potatoes, sliced
- 1 celery stalk, sliced
- 1 tsp chopped dill
- 4 cups vegetable broth
- Salt and black pepper to taste
- 1 tbsp Parmesan, grated

Directions:
1. Preheat oven to 400°F. Mix carrots, sweet potatoes, and celery in a bowl. Drizzle with olive oil and toss. Sprinkle with dill, salt, and pepper. Arrange the vegetable on a lined with parchment paper sheet and bake for 30 minutes or until the veggies are tender and golden brown. Let cool slightly.
2. Place the veggies and some broth in a food processor and pulse until smooth; work in batches. Transfer to a pot over low heat and add in the remaining broth. Cook just until heated through. Serve topped with Parmesan cheese.

Nutrition Info:
- Per Serving: Calories: 203;Fat: 10g;Protein: 2g;Carbs: 23g.

Corn & Cucumber Salad

Servings:4 | Cooking Time:10 Minutes

Ingredients:
- 3 tbsp olive oil
- 3 tbsp pepitas, roasted
- 2 tbsp cilantro, chopped
- 1 cup corn
- 1 cup radishes, sliced
- 2 avocados, mashed
- 2 cucumbers, chopped
- 2 tbsp Greek yogurt
- 1 tsp balsamic vinegar
- 2 tbsp lime juice
- Salt and black pepper to taste

Directions:
1. In a bowl, whisk the olive oil, avocados, salt, pepper, lime juice, yogurt, and vinegar until smooth. Combine pepitas, cilantro, corn, radishes, and cucumbers in a salad bowl. Pour the avocado dressing over salad and toss to combine. Serve.

Nutrition Info:
- Per Serving: Calories: 410;Fat: 32g;Protein: 4g;Carbs: 25g.

Parsley Carrot & Cabbage Salad

Servings:4 | Cooking Time:10 Minutes

Ingredients:
- 2 tbsp olive oil
- 1 green cabbage head, torn
- 1 tbsp lemon juice
- 1 carrot, grated
- Salt and black pepper to taste
- ¼ cup parsley, chopped

Directions:
1. Mix olive oil, lemon juice, carrot, parsley, salt, pepper, and cabbage in a bowl. Serve right away.

Nutrition Info:
- Per Serving: Calories: 110;Fat: 5g;Protein: 5g;Carbs: 5g.

Carrot & Celery Bean Soup

Servings:6 | Cooking Time:35 Minutes

Ingredients:
- 3 tbsp olive oil
- 1 onion, finely chopped
- 3 garlic cloves, minced
- 2 cups carrots, diced
- 2 cups celery, diced
- 1 medium potato, cubed
- 2 oz cubed pancetta
- 2 cans white beans, rinsed
- 6 cups vegetable broth
- Salt and black pepper to taste

Directions:
1. Heat the olive oil in a stockpot over medium heat. Add the pancetta, onion, and garlic and cook for 3-4 minutes, stirring often. Add the carrots and celery and cook for another 3-5 minutes until tender. Add the beans, potato, broth, salt, and pepper. Stir and simmer for about 20 minutes, stirring occasionally. Serve warm.

Nutrition Info:
- Per Serving: Calories: 244;Fat: 7.2g;Protein: 9g;Carbs: 36.4g.

Chicken & Mushroom Soup

Servings:4 | Cooking Time:30 Minutes

Ingredients:
- 2 tbsp olive oil
- 1 can diced tomatoes
- ½ lb chicken breasts, cubed
- 4 cups chicken broth
- 2 carrots, chopped
- 1 onion, chopped
- 1 red bell pepper, chopped
- 1 fennel bulb, chopped
- 2 garlic cloves, minced
- ½ tsp paprika
- 1 cup mushrooms, sliced
- 1 tbsp Italian seasoning
- Salt and black pepper to taste

Directions:
1. Warm the olive oil in a pot over medium heat. Place in chicken and brown for 5 minutes. Set aside.
2. Add in onion, carrots, bell pepper, and fennel, sauté for 5 minutes until softened. Throw in garlic and paprika and cook for 30 seconds. Mix in tomatoes, mushrooms, Italian seasoning, broth, chicken, salt, and pepper. Bring to a boil, then decrease the heat and simmer for 20 minutes. Serve.

Nutrition Info:
- Per Serving: Calories: 293;Fat: 14g;Protein: 24g;Carbs: 19g.

Eggplant & Chicken Soup

Servings:4 | Cooking Time:40 Minutes

Ingredients:
- 2 tbsp butter
- ¼ tsp celery seeds
- 2 cups eggplants, cubed
- Salt and black pepper to taste
- 1 red onion, chopped
- 2 garlic cloves, minced
- 1 red bell pepper, chopped
- 1 red chili pepper

- 2 tbsp parsley, chopped
- 2 tbsp oregano, chopped
- 4 cups chicken stock
- 1 lb chicken breasts, cubed
- 1 cup half and half
- 1 egg yolk

Directions:

1. Melt butter in a pot over medium heat and sauté chicken, garlic, and onion for 10 minutes. Put in bell pepper, eggplant, salt, pepper, red chili pepper, celery seeds, oregano, and chicken stock and bring to a simmer. Cook for 20 minutes. Whisk egg yolk, half and half, and 1 cup of the soup in a bowl and pour gradually into the pot. Sprinkle with parsley.

Nutrition Info:

- Per Serving: Calories: 320;Fat: 18g;Protein: 16g;Carbs: 21g.

Chorizo & Fire-roasted Tomato Soup

Servings:4 | Cooking Time:25 Minutes

Ingredients:

- 28 oz fire-roasted diced tomatoes
- 1 tbsp olive oil
- 2 shallots, chopped
- 3 cloves garlic, minced
- Salt and black pepper to taste
- 4 cups beef broth
- ½ cup fresh ripe tomatoes
- 1 tbsp red wine vinegar
- 3 chorizo sausage, chopped
- ½ cup thinly chopped basil

Directions:

1. Warm the olive oil on Sauté in your Instant Pot. Cook the chorizo until crispy, stirring occasionally, about 5 minutes. Remove to a plate. Add the garlic and shallots to the pot and sauté for 3 minutes until soft. Season with salt and pepper.

2. Stir in red wine vinegar, broth, diced tomatoes, and ripe tomatoes. Seal the lid and cook on High Pressure for 8 minutes. Release the pressure quickly. Pour the soup into a blender and process until smooth. Divide into bowls, top with chorizo, and decorate with basil.

Nutrition Info:

- Per Serving: Calories: 771;Fat: 27g;Protein: 40g;Carbs: 117g.

Classic Aioli

Servings:6 | Cooking Time:10 Minutes

Ingredients:

- ½ cup sunseed oil
- 1 garlic clove, minced
- 2 tsp lemon juice
- 1 tsp lemon zest
- 1 large egg yolk
- Salt to taste

Directions:

1. Blitz all the ingredients in a large bowl with an immersion blender until everything is well combined and thick. Store in an airtight container in the refrigerator for up to 2-3 days.

Nutrition Info:

- Per Serving: Calories: 181;Fat: 9.7g;Protein: 3.3g;Carbs: 4g.

Parsley Garden Vegetable Soup

Servings:4 | Cooking Time:25 Minutes

Ingredients:

- ¼ head green cabbage, shredded
- 2 tbsp olive oil
- 1 cup leeks, chopped
- 2 garlic cloves, minced
- 8 cups vegetable stock
- 1 carrot, diced
- 1 potato, diced
- 1 celery stalk, diced
- 1 cup mushrooms
- 1 cup broccoli florets
- 1 cup cauliflower florets
- ½ red bell pepper, diced
- ½ cup green beans
- Salt and black pepper to taste
- 2 tbsp fresh parsley, chopped

Directions:

1. Heat oil on Sauté in your Instant Pot. Add in garlic and leeks and cook for 6 minutes until slightly browned. Add in stock, carrot, celery, broccoli, bell pepper, green beans, salt, cabbage, cauliflower, mushrooms, potato, and pepper. Seal lid and cook on High Pressure for 6 minutes. Release pressure naturally for about 10 minutes. Stir in parsley and serve.

Nutrition Info:

- Per Serving: Calories: 218;Fat: 7g;Protein: 5g;Carbs: 36g.

Paprika Bean Soup

Servings:4 | Cooking Time:50 Minutes

Ingredients:

- 2 tbsp olive oil
- 6 cups veggie stock
- 1 cup celery, chopped
- 1 cup carrots, chopped
- 1 yellow onion, chopped
- 2 garlic cloves, minced
- ½ cup navy beans, soaked
- 2 tbsp chopped parsley
- ½ tsp paprika
- 1 tsp thyme
- Salt and black pepper to taste

Directions:

1. Warm olive oil in a saucepan and sauté onion, garlic, carrots, and celery for 5 minutes, stirring occasionally. Stir in paprika, thyme, salt, and pepper for 1 minute. Pour in broth and navy beans. Bring to a boil, then reduce the heat and simmer for 40 minutes. Sprinkle with parsley and serve.

Nutrition Info:

- Per Serving: Calories: 270;Fat: 18g;Protein: 12g;Carbs: 24g.

Pesto Ravioli Salad

Servings:6 | Cooking Time:15 Minutes

Ingredients:

- 1 cup smoked mozzarella cheese, cubed
- ¼ tsp lemon zest
- 1 cup basil pesto
- ½ cup mayonnaise
- 2 red bell peppers, chopped
- 18 oz cheese ravioli

Directions:

1. Bring to a boil salted water in a pot over high heat. Add the ravioli and cook, uncovered, for 4-5 minutes, stirring occasionally; drain and place them in a salad bowl to cool slightly. Blend the lemon zest, pesto, and mayonnaise in a large bowl and stir in mozzarella cheese and bell peppers. Pour the mixture over the ravioli and toss to coat. Serve.

Nutrition Info:

- Per Serving: Calories: 447;Fat: 32g;Protein: 18g;Carbs: 24g.

White Bean & Potato Soup

Servings:4 | Cooking Time:50 Minutes

Ingredients:

- 2 tbsp olive oil
- 2 shallots, chopped
- 1 potato, chopped
- 5 celery sticks, chopped
- 1 carrot, chopped
- ½ tsp dried oregano
- 1 bay leaf
- 30 oz canned white beans
- 2 tbsp tomato paste
- 4 cups chicken stock

Directions:

1. Warm the olive oil in a pot over medium heat and cook shallots, celery, carrot, bay leaf, and oregano for 5 minutes. Stir in beans, tomato paste, potato, and chicken stock and bring to a boil. Cook for 20 minutes. Remove the bay leaf. Serve.

Nutrition Info:

Zuppa Frutti Di Mare With Sausages

Servings:4 | Cooking Time:30 Minutes

Ingredients:
- 2 tbsp olive oil
- 2 tbsp butter
- ½ lb shrimp, deveined
- 3 Italian sausages, sliced
- 1 red onion, chopped
- 1 ½ cups clams
- 1 carrot, chopped
- 1 celery stalk, chopped
- 2 garlic cloves, minced
- 1 canned tomatoes
- 1 tsp dried basil
- 1 tsp dried dill
- 4 cups chicken broth
- 4 tbsp cornflour
- 2 tbsp lemon juice
- 2 tbsp fresh cilantro, chopped
- Salt and black pepper to taste

Directions:
1. Melt the butter in a pot over medium heat and brown the sausage; set aside. Heat the olive oil in the same pot and add in cornflour; cook for 4 minutes. Add in the onion, garlic, carrot, and celery and stir-fry them for 3 minutes.
2. Stir in tomatoes, basil, dill, and chicken broth. Bring to a boil. Lower the heat and simmer for 5 minutes. Mix in the reserved sausages, salt, black pepper, clams, and shrimp and simmer for 10 minutes. Discard any unopened clams. Share into bowls and sprinkle with lemon juice. Serve warm garnished with fresh cilantro.

Nutrition Info:
- Per Serving: Calories: 619;Fat: 43g;Protein: 32g;Carbs: 27g.

Italian Sausage & Cannellini Stew

Servings:6 | Cooking Time:45 Minutes

Ingredients:
- 1 cup Cannellini beans, soaked and rinsed
- 3 tbsp olive oil
- 1 lb Italian sausages, halved
- 1 celery stalk, chopped
- 1 carrot, chopped
- 1 onion, chopped
- 1 sprig of fresh rosemary
- 1 bay leaf
- 2 cups vegetable stock
- 3 cups fresh spinach
- Salt to taste

Directions:
1. Preheat your Instant Pot on Sauté mode and warm the olive oil. Add in sausage and sear for 5 minutes until browned; set aside on a plate. To the pot, add celery, onion, bay leaf, sage, carrot, and rosemary; cook for 3 minutes to soften slightly. Stir in vegetable stock and beans. Arrange seared sausage pieces on top of the beans. Seal the lid, press Bean/Chili, and cook on High for 10 minutes. Release Pressure naturally for 20 minutes. Get rid of bay leaf and rosemary sprig. Mix spinach into the mixture. Serve warm.

Nutrition Info:
- Per Serving: Calories: 401;Fat: 26g;Protein: 19g;Carbs: 23g.

Italian Colorful Salad

Servings:4 | Cooking Time:10 Minutes

Ingredients:
- ¼ cup olive oil
- 1 cup black olives, halved
- 10 cherry tomatoes, halved
- 1 red onion, chopped
- 2 tbsp parsley, chopped
- 2 tbsp balsamic vinegar
- 2 tsp dried Italian herbs
- Salt and black pepper to taste

Directions:
1. Mix black olives, cherry tomatoes, onion, parsley, vinegar, olive oil, Italian herbs, salt, and pepper in a bowl and toss to combine. Serve right away.

Nutrition Info:
- Per Serving: Calories: 200;Fat: 9g;Protein: 6g;Carbs: 13g.

Zoodles With Tomato-mushroom Sauce

Servings:4 | Cooking Time:25 Minutes

Ingredients:
- 1 lb oyster mushrooms, chopped
- 2 tbsp olive oil
- 1 cup chicken broth
- 1 tsp Mediterranean sauce
- 1 yellow onion, minced
- 1 cup pureed tomatoes
- 2 garlic cloves, minced
- 2 zucchinis, spiralized

Directions:
1. Warm the olive oil in a saucepan over medium heat and sauté the zoodles for 1-2 minutes; reserve. Sauté the onion and garlic in the same saucepan for 2-3 minutes. Add in the mushrooms and continue to cook for 2 to 3 minutes until they release liquid. Add in the remaining ingredients and cover the pan; let it simmer for 10 minutes longer until everything is cooked through. Top the zoodles with the prepared mushroom sauce and serve.

Nutrition Info:
- Per Serving: Calories: 95;Fat: 6.4g;Protein: 6g;Carbs: 5g.

Easy Moroccan Spice Mix

Servings:4 | Cooking Time:15 Minutes

Ingredients:
- 2 tsp ground cayenne pepper
- 16 cardamom pods
- 4 tsp coriander seeds
- 4 tsp cumin seeds
- 2 tsp anise seeds
- ½ tsp allspice berries
- ¼ tsp black peppercorns
- 4 tsp ground ginger
- 2 tsp ground nutmeg
- 2 tsp ground cinnamon

Directions:
1. Place the cardamom, coriander, cumin, anise, allspice, and peppercorns in a dry skillet over medium heat and toast for 1-2 minutes, occasionally shaking the skillet to prevent scorching. Let cool at room temperature. Put the toasted spices, ginger, nutmeg, cayenne pepper, and cinnamon in your spice grinder and process to a fine powder. Store the spices in a glass jar at room temperature for up to 7-9 months.

Nutrition Info:
- Per Serving: Calories: 144;Fat: 7.1g;Protein: 7.8g;Carbs: 4.2g.

Andalusian Lentil Soup

Servings:4 | Cooking Time:25 Minutes

Ingredients:
- 2 tbsp olive oil
- 3 cups vegetable broth
- 1 cup tomato sauce
- 1 onion, chopped
- 1 cup dry red lentils
- ½ cup prepared salsa verde
- 2 garlic cloves, minced
- 1 tbsp smoked paprika
- 2 tsp ground cumin
- ¼ tsp cayenne pepper
- Salt and black pepper to taste
- 2 tbsp crushed tortilla chips

Directions:
1. Warm the olive oil on Sauté in your Instant Pot. Stir in garlic and onion and cook for 5 minutes until golden brown. Add in tomato sauce, broth, salsa verde, cumin, cayenne pepper, lentils, paprika, salt, and pepper. Seal the lid and cook for 20 minutes on High Pressure. Release pressure naturally for 10 minutes. Top with crushed tortilla chips and serve.

Nutrition Info:
- Per Serving: Calories: 324;Fat: 10g;Protein: 14g;Carbs: 47g.

Tuscan-style Panzanella Salad

Servings:4 | Cooking Time:25 Minutes

Ingredients:
- 2 cups mixed cherry tomatoes, quartered
- 4 bread slices, crusts removed, cubed
- 4 tbsp extra-virgin olive oil
- 1 cucumber, sliced
- ½ red onion, thinly sliced
- ¼ cup chopped fresh basil
- ½ tsp dried oregano
- 1 tbsp capers
- 1 garlic clove, minced
- ¼ cup red wine vinegar
- 2 anchovy fillets, chopped
- Salt and black pepper to taste

Directions:
1. Preheat oven to 320° F. Pour the bread cubes into a baking dish and drizzle with 2 tbsp of olive oil. Bake for 6-8 minutes, shaking occasionally until browned and crisp. Let cool. Toss the cooled bread, cherry tomatoes, cucumber, red onion, basil, anchovies, and capers in a serving dish.
2. In another bowl, whisk the remaining olive oil, oregano, red wine vinegar, and garlic. Adjust the seasoning with salt and pepper. Drizzle the dressing over the salad and toss to coat.

Nutrition Info:
- Per Serving: Calories: 228;Fat: 21.6g;Protein: 2g;Carbs: 8.2g.

Simple Green Salad

Servings:4 | Cooking Time:10 Minutes

Ingredients:
- 2 tbsp olive oil
- 10 cherry tomatoes, halved
- 2 cucumbers, sliced
- 1 romaine lettuce head, torn
- 2 tbsp parsley, chopped
- 1 lemon, juiced

Directions:
1. Combine olive oil, cucumbers, lettuce, tomatoes, parsley, and lemon juice in a bowl. Serve chilled.

Nutrition Info:
- Per Serving: Calories: 150;Fat: 6g;Protein: 5g;Carbs: 2g.

Fennel Salad With Olives & Hazelnuts

Servings:4 | Cooking Time:5 Minutes

Ingredients:
- 2 tbsp olive oil
- 8 dates, pitted and sliced
- 2 fennel bulbs, sliced
- 2 tbsp chives, chopped
- ½ cup hazelnuts, chopped
- 2 tbsp lime juice
- Salt and black pepper to taste
- 40 green olives, chopped

Directions:
1. Place fennel, dates, chives, hazelnuts, lime juice, olives, olive oil, salt, and pepper in a bowl and toss to combine.

Nutrition Info:
- Per Serving: Calories: 210;Fat: 8g;Protein: 5g;Carbs: 15g.

Minty Lamb Egg Soup

Servings:4 | Cooking Time:50 Minutes

Ingredients:
- 2 tbsp olive oil
- ½ lb lamb meat, cubed
- 3 eggs, whisked
- 4 cups beef broth
- 5 spring onions, chopped
- 2 tbsp mint, chopped
- 2 lemons, juiced
- Salt and black pepper to taste
- 1 cup baby spinach

Directions:
1. Warm the olive oil in a pot over medium heat and cook lamb for 10 minutes, stirring occasionally. Add in spring onions and cook for another 3 minutes. Pour in beef broth, salt, and pepper and simmer for 30 minutes. Whisk eggs with lemon juice and some soup, pour into the pot, and spinach and cook for an additional 5 minutes. Sprinkle with mint and serve.

Nutrition Info:
- Per Serving: Calories: 290;Fat: 29g;Protein: 6g;Carbs: 3g.

Balsamic Brussels Sprouts And Delicata Squash

Servings:2 | Cooking Time: 30 Minutes

Ingredients:
- ½ pound Brussels sprouts, ends trimmed and outer leaves removed
- 1 medium delicata squash, halved lengthwise, seeded, and cut into 1-inch pieces
- 1 cup fresh cranberries
- 2 teaspoons olive oil
- Salt and freshly ground black pepper, to taste
- ½ cup balsamic vinegar
- 2 tablespoons roasted pumpkin seeds
- 2 tablespoons fresh pomegranate arils (seeds)

Directions:
1. Preheat oven to 400ºF. Line a sheet pan with parchment paper.
2. Combine the Brussels sprouts, squash, and cranberries in a large bowl. Drizzle with olive oil, and season lightly with salt and pepper. Toss well to coat and arrange in a single layer on the sheet pan.
3. Roast in the preheated oven for 30 minutes, turning vegetables halfway through, or until Brussels sprouts turn brown and crisp in spots.
4. Meanwhile, make the balsamic glaze by simmering the vinegar for 10 to 12 minutes, or until mixture has reduced to about ¼ cup and turns a syrupy consistency.
5. Remove the vegetables from the oven, drizzle with balsamic syrup, and sprinkle with pumpkin seeds and pomegranate arils before serving.

Nutrition Info:
- Per Serving: Calories: 203;Fat: 6.8g;Protein: 6.2g;Carbs: 22.0g.

Chapter 8 Fruits, Desserts And Snacks Recipes

Chapter 8 Fruits, Desserts And Snacks Recipes

Chili & Lemon Shrimp

Servings:6 | Cooking Time:10 Minutes

Ingredients:
- 24 large shrimp, peeled and deveined
- ½ cup olive oil
- 5 garlic cloves, minced
- 1 tsp red pepper flakes
- 1 lemon, juiced and zested
- 1 tsp dried dill
- 1 tsp dried thyme
- Salt and black pepper to taste

Directions:
1. Warm the olive oil in a large skillet over medium heat. Add the garlic and red pepper flakes and cook for 1 minute. Add the shrimp and cook an additional 3 minutes, stirring frequently. Remove from the pan, and sprinkle with lemon juice, lemon zest, thyme, dill, salt, and pepper. Serve.

Nutrition Info:
- Per Serving: Calories: 198;Fat: 6g;Protein: 9g;Carbs: 28g.

Crispy Sesame Cookies

Servings:14 | Cooking Time: 8 To 10 Minutes

Ingredients:
- 1 cup hulled sesame seeds
- 1 cup sugar
- 8 tablespoons almond butter
- 2 large eggs
- 1¼ cups flour

Directions:
1. Preheat the oven to 350ºF.
2. Toast the sesame seeds on a baking sheet for 3 minutes. Set aside and let cool.
3. Using a mixer, whisk together the sugar and butter. Add the eggs one at a time until well blended. Add the flour and toasted sesame seeds and mix until well blended.
4. Drop spoonfuls of cookie dough onto a baking sheet and form them into round balls, about 1-inch in diameter, similar to a walnut.
5. Put in the oven and bake for 5 to 7 minutes, or until golden brown.
6. Let the cookies cool for 5 minutes before serving.

Nutrition Info:
- Per Serving: Calories: 218;Fat: 12.0g;Protein: 4.0g;Carbs: 25.0g.

Glazed Pears With Hazelnuts

Servings:4 | Cooking Time: 20 Minutes

Ingredients:
- 4 pears, peeled, cored, and quartered lengthwise
- 1 cup apple juice
- 1 tablespoon grated fresh ginger
- ½ cup pure maple syrup
- ¼ cup chopped hazelnuts

Directions:
1. Put the pears in a pot, then pour in the apple juice. Bring to a boil over medium-high heat, then reduce the heat to medium-low. Stir constantly.
2. Cover and simmer for an additional 15 minutes or until the pears are tender.
3. Meanwhile, combine the ginger and maple syrup in a sauce-pan. Bring to a boil over medium-high heat. Stir frequently. Turn off the heat and transfer the syrup to a small bowl and let sit until ready to use.
4. Transfer the pears in a large serving bowl with a slotted spoon, then top the pears with syrup.
5. Spread the hazelnuts over the pears and serve immediately.

Nutrition Info:
- Per Serving: Calories: 287;Fat: 3.1g;Protein: 2.2g;Carbs: 66.9g.

Roasted Garlic & Spicy Lentil Dip

Servings:6 | Cooking Time:40 Minutes

Ingredients:
- 1 roasted red bell pepper, chopped
- 4 tbsp olive oil
- 1 cup split red lentils
- ½ red onion
- 1 garlic bulb, top removed
- ½ tsp cumin seeds
- 1 tsp coriander seeds
- ¼ cup walnuts
- 2 tbsp tomato paste
- ½ tsp Cayenne powder
- Salt and black pepper to taste

Directions:
1. Preheat oven to 370 °F. Drizzle the garlic with some olive oil and wrap it in a piece of aluminum foil. Roast for 35-40 minutes. Remove and allow to cool for a few minutes. Cover the lentils with salted water in a pot over medium heat and bring to a boil. Simmer for 15 minutes. Drain and set aside.
2. Squeeze out the garlic cloves and place them in a food processor. Add in the cooled lentils, cumin seeds, coriander seeds, roasted red bell pepper, onion, walnuts, tomato paste, Cayenne powder, remaining olive oil, salt, and black pepper. Pulse until smooth. Serve with crostiniif desire.

Nutrition Info:
- Per Serving: Calories: 234;Fat: 13g;Protein: 9g;Carbs: 21.7g.

Spiced Fries

Servings:6 | Cooking Time:35 Minutes

Ingredients:
- 2 lb red potatoes, cut into wedges
- ¼ cup olive oil
- 3 tbsp garlic, minced
- ½ tsp smoked paprika
- Salt and black pepper to taste
- ½ cup fresh cilantro, chopped
- ¼ tsp cayenne pepper

Directions:
1. Preheat oven to 450 °F. Place the potatoes into a bowl. Add the garlic, salt, pepper, and olive oil and toss everything together to coat evenly. Spread the potato mixture onto a baking sheet; bake for 25 minutes, flipping them halfway through the cooking time until golden and crisp. Sprinkle the potatoes with cilantro, cayenne pepper, and smoked paprika. Serve warm and enjoy!

Nutrition Info:
- Per Serving: Calories: 203;Fat: 11g;Protein: 3g;Carbs: 24g.

Tuna, Tomato & Burrata Salad

Servings:4 | Cooking Time:10 Minutes

Ingredients:
- 2 tbsp extra-virgin olive oil
- 2 tbsp canned tuna, flaked
- 4 heirloom tomato slices
- Salt and black pepper to taste
- 4 burrata cheese slices
- 8 fresh basil leaves, sliced
- 1 tbsp balsamic vinegar

Directions:
1. Place the tomatoes on a plate. Top with burrata slices and tuna. Sprinkle with basil. Drizzle with olive oil and balsamic vinegar and serve.

Nutrition Info:
- Per Serving: Calories: 153;Fat: 13g;Protein: 7g;Carbs: 2g.

Chocolate And Avocado Mousse

Servings:4 | Cooking Time: 5 Minutes

Ingredients:
- 8 ounces dark chocolate, chopped
- ¼ cup unsweetened coconut milk
- 2 tablespoons coconut oil
- 2 ripe avocados, deseeded
- ¼ cup raw honey
- Sea salt, to taste

Directions:
1. Put the chocolate in a saucepan. Pour in the coconut milk and add the coconut oil.
2. Cook for 3 minutes or until the chocolate and coconut oil melt. Stir constantly.
3. Put the avocado in a food processor, then drizzle with honey and melted chocolate. Pulse to combine until smooth.
4. Pour the mixture in a serving bowl, then sprinkle with salt. Refrigerate to chill for 30 minutes and serve.

Nutrition Info:
- Per Serving: Calories: 654;Fat: 46.8g;Protein: 7.2g;Carbs: 55.9g.

Fancy Baileys Ice Coffee

Servings:4 | Cooking Time:5 Min + Chilling Time

Ingredients:
- 1 cup espresso
- 2 cups milk
- 4 tbsp Baileys
- ½ tsp ground cinnamon
- ½ tsp vanilla extract
- Ice cubes

Directions:
1. Fill four glasses with ice cubes. Mix milk, cinnamon, and vanilla in a food processor until nice and frothy. Pour into the glasses. Combine the Baileys with the espresso and mix well. Pour ¼ of the espresso mixture over the milk and serve.

Nutrition Info:
- Per Serving: Calories: 100;Fat: 5g;Protein: 4g;Carbs: 8g.

Delicious Eggplant Balls

Servings:4 | Cooking Time:55 Minutes

Ingredients:
- 3 tbsp olive oil
- 2 cups eggplants, chopped
- 3 garlic cloves, minced
- 2 eggs, whisked
- Salt and black pepper to taste
- 2 tbsp parsley, chopped
- ½ cup Pecorino cheese, grated
- ¾ cups panko breadcrumbs

Directions:
1. Preheat the oven to 360 °F. Warm olive oil in a skillet over medium heat and sauté garlic and eggplants for 15 minutes. Mix cooked eggplants, eggs, salt, pepper, parsley, Pecorino cheese, and breadcrumbs in a bowl and form medium balls out of the mixture. Bake the balls for 30 minutes. Serve.

Nutrition Info:
- Per Serving: Calories: 230;Fat: 11g;Protein: 4g;Carbs: 6g.

Minty Yogurt & Banana Cups

Servings:2 | Cooking Time:5 Minutes

Ingredients:
- 2 bananas, sliced
- 2 cups Greek yogurt
- 1 tsp cinnamon
- 3 tbsp honey
- 2 tbsp mint leaves, chopped

Directions:
1. Divide the yogurt between 2 cups and top with banana slices, cinnamon, honey, and mint. Serve immediately.

Nutrition Info:
- Per Serving: Calories: 355;Fat: 4.2g;Protein: 22g;Carbs: 61g.

Wrapped Pears In Prosciutto

Servings:4 | Cooking Time:5 Minutes

Ingredients:
- 2 pears, cored and cut into wedges
- 4 oz prosciutto slices, halved
- lengthwise
- 1 tbsp chives, chopped
- 1 tsp red pepper flakes

Directions:
1. Wrap the pear wedges with prosciutto slices. Transfer them to a platter. Garnish with chives and pepper flakes. Serve.

Nutrition Info:
- Per Serving: Calories: 35;Fat: 2g;Protein: 12g;Carbs: 5g.

Fig & Mascarpone Toasts With Pistachios

Servings:6 | Cooking Time:10 Minutes

Ingredients:
- 4 tbsp butter, melted
- 1 French baguette, sliced
- 1 cup Mascarpone cheese
- 1 jar fig jam
- ½ cup crushed pistachios

Directions:
1. Preheat oven to 350 °F. Arrange the sliced bread on a greased baking sheet and brush each slice with melted butter.
2. Toast the bread for 5-7 minutes until golden brown. Let the bread cool slightly. Spread about a teaspoon of the mascarpone cheese on each piece of bread. Top with fig jam and pistachios.

Nutrition Info:
- Per Serving: Calories: 445;Fat: 24g;Protein: 3g;Carbs: 48g.

Coconut Blueberries With Brown Rice

Servings:4 | Cooking Time: 10 Minutes

Ingredients:
- 1 cup fresh blueberries
- 2 cups unsweetened coconut milk
- 1 teaspoon ground ginger
- ¼ cup maple syrup
- Sea salt, to taste
- 2 cups cooked brown rice

Directions:
1. Put all the ingredients, except for the brown rice, in a pot. Stir to combine well.
2. Cook over medium-high heat for 7 minutes or until the blueberries are tender.

3. Pour in the brown rice and cook for 3 more minute or until the rice is soft. Stir constantly.
4. Serve immediately.
Nutrition Info:
• Per Serving: Calories: 470;Fat: 24.8g;Protein: 6.2g;Carbs: 60.1g.

Strawberry Parfait
Servings:2 | Cooking Time:10 Minutes
Ingredients:
• ¾ cup Greek yogurt
• 1 tbsp cocoa powder
• ¼ cup strawberries, chopped
• 5 drops vanilla stevia
Directions:
1. Combine cocoa powder, strawberries, yogurt, and stevia in a bowl. Serve immediately.
Nutrition Info:
• Per Serving: Calories: 210;Fat: 9g;Protein: 5g;Carbs: 8g.

Fruit And Nut Chocolate Bark
Servings:2 | Cooking Time: 2 Minutes
Ingredients:
• 2 tablespoons chopped nuts
• 3 ounces dark chocolate chips
• ¼ cup chopped dried fruit
(blueberries, apricots, figs, prunes, or any combination of those)
Directions:
1. Line a sheet pan with parchment paper and set aside.
2. Add the nuts to a skillet over medium-high heat and toast for 60 seconds, or just fragrant. Set aside to cool.
3. Put the chocolate chips in a microwave-safe glass bowl and microwave on High for 1 minute.
4. Stir the chocolate and allow any unmelted chips to warm and melt. If desired, heat for an additional 20 to 30 seconds.
5. Transfer the chocolate to the prepared sheet pan. Scatter the dried fruit and toasted nuts over the chocolate evenly and gently pat in so they stick.
6. Place the sheet pan in the refrigerator for at least 1 hour to let the chocolate harden.
7. When ready, break into pieces and serve.
Nutrition Info:
• Per Serving: Calories: 285;Fat: 16.1g;Protein: 4.0g;Carbs: 38.7g.

Roasted Veggies With Marsala Sauce
Servings:4 | Cooking Time:30 Minutes
Ingredients:
• Vegetables:
• ¼ cup olive oil
• 1 lb green beans, trimmed
• ½ lb carrots, trimmed
• 1 fennel bulb, sliced
• ¼ cup dry white wine
• ¼ tsp oregano
• ½ tsp thyme
• ½ tsp rosemary
• ¼ tsp coriander seeds
• ¼ tsp celery seeds
• ¼ tsp dried dill weed
• 1 head garlic, halved
• 1 red onion, sliced
• Salt and black pepper to taste
• Sauce:
• 2 tbsp olive oil
• 2 tbsp Marsala wine
• 2 tbsp plain yogurt
• 1 tbsp yellow mustard
• 1 tsp honey
• 1 tbsp lemon juice
• 1 yolk from 1 hard-boiled egg
• Salt to taste
• 1 tbsp paprika
Directions:

1. Preheat the oven to 380 °F. In a bowl, combine the olive oil, white wine, oregano, thyme, rosemary, coriander seeds, celery seeds, dill weed, salt, and black pepper and mix well. Add in carrots, green beans, fennel, garlic, and onion and toss to coat. Spread the mixture on a baking dish and roast in the oven for 15-20 minutes until tender.
2. In a food processor, place the honey, yogurt, mustard, lemon juice, Marsala wine, yolk, olive oil, salt, and paprika, and blitz until smooth and uniform. Transfer to a bowl and place in the fridge until ready to use. When the veggies are ready, remove and serve with the prepared sauce on the side.
Nutrition Info:
• Per Serving: Calories: 280;Fat: 20.2g;Protein: 4g;Carbs: 21g.

Lamb Ragu Tagliatelle
Servings:4 | Cooking Time:25 Minutes
Ingredients:
• 2 tbsp olive oil
• 16 oz tagliatelle
• 1 tsp paprika
• 1 tsp cumin
• Salt and black pepper to taste
• 1 lb ground lamb
• 1 cup onions, chopped
• ¼ cup parsley, chopped
• 2 garlic cloves, minced
Directions:
1. Boil the tagliatelle in a pot over medium heat for 9-11 minutes or until "al dente". Drain and set aside.
2. Warm the olive oil in a skillet over medium heat and sauté lamb, onions, and garlic until the meat is browned, about 10-15 minutes. Stir in cumin, paprika, salt, and pepper for 1-2 minutes. Spoon tagliatelle on a platter and scatter lamb over. Top with parsley and serve.
Nutrition Info:
• Per Serving: Calories: 140;Fat: 10g;Protein: 6g;Carbs: 7g.

Chocolate, Almond, And Cherry Clusters
Servings:10 | Cooking Time: 3 Minutes
Ingredients:
• 1 cup dark chocolate, chopped
• 1 tablespoon coconut oil
• ½ cup dried cherries
• 1 cup roasted salted almonds
Directions:
1. Line a baking sheet with parchment paper.
2. Melt the chocolate and coconut oil in a saucepan for 3 minutes. Stir constantly.
3. Turn off the heat and mix in the cherries and almonds.
4. Drop the mixture on the baking sheet with a spoon. Place the sheet in the refrigerator and chill for at least 1 hour or until firm.
5. Serve chilled.
Nutrition Info:
• Per Serving: Calories: 197;Fat: 13.2g;Protein: 4.1g;Carbs: 17.8g.

No-gluten Caprese Pizza
Servings:4 | Cooking Time:40 Minutes
Ingredients:
• 2 tbsp olive oil
• 2 ¼ cups chickpea flour
• Salt and black pepper to taste
• 1 tsp onion powder
• 1 tomato, sliced
• ¼ tsp dried oregano
• 2 oz mozzarella cheese, sliced
• ¼ cup tomato sauce
• 2 tbsp fresh basil, chopped

Directions:
1. Preheat oven to 360 °F. Combine the chickpea flour, salt, pepper, 1 ¼ cups of water, olive oil, and onion powder in a bowl. Mix well to form a soft dough, then knead a bit until elastic. Let sit covered in a greased bowl to rise, for 25 minutes in a warm place. Remove the dough to a floured surface and roll out it with a rolling pin into a thin circle.
2. Transfer to a floured baking tray and bake in the oven for 10 minutes. Evenly spread the tomato sauce over the pizza base. Sprinkle with oregano and arrange the mozzarella cheese and tomato slices on top. Bake for 10 minutes. Top with basil and serve sliced.

Nutrition Info:
- Per Serving: Calories: 420;Fat: 26g;Protein: 14g;Carbs: 35g.

Simple Greek Pizza

Servings:4 | Cooking Time:25 Minutes

Ingredients:
- 2 cups halloumi cheese, shredded
- 1 pizza crust
- 1 cup marinara sauce
- ½ tsp dried Greek oregano
- 1 cup feta cheese, crumbled
- ½ tsp garlic powder
- 6 Kalamata olives, sliced

Directions:
1. Preheat oven to 400 °F. Spread the pizza crust evenly with marinara sauce. Sprinkle with oregano and garlic powder. Scatter the feta cheese and olives over the sauce and top with halloumi cheese. Bake for 10–16 minutes or until the crust is golden. Serve sliced and enjoy!

Nutrition Info:
- Per Serving: Calories: 655;Fat: 45g;Protein: 25g;Carbs: 38g.

Spanish-style Pizza With Jamón Serrano

Servings:4 | Cooking Time:90 Minutes

Ingredients:
- For the crust
- 2 tbsp olive oil
- 2 cups flour
- 1 cup lukewarm water
- 1 pinch of sugar
- 1 tsp active dry yeast
- ¾ tsp salt
- For the topping
- 1/3 cup Spanish olives with pimento
- ½ cup tomato sauce
- ½ cup sliced mozzarella
- 4 oz jamon serrano, sliced
- 7 fresh basil leaves

Directions:
1. Sift the flour and salt in a bowl and stir in yeast. Mix lukewarm water, olive oil, and sugar in another bowl. Add the wet mixture to the dry mixture and whisk until you obtain a soft dough. Place the dough on a lightly floured work surface and knead it thoroughly for 4-5 minutes until elastic. Transfer the dough to a greased bowl. Cover with cling film and leave to rise for 50-60 minutes in a warm place until doubled in size. Roll out the dough to a thickness of around 12 inches.
2. Preheat the oven to 400 °F. Line a pizza pan with parchment paper. Spread the tomato sauce on the crust. Arrange the mozzarella slices on the sauce and then the Jamon serrano. Bake for 15 minutes or until the cheese melts. Remove from the oven and top with olives and basil. Slice and serve warm.

Nutrition Info:
- Per Serving: Calories: 160;Fat: 6g;Protein: 22g;Carbs: 0.5g.

Basic Pudding With Kiwi

Servings:4 | Cooking Time:20 Min + Chilling Time

Ingredients:
- 2 kiwi, peeled and sliced
- 1 egg
- 2 ¼ cups milk
- ½ cup honey
- 1 tsp vanilla extract
- 3 tbsp cornstarch

Directions:
1. In a bowl, beat the egg with honey. Stir in 2 cups of milk and vanilla. Pour into a pot over medium heat and bring to a boil. Combine cornstarch and remaining milk in a bowl. Pour slowly into the pot and boil for 1 minute until thickened, stirring often. Divide between 4 cups and transfer to the fridge. Top with kiwi and serve.

Nutrition Info:
- Per Serving: Calories: 262;Fat: 4.1g;Protein: 6.5g;Carbs: 52g.

Cantaloupe & Watermelon Balls

Servings:4 | Cooking Time:5 Min + Chilling Time

Ingredients:
- 2 cups watermelon balls
- 2 cups cantaloupe balls
- ½ cup orange juice
- ¼ cup lemon juice
- 1 tbsp orange zest

Directions:
1. Place the watermelon and cantaloupe in a bowl. In another bowl, mix the lemon juice, orange juice and zest. Pour over the fruit. Transfer to the fridge covered for 5 hours. Serve.

Nutrition Info:
- Per Serving: Calories: 71;Fat: 0g;Protein: 1.5g;Carbs: 18g.

Strawberries With Balsamic Vinegar

Servings:2 | Cooking Time: 0 Minutes

Ingredients:
- 2 cups strawberries, hulled and sliced
- 2 tablespoons sugar
- 2 tablespoons balsamic vinegar

Directions:
1. Place the sliced strawberries in a bowl, sprinkle with the sugar, and drizzle lightly with the balsamic vinegar.
2. Toss to combine well and allow to sit for about 10 minutes before serving.

Nutrition Info:
- Per Serving: Calories: 92;Fat: 0.4g;Protein: 1.0g;Carbs: 21.7g.

Cherry Walnut Brownies

Servings:9 | Cooking Time: 20 Minutes

Ingredients:
- 2 large eggs
- ½ cup 2% plain Greek yogurt
- ½ cup sugar
- 1/3 cup honey
- ¼ cup extra-virgin olive oil
- 1 teaspoon vanilla extract
- ½ cup whole-wheat pastry flour
- 1/3 cup unsweetened dark chocolate cocoa powder
- ¼ teaspoon baking powder
- ¼ teaspoon salt
- 1/3 cup chopped walnuts
- 9 fresh cherries, stemmed and pitted
- Cooking spray

Directions:
1. Preheat the oven to 375ºF and set the rack in the middle of the oven. Spritz a square baking pan with cooking spray.
2. In a large bowl, whisk together the eggs, yogurt, sugar, honey,

oil and vanilla.

3. In a medium bowl, stir together the flour, cocoa powder, baking powder and salt. Add the flour mixture to the egg mixture and whisk until all the dry ingredients are incorporated. Fold in the walnuts.

4. Pour the batter into the prepared pan. Push the cherries into the batter, three to a row in three rows, so one will be at the center of each brownie once you cut them into squares.

5. Bake the brownies for 20 minutes, or until just set. Remove from the oven and place on a rack to cool for 5 minutes. Cut into nine squares and serve.

Nutrition Info:
- Per Serving: Calories: 154;Fat: 6.0g;Protein: 3.0g;Carbs: 24.0g.

Simple Apple Compote

Servings:4 | Cooking Time: 10 Minutes

Ingredients:
- 6 apples, peeled, cored, and chopped
- ¼ cup raw honey
- 1 teaspoon ground cinnamon
- ¼ cup apple juice
- Sea salt, to taste

Directions:
1. Put all the ingredients in a stockpot. Stir to mix well, then cook over medium-high heat for 10 minutes or until the apples are glazed by honey and lightly saucy. Stir constantly.
2. Serve immediately.

Nutrition Info:
- Per Serving: Calories: 246;Fat: 0.9g;Protein: 1.2g;Carbs: 66.3g.

Eggplant & Pepper Spread On Toasts

Servings:4 | Cooking Time:10 Minutes

Ingredients:
- 1 red bell pepper, roasted and chopped
- 1 lb eggplants, baked, peeled and chopped
- ¾ cup olive oil
- 1 lemon, zested
- 1 red chili pepper, chopped
- 1 ½ tsp capers
- 1 garlic clove, minced
- Salt and black pepper to taste
- 1 baguette, sliced and toasted

Directions:
1. In a food processor, place the eggplants, lemon zest, red chili pepper, bell pepper, garlic, salt, and pepper. Blend while gradually adding the olive oil until smooth. Spread each baguette slice with the spread and top with capers to serve.

Nutrition Info:
- Per Serving: Calories: 364;Fat: 38g;Protein: 1.5g;Carbs: 9.3g.

Chocolate-almond Cups

Servings:6 | Cooking Time:10 Min + Freezing Time

Ingredients:
- ½ cup butter
- ½ cup olive oil
- ¼ cup ground flaxseed
- 2 tbsp cocoa powder
- 1 tsp vanilla extract
- 1 tsp ground cinnamon
- 2 tsp maple syrup

Directions:
1. In a bowl, mix the butter, olive oil, flaxseed, cocoa powder, vanilla, cinnamon, and maple syrup and stir well with a spatula. Pour into 6 mini muffin liners and freeze until solid, at least 2 hours. Serve and enjoy!

Nutrition Info:
- Per Serving: Calories: 240;Fat: 24g;Protein: 3g;Carbs: 5g.

Country Pizza

Servings:4 | Cooking Time:45 Minutes

Ingredients:
- For the crust
- 2 tbsp olive oil
- 2 cups flour
- 1 cup lukewarm water
- 1 pinch of sugar
- 1 tsp active dry yeast
- ¾ tsp salt
- For the ranch sauce
- 1 tbsp butter
- 2 garlic cloves, minced
- 1 tbsp cream cheese
- ¼ cup half and half
- 1 tbsp Ranch seasoning mix
- For the topping
- 3 bacon slices, chopped
- 2 chicken breasts
- Salt and black pepper to taste
- 1 cup grated mozzarella
- 6 fresh basil leaves

Directions:
1. Sift the flour and salt in a bowl and stir in yeast. Mix lukewarm water, olive oil, and sugar in another bowl. Add the wet mixture to the dry mixture and whisk until you obtain a soft dough. Place the dough on a lightly floured work surface and knead it thoroughly for 4-5 minutes until elastic. Transfer the dough to a greased bowl. Cover with cling film and leave to rise for 50-60 minutes in a warm place until doubled in size. Roll out the dough to a thickness of around 12 inches.

2. Preheat the oven to 400 °F. Line a pizza pan with parchment paper. In a bowl, mix the sauce's ingredients butter, garlic, cream cheese, half and half, and ranch mix. Set aside. Heat a grill pan over medium heat and cook the bacon until crispy and brown, 5 minutes. Transfer to a plate and set aside.

3. Season the chicken with salt, pepper and grill in the pan on both sides until golden brown, 10 minutes. Remove to a plate, allow cooling and cut into thin slices. Spread the ranch sauce on the pizza crust, followed by the chicken and bacon, and then, mozzarella cheese and basil. Bake for 5 minutes or until the cheese melts. Slice and serve warm.

Nutrition Info:
- Per Serving: Calories: 528;Fat: 28g;Protein: 61g;Carbs: 5g.

Amaretto Squares

Servings:6 | Cooking Time:1 Hour 10 Minutes

Ingredients:
- 1 tsp olive oil
- Zest from 1 lemon
- 3/4 cup slivered almonds
- 2 cups flour
- 3/4 cup sugar
- 1 tsp baking powder
- ¼ tsp salt
- 3 eggs
- 2 tbsp Amaretto liqueur

Directions:
1. Preheat the oven to 280 °F. Combine flour, baking powder, sugar, lemon zest, salt, and almonds in a bowl and mix well. In another bowl, beat the eggs and amaretto liqueur. Pour into the flour mixture and mix to combine.

2. Grease a baking sheet with olive oil and spread in the dough. Bake for 40-45 minutes. Remove from the oven, let cool for a few minutes, and cut diagonally into slices about ½-inch thick. Place the pieces back on the sheet, cut sides up, and bake for 20 more minutes. Let cool before serving.

Nutrition Info:
- Per Serving: Calories: 78;Fat: 1g;Protein: 2g;Carbs: 14g.

Chickpea & Spinach Salad With Almonds

Servings:4 | Cooking Time:5 Minutes

Ingredients:
- 2 tbsp olive oil
- 3 spring onions, chopped
- 1 cup baby spinach
- 15 oz canned chickpeas
- Salt and black pepper to taste
- 2 tbsp lemon juice
- 1 tbsp cilantro, chopped
- 2 tbsp almonds flakes, toasted

Directions:
1. Toss chickpeas, spring onions, spinach, salt, pepper, olive oil, lemon juice, and cilantro in a salad bowl. Top with almond flakes. Serve and enjoy!

Nutrition Info:
- Per Serving: Calories: 230;Fat: 6g;Protein: 16g;Carbs: 10g.

Sicilian Almond Granita

Servings:4 | Cooking Time:5 Min + Freezing Time

Ingredients:
- 4 small oranges, chopped
- ½ tsp almond extract
- 2 tbsp lemon juice
- 1 cup orange juice
- ¼ cup honey
- Fresh mint leaves for garnish

Directions:
1. In a food processor, mix oranges, orange juice, honey, almond extract, and lemon juice. Pulse until smooth. Pour in a dip dish and freeze for 1 hour. Mix with a fork and freeze for 30 minutes more. Repeat a couple of times. Pour into dessert glasses and garnish with basil leaves. Serve.

Nutrition Info:
- Per Serving: Calories: 145;Fat: 0g;Protein: 1.5g;Carbs: 36g.

Broccoli-pepper Pizza

Servings:4 | Cooking Time:25 Minutes

Ingredients:
- For the crust
- 1 tbsp olive oil
- ½ cup almond flour
- ¼ tsp salt
- 2 tbsp ground psyllium husk
- 1 cup lukewarm water
- For the topping
- 1 tbsp olive oil
- 1 cup sliced fresh mushrooms
- 1 white onion, thinly sliced
- 3 cups broccoli florets
- 4 garlic cloves, minced
- ½ cup pizza sauce
- 4 tomatoes, sliced
- 1 ½ cup grated mozzarella
- ½ cup grated Parmesan cheese

Directions:
1. Preheat the oven to 400 °F. Line a baking sheet with parchment paper. In a bowl, mix the almond flour, salt, psyllium powder, olive oil, and lukewarm water until dough forms. Spread the mixture on the pizza pan and bake in the oven until crusty, 10 minutes. Remove and allow cooling.
2. Heat olive oil in a skillet and sauté the mushrooms, onion, garlic, and broccoli until softened, 5 minutes. Spread the pizza sauce on the crust and top with the broccoli mixture, tomato, mozzarella and Parmesan. Bake for 5 minutes.

Nutrition Info:
- Per Serving: Calories: 180;Fat: 9g;Protein: 17g;Carbs: 3.6g.

Cardamom Apple Slices

Servings:2 | Cooking Time:30 Minutes

Ingredients:
- 1 ½ tsp cardamom
- ½ tsp salt
- 4 peeled, cored apples, sliced
- 2 tbsp honey
- 2 tbsp milk

Directions:
1. Preheat oven to 390 °F. In a bowl, combine apple slices, salt, and ½ tsp of cardamom. Arrange them on a greased baking dish and cook for 20 minutes. Remove to a serving plate.
2. In the meantime, place milk, honey, and remaining cardamom in a pot over medium heat. Cook until simmer. Pour the sauce over the apples and serve immediately.

Nutrition Info:
- Per Serving: Calories: 287;Fat: 3g;Protein: 2g;Carbs: 69g.

Arugula & Olive Pizza With Balsamic Glaze

Servings:4 | Cooking Time:90 Minutes

Ingredients:
- 2 tbsp olive oil
- 2 cups flour
- 1 cup lukewarm water
- 1 pinch of sugar
- 1 tsp active dry yeast
- 2 tbsp honey
- ½ cup balsamic vinegar
- 4 cups arugula
- Salt to taste
- 1 cup mozzarella, grated
- ¾ tsp dried oregano
- 6 black olives, drained

Directions:
1. Sift the flour and ¾ tsp salt in a bowl and stir in yeast. Mix lukewarm water, olive oil, and sugar in another bowl. Add the wet mixture to the dry mixture and whisk until you obtain a soft dough. Place the dough on a lightly floured work surface and knead it thoroughly for 4-5 minutes until elastic. Transfer the dough to a greased bowl. Cover with cling film and leave to rise for 50-60 minutes in a warm place. Roll out the dough to a thickness of around 12 inches.
2. Place the balsamic vinegar and honey in a saucepan over medium heat and simmer for 5 minutes until syrupy. Preheat oven to 390 °F. Transfer the pizza crust to a baking sheet and sprinkle with oregano and mozzarella cheese; bake for 10-15 minutes. Remove the pizza from the oven and top with arugula. Sprinkle with balsamic glaze and olives and serve.

Nutrition Info:
- Per Serving: Calories: 350;Fat: 15.4g;Protein: 6g;Carbs: 47g.

Honey & Spice Roasted Almonds

Servings:4 | Cooking Time:15 Minutes

Ingredients:
- 2 tbsp olive oil
- 3 cups almonds
- 1 tbsp curry powder
- ¼ cup honey
- 1 tsp salt

Directions:
1. Preheat oven to 260 °F. Coat almonds with olive oil, curry powder, and salt in a bowl; mix well. Arrange on a lined with aluminum foil sheet and bake for 15 minutes. Remove from the oven and let cool for 10 minutes. Drizzle with honey and let cool at room temperature. Enjoy!

Nutrition Info:
- Per Serving: Calories: 134;Fat: 8g;Protein: 1g;Carbs: 18g.

Hot Italian Sausage Pizza Wraps

Servings:2 | Cooking Time:20 Minutes

Ingredients:

- 1 tbsp basil, chopped
- 1 tsp olive oil
- 6 oz spicy Italian sausage
- 1 shallot, chopped
- 1 tsp Italian seasoning
- 4 oz marinara sauce
- 2 flour tortillas
- ½ cup mozzarella, shredded
- 1/3 cup Parmesan, grated
- 1 tsp red pepper flakes

Directions:

1. Warm the olive oil in a skillet over medium heat. Add and cook the sausage for 5-6 minutes, stirring and breaking up larger pieces, until cooked through. Remove to a bowl. Sauté the shallot for 3 minutes until soft, stirring frequently. Stir in Italian seasoning, marinara sauce, and reserved sausage. Bring to a simmer and cook for about 2 minutes. Divide the mixture between the tortillas, top with the cheeses, add red pepper flakes and basil, and fold over. Serve immediately.

Nutrition Info:

- Per Serving: Calories: 744;Fat: 46g;Protein: 41g;Carbs: 40g.

Traditional Pizza Margherita

Servings:4 | Cooking Time:30 Minutes

Ingredients:

- 1 can diced San Marzano tomatoes with juices
- 16 oz pizza dough
- Salt to taste
- 1 tsp oregano
- 2 tbsp extra-virgin olive oil
- 10 mozzarella cheese slices
- 12 fresh basil leaves
- 6 whole black olives

Directions:

1. Preheat oven to 450 °F. Place the dough on a floured surface and roll out it thinly. Place it on a lightly floured pizza pan and drizzle with some olive oil. Puree the tomatoes, a splash of olive oil and a sprinkle of salt until smooth. Spread the tomato sauce over the base, leaving a 1-inch border and sprinkle with oregano. Arrange the mozzarella cheese slices on top and bake for 8-10 minutes until the crust is golden. Top with basil and olives and serve.

Nutrition Info:

- Per Serving: Calories: 542;Fat: 21g;Protein: 26g;Carbs: 63g.

Italian Submarine-style Sandwiches

Servings:4 | Cooking Time:35 Minutes

Ingredients:

- ½ lb sliced deli ham
- ½ lb sliced deli turkey
- 1 Italian loaf bread, unsliced
- 1/3 cup honey mustard
- ½ lb sliced mozzarella cheese

Directions:

1. Preheat oven to 400 °F. Cut the bread horizontally in half. Spread the honey mustard over the bottom half. Layer ham, turkey, and mozzarella cheese over, then top with the remaining bread half. Wrap the sandwich in foil and bake for 20 minutes or until the bread is toasted. Open the foil and bake for 5 minutes or until the top is crisp. Serve sliced.

Nutrition Info:

- Per Serving: Calories: 704;Fat: 17g;Protein: 50g;Carbs: 85g.

Charred Asparagus

Servings:4 | Cooking Time:25 Minutes

Ingredients:

- 2 tbsp olive oil
- 1 lb asparagus, trimmed
- 4 tbsp Grana Padano, grated
- ½ tsp garlic powder
- Salt to taste
- 2 tbsp parsley, chopped

Directions:

1. Preheat the grill to high. Season the asparagus with salt and garlic powder and coat with olive oil. Grill the asparagus for 10 minutes, turning often until lightly charred and tender. Sprinkle with cheese and parsley and serve.

Nutrition Info:

- Per Serving: Calories: 105;Fat: 8g;Protein: 4.3g;Carbs: 4.7g.

Speedy Cucumber Canapes

Servings:4 | Cooking Time:5 Minutes

Ingredients:

- 2 tbsp olive oil
- 2 cucumbers, sliced into rounds
- 12 cherry tomatoes, halved
- Salt and black pepper to taste
- 1 red chili pepper, dried
- 8 oz cream cheese, softened
- 1 tbsp balsamic vinegar
- 1 tsp chives, chopped

Directions:

1. In a bowl, mix cream cheese, balsamic vinegar, olive oil, chili pepper, and chives. Season with salt and pepper. Spread the mixture over the cucumber rounds and top with the cherry tomato halves. Serve.

Nutrition Info:

- Per Serving: Calories: 130;Fat: 3g;Protein: 3g;Carbs: 7g.

Salt & Pepper Toasted Walnuts

Servings:6 | Cooking Time:20 Minutes

Ingredients:

- 2 tbsp olive oil
- 4 cups walnut halves
- Sea salt flakes to taste
- Black pepper to taste

Directions:

1. Preheat the oven to 250 °F. In a bowl, toss the walnuts with olive oil, salt, and pepper to coat. Spread out the walnuts on a parchment-lined baking sheet. Toast for 10-15 minutes. Remove from the oven and allow to cool completely. Serve.

Nutrition Info:

- Per Serving: Calories: 193;Fat: 2g;Protein: 8g;Carbs: 23g.

Banana, Cranberry, And Oat Bars

Servings:16 | Cooking Time: 40 Minutes

Ingredients:

- 2 tablespoon extra-virgin olive oil
- 2 medium ripe bananas, mashed
- ½ cup almond butter
- ½ cup maple syrup
- 1/3 cup dried cranberries
- 1½ cups old-fashioned rolled
- oats
- ¼ cup oat flour
- ¼ cup ground flaxseed
- ¼ teaspoon ground cloves
- ½ cup shredded coconut
- ½ teaspoon ground cinnamon
- 1 teaspoon vanilla extract

Directions:

1. Preheat the oven to 400°F. Line a 8-inch square pan with parchment paper, then grease with olive oil.

2. Combine the mashed bananas, almond butter, and maple syrup

in a bowl. Stir to mix well.

3. Mix in the remaining ingredients and stir to mix well until thick and sticky.

4. Spread the mixture evenly on the square pan with a spatula, then bake in the preheated oven for 40 minutes or until a toothpick inserted in the center comes out clean.

5. Remove them from the oven and slice into 16 bars to serve.

Nutrition Info:
- Per Serving: Calories: 145;Fat: 7.2g;Protein: 3.1g;Carbs: 18.9g.

Spicy Hummus

Servings:6 | Cooking Time:10 Minutes

Ingredients:
- 2 tbsp olive oil
- ½ tsp hot paprika
- 1 tsp hot pepper sauce
- 1 tsp ground cumin
- 3 garlic cloves, minced
- 1 can chickpeas
- 2 tbsp tahini
- 2 tbsp chopped fresh parsley
- 1 lemon, juiced and zested
- Salt to taste

Directions:
1. In a food processor, blend chickpeas, tahini, oil, garlic, lemon juice, lemon zest, salt, cumin, and hot pepper sauce for a minute until smooth. Decorate with parsley and paprika.

Nutrition Info:
- Per Serving: Calories: 236;Fat: 8.6g;Protein: 10g;Carbs: 31g.

Walnut And Date Balls

Servings:6 | Cooking Time: 8 To 10 Minutes

Ingredients:
- 1 cup walnuts
- 1 cup unsweetened shredded coconut
- 14 medjool dates, pitted
- 8 tablespoons almond butter

Directions:
1. Preheat the oven to 350°F.
2. Put the walnuts on a baking sheet and toast in the oven for 5 minutes.
3. Put the shredded coconut on a clean baking sheet. Toast for about 3 to 5 minutes, or until it turns golden brown. Once done, remove it from the oven and put it in a shallow bowl.
4. In a food processor, process the toasted walnuts until they have a medium chop. Transfer the chopped walnuts into a medium bowl.
5. Add the dates and butter to the food processor and blend until the dates become a thick paste. Pour the chopped walnuts into the food processor with the dates and pulse just until the mixture is combined, about 5 to 7 pulses.
6. Remove the mixture from the food processor and scrape it into a large bowl.
7. To make the balls, spoon 1 to 2 tablespoons of the date mixture into the palm of your hand and roll around between your hands until you form a ball. Put the ball on a clean, lined baking sheet. Repeat until all the mixture is formed into balls.
8. Roll each ball in the toasted coconut until the outside of the ball is coated. Put the ball back on the baking sheet and repeat.
9. Put all the balls into the refrigerator for 20 minutes before serving. Store any leftovers in the refrigerator in an airtight container.

Nutrition Info:
- Per Serving: Calories: 489;Fat: 35.0g;Protein: 5.0g;Carbs: 48.0g.

Chocolate-avocado Cream

Servings:4 | Cooking Time:10 Min + Chilling Time

Ingredients:
- 2 avocados, mashed
- ¼ cup cocoa powder
- ¼ cup heavy whipping cream
- 2 tsp vanilla extract
- 2 tbsp sugar
- ½ tsp ground cinnamon
- ¼ tsp salt

Directions:
1. Blend the avocado, cocoa powder, heavy whipping cream, vanilla, sugar, cinnamon, and salt into a large bowl until smooth and creamy. Cover and refrigerate for at least 1 hour.

Nutrition Info:
- Per Serving: Calories: 230;Fat: 22g;Protein: 3g;Carbs: 10g.

Mint-watermelon Gelato

Servings:4 | Cooking Time:10 Min + Freezing Time

Ingredients:
- ¼ cup honey
- 4 cups watermelon cubes
- ¼ cup lemon juice
- 12 mint leaves to serve

Directions:
1. In a food processor, blend the watermelon, honey, and lemon juice to form a purée with chunks. Transfer to a freezer-proof container and place in the freezer for 1 hour.
2. Remove the container from and scrape with a fork. Return the to the freezer and repeat the process every half hour until the sorbet is completely frozen, for around 4 hours. Share into bowls, garnish with mint leaves, and serve.

Nutrition Info:
- Per Serving: Calories: 149;Fat: 0.4g;Protein: 1.8g;Carbs: 38g.

Pecan & Raspberry & Frozen Yogurt Cups

Servings:4 | Cooking Time:10 Minutes

Ingredients:
- 2 cups fresh raspberries
- 4 cups vanilla frozen yogurt
- 1 lime, zested
- ¼ cup chopped praline pecans

Directions:
1. Divide the frozen yogurt into 4 dessert glasses. Top with raspberries, lime zest, and pecans. Serve immediately.

Nutrition Info:
- Per Serving: Calories: 142;Fat: 3.4g;Protein: 3.7g;Carbs: 26g.

Baby Artichoke Antipasto

Servings:4 | Cooking Time:5 Minutes

Ingredients:
- 1 jar roasted red peppers
- 8 canned artichoke hearts
- 1 can garbanzo beans
- 1 cup whole Kalamata olives
- ¼ cup balsamic vinegar
- Salt to taste
- 1 lemon, zested

Directions:
1. Slice the peppers and put them into a large bowl. Cut the artichoke hearts into quarters, and add them to the bowl. Add the garbanzo beans, olives, balsamic vinegar, lemon zest, and salt. Toss all the ingredients together. Serve chilled.

Nutrition Info:
- Per Serving: Calories: 281;Fat: 15g;Protein: 7g;Carbs: 30g.

Honeyed Pistachio Dumplings

Servings:4 | Cooking Time:25 Minutes

Ingredients:

- 1 cup vegetable oil
- ½ cup warm milk
- 2 cups flour
- 2 eggs, beaten
- 1 tsp sugar
- 1 ½ oz active dry yeast
- 1 cup warm water
- ½ tsp vanilla extract
- 1 tsp cinnamon
- 1 orange, zested
- 4 tbsp honey
- 2 tbsp pistachios, chopped

Directions:

1. In a bowl, sift the flour and combine it with the cinnamon and orange zest. In another bowl, mix the sugar, yeast, and ½ cup of warm water. Leave to stand until the yeast dissolves. Stir in milk, eggs, vanilla, and flour mixture. Beat with an electric mixer until smooth. Cover the bowl with plastic wrap and let sit to rise in a warm place for at least 1 hour.

2. Pour the vegetable oil into a deep pan or wok to come halfway up the sides and heat the oil. Add some more oil if necessary. Using a teaspoon, form balls, one by one, and drop in the hot oil one after another. Fry the balls on all sides, until golden brown. Remove them with a slotted spoon to paper towels to soak the excess fat. Repeat the process until the dough is exhausted. Drizzle with honey and sprinkle with pistachios.

Nutrition Info:

- Per Serving: Calories: 890;Fat: 59g;Protein: 15g;Carbs: 78g.

Fluffy Orange Muffins

Servings:6 | Cooking Time:35 Minutes

Ingredients:

- ½ cup olive oil
- 1 large egg
- 2 tbsp powdered sugar
- 1 tsp orange extract
- 1 orange, zested and juiced
- 1 cup flour
- ¾ tsp baking powder
- ½ tsp salt

Directions:

1. Preheat oven to 350 °F. In a large bowl, whisk together the egg and powdered sugar. Add the olive oil, orange extract, and orange zest and whisk to combine well. In a separate bowl, mix together the flour, baking powder, and salt.

2. Add to wet ingredients along with the orange juice and stir until just combined. Divide the batter evenly between 6 greased muffin cups and bake until a toothpick inserted in the center of the cupcake comes out clean, 20-25 minutes.

3. Remove and let sit for 5 minutes in the tin, then transfer to a wire rack to cool completely. Serve and enjoy!

Nutrition Info:

- Per Serving: Calories: 211;Fat: 22g;Protein: 3g;Carbs: 2g.

Apples Stuffed With Pecans

Servings:4 | Cooking Time:55 Minutes

Ingredients:

- 2 tbsp brown sugar
- 4 apples, cored
- ¼ cup chopped pecans
- 1 tsp ground cinnamon
- ¼ tsp ground nutmeg
- ¼ tsp ground ginger

Directions:

1. Preheat oven to 375 °F. Arrange the apples cut-side up on a baking dish. Combine pecans, ginger, cinnamon, brown sugar, and nutmeg in a bowl. Scoop the mixture into the apples and bake for 35-40 minutes until golden brown.

Nutrition Info:

- Per Serving: Calories: 142;Fat: 1.1g;Protein: 0.8g;Carbs: 36g.

Vegetarian Spinach-olive Pizza

Servings:4 | Cooking Time:40 Minutes

Ingredients:

- For the crust
- 1 tbsp olive oil
- ½ cup almond flour
- ¼ tsp salt
- 2 tbsp ground psyllium husk
- 1 cup lukewarm water
- For the topping
- ½ cup tomato sauce
- ½ cup baby spinach
- 1 cup grated mozzarella
- 1 tsp dried oregano
- 3 tbsp sliced black olives

Directions:

1. Preheat the oven to 400 °F. Line a baking sheet with parchment paper. In a medium bowl, mix the almond flour, salt, psyllium powder, olive oil, and water until dough forms.

2. Spread the mixture on the pizza pan and bake in the oven until crusty, 10 minutes. When ready, remove the crust and spread the tomato sauce on top. Add the spinach, mozzarella cheese, oregano, and olives. Bake until the cheese melts, 15 minutes. Take out of the oven, slice and serve warm.

Nutrition Info:

- Per Serving: Calories: 167;Fat: 13g;Protein: 4g;Carbs: 6.7g.

Shallot & Kale Spread

Servings:4 | Cooking Time:10 Minutes

Ingredients:

- 2 shallots, chopped
- 1 lb kale, roughly chopped
- 2 tbsp mint, chopped
- ¾ cup cream cheese, soft
- Salt and black pepper to taste

Directions:

1. In a food processor, blend kale, shallots, mint, cream cheese, salt, and pepper until smooth. Serve.

Nutrition Info:

- Per Serving: Calories: 210;Fat: 12g;Protein: 6g;Carbs: 5g.

Caramel Peach & Walnut Cake

Servings:6 | Cooking Time:50 Min + Cooling Time

Ingredients:

- ¼ cup coconut oil
- ¼ cup olive oil
- 2 peeled peaches, chopped
- ½ cup raisins, soaked
- 1 cup plain flour
- 3 eggs
- 1 tbsp dark rum
- ¼ tsp ground cinnamon
- 1 tsp vanilla extract
- 1 ½ tsp baking powder
- 4 tbsp Greek yogurt
- 2 tbsp honey
- 1 cup brown sugar
- 4 tbsp walnuts, chopped
- ¼ caramel sauce
- ¼ tsp salt

Directions:

1. Preheat the oven to 350 °F. In a bowl, mix the flour, cinnamon, vanilla, baking powder, and salt. In another bowl, whisk the eggs with Greek yogurt using an electric mixer. Gently add in coconut and olive oil. Combine well. Put in rum, honey and sugar; stir to combine. Mix the wet ingredients with the dry mixture. Stir in peaches, raisins, and walnuts.

2. Pour the mixture into a greased baking pan and bake for 30-40 minutes until a knife inserted into the middle of the cake comes out clean. Remove from the oven and let sit for 10 minutes, then invert onto a wire rack to cool completely. Warm the caramel sauce through in a pan and pour it over the cooled cake to serve.

Nutrition Info:

- Per Serving: Calories: 568;Fat: 26g;Protein: 215g;Carbs: 66g.

Spiced Nut Mix
Servings:6 | Cooking Time:20 Minutes

Ingredients:
- 1 tbsp olive oil
- 2 cups raw mixed nuts
- 1 tsp ground cumin
- ½ tsp garlic powder
- ½ tsp kosher salt
- ⅛ tsp chili powder
- ⅛ tsp ground coriander

Directions:
1. Place the nuts in a skillet over medium heat and toast for 3 minutes, shaking the pan continuously. Remove to a bowl, season with salt, and reserve. Warm olive oil in the same skillet. Add in cumin, garlic powder, chili powder, and ground coriander and cook for about 20-30 seconds. Mix in nuts and cook for another 4 minutes. Serve chilled.

Nutrition Info:
- Per Serving: Calories: 315;Fat: 29.2g;Protein: 8g;Carbs: 11g.

Easy Mixed Berry Crisp
Servings:2 | Cooking Time: 30 Minutes

Ingredients:
- 1½ cups frozen mixed berries, thawed
- 1 tablespoon coconut sugar
- 1 tablespoon almond butter
- ¼ cup oats
- ¼ cup pecans

Directions:
1. Preheat the oven to 350ºF.
2. Divide the mixed berries between 2 ramekins
3. Place the coconut sugar, almond butter, oats, and pecans in a food processor, and pulse a few times, until the mixture resembles damp sand.
4. Divide the crumble topping over the mixed berries.
5. Put the ramekins on a sheet pan and bake for 30 minutes, or until the top is golden and the berries are bubbling.
6. Serve warm.

Nutrition Info:
- Per Serving: Calories: 268;Fat: 17.0g;Protein: 4.1g;Carbs: 26.8g.

Dark Chocolate Barks
Servings:6 | Cooking Time:20 Min + Freezing Time

Ingredients:
- ½ cup quinoa
- ½ tsp sea salt
- 1 cup dark chocolate chips
- ½ tsp mint extract
- ½ cup pomegranate seeds

Directions:
1. Toast the quinoa in a greased saucepan for 2-3 minutes, stirring frequently. Remove the pan from the stove and mix in the salt. Set aside 2 tablespoons of the toasted quinoa.
2. Microwave the chocolate for 1 minute. Stir until the chocolate is completely melted. Mix the toasted quinoa and mint extract into the melted chocolate. Line a large, rimmed baking sheet with parchment paper. Spread the chocolate mixture onto the sheet. Sprinkle the remaining 2 tablespoons of quinoa and pomegranate seeds, pressing with a spatula. Freeze the mixture for 10-15 minutes or until set. Remove and break into about 2-inch jagged pieces. Store in the refrigerator until ready to serve.

Nutrition Info:
- Per Serving: Calories: 268;Fat: 12g;Protein: 4g;Carbs: 37g.

Cheese Stuffed Potato Skins
Servings:4 | Cooking Time:40 Minutes

Ingredients:
- 2 tbsp olive oil
- 1 lb red baby potatoes
- 1 cup ricotta cheese, crumbled
- 2 garlic cloves, minced
- 1 tbsp chives, chopped
- ½ tsp hot chili sauce
- Salt and black pepper to taste

Directions:
1. Place potatoes and enough water in a pot over medium heat and bring to a boil. Simmer for 15 minutes and drain. Let them cool. Cut them in halves and scoop out the pulp. Place the pulp in a bowl and mash it a bit with a fork. Add in the ricotta cheese, olive oil, garlic, chives, chili sauce, salt, and pepper. Mix to combine. Fill potato skins with the mixture.
2. Preheat oven to 360 °F. Line a baking sheet with parchment paper. Place filled skins on the sheet and bake for 10 minutes.

Nutrition Info:
- Per Serving: Calories: 310;Fat: 10g;Protein: 9g;Carbs: 23g.

Garbanzo Patties With Cilantro-yogurt Sauce
Servings:4 | Cooking Time:20 Minutes

Ingredients:
- ¼ cup olive oil
- 3 garlic cloves, minced
- 1 cup canned garbanzo beans
- 2 tbsp parsley, chopped
- 1 onion, chopped
- 1 tsp ground coriander
- Salt and black pepper to taste
- ¼ tsp cayenne pepper
- ¼ tsp cumin powder
- 1 tsp lemon juice
- 3 tbsp flour
- ¼ cup Greek yogurt
- 2 tbsp chopped cilantro
- ½ tsp garlic powder

Directions:
1. In a blender, blitz garbanzo, parsley, onion, garlic, salt, pepper, ground coriander, cayenne pepper, cumin powder, and lemon juice until smooth. Remove to a bowl and mix in flour. Form 16 balls out of the mixture and flatten them into patties.
2. Warm the olive oil in a skillet over medium heat and fry patties for 10 minutes on both sides. Remove them to a paper towel–lined plate to drain the excess fat. In a bowl, mix the Greek yogurt, cilantro, garlic powder, salt, and pepper. Serve the patties with yogurt sauce.

Nutrition Info:
- Per Serving: Calories: 120;Fat: 7g;Protein: 4g;Carbs: 13g.

Berry Sorbet
Servings:4 | Cooking Time:10 Min + Freezing Time

Ingredients:
- 1 tsp lemon juice
- ¼ cup honey
- 1 cup fresh strawberries
- 1 cup fresh raspberries
- 1 cup fresh blueberries

Directions:
1. Bring 1 cup of water to a boil in a pot over high heat. Stir in honey until dissolved. Remove from the heat and mix in berries and lemon juice; let cool.
2. Once cooled, add the mixture to a food processor and pulse until smooth. Transfer to a shallow glass and freeze for 1 hour. Stir with a fork and freeze for 30 more minutes. Repeat a couple of times. Serve in dessert dishes.

Nutrition Info:

- Per Serving: Calories: 115;Fat: 1g;Protein: 1g;Carbs: 29g.

Portuguese Orange Mug Cake

Servings:2 | Cooking Time:12 Minutes

Ingredients:
- 2 tbsp butter, melted
- 6 tbsp flour
- 2 tbsp sugar
- ½ tsp baking powder
- ¼ tsp salt
- 1 tsp orange zest
- 1 egg
- 2 tbsp orange juice
- 2 tbsp milk
- ½ tsp orange extract
- ½ tsp vanilla extract
- Orange slices for garnish

Directions:
1. In a bowl, beat the egg, butter, orange juice, milk, orange extract, and vanilla extract. In another bowl, combine the flour, sugar, baking powder, salt, and orange zest. Pour the dry ingredients into the wet ingredients and stir to combine. Spoon the mixture into 2 mugs and microwave one at a time for 1-2 minutes. Garnish with orange slices.

Nutrition Info:
- Per Serving: Calories: 302;Fat: 17g;Protein: 6g;Carbs: 33g.

Classic Tzatziki Dip

Servings:6 | Cooking Time:10 Min + Chilling Time

Ingredients:
- 1 large cucumber, grated
- 1 garlic clove, minced
- 1 cup Greek yogurt
- 1 tsp chopped fresh dill
- 1 tsp chopped fresh parsley
- Salt and black pepper to taste
- ¼ cup ground walnuts

Directions:
1. In a colander over the sink, squeeze the excess liquid out of the grated cucumber. Combine the yogurt, cucumber, garlic, salt, dill, and pepper in a bowl. Keep in the fridge covered for 2 hours. Serve topped with ground walnuts and parsley.

Nutrition Info:
- Per Serving: Calories: 66;Fat: 3.8g;Protein: 5g;Carbs: 4g.

Grilled Stone Fruit With Honey

Servings:2 | Cooking Time: 6 Minutes

Ingredients:
- 3 apricots, halved and pitted
- 2 plums, halved and pitted
- 2 peaches, halved and pitted
- ½ cup low-fat ricotta cheese
- 2 tablespoons honey
- Cooking spray

Directions:
1. Preheat the grill to medium heat. Spray the grill grates with cooking spray.
2. Arrange the fruit, cut side down, on the grill, and cook for 2 to 3 minutes per side, or until lightly charred and softened.
3. Serve warm with a sprinkle of cheese and a drizzle of honey.

Nutrition Info:
- Per Serving: Calories: 298;Fat: 7.8g;Protein: 11.9g;Carbs: 45.2g.

Crispy Potato Chips

Servings:4 | Cooking Time:40 Minutes

Ingredients:
- 2 tbsp olive oil
- 4 potatoes, cut into wedges
- 2 tbsp grated Parmesan
- cheese
- Salt and black pepper to taste

Directions:
1. Preheat the oven to 340 °F. In a bowl, combine the potatoes, olive oil, salt, and black pepper. Spread on a lined baking sheet and bake for 40 minutes until the edges are browned. Serve sprinkled with Parmesan cheese.

Nutrition Info:
- Per Serving: Calories: 359;Fat: 8g;Protein: 9g;Carbs: 66g.

Baked Beet Fries With Feta Cheese

Servings:4 | Cooking Time:40 Minutes

Ingredients:
- 1 cup olive oil
- 1 cup feta cheese, crumbled
- 2 beets, sliced
- Salt and black pepper to taste
- 1/3 cup balsamic vinegar

Directions:
1. Preheat the oven to 340 °F. Line a baking sheet with parchment paper. Arrange beet slices, salt, pepper, vinegar, and olive oil on the sheet and toss to combine. Bake for 30 minutes. Serve topped with feta cheese.

Nutrition Info:
- Per Serving: Calories: 210;Fat: 6g;Protein: 4g;Carbs: 9g.

Grilled Pesto Halloumi Cheese

Servings:2 | Cooking Time:9 Minutes

Ingredients:
- 1 tbsp olive oil
- 3 oz Halloumi cheese
- 2 tsp pesto sauce
- 1 tomato, sliced

Directions:
1. Cut the cheese into 2 rectangular pieces. Heat a griddle pan over medium heat. Drizzle the halloumi slices with and add to the pan. After about 2 minutes, check to see if the cheese is golden on the bottom. Flip the slices, top each with pesto, and cook for another 2 minutes, or until the second side is golden. Serve with tomato slices.

Nutrition Info:
- Per Serving: Calories: 177;Fat: 14g;Protein: 10g;Carbs: 4g.

Rice Pudding With Roasted Orange

Servings:6 | Cooking Time: 19 To 20 Minutes

Ingredients:
- 2 medium oranges
- 2 teaspoons extra-virgin olive oil
- ⅛ teaspoon kosher salt
- 2 large eggs
- 2 cups unsweetened almond milk
- 1 cup orange juice
- 1 cup uncooked instant brown rice
- ¼ cup honey
- ½ teaspoon ground cinnamon
- 1 teaspoon vanilla extract
- Cooking spray

Directions:
1. Preheat the oven to 450ºF. Spritz a large, rimmed baking sheet with cooking spray. Set aside.
2. Slice the unpeeled oranges into ¼-inch rounds. Brush with the oil and sprinkle with salt. Place the slices on the baking sheet and

roast for 4 minutes. Flip the slices and roast for 4 more minutes, or until they begin to brown. Remove from the oven and set aside.

3. Crack the eggs into a medium bowl. In a medium saucepan, whisk together the milk, orange juice, rice, honey and cinnamon. Bring to a boil over medium-high heat, stirring constantly. Reduce the heat to medium-low and simmer for 10 minutes, stirring occasionally.

4. Using a measuring cup, scoop out ½ cup of the hot rice mixture and whisk it into the eggs. While constantly stirring the mixture in the pan, slowly pour the egg mixture back into the saucepan. Cook on low heat for 1 to 2 minutes, or until thickened, stirring constantly. Remove from the heat and stir in the vanilla.

5. Let the pudding stand for a few minutes for the rice to soften. The rice will be cooked but slightly chewy. For softer rice, let stand for another half hour.

6. Top with the roasted oranges. Serve warm or at room temperature.

Nutrition Info:
- Per Serving: Calories: 204;Fat: 6.0g;Protein: 5.0g;Carbs: 34.0g.

Quick & Easy Red Dip

Servings:4 | Cooking Time:10 Minutes

Ingredients:
- 1 cup roasted red peppers, chopped
- 3 tbsp olive oil
- 1 lb tomatoes, chopped
- Salt and black pepper to taste
- 1 ½ tsp balsamic vinegar
- ½ tsp oregano, chopped
- 2 garlic cloves, minced
- 2 tbsp parsley, chopped

Directions:
1. In a food processor, blend tomatoes, red peppers, salt, pepper, vinegar, oregano, olive oil, garlic, and parsley until smooth. Store this in the fridge for a few days, up to a week.

Nutrition Info:
- Per Serving: Calories: 130;Fat: 5g;Protein: 4g;Carbs: 4g.

Homemade Studentenfutter

Servings:4 | Cooking Time:10 Minutes

Ingredients:
- ¼ cup dried figs
- ½ cup almonds
- ¼ seed mix
- ¼ cup dried cranberries
- ½ cup walnut halves
- ½ cup hazelnuts
- ½ tsp paprika
- 1 tbsp Parmesan cheese, grated

Directions:
1. Spread the almonds, walnuts, hazelnuts, and seeds on a greased baking dish. Bake in preheated oven for 10 minutes at 350 °F. Remove and mix with figs and cranberries. Toss to combine. Sprinkle with Parmesan and paprika and serve.

Nutrition Info:
- Per Serving: Calories: 195;Fat: 15.6g;Protein: 7g;Carbs: 9.8g.

Charred Maple Pineapple

Servings:4 | Cooking Time:10 Minutes

Ingredients:
- 1 pineapple, peeled and cut into wedges
- 1 tbsp maple syrup
- ½ tsp ground cinnamon

Directions:
1. Preheat a grill pan over high heat. Place the fruit in a bowl and drizzle with maple syrup; sprinkle with ground cinnamon. Grill for about 7-8 minutes, turning occasionally until the fruit chars slightly. Serve.

Nutrition Info:
- Per Serving: Calories: 130;Fat: 0g;Protein: 1g;Carbs: 32g.

Balsamic Squash Wedges With Walnuts

Servings:4 | Cooking Time:50 Minutes

Ingredients:
- 3 tbsp olive oil
- 1 lb butternut squash, peeled and cut into wedges
- 1 cup walnuts, chopped
- 1 tbsp chili paste
- 1 tbsp balsamic vinegar
- 1 tbsp chives, chopped

Directions:
1. Preheat the oven to 380 °F. Line a baking sheet with parchment paper. Combine squash wedges, chili paste, olive oil, vinegar, and chives in a bowl and arrange on the sheet. Bake for 40 minutes, turning often. Sprinkle with walnuts.

Nutrition Info:
- Per Serving: Calories: 190;Fat: 5g;Protein: 2g;Carbs: 7g.

Poached Pears In Red Wine

Servings:4 | Cooking Time:1 Hour 35 Minutes

Ingredients:
- 4 pears, peeled with stalk intact
- 2 cups red wine
- 8 whole cloves
- 1 cinnamon stick
- ½ tsp vanilla extract
- 2 tsp sugar
- Creme fraiche for garnish

Directions:
1. In a pot over low heat, mix red wine, cinnamon stick, cloves, vanilla, and sugar and bring to a simmer, stirring often until the sugar is dissolved. Add in the pears, make sure that they are submerged and poach them for 15-20 minutes.

2. Remove the pears to a platter and allow the liquid simmering over medium heat for 15 minutes until reduced by half and syrupy. Remove from the heat and let cool for 10 minutes. Drain to discard the spices, let cool, and pour over the pears. Top with creme fraiche and serve.

Nutrition Info:
- Per Serving: Calories: 158;Fat: 1g;Protein: 2g;Carbs: 33g.

Berry And Rhubarb Cobbler

Servings:8 | Cooking Time: 35 Minutes

Ingredients:
- Cobbler:
- 1 cup fresh raspberries
- 2 cups fresh blueberries
- 1 cup sliced (½-inch) rhubarb pieces
- 1 tablespoon arrowroot powder
- ¼ cup unsweetened apple juice
- 2 tablespoons melted coconut
- oil
- ¼ cup raw honey
- Topping:
- 1 cup almond flour
- 1 tablespoon arrowroot powder
- ½ cup shredded coconut
- ¼ cup raw honey
- ½ cup coconut oil

Directions:
1. Make the Cobbler
2. Preheat the oven to 350ºF. Grease a baking dish with melted coconut oil.
3. Combine the ingredients for the cobbler in a large bowl. Stir to mix well.

4. Spread the mixture in the single layer on the baking dish. Set aside.

5. Make the Topping

6. Combine the almond flour, arrowroot powder, and coconut in a bowl. Stir to mix well.

7. Fold in the honey and coconut oil. Stir with a fork until the mixture crumbled.

8. Spread the topping over the cobbler, then bake in the preheated oven for 35 minutes or until frothy and golden brown.

9. Serve immediately.

Nutrition Info:
• Per Serving: Calories: 305;Fat: 22.1g;Protein: 3.2g;Carbs: 29.8g.

Ultimate Seed Crackers

Servings:6 | Cooking Time:20 Minutes

Ingredients:
• 1 cup almond flour
• 1 tbsp sesame seeds
• 1 tbsp sunflower seeds
• 1 tbsp flaxseed
• 1 tbsp chia seeds
• ¼ tsp baking soda
• Salt and black pepper to taste
• 1 egg, beaten

Directions:
1. Preheat oven to 350 °F. In a bowl, mix the almond flour, sesame seeds, flaxseed, chia seeds, sunflower seeds, baking soda, salt, and pepper and stir well. Add the egg and stir well to combine and form the dough into a ball. Place one layer of parchment paper on your counter-top and place the dough on top. Cover with a second layer of parchment and, using a rolling pin, roll the dough to ¼-inch thickness, aiming for a rectangular shape. Cut the dough into crackers and bake on parchment until crispy and slightly golden, 10-15 minutes, depending on thickness. Alternatively, you can bake the large rolled dough before cutting and break into free-form crackers once baked and crispy. Store in an airtight container for up to 1 week.

Nutrition Info:
• Per Serving: Calories: 119;Fat: 9g;Protein: 4g;Carbs: 5g.

Mushroom & Black Olive Pizza

Servings:4 | Cooking Time:45 Minutes

Ingredients:
• For the crust
• 2 tbsp olive oil
• 2 cups flour
• 1 cup lukewarm water
• 1 pinch of sugar
• 1 tsp active dry yeast
• ¾ tsp salt
• For the topping
• 2 medium cremini mushrooms, sliced
• 1 tsp olive oil
• 1 garlic clove, minced
• ½ cup tomato sauce
• 1 tsp sugar
• 1 bay leaf
• 1 tsp dried oregano
• 1tsp dried basil
• Salt and black pepper to taste
• ½ cup grated mozzarella
• ½ cup grated Parmesan cheese
• 6 black olives, sliced

Directions:
1. Sift the flour and salt in a bowl and stir in yeast. Mix lukewarm water, olive oil, and sugar in another bowl. Add the wet mixture to the dry mixture and whisk until you obtain a soft dough. Place the dough on a lightly floured work surface and knead it thoroughly for 4-5 minutes until elastic. Transfer the dough to a greased bowl. Cover with cling film and leave to rise for 50-60 minutes in a warm place until doubled in size. Roll out the dough to a thickness of around 12 inches.

2. Preheat the oven to 400 °F. Line a pizza pan with parchment paper. Heat the olive oil in a medium skillet and sauté the mushrooms until softened, 5 minutes. Stir in the garlic and cook until fragrant, 30 seconds.

3. Mix in the tomato sauce, sugar, bay leaf, oregano, basil, salt, and black pepper. Cook for 2 minutes and turn the heat off. Spread the sauce on the crust, top with the mozzarella and Parmesan cheeses, and then, the olives. Bake in the oven until the cheeses melts, 15 minutes. Serve warm.

Nutrition Info:
• Per Serving: Calories: 203;Fat: 9g;Protein: 24g;Carbs: 2.6g.

Thyme Lentil Spread

Servings:6 | Cooking Time:10 Minutes

Ingredients:
• 3 tbsp olive oil
• 1 garlic clove, minced
• 1 cup split red lentils, rinsed
• ½ tsp dried thyme
• 1 tbsp balsamic vinegar
• Salt and black pepper to taste

Directions:
1. Bring to a boil salted water in a pot over medium heat. Add in the lentils and cook for 15 minutes until cooked through. Drain and set aside to cool. In a food processor, place the lentils, garlic, thyme, vinegar, salt, and pepper. Gradually add olive oil while blending until smooth. Serve.

Nutrition Info:
• Per Serving: Calories: 295;Fat: 10g;Protein: 10g;Carbs: 16g.

Two-cheese Stuffed Bell Peppers

Servings:6 | Cooking Time:20 Min + Chilling Time

Ingredients:
• 1 ½ lb bell peppers, cored and seeded
• 1 tbsp extra-virgin olive oil
• 4 oz ricotta cheese
• 4 oz mascarpone cheese
• 1 tbsp scallions, chopped
• 1 tbsp lemon zest

Directions:
1. Preheat oven to 400 °F. Coat the peppers with olive oil, put them on a baking sheet, and roast for 8 minutes. Remove and let cool. In a bowl, add the ricotta cheese, mascarpone cheese, scallions, and lemon zest. Stir to combine, then spoon mixture into a piping bag. Stuff each pepper to the top with the cheese mixture. Chill the peppers and serve.

Nutrition Info:
• Per Serving: Calories: 141;Fat: 11g;Protein: 4g;Carbs: 6g.

Parsley Lamb Arancini

Servings:4 | Cooking Time:25 Minutes

Ingredients:
• 3 tbsp olive oil
• 1 lb ground lamb
• ½ tsp cumin, ground
• 1 garlic clove, minced
• Salt and black pepper to taste
• 1 cup rice
• 2 cups vegetable broth
• ¼ cup parsley, chopped
• ¼ cup shallots, chopped
• ½ tsp allspice
• 2 eggs, lightly beaten
• 1 cup breadcrumbs

Directions:
1. Cook the rice in the vegetable broth for about 15 minutes. Remove from the heat and leave to cool uncovered. In a large bowl, mix the cooled rice, ground lamb, cumin, garlic, salt, pepper, parsley, shallots, and allspice until combined. Form medium balls out of the mixture. Dip the arancini in the beaten eggs and toss in

the breadcrumbs. Warm the olive oil in a skillet over medium heat and fry meatballs for 14 minutes on all sides until golden brown. Remove to paper towels to absorb excess oil. Serve warm.

Nutrition Info:
• Per Serving: Calories: 310;Fat: 10g;Protein: 7g;Carbs: 23g.

Grilled Peaches With Whipped Ricotta

Servings:4 | Cooking Time: 14 To 22 Minutes

Ingredients:
• 4 peaches, halved and pitted
• 2 teaspoons extra-virgin olive oil
• ¾ cup whole-milk Ricotta cheese
• 1 tablespoon honey
• ¼ teaspoon freshly grated nutmeg
• 4 sprigs mint
• Cooking spray

Directions:
1. Spritz a grill pan with cooking spray. Heat the grill pan to medium heat.
2. Place a large, empty bowl in the refrigerator to chill.
3. Brush the peaches all over with the oil. Place half of the peaches, cut-side down, on the grill pan and cook for 3 to 5 minutes, or until grill marks appear.
4. Using tongs, turn the peaches over. Cover the grill pan with aluminum foil and cook for 4 to 6 minutes, or until the peaches are easily pierced with a sharp knife. Set aside to cool. Repeat with the remaining peaches.
5. Remove the bowl from the refrigerator and add the Ricotta. Using an electric beater, beat the Ricotta on high for 2 minutes. Add the honey and nutmeg and beat for 1 more minute.
6. Divide the cooled peaches among 4 serving bowls. Top with the Ricotta mixture and a sprig of mint and serve.

Nutrition Info:
• Per Serving: Calories: 176;Fat: 8.0g;Protein: 8.0g;Carbs: 20.0g.

Orange Pannacotta With Blackberries

Servings:2 | Cooking Time:15 Min + Chilling Time

Ingredients:
• ¾ cup half-and-half
• 1 tsp powdered gelatin
• ½ cup heavy cream
• 3 tbsp sugar
• 1 tsp orange zest
• 1 tbsp orange juice
• 1 tsp orange extract
• ½ cup fresh blackberries
• 2 mint leaves

Directions:
1. Put ¼ cup of half-and-half in a bowl. Mix in gelatin powder and set it aside for 10 minutes to hydrate. In a saucepan over medium heat, combine the remaining half-and-half, heavy cream, sugar, orange zest, orange juice, and orange extract. Warm the mixture for 4 minutes. Don't let it come to a full boil. Remove from the heat. Let cool slightly.
2. Add the gelatin into the cream mixture and whisk until the gelatin melts. Pour the mixture into 2 dessert glasses and refrigerate for at least 2 hours. Serve with fresh berries and garnish with mint leaves.

Nutrition Info:
• Per Serving: Calories: 422;Fat: 33g;Protein: 6g;Carbs: 28g.

Orange Mug Cakes

Servings:2 | Cooking Time: 3 Minutes

Ingredients:
• 6 tablespoons flour
• 2 tablespoons sugar
• 1 teaspoon orange zest
• ½ teaspoon baking powder
• Pinch salt
• 1 egg
• 2 tablespoons olive oil
• 2 tablespoons unsweetened almond milk
• 2 tablespoons freshly squeezed orange juice
• ½ teaspoon orange extract
• ½ teaspoon vanilla extract

Directions:
1. Combine the flour, sugar, orange zest, baking powder, and salt in a small bowl.
2. In another bowl, whisk together the egg, olive oil, milk, orange juice, orange extract, and vanilla extract.
3. Add the dry ingredients to the wet ingredients and stir to incorporate. The batter will be thick.
4. Divide the mixture into two small mugs. Microwave each mug separately. The small ones should take about 60 seconds, and one large mug should take about 90 seconds, but microwaves can vary.
5. Cool for 5 minutes before serving.

Nutrition Info:
• Per Serving: Calories: 303;Fat: 16.9g;Protein: 6.0g;Carbs: 32.5g.

The Best Trail Mix

Servings:4 | Cooking Time:20 Minutes

Ingredients:
• 1 tbsp olive oil
• 1 tbsp maple syrup
• 1 tsp vanilla
• ½ tsp paprika
• ½ tsp cardamom
• ½ tsp allspice
• 2 cups mixed, unsalted nuts
• ¼ cup sunflower seeds
• ½ cup dried apricots, diced
• ½ cup dried figs, diced
• Salt to taste

Directions:
1. Mix the olive oil, maple syrup, vanilla, cardamom, paprika, and allspice in a pan over medium heat. Stir to combine. Add the nuts and seeds and stir well to coat. Let the nuts and seeds toast for about 10 minutes, stirring often. Remove from the heat, and add the dried apricots and figs. Stir everything well and season with salt. Store in an airtight container.

Nutrition Info:
• Per Serving: Calories: 261;Fat: 18g;Protein: 6g;Carbs: 23g.

Crunchy Eggplant Fries

Servings:4 | Cooking Time:35 Minutes

Ingredients:
• 2 tbsp olive oil
• 2 eggplants, sliced
• ½ tbsp smoked paprika
• Salt and black pepper to taste
• ½ tsp onion powder
• 2 tsp dried sage
• 1 cup fine breadcrumbs
• 1 large egg white, beaten

Directions:
1. Preheat the oven to 350 °F. Line a baking sheet with parchment paper. In a bowl, mix olive oil, paprika, salt, pepper, onion powder, and sage. Dip the eggplant slices in the egg white, then coat in the breadcrumb mixture. Arrange them on the sheet and roast in the oven for 25 minutes, flipping once.

Nutrition Info:

- Per Serving: Calories: 140;Fat: 8g;Protein: 3g;Carbs: 12g.

Apple And Berries Ambrosia
Servings:4 | Cooking Time: 0 Minutes

Ingredients:
- 2 cups unsweetened coconut milk, chilled
- 2 tablespoons raw honey
- 1 apple, peeled, cored, and
- chopped
- 2 cups fresh raspberries
- 2 cups fresh blueberries

Directions:
1. Spoon the chilled milk in a large bowl, then mix in the honey. Stir to mix well.
2. Then mix in the remaining ingredients. Stir to coat the fruits well and serve immediately.

Nutrition Info:
- Per Serving: Calories: 386;Fat: 21.1g;Protein: 4.2g;Carbs: 45.9g.

Vanilla Cheesecake Squares
Servings:6 | Cooking Time:55 Min + Chilling Time

Ingredients:
- ½ cup butter, melted
- 1 box butter cake mix
- 3 large eggs
- 1 cup maple syrup
- 1/8 tsp cinnamon
- 1 cup cream cheese
- 1 tsp vanilla extract

Directions:
1. Preheat oven to 350 °F. In a medium bowl, blend the cake mix, butter, cinnamon, and 1 egg. Then, pour the mixture into a greased baking pan. Mix together maple syrup, cream cheese, the remaining 2 eggs, and vanilla in a separate bowl and pour this gently over the first layer. Bake for 45-50 minutes. Remove and allow to cool. Cut into squares.

Nutrition Info:
- Per Serving: Calories: 160;Fat: 8g;Protein: 2g;Carbs: 20g.

Stuffed Cherry Tomatoes
Servings:4 | Cooking Time:10 Minutes

Ingredients:
- 2 tbsp olive oil
- 16 cherry tomatoes
- 1 tbsp lemon zest
- ½ cup feta cheese, crumbled
- 2 tbsp olive tapenade
- ¼ cup parsley, torn

Directions:
1. Using a sharp knife, slice off the tops of the tomatoes and hollow out the insides. Combine olive oil, lemon zest, feta cheese, olive tapenade, and parsley in a bowl. Fill the cherry tomatoes with the feta mixture and arrange them on a plate.

Nutrition Info:
- Per Serving: Calories: 140;Fat: 9g;Protein: 6g;Carbs: 6g.

Cinnamon Pear & Oat Crisp With Pecans
Servings:4 | Cooking Time:30 Minutes

Ingredients:
- 2 tbsp butter, melted
- 4 fresh pears, mashed
- ½ lemon, juiced and zested
- ¼ cup maple syrup
- 1 cup gluten-free rolled oats
- ½ cup chopped pecans
- ½ tsp ground cinnamon
- ¼ tsp salt

Directions:
1. Preheat oven to 350 °F. Combine the pears, lemon juice and zest, and maple syrup in a bowl. Stir to mix well, then spread the mixture on a greased baking dish. Combine the remaining ingredients in a small bowl. Stir to mix well. Pour the mixture over the pear mixture. Bake for 20 minutes or until the oats are golden brown.

Nutrition Info:
- Per Serving: Calories: 496;Fat: 33g;Protein: 5g;Carbs: 50.8g.

Salmon-cucumber Rolls
Servings:4 | Cooking Time:5 Minutes

Ingredients:
- 8 Kalamata olives, chopped
- 4 oz smoked salmon strips
- 1 cucumber, sliced length-wise
- 2 tsp lime juice
- 4 oz cream cheese, soft
- 1 tsp lemon zest, grated
- Salt and black pepper to taste
- 2 tsp dill, chopped

Directions:
1. Place cucumber slices on a flat surface and top each with a salmon strip. Combine olives, lime juice, cream cheese, lemon zest, salt, pepper, and dill in a bowl. Smear cream mixture over salmon and roll them up. Serve immediately.

Nutrition Info:
- Per Serving: Calories: 250;Fat: 16g;Protein: 18g;Carbs: 17g.

Roasted Eggplant Hummus
Servings:4 | Cooking Time:25 Minutes

Ingredients:
- 1 lb eggplants, peeled and sliced
- 1 lemon, juiced
- 1 garlic clove, minced
- ¼ cup tahini
- ¼ tsp ground cumin
- Salt and black pepper to taste
- 2 tbsp fresh parsley, chopped
- ½ cup mayonnaise

Directions:
1. Preheat oven to 350 °F. Arrange the eggplant slices on a baking sheet and bake for 15 minutes until tender. Let cool slightly before chopping. In a food processor, mix eggplants, salt, lemon juice, tahini, cumin, garlic, and pepper for 30 seconds. Remove to a bowl. Stir in mayonnaise. Serve topped with parsley.

Nutrition Info:
- Per Serving: Calories: 235;Fat: 18g;Protein: 4.1g;Carbs: 17g.

Two Cheese Pizza
Servings:4 | Cooking Time:35 Minutes

Ingredients:
- For the crust:
- 1 tbsp olive oil
- ½ cup almond flour
- ¼ tsp salt
- 2 tbsp ground psyllium husk
- For the topping
- ½ cup pizza sauce
- 4 oz mozzarella, sliced
- 1 cup grated mozzarella
- 3 tbsp grated Parmesan cheese
- 2 tsp Italian seasoning

Directions:
1. Preheat the oven to 400 °F. Line a baking sheet with parchment paper. In a medium bowl, mix the almond flour, salt, psyllium powder, olive oil, and 1 cup of lukewarm water until dough forms. Spread the mixture on the pizza pan and bake in the oven until crusty, 10 minutes. When ready, remove the crust and spread the pizza sauce on top. Add the sliced mozzarella, grated mozzarella, Parmesan cheese, and Italian seasoning. Bake in the oven for 18 minutes or until the cheeses melt. Serve warm.

Nutrition Info:
- Per Serving: Calories: 193;Fat: 10g;Protein: 19g;Carbs: 3g.

Fresh Fruit Cups

Servings:4 | Cooking Time:10 Minutes

Ingredients:
- 1 cup orange juice
- ½ cup watermelon cubes
- 1 ½ cups grapes, halved
- 1 cup chopped cantaloupe
- ½ cup cherries, chopped
- 1 peach, chopped
- ½ tsp ground cinnamon

Directions:
1. Combine watermelon cubes, grapes, cherries, cantaloupe, and peach in a bowl. Add in the orange juice and mix well. Share into dessert cups, dust with cinnamon, and serve.

Nutrition Info:
- Per Serving: Calories: 156;Fat: 0.5g;Protein: 1.8g;Carbs: 24g.

Skillet Pesto Pizza

Servings:2 | Cooking Time:10 Minutes

Ingredients:
- 1 tbsp butter
- 2 pieces of focaccia bread
- 2 tbsp pesto
- 1 medium tomato, sliced
- 2 large eggs

Directions:
1. Place a large skillet over medium heat. Place the focaccia in the skillet and let it warm for about 4 minutes on both sides until softened and just starting to turn golden. Remove to a platter. Spread 1 tablespoon of the pesto on one side of each slice. Cover with tomato slices. Melt the butter in the skillet over medium heat. Crack in the eggs, keeping them separated, and cook until the whites are no longer translucent and the yolk is cooked to desired doneness. Spoon one egg onto each pizza. Serve and enjoy!

Nutrition Info:
- Per Serving: Calories: 427;Fat: 17g;Protein: 17g;Carbs: 10g.

Easy Blueberry And Oat Crisp

Servings:4 | Cooking Time: 20 Minutes

Ingredients:
- 2 tablespoons coconut oil, melted, plus additional for greasing
- 4 cups fresh blueberries
- Juice of ½ lemon
- 2 teaspoons lemon zest
- ¼ cup maple syrup
- 1 cup gluten-free rolled oats
- ½ cup chopped pecans
- ½ teaspoon ground cinnamon
- Sea salt, to taste

Directions:
1. Preheat the oven to 350ºF. Grease a baking sheet with coconut oil.
2. Combine the blueberries, lemon juice and zest, and maple syrup in a bowl. Stir to mix well, then spread the mixture on the baking sheet.
3. Combine the remaining ingredients in a small bowl. Stir to mix well. Pour the mixture over the blueberries mixture.
4. Bake in the preheated oven for 20 minutes or until the oats are golden brown.
5. Serve immediately with spoons.

Nutrition Info:
- Per Serving: Calories: 496;Fat: 32.9g;Protein: 5.1g;Carbs: 50.8g.

Mint Raspberries Panna Cotta

Servings:4 | Cooking Time:15 Min + Chilling Time

Ingredients:
- 2 tbsp warm water
- 2 tsp gelatin powder
- 2 cups heavy cream
- 1 cup raspberries
- 2 tbsp sugar
- 1 tsp vanilla extract
- 4 fresh mint leaves

Directions:
1. Pour 2 tbsp of warm water into a small bowl. Stir in the gelatin to dissolve. Allow the mixture to sit for 10 minutes. In a large bowl, combine the heavy cream, raspberries, sugar, and vanilla. Blend with an immersion blender until the mixture is smooth and the raspberries are well puréed. Transfer the mixture to a saucepan and heat over medium heat until just below a simmer. Remove from the heat and let cool for 5 minutes. Add in the gelatin mixture, whisking constantly until smooth. Divide the custard between ramekins and refrigerate until set, 4-6 hours. Serve chilled garnished with mint leaves.

Nutrition Info:
- Per Serving: Calories: 431;Fat: 44g;Protein: 4g;Carbs: 7g.

Lebanese Spicy Baba Ganoush

Servings:4 | Cooking Time:50 Minutes

Ingredients:
- 2 tbsp olive oil
- 2 eggplants, poked with a fork
- 2 tbsp tahini paste
- 1 tsp cayenne pepper
- 2 tbsp lemon juice
- 2 garlic cloves, minced
- Salt and black pepper to taste
- 1 tbsp parsley, chopped

Directions:
1. Preheat oven to 380 °F. Arrange eggplants on a roasting pan and bake for 40 minutes. Set aside to cool. Peel the cooled eggplants and place them in a blender along with the tahini paste, lemon juice, garlic, cayenne pepper, salt, and pepper. Puree the ingredients while gradually adding olive oil until a smooth and homogeneous consistency. Top with parsley.

Nutrition Info:
- Per Serving: Calories: 130;Fat: 5g;Protein: 5g;Carbs: 2g.

Carrot & Walnut Cake

Servings:6 | Cooking Time:55 Minutes

Ingredients:
- ½ cup vegetable oil
- 2 tsp vanilla extract
- ¼ cup maple syrup
- 6 eggs, beaten
- ½ cup flour
- 1 tsp baking powder
- 1 tsp baking soda
- ½ tsp ground nutmeg
- 1 tsp ground cinnamon
- ½ tsp salt
- ½ cup chopped walnuts
- 3 cups finely grated carrots

Directions:
1. Preheat oven to 350 °F. Mix the vanilla extract, maple syrup, and oil in a large bowl. Stir to mix well. Add in the eggs and whisk to combine. Set aside.
2. Combine the flour, baking powder, baking soda, nutmeg, cinnamon, and salt in a separate bowl. Stir to combine. Make a well in the center of the flour mixture, then pour the egg mixture into the well and stir well. Add in the walnuts and carrots and toss to mix well. Pour the mixture into a greased baking dish. Bake for 35-45 minutes or until puffed and the cake spring back when lightly press with your fingers. Remove the cake from the oven. Allow to cool, then serve.

Nutrition Info:
- Per Serving: Calories: 255;Fat: 21g;Protein: 5.1g;Carbs: 13g.

Stuffed Cucumber Bites

Servings:4 | Cooking Time:10 Minutes

Ingredients:
- ¼ cup extra-virgin olive oil
- 2 cucumbers
- Salt to taste
- 6 basil leaves, chopped
- 1 tbsp fresh mint, minced
- 1 garlic clove, minced
- ¼ cup walnuts, ground
- ¼ cup feta cheese, crumbled
- ½ tsp paprika

Directions:
1. Cut cucumbers lengthwise. With a spoon, remove the seeds and hollow out a shallow trough in each piece. Lightly salt each piece and set aside on a platter. In a bowl, combine the basil, mint, garlic, walnuts, feta, and olive oil and blend until smooth. Spoon the mixture into each cucumber half and sprinkle with paprika. Cut each half into 4 pieces. Serve.

Nutrition Info:
- Per Serving: Calories: 176;Fat: 3g;Protein: 5g;Carbs: 18g.

Garlic-yogurt Dip With Walnuts

Servings:4 | Cooking Time:5 Minutes

Ingredients:
- 2 cups Greek yogurt
- 3 garlic cloves, minced
- ¼ cup dill, chopped
- 1 green onion, chopped
- ¼ cup walnuts, chopped
- Salt and black pepper to taste

Directions:
1. Combine garlic, yogurt, dill, walnuts, salt, and pepper in a bowl. Serve topped with green onion.

Nutrition Info:
- Per Serving: Calories: 210;Fat: 7g;Protein: 9g;Carbs: 16g.

Greek Yogurt & Za'atar Dip On Grilled Pitta

Servings:6 | Cooking Time:10 Minutes

Ingredients:
- 1/3 cup olive oil
- 2 cups Greek yogurt
- 2 tbsp toasted ground pistachios
- Salt and white pepper to taste
- 2 tbsp mint, chopped
- 3 kalamata olives, chopped
- ¼ cup za'atar seasoning
- 3 pitta breads, cut into triangles

Directions:
1. Mix the yogurt, pistachios, salt, pepper, mint, olives, za´atar spice, and olive oil in a bowl. Grill the pitta bread until golden, about 5-6 minutes. Serve with the yogurt spread.

Nutrition Info:
- Per Serving: Calories: 300;Fat: 19g;Protein: 11g;Carbs: 22g.

	Breakfast	Lunch	Dinner
Day 1	Yummy Lentil Stuffed Pitas	Picante Green Pea & Chicken	Pesto Shrimp Over Zoodles
Day 2	Red Pepper Coques With Pine Nuts	Greek-style Veggie & Beef In Pita	Honey-mustard Roasted Salmon
Day 3	Baked Eggs In Avocado	Chicken With Farro & Carrots	Parsley Salmon Bake
Day 4	Basil Scrambled Eggs	Coriander Pork Roast	Tuna Gyros With Tzatziki
Day 5	Luxurious Fruit Cocktail	Sweet Chicken Stew	Cannellini Bean Stew With Spinach
Day 6	Mushroom And Caramelized Onion Musakhan	Baked Chicken & Veggie	Seafood Fideuà
Day 7	Carrot & Pecan Cupcakes	Pork Chops In Wine Sauce	Classic Prawn Scampi
Day 8	Lemon Cardamom Buckwheat Pancakes	Baked Garlicky Pork Chops	Lemon And Spinach Orzo
Day 9	White Pizzas With Arugula And Spinach	Bell Pepper & Onion Pork Chops	Better-for-you Cod & Potatoes
Day 10	Tomato Eggs With Fried Potatoes	Beef, Tomato, And Lentils Stew	Party Summer Salad
Day 11	Pesto Salami & Cheese Egg Cupcakes	Picante Beef Stew	Hazelnut Crusted Sea Bass
Day 12	Tomato Scrambled Eggs With Feta Cheese	Caprese Stuffed Chicken Breasts	Summer Fruit & Cheese Salad
Day 13	Crustless Tiropita (greek Cheese Pie)	Chicken Drumsticks With Peach Glaze	Hot Jumbo Shrimp
Day 14	Spinach Cheese Pie	Baked Turkey With Veggies	Radicchio Salad With Sunflower Seeds
Day 15	Dulse, Avocado, And Tomato Pitas	Herby Chicken With Asparagus Sauce	Easy Breaded Shrimp

	Breakfast	Lunch	Dinner
Day 16	5-ingredient Quinoa Breakfast Bowls	Authentic Turkey Kofta	Favorite Green Bean Stir-fry
Day 17	Avocado Toast With Goat Cheese	Parsley Eggplant Lamb	Baked Lemon Salmon
Day 18	Feta & Olive Breakfast	Hot Pork Meatballs	Pepper & Cheese Stuffed Tomatoes
Day 19	Fresh Mozzarella & Salmon Frittata	Shallot Beef	Garlic Skillet Salmon
Day 20	Herby Artichoke Frittata With Ricotta	Roasted Chicken Thighs With Basmati Rice	Three-bean Salad With Black Olives
Day 21	Vegetable & Egg Sandwiches	Panko Grilled Chicken Patties	Moroccan Spinach & Lentil Soup
Day 22	Apple & Pumpkin Muffins	Mushroom Chicken Piccata	Grilled Lemon Pesto Salmon
Day 23	Sunday Pancakes In Berry Sauce	Curried Green Bean & Chicken Breasts	Warm Kale Salad With Red Bell Pepper
Day 24	Avocado & Peach Power Smoothie	Spanish Chicken Skillet	Slow Cooker Salmon In Foil
Day 25	Honey Breakfast Smoothie	Chicken Souvlaki	Cucumber Salad With Mustard Dressing
Day 26	Brown Rice Salad With Cheese	Greek Peachy Lamb	Baked Cod With Vegetables
Day 27	Power Green Smoothie	Slow Cooker Beef With Tomatoes	Olive Tapenade Flatbread With Cheese
Day 28	Zucchini & Tomato Cheese Tart	Chicken Bake With Cottage Cheese	Fried Scallops With Bean Mash
Day 29	Vegetable & Cheese Frittata	Rosemary Pork Loin With Green Onions	Cucumber Salad With Goat Cheese
Day 30	Ritzy Garden Burgers	Greek-style Lamb Burgers	Lemon Cioppino

	Breakfast	Lunch	Dinner
Day 31	Bell Pepper & Cheese Egg Scramble	Cocktail Meatballs In Almond Sauce	Lemony Shrimp With Orzo Salad
Day 32	Brown Rice And Black Bean Burgers	Chicken Sausage & Zucchini Soup	Saucy Cod With Calamari Rings
Day 33	Lime Watermelon Yogurt Smoothie	Grilled Pork Chops With Apricot Chutney	Vegetable & Shrimp Roast
Day 34	Apple-oat Porridge With Cranberries	Dragon Pork Chops With Pickle Topping	Leek Cream Soup With Hazelnuts
Day 35	Grilled Caesar Salad Sandwiches	Mustardy Steak In Mushroom Sauce	Balsamic-honey Glazed Salmon
Day 36	Basic Tortilla De Patatas	Chicken & Spinach Dish	Kale & Bean Soup With Chorizo
Day 37	Quick & Easy Bread In A Mug	Apricot-glazed Pork Skewers	Parsley Tomato Tilapia
Day 38	Berry & Cheese Omelet	Paprika Chicken With Caper Dressing	Marinated Mushrooms And Olives
Day 39	Za'atar Pizza	Rosemary Pork Chops With Cabbage Mix	Shrimp & Spinach A La Puttanesca
Day 40	Pumpkin-yogurt Parfaits	Easy Pork Souvlaki	Moroccan Lentil, Tomato, And Cauliflower Soup
Day 41	Cheese & Mushroom Muffins	Rich Beef Meal	Tuna And Zucchini Patties
Day 42	Samosas In Potatoes	Harissa Turkey With Couscous	The Ultimate Chicken Bean Soup
Day 43	Energy Nut Smoothie	Baked Root Veggie & Chicken	Mushroom & Bell Pepper Salad
Day 44	Eggs Florentine With Pancetta	Provençal Flank Steak Au Pistou	Chicken Salad With Mustard Dressing
Day 45	Avocado & Tuna Sandwiches	Chicken Thighs With Roasted Artichokes	Pancetta-wrapped Scallops

	Breakfast	Lunch	Dinner
Day 46	Honey & Feta Frozen Yogurt	Baked Teriyaki Turkey Meatballs	Spiced Citrus Sole
Day 47	Cauliflower Breakfast Porridge	Parsley-dijon Chicken And Potatoes	Green Bean And Halloumi Salad
Day 48	Cheese Egg Quiche	Cream Zucchini & Chicken Dish	Crispy Herb Crusted Halibut
Day 49	Quick Pumpkin Oatmeal	Mushroom & Sausage With Orecchiette	Italian Tilapia Pilaf
Day 50	Warm Bulgur Breakfast Bowls With Fruits	Cilantro Turkey Penne With Asparagus	Orange-honey Glazed Carrots
Day 51	Eggplant, Spinach, And Feta Sandwiches	Herby Turkey Stew	Lemon Shrimp With Black Olives
Day 52	Easy Pizza Pockets	Roasted Herby Chicken	Greek-style Pasta Salad
Day 53	Tomato And Egg Scramble	Chili Beef Stew	Salmon Tartare With Avocado
Day 54	Olive & Poppy Seed Bread	Baked Beef With Kale Slaw & Bell Peppers	Goat Cheese & Beet Salad With Nuts
Day 55	Veg Mix And Blackeye Pea Burritos	Vegetable Pork Loin	Pumpkin Soup With Crispy Sage Leaves
Day 56	Hummus Toast With Pine Nuts & Ricotta	Pork Chops In Tomato Olive Sauce	Zucchini & Green Bean Soup
Day 57	One-pan Tomato-basil Eggs	Exotic Pork Chops	Homemade Lebanese Bulgur Salad
Day 58	Maple-vanilla Yogurt With Walnuts	Homemade Pizza Burgers	Moroccan Chicken & Chickpea Stew
Day 59	Berry-yogurt Smoothie	Chermoula Roasted Pork Tenderloin	Roasted Root Vegetable Soup
Day 60	Super Cheeses And Mushroom Tart	Smooth Chicken Breasts With Nuts	Sumptuous Greek Vegetable Salad

W

Y

Z